Papillon

Miwa Ueda

Translated and adapted by Elina Ishikawa
Lettered by North Market Street Graphics

Ballantine Books · New York

Papillon volume 2 is a work of fiction. Names, characters, places, and incidents are the products of the author's imagination or are used fictitiously. Any resemblance to actual events, locales, or persons, living or dead, is entirely coincidental.

A Del Rey Manga/Kodansha Trade Paperback Original

Published in the United States by Del Rey, an imprint of The Random House Publishing Group, a division of Random House, Inc., New York.

Publication rights arranged through Kodansha Ltd.

First published in Japan in 2007 by Kodansha Ltd., Tokyo

ISBN 978-0-345-50592-7

Printed in the United States of America

www.delreymanga.com

2 4 6 8 9 7 5 3 1

Translator/Adapter: Elina Ishikawa
Lettering: North Market Street Graphics

CONTENTS

I
started
jumping
rope.

MI

Everyone sees the world through eyeglasses of
their own creation. What they see is affected by the
thickness and shape of the lenses. Ageha literally
wears eyeglasses, but they're a symbol, too, of her
feeling of being unloved. In this volume, she's able to
remove them when she faces—and heals—all the pain
of her past. I hope the new world she sees will look
brighter to her.

—Miwa Ueda

Honorifics Explained

Throughout the Del Rey Manga books, you will find Japanese honorifics left intact in the translations. For those not familiar with how the Japanese use honorifics and, more important, how they differ from American honorifics, we present this brief overview.

Politeness has always been a critical facet of Japanese culture. Ever since the feudal era, when Japan was a highly stratified society, use of honorifics—which can be defined as polite speech that indicates relationship or status—has played an essential role in the Japanese language. When you address someone in Japanese, an honorific usually takes the form of a suffix attached to one's name (example: "Asuna-san"), is used as a title at the end of one's name, or appears in place of the name itself (example: "Negi-sensei," or simply "Sensei!").

Honorifics can be expressions of respect or endearment. In the context of manga and anime, honorifics give insight into the nature of the relationship between characters. Many English translations leave out these important honorifics and therefore distort the feel of the original Japanese. Because Japanese honorifics contain nuances that English honorifics lack, it is our policy at Del Rey not to translate them. Here, instead, is a guide to some of the honorifics you may encounter in Del Rey Manga.

-san: This is the most common honorific and is equivalent to Mr., Miss, Ms., or Mrs. It is the all-purpose honorific and can be used in any situation where politeness is required.

-sama: This is one level higher than "-san" and is used to confer great respect.

-dono: This comes from the word "tono," which means "lord." It is an even higher level than "-sama" and confers utmost respect.

-*kun*: This suffix is used at the end of boys' names to express familiarity or endearment. It is also sometimes used by men among friends, or when addressing someone younger or of a lower station.

-*chan*: This is used to express endearment, mostly toward girls. It is also used for little boys, pets, and even among lovers. It gives a sense of childish cuteness.

Bozu: This is an informal way to refer to a boy, similar to the English terms "kid" and "squirt."

Sempai/
Senpai: This title suggests that the addressee is one's senior in a group or organization. It is most often used in a school setting, where underclassmen refer to their upperclassmen as "sempai." It can also be used in the workplace, such as when a newer employee addresses an employee who has seniority in the company.

Kohai: This is the opposite of "sempai" and is used toward underclassmen in school or newcomers in the workplace. It connotes that the addressee is of a lower station.

Sensei: Literally meaning "one who has come before," this title is used for teachers, doctors, or masters of any profession or art.

-*[blank]*: This is usually forgotten in these lists, but it is perhaps the most significant difference between Japanese and English. The lack of honorific, known as *yobisute*, means that the speaker has permission to address the person in a very intimate way. Usually, only family, spouses, or very close friends have this kind of permission. It can be gratifying when someone who has earned the intimacy starts to call one by one's name without an honorific. But when that intimacy hasn't been earned, it can be very insulting.

2

Papillon

Miwa Ueda

CONTENTS

The Story So Far

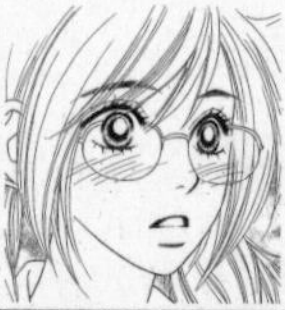

Ageha Mizuki
(a.k.a. Chrysalis)

Our heroine. One of the twins, she's shy and introverted.

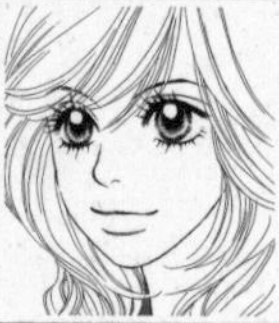

Hana Mizuki
(a.k.a. Watery Nose)

Ageha's twin sister—the most popular girl in school.

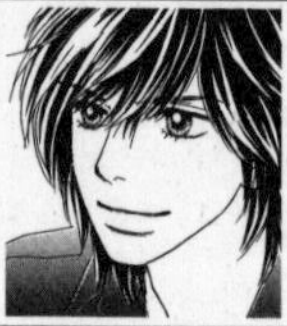

Hayato Ichijiku
(a.k.a. Kyû-chan)

A counselor-in-training. He is a graduate student.

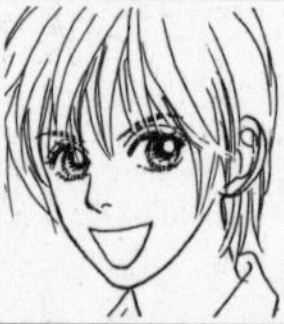

Ryûsei Koike

Ageha's childhood friend. He's also dating Hana.

Summary: Ageha had a crush on Ryûsei, but her twin sister, Hana, lured him away. Acting on advice from her school counselor, Hayato Ichijiku, Ageha found her fighting spirit and made new friends who encouraged her to win Ryûsei back. Hayato then gave Ageha a new assignment: to ask Ryûsei out on a date. Ageha resolved to do so, but on that very same day, Ageha caught Ryûsei and Hana kissing!

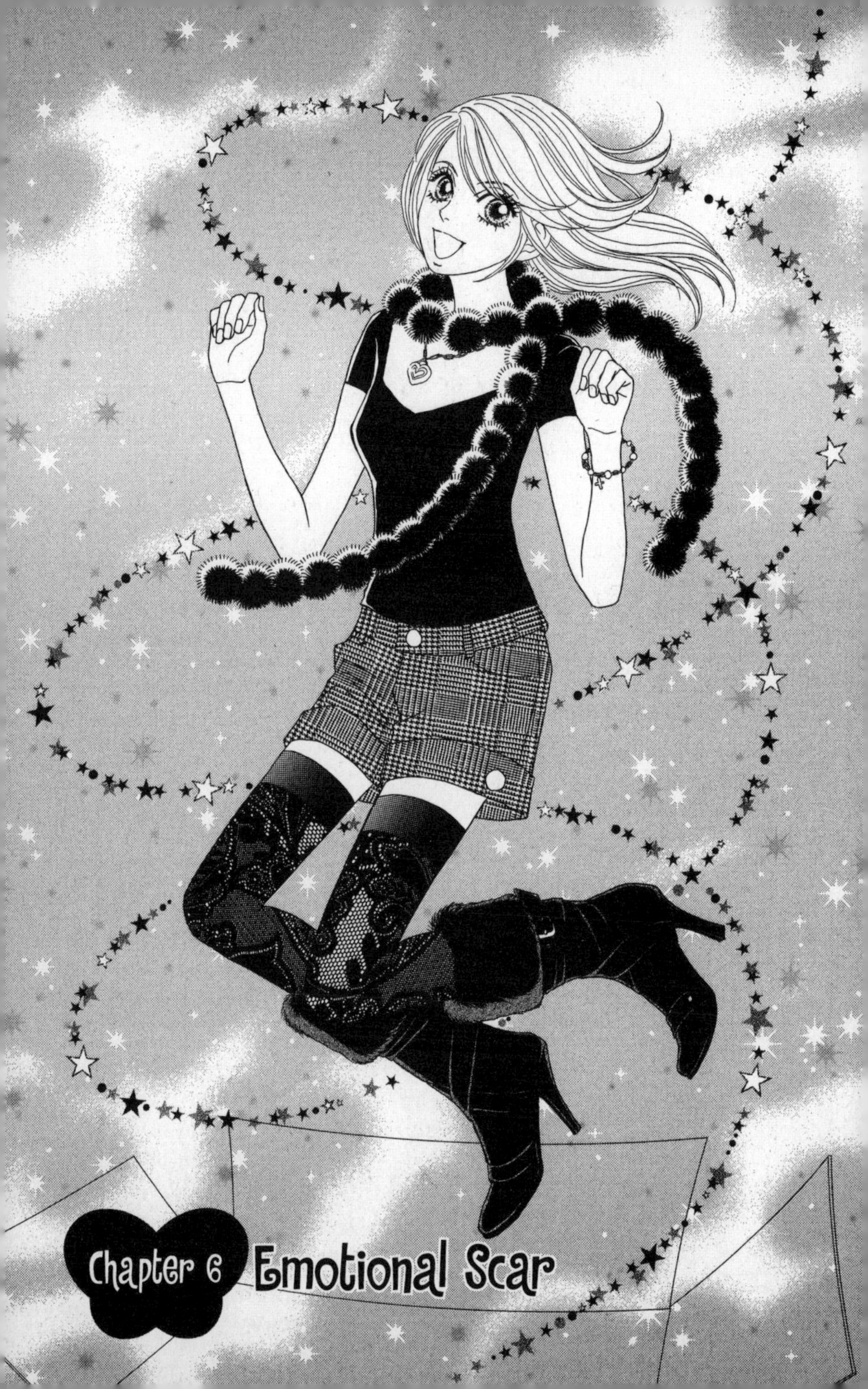
Chapter 6
Emotional Scar

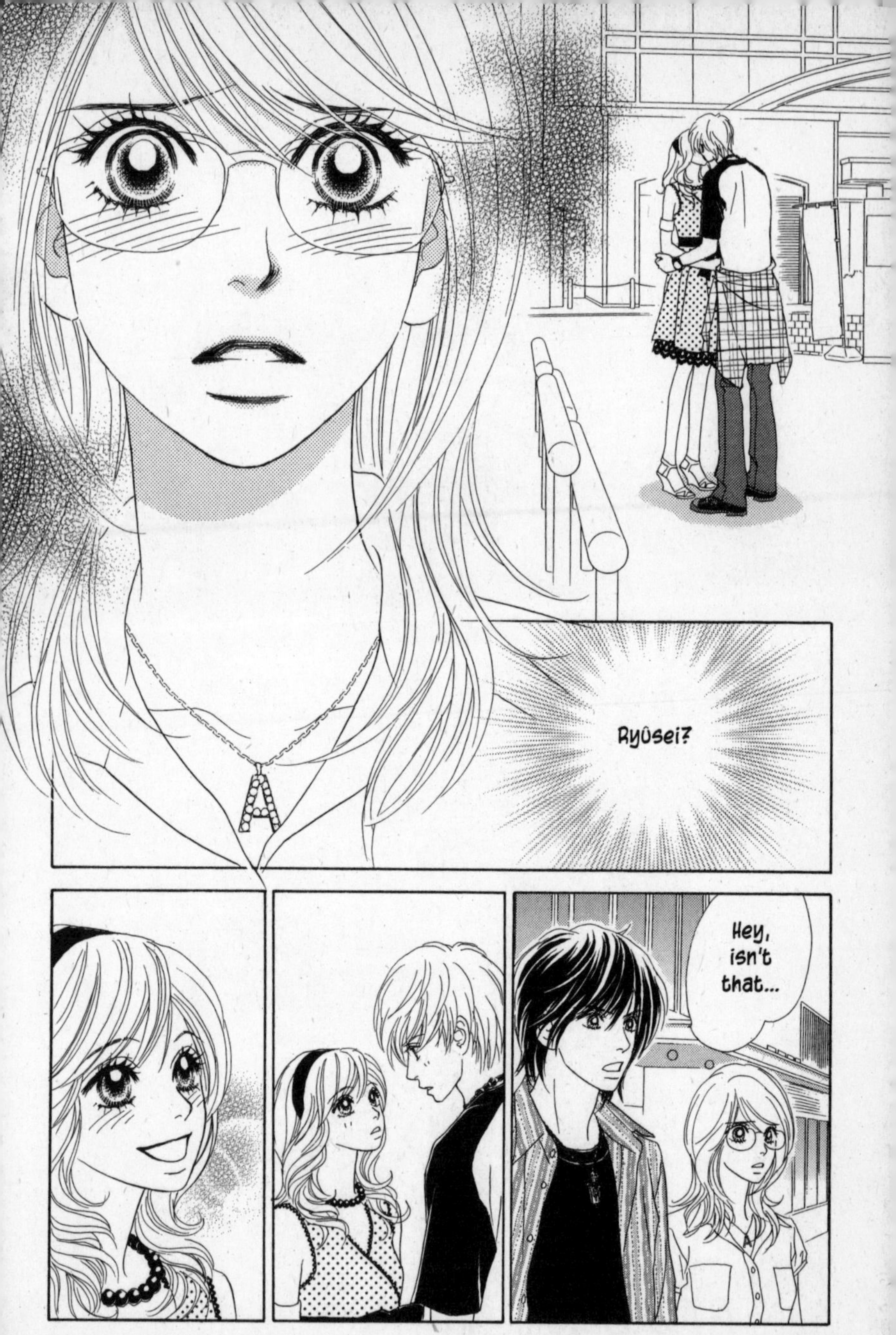

Ryûsei?
Hey, isn't that...

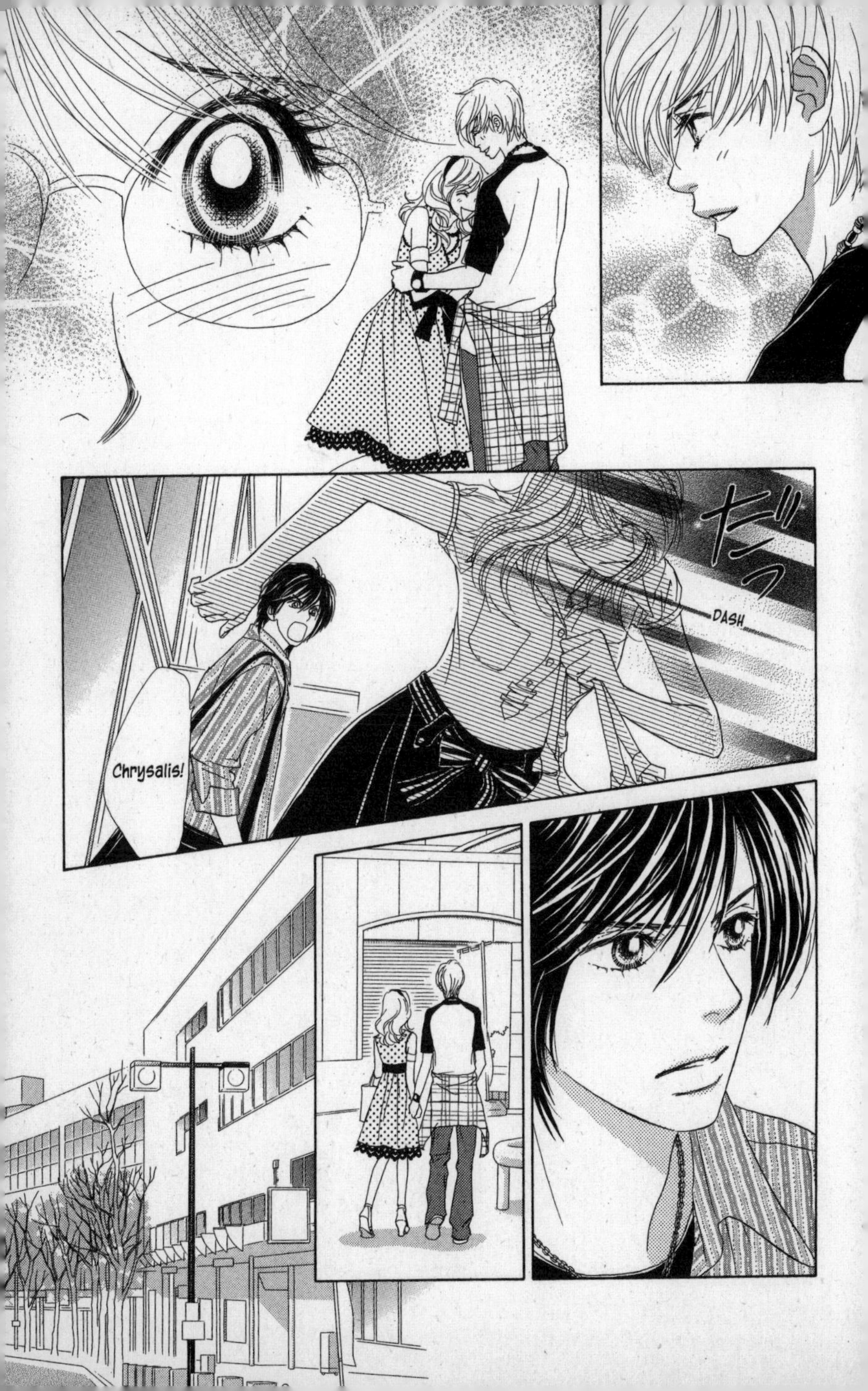
だッ
DASH
Chrysalis!

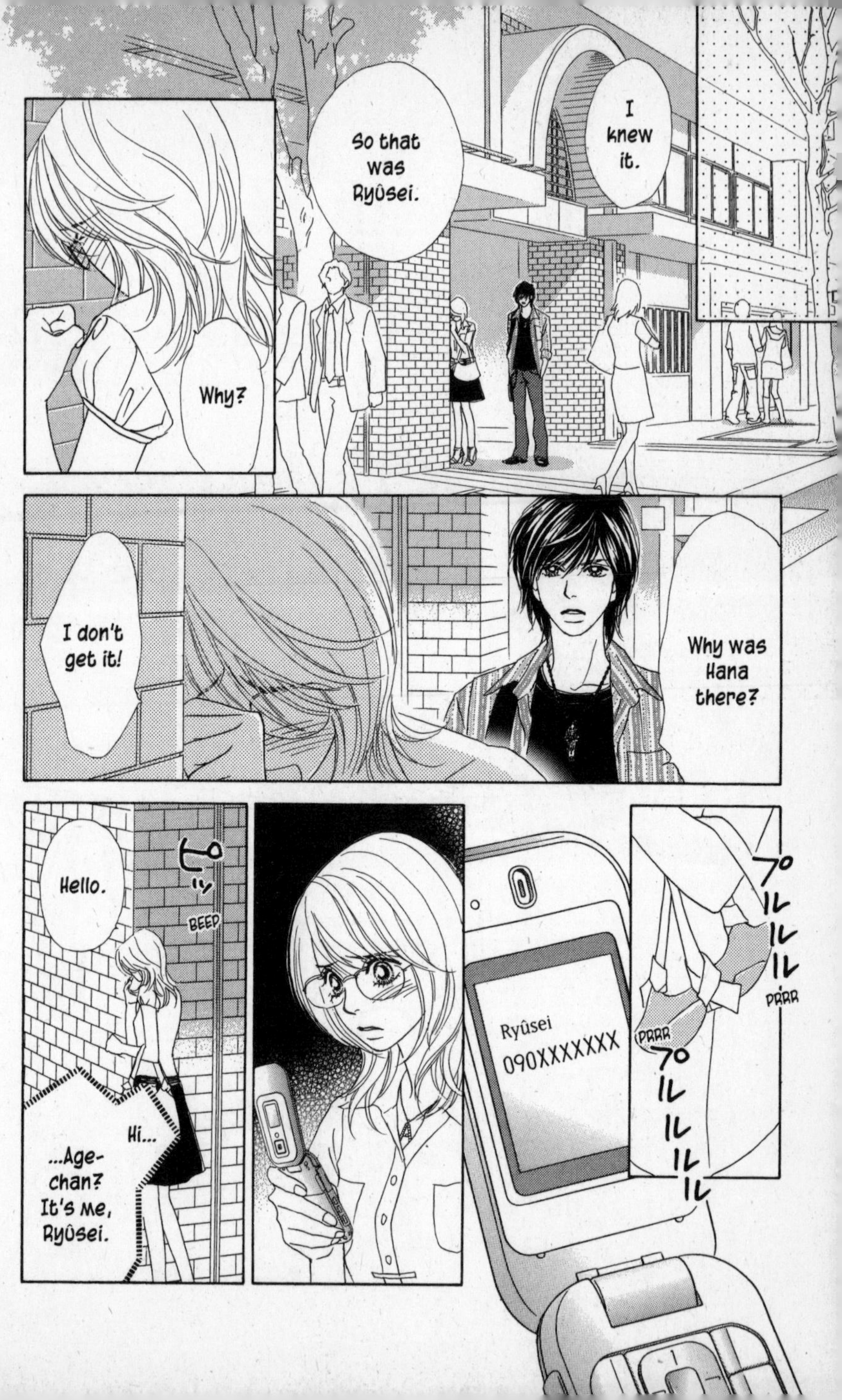
I knew it.
So that was Ryûsei.
Why?
Why was Hana there?
I don't get it!
プルルル
PRRR
プルルルル
PRRR
Ryûsei
090XXXXXXX
ピッ
BEEP
Hello.
Hi...
...Age-chan? It's me, Ryûsei.

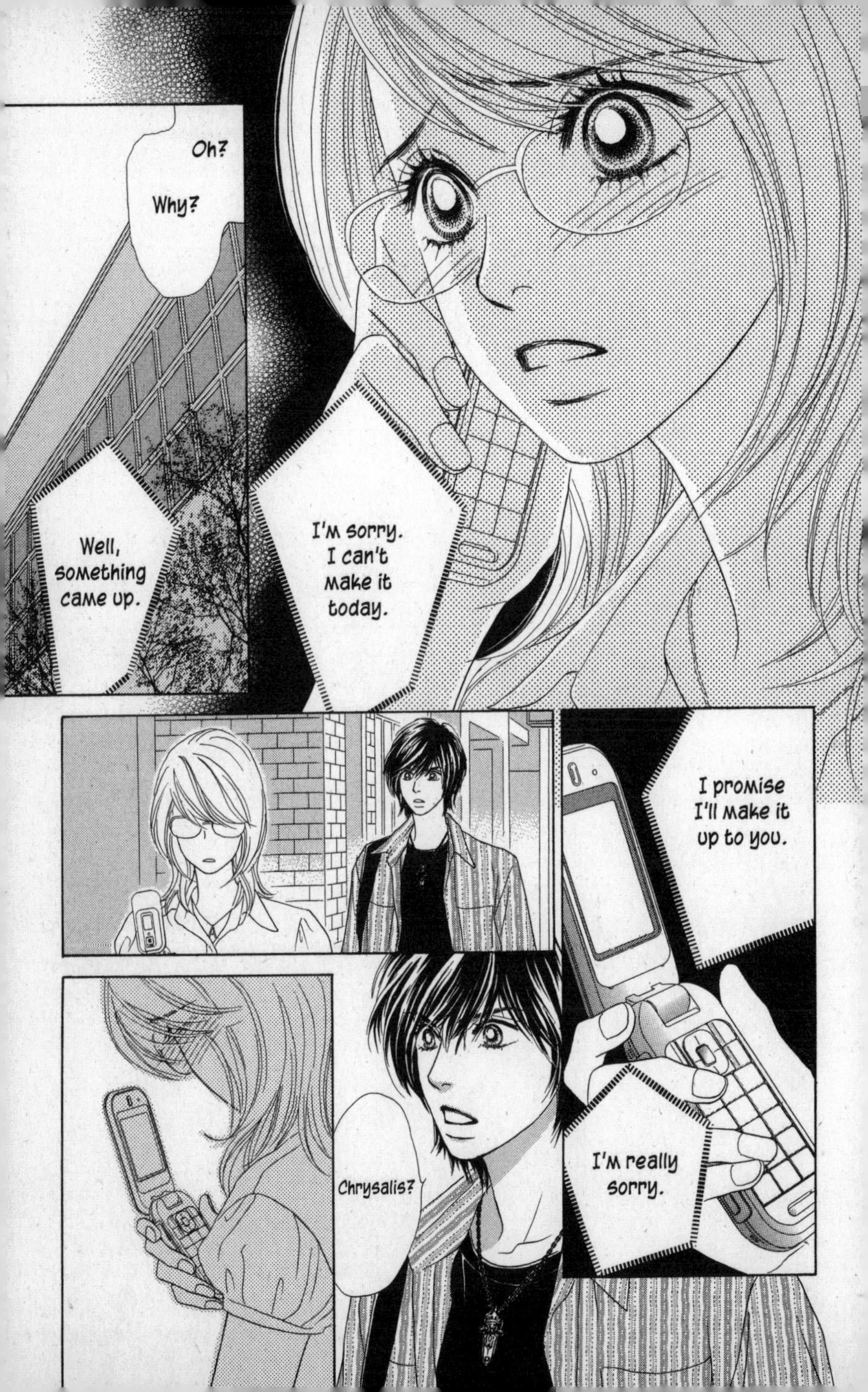
I'm sorry. I can't make it today.
Oh?
Why?
Well, something came up.
I promise I'll make it up to you.
I'm really sorry.
Chrysalis?

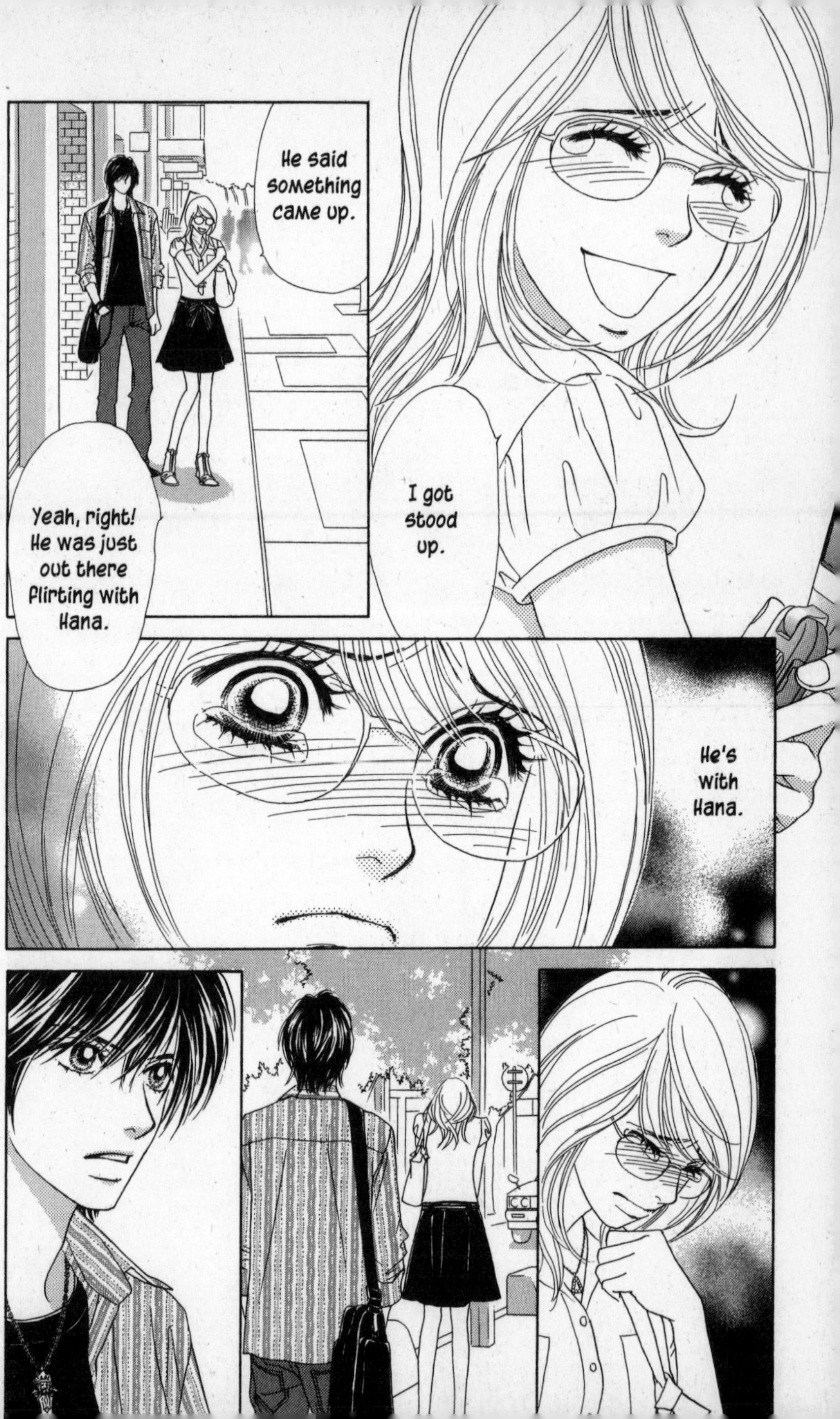
I got stood up.
He said something came up.
Yeah, right! He was just out there flirting with Hana.
He's with Hana.

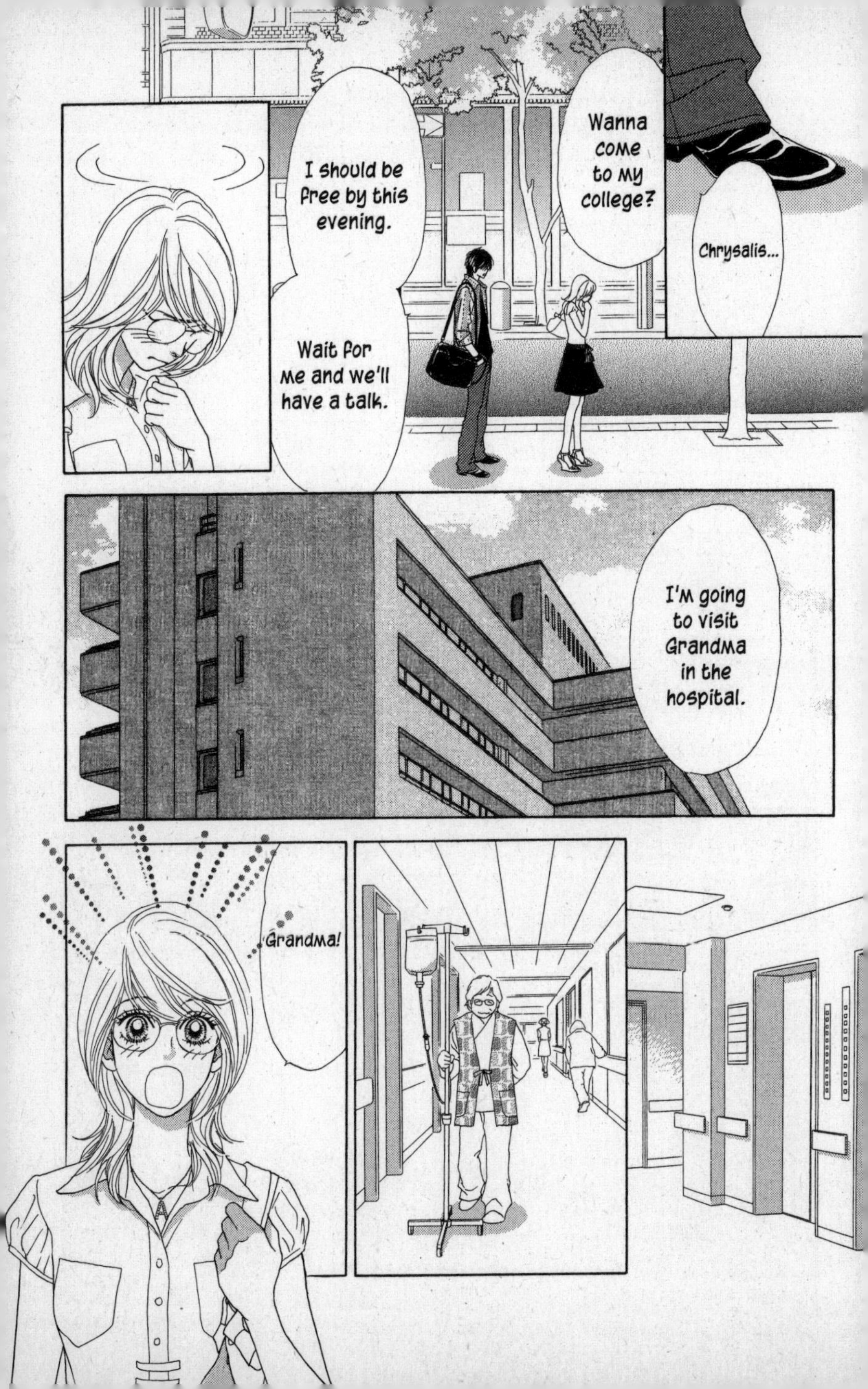
Chrysalis...
Wanna come to my college?
I should be free by this evening.
Wait for me and we'll have a talk.
I'm going to visit Grandma in the hospital.
Grandma!

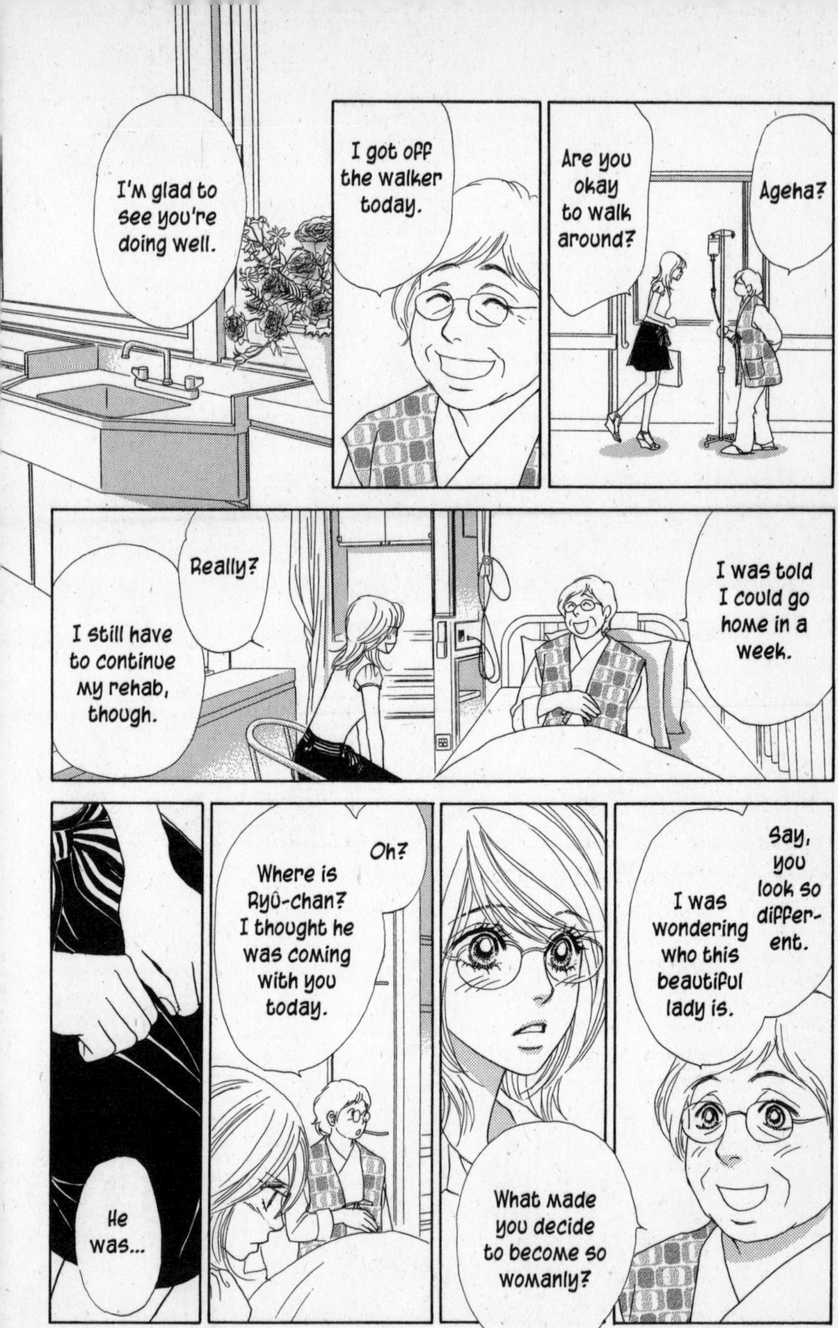
Ageha?
Are you okay to walk around?
I got off the walker today.
I'm glad to see you're doing well.
I was told I could go home in a week.
Really?
I still have to continue my rehab, though.
Say, you look so different.
I was wondering who this beautiful lady is.
What made you decide to become so womanly?
Oh?
Where is Ryû-chan? I thought he was coming with you today.
He was...

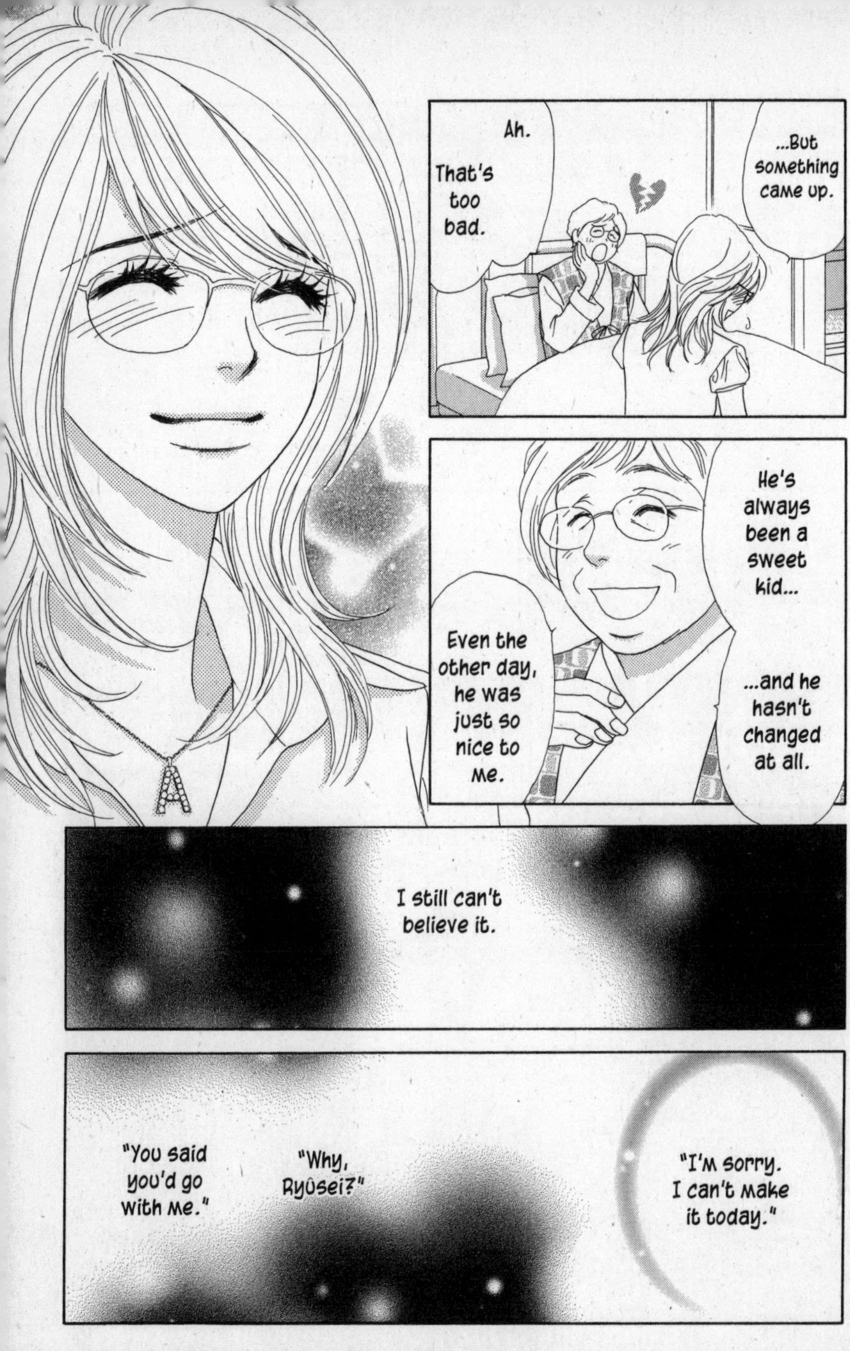
...But something came up.
Ah. That's too bad.
He's always been a sweet kid...
...and he hasn't changed at all.
Even the other day, he was just so nice to me.
I still can't believe it.
"I'm sorry. I can't make it today."
"Why, Ryôsei?"
"You said you'd go with me."

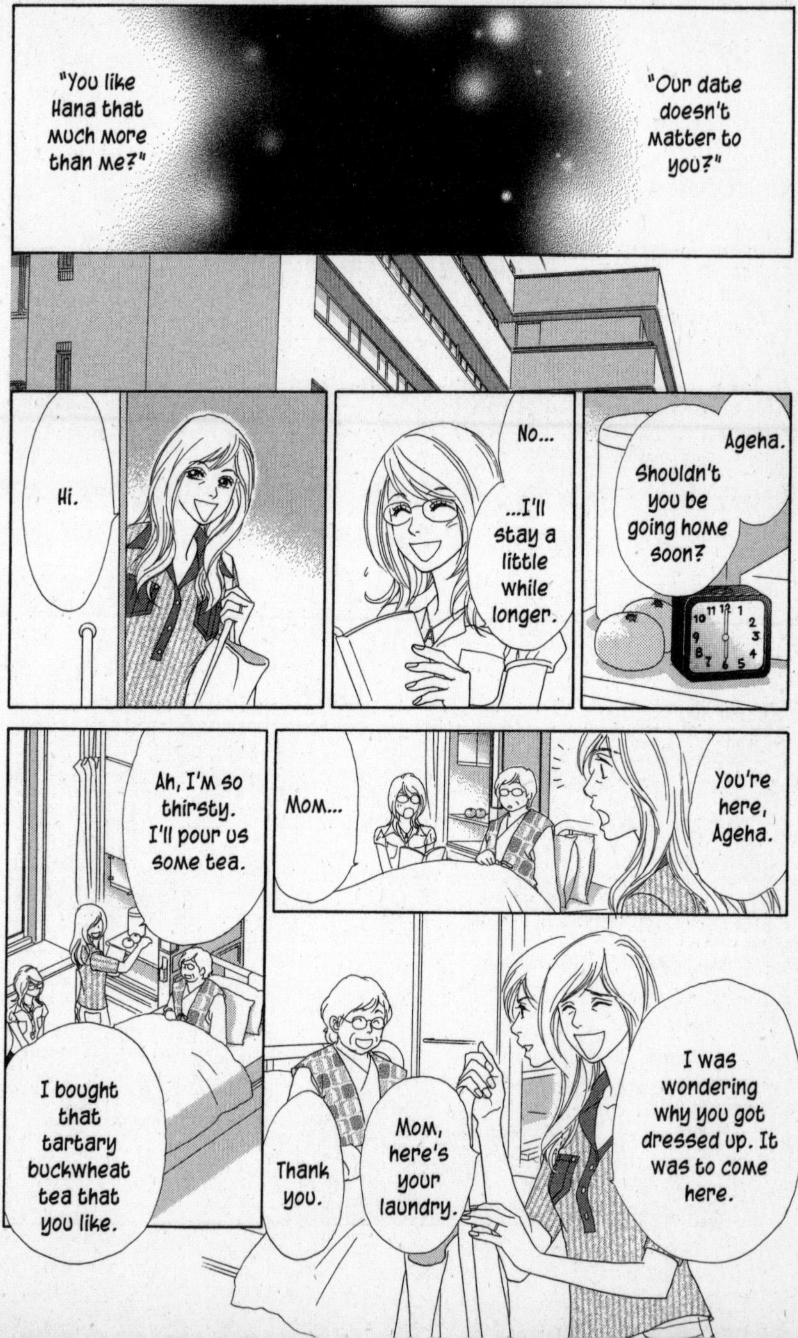
"Our date doesn't matter to you?"
"You like Hana that much more than me?"
Ageha.
Shouldn't you be going home soon?
No...
...I'll stay a little while longer.
Hi.
You're here, Ageha.
Mom...
I was wondering why you got dressed up. It was to come here.
Mom, here's your laundry.
Thank you.
Ah, I'm so thirsty. I'll pour us some tea.
I bought that tartary buckwheat tea that you like.

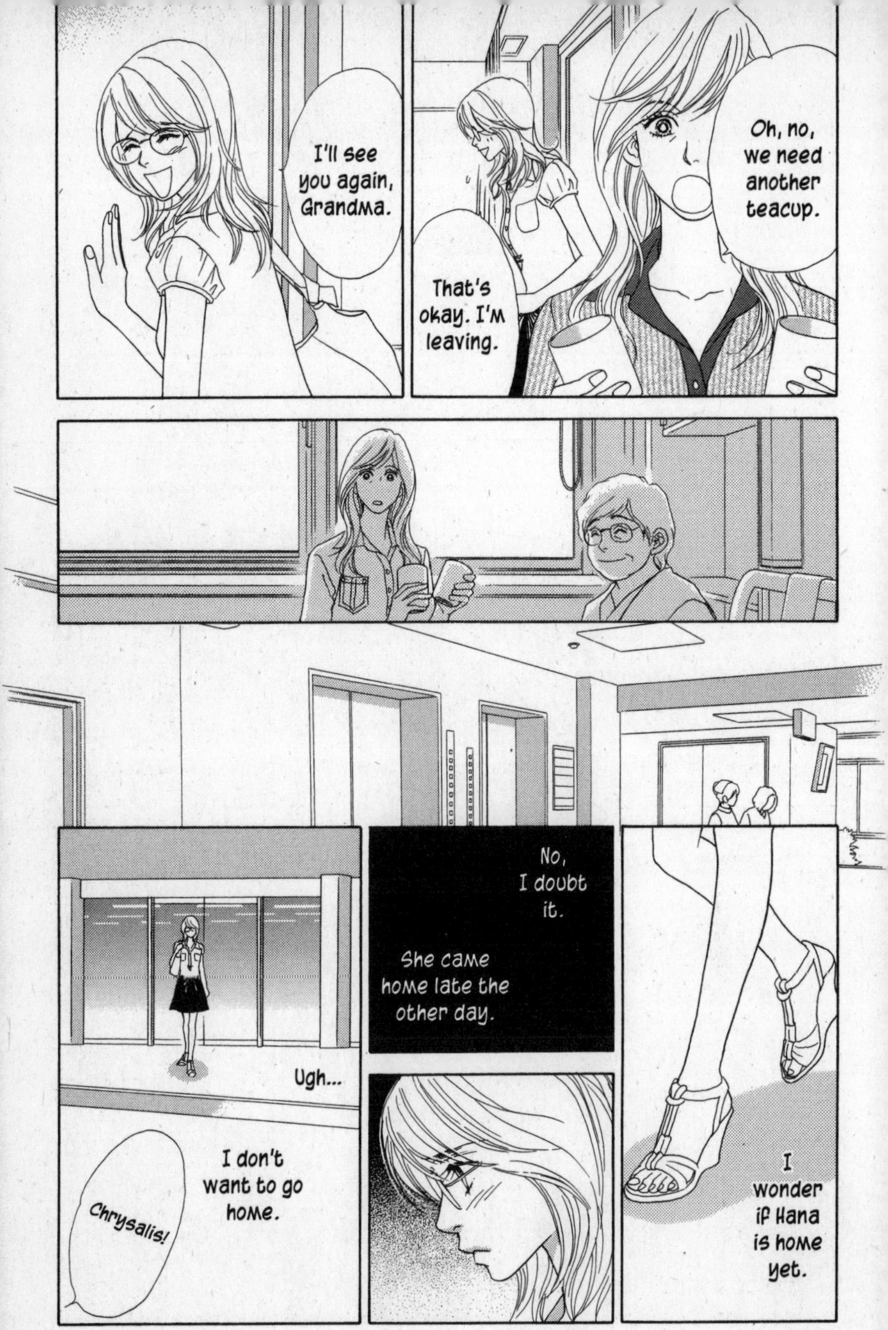
Oh, no, we need another teacup.
That's okay. I'm leaving.
I'll see you again, Grandma.
I wonder if Hana is home yet.
No, I doubt it.
She came home late the other day.
Ugh...
I don't want to go home.
Chrysalis!

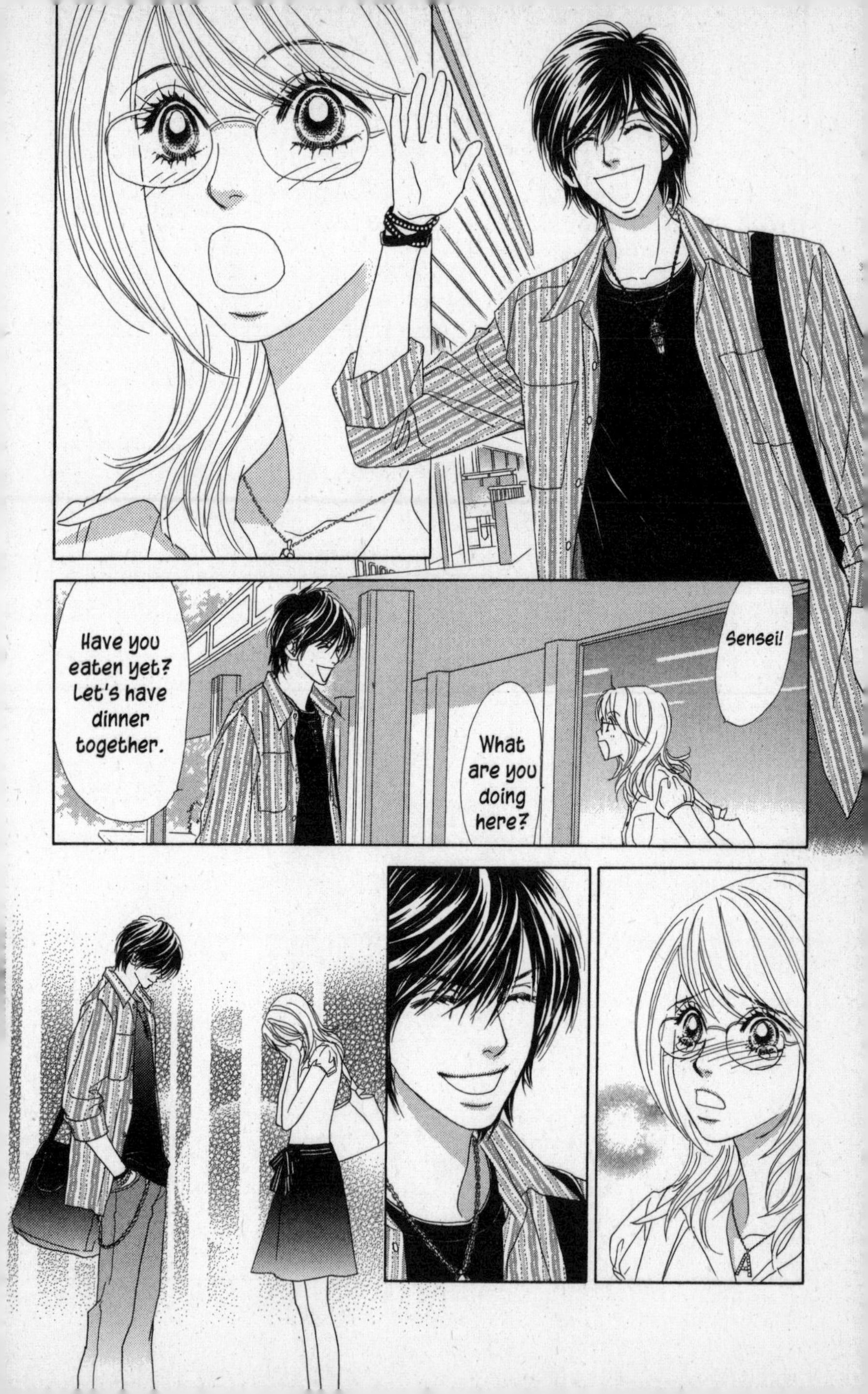
Sensei!
What are you doing here?
Have you eaten yet? Let's have dinner together.

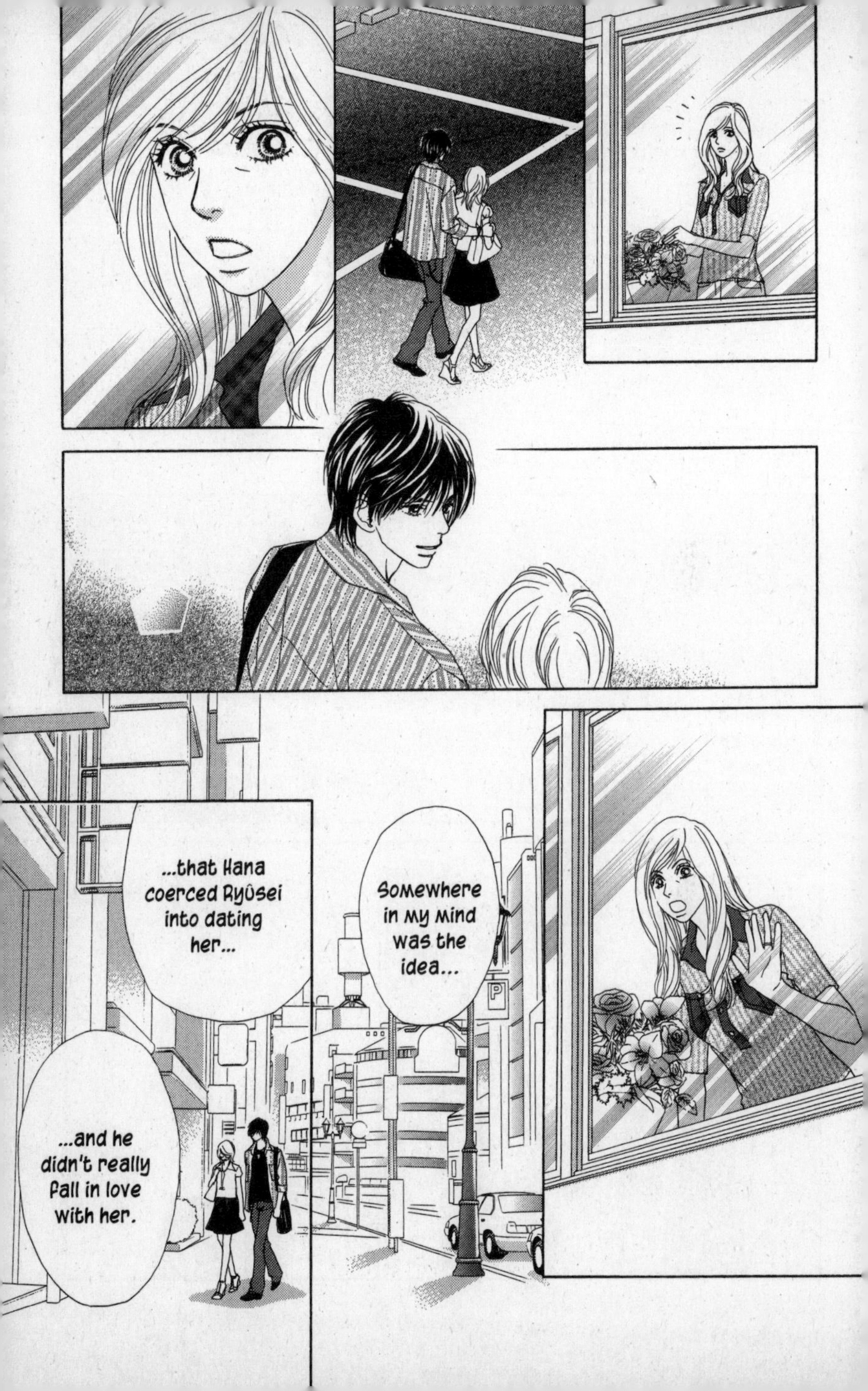
Somewhere in my mind was the idea...
...that Hana coerced Ryûsei into dating her...
...and he didn't really fall in love with her.

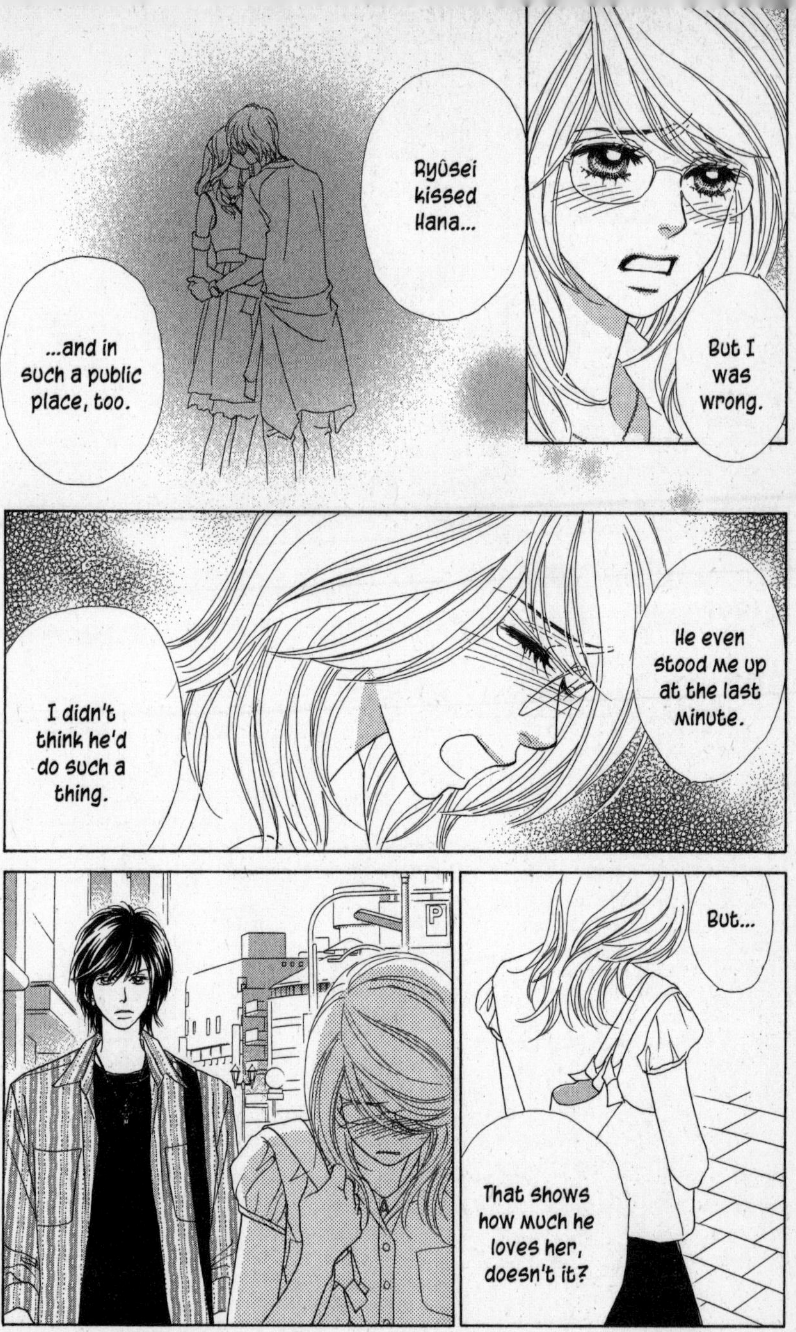
But I was wrong.
Ryûsei kissed Hana...
...and in such a public place, too.
He even stood me up at the last minute.
I didn't think he'd do such a thing.
But...
That shows how much he loves her, doesn't it?

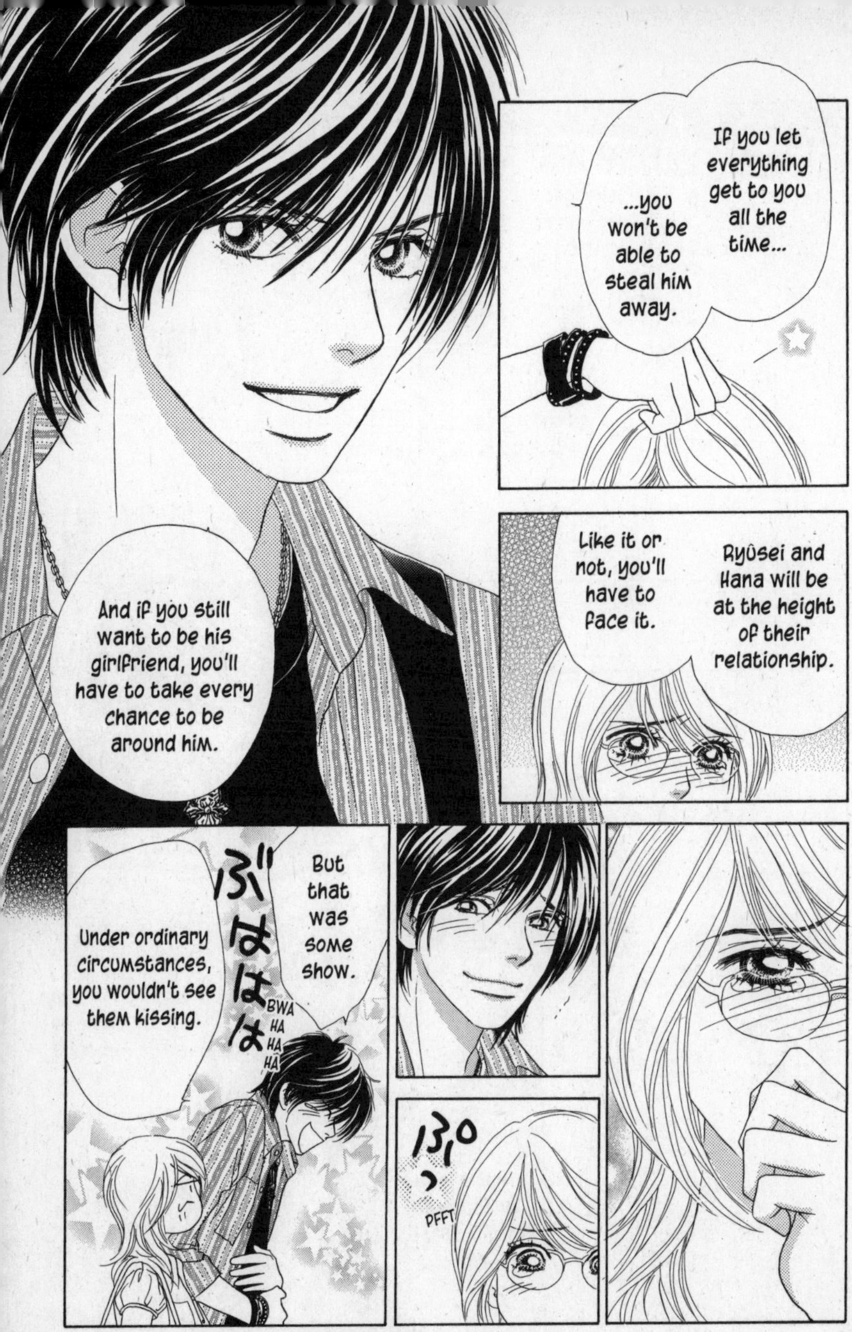
If you let everything get to you all the time...
...you won't be able to steal him away.
Ryûsei and Hana will be at the height of their relationship.
Like it or not, you'll have to face it.
And if you still want to be his girlfriend, you'll have to take every chance to be around him.
ぷっ
PFFT
But that was some show.
ぶははは
BWA HA HA HA
Under ordinary circumstances, you wouldn't see them kissing.

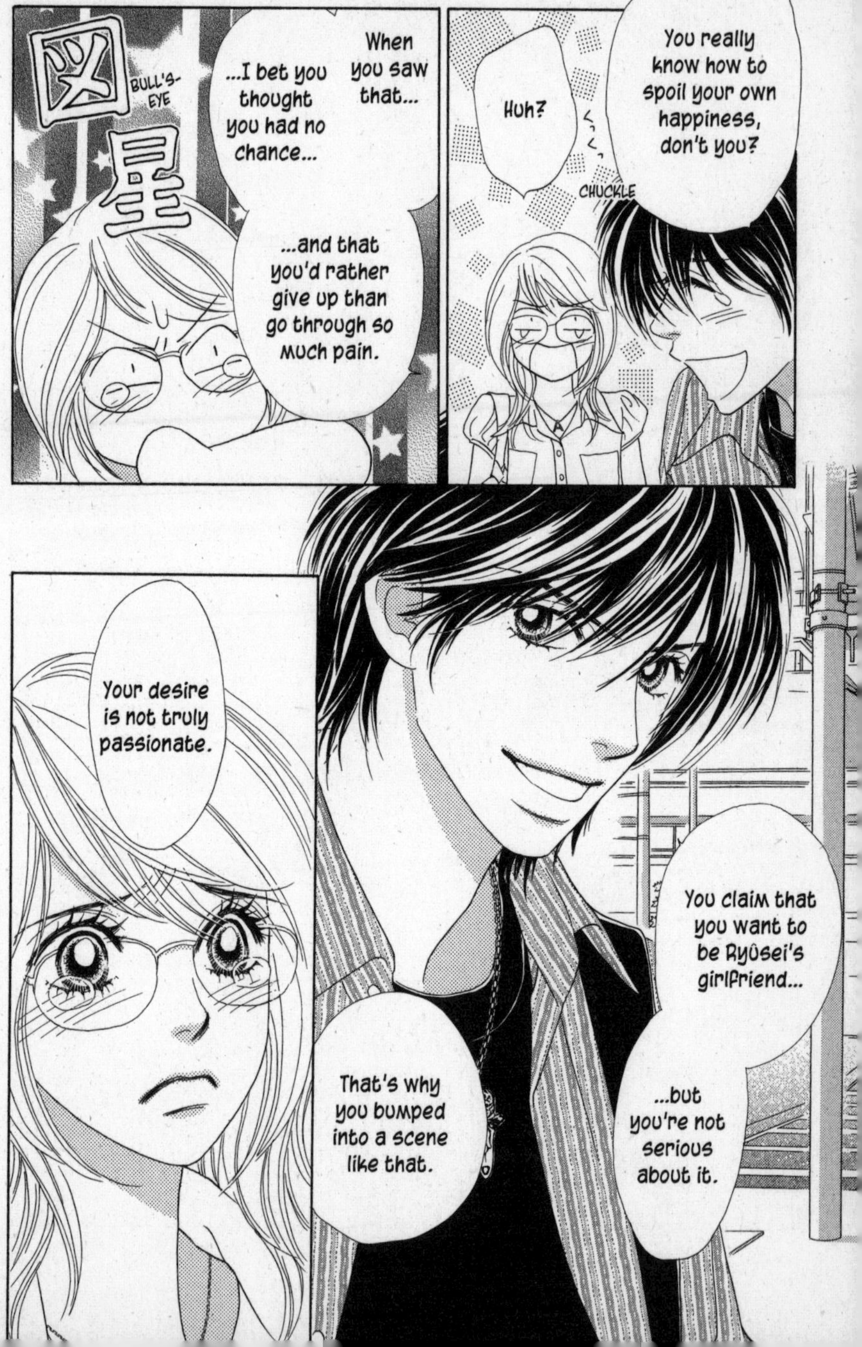
You really know how to spoil your own happiness, don't you?
Huh?
CHUCKLE
When you saw that...
...I bet you thought you had no chance...
図星
BULL'S-EYE
...and that you'd rather give up than go through so much pain.
You claim that you want to be Ryôsei's girlfriend...
...but you're not serious about it.
That's why you bumped into a scene like that.
Your desire is not truly passionate.

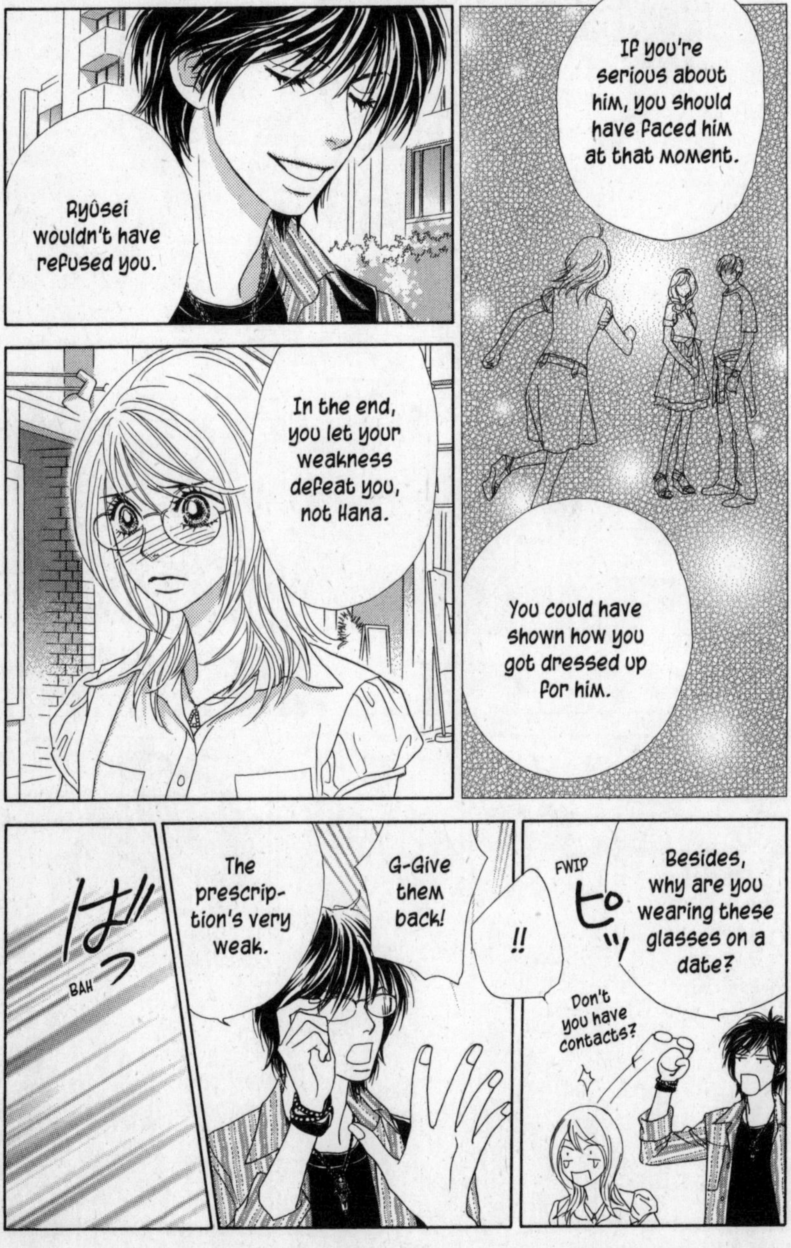
If you're serious about him, you should have faced him at that moment.
You could have shown how you got dressed up for him.
Ryûsei wouldn't have refused you.
In the end, you let your weakness defeat you, not Hana.
Besides, why are you wearing these glasses on a date?
FWIP
ピッ
Don't you have contacts?
!!
G-Give them back!
The prescrip-tion's very weak.
ばっ
BAH

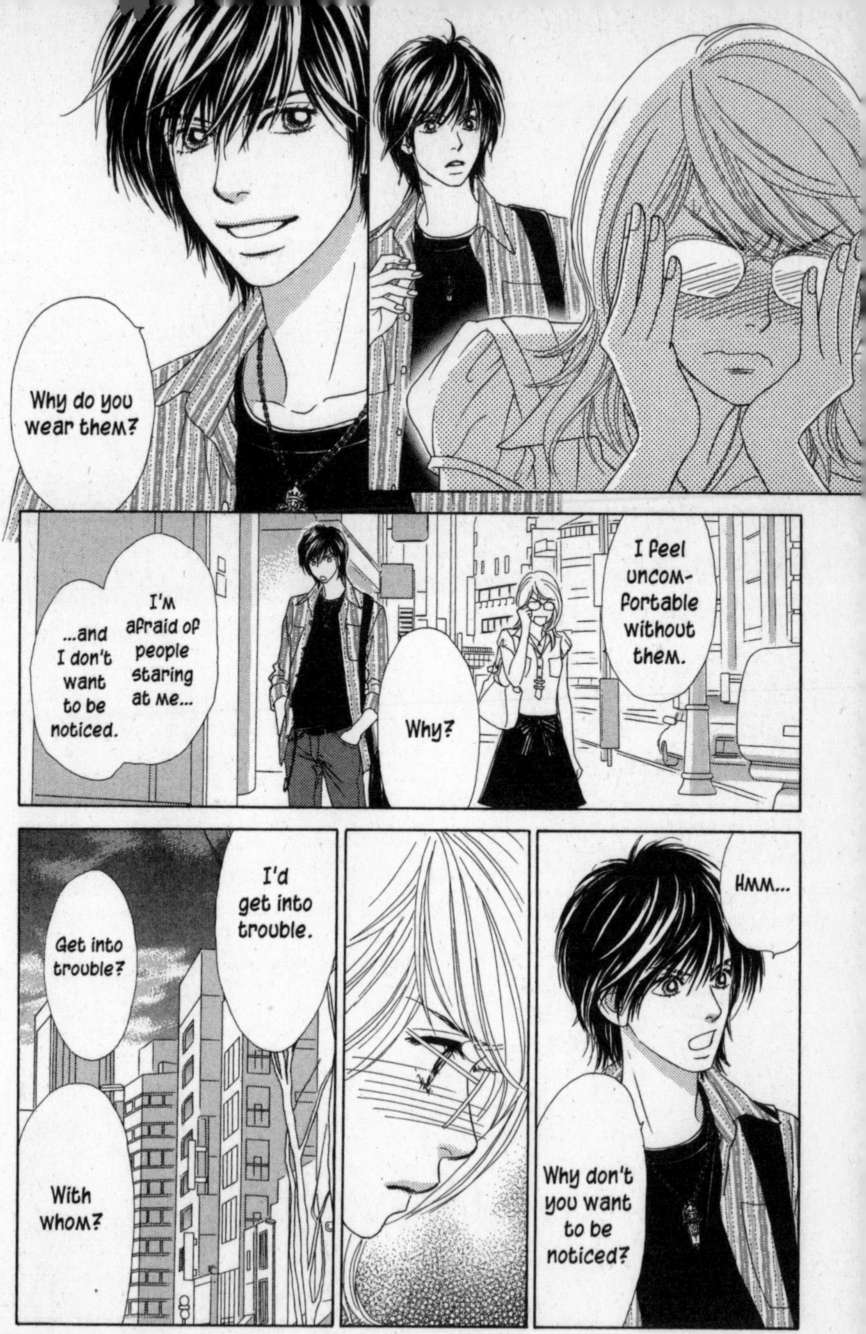
Why do you wear them?
I feel uncom-fortable without them.
Why?
I'm afraid of people staring at me...
...and I don't want to be noticed.
Hmm...
Why don't you want to be noticed?
I'd get into trouble.
Get into trouble?
With whom?

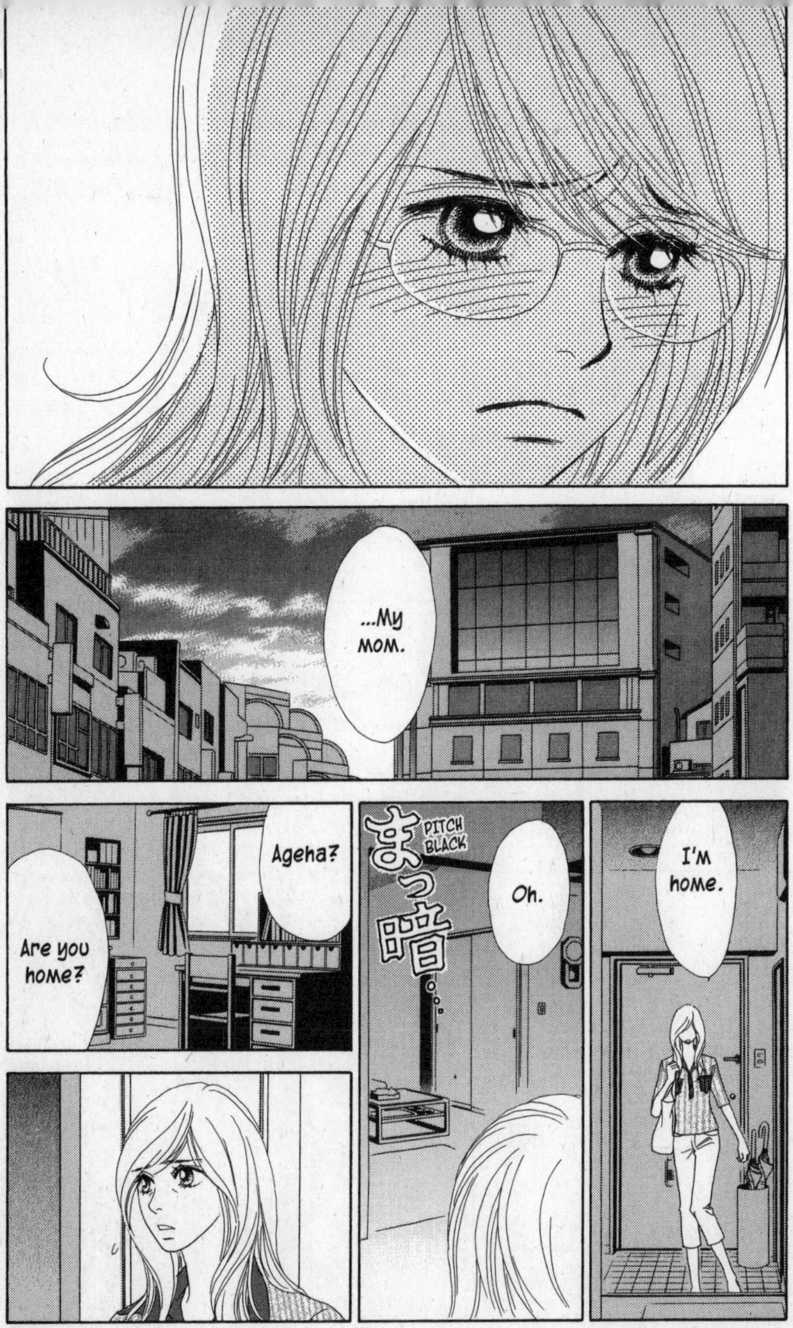
...My mom.
I'm home.
まっ暗
PITCH BLACK
Oh.
Ageha?
Are you home?

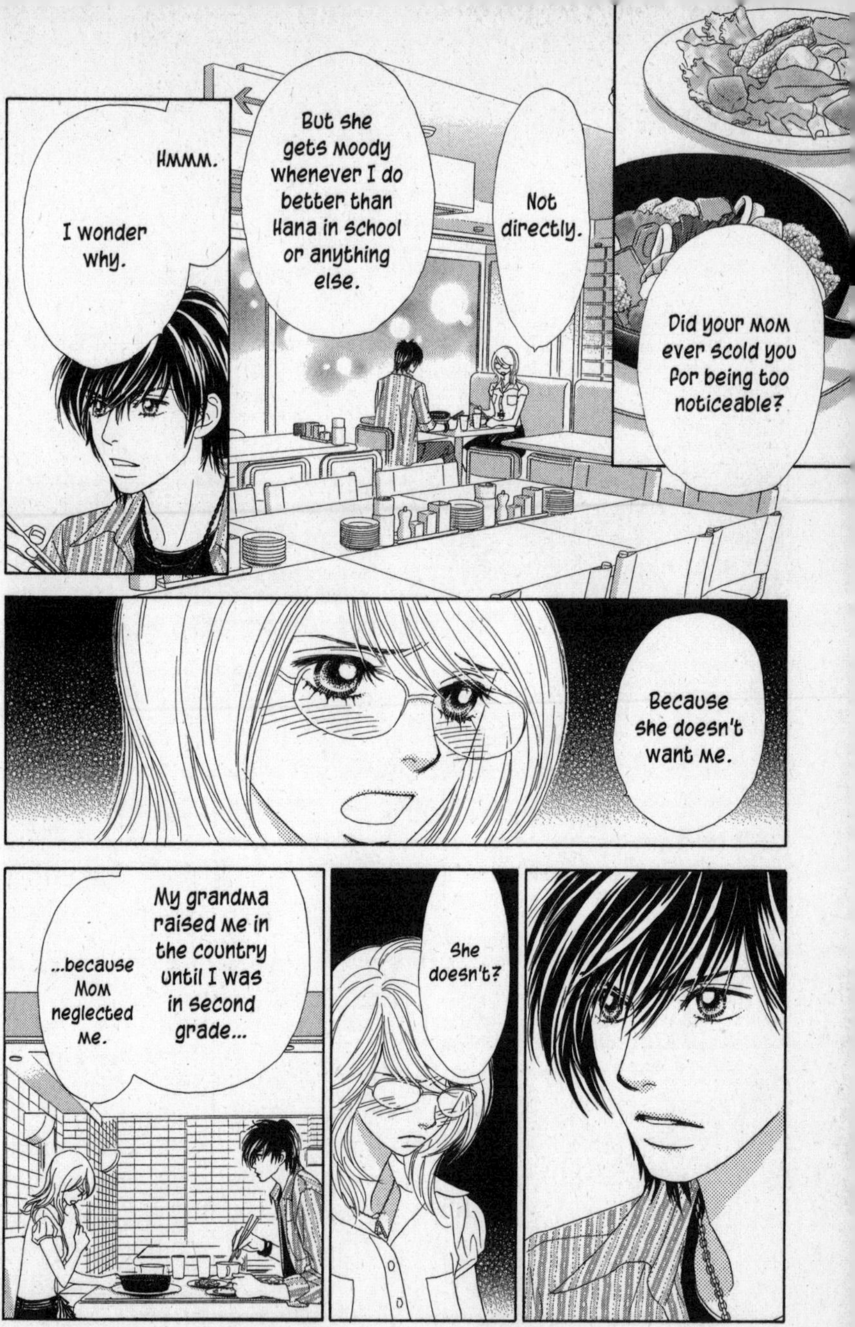
Did your mom ever scold you for being too noticeable?
Not directly.
But she gets moody whenever I do better than Hana in school or anything else.
Hmmm.
I wonder why.
Because she doesn't want me.
She doesn't?
My grandma raised me in the country until I was in second grade...
...because Mom neglected me.

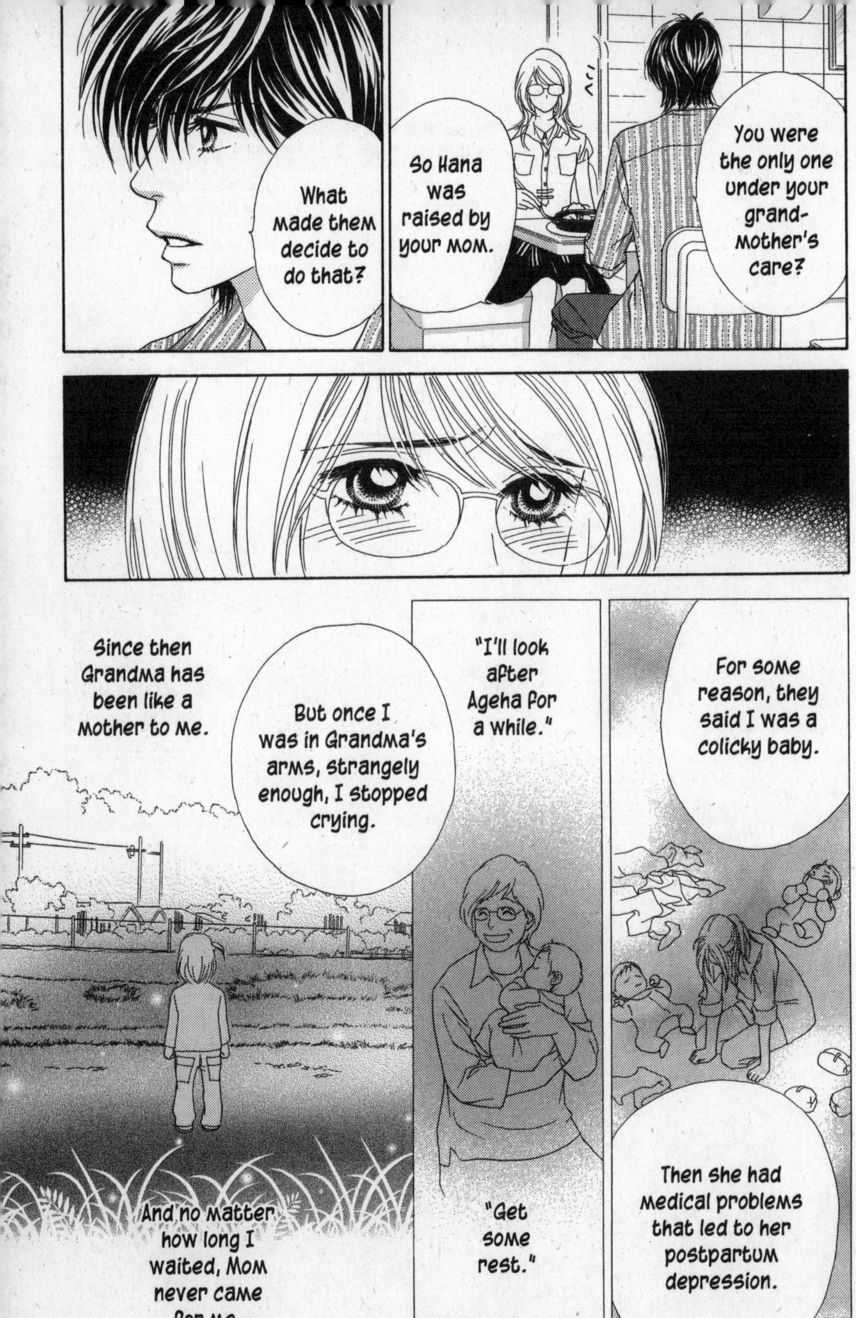
You were the only one under your grand-mother's care?
So Hana was raised by your mom.
What made them decide to do that?
For some reason, they said I was a colicky baby.
Then she had medical problems that led to her postpartum depression.
"I'll look after Ageha for a while."
"Get some rest."
But once I was in Grandma's arms, strangely enough, I stopped crying.
Since then Grandma has been like a mother to me.
And no matter how long I waited, Mom never came for me.

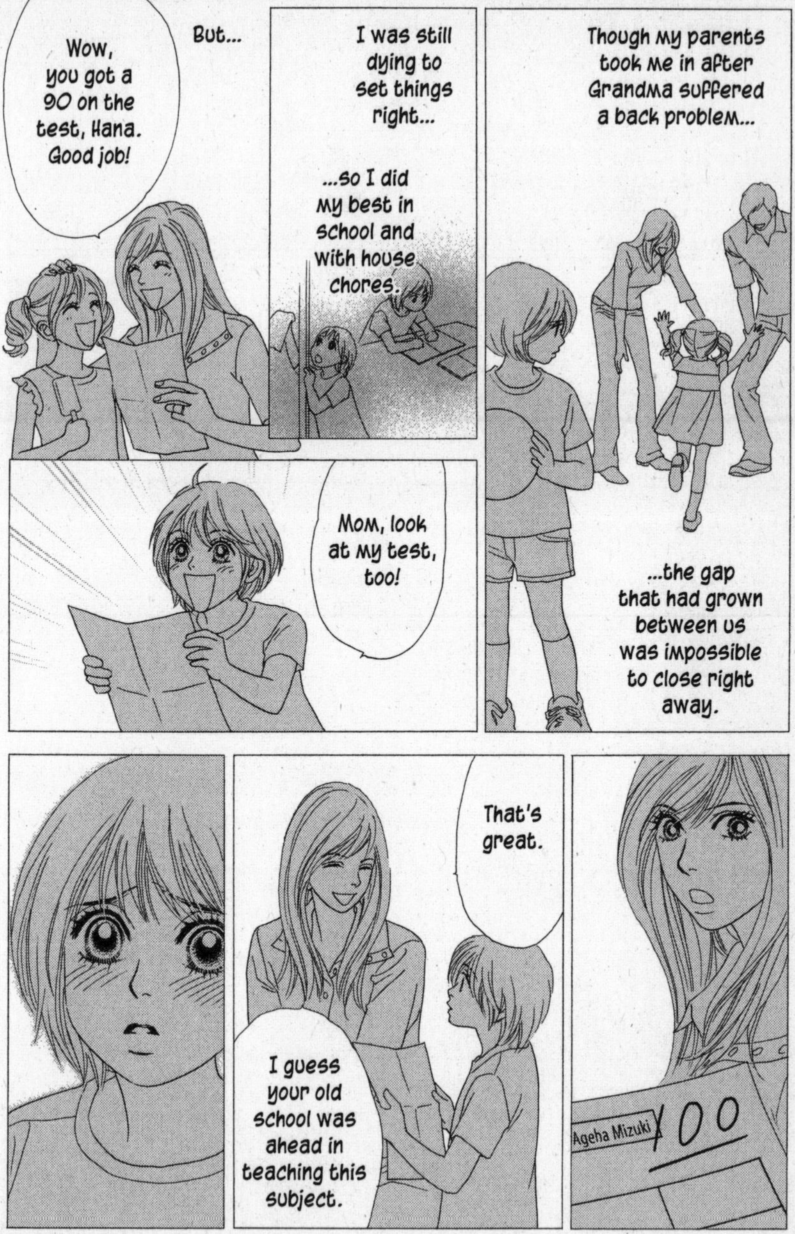
Though my parents took me in after Grandma suffered a back problem...
...the gap that had grown between us was impossible to close right away.
I was still dying to set things right...
...so I did my best in school and with house chores.
But...
Wow, you got a 90 on the test, Hana. Good job!
Mom, look at my test, too!
Ageha Mizuki
100
That's great.
I guess your old school was ahead in teaching this subject.

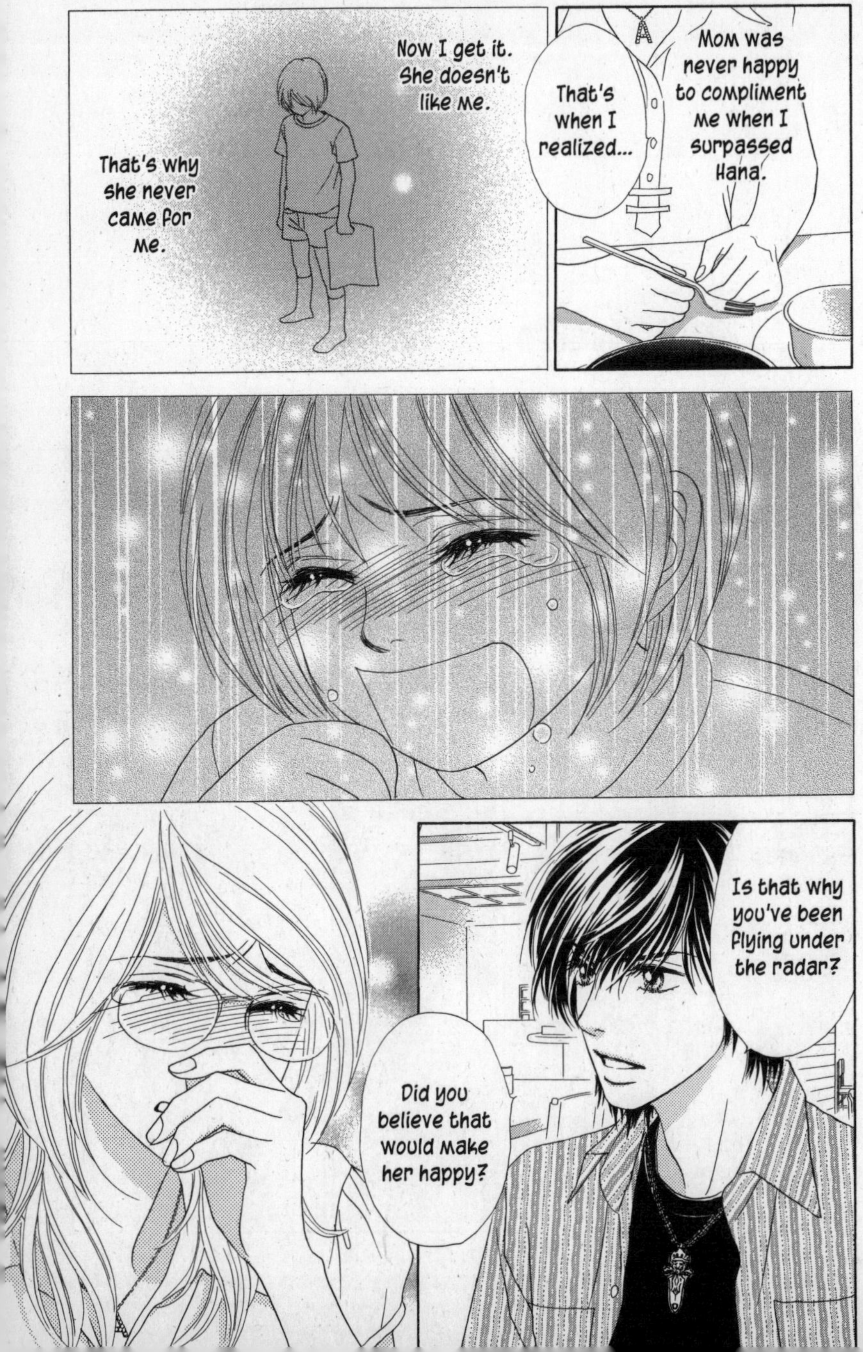
Mom was never happy to compliment me when I surpassed Hana.
That's when I realized...
Now I get it. She doesn't like me.
That's why she never came for me.
Is that why you've been flying under the radar?
Did you believe that would make her happy?

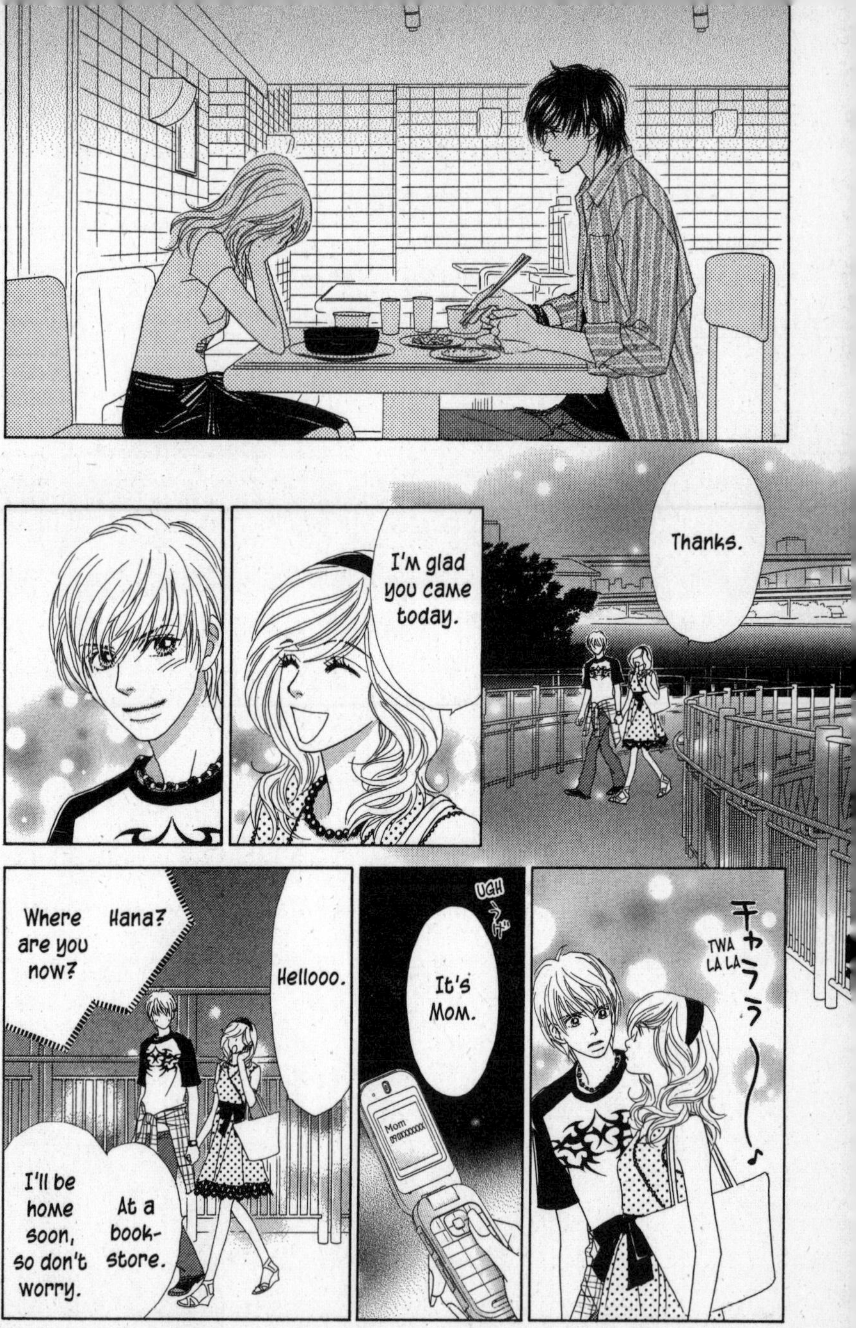
Thanks.
I'm glad you came today.
チャララ～♪
TWA LA LA
うげ
UGH
It's Mom.
Mom
Hellooo.
Hana? Where are you now?
At a bookstore.
I'll be home soon, so don't worry.

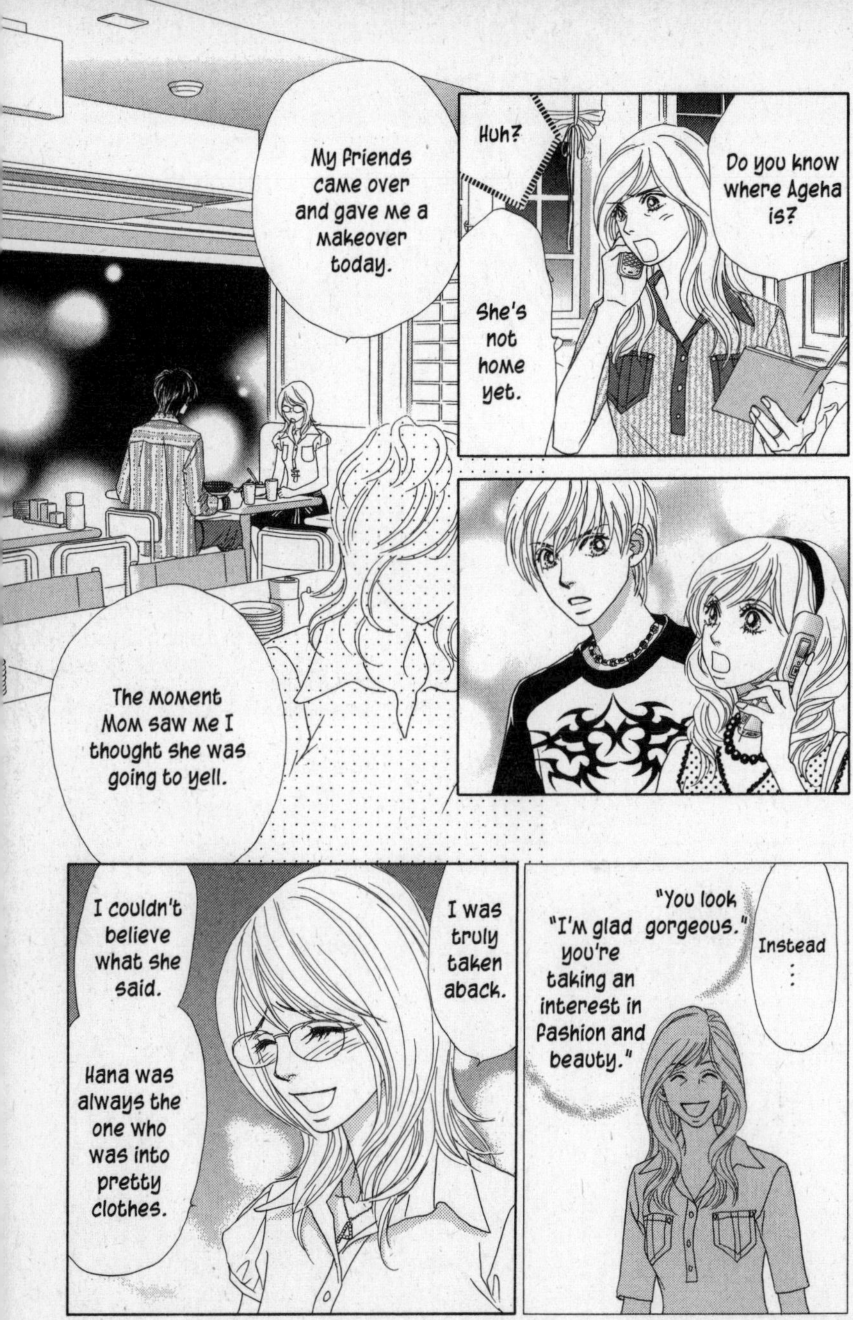
Do you know where Ageha is?
Huh?
She's not home yet.
My friends came over and gave me a makeover today.
The moment Mom saw me I thought she was going to yell.
Instead...
"You look gorgeous."
"I'm glad you're taking an interest in fashion and beauty."
I was truly taken aback.
I couldn't believe what she said.
Hana was always the one who was into pretty clothes.

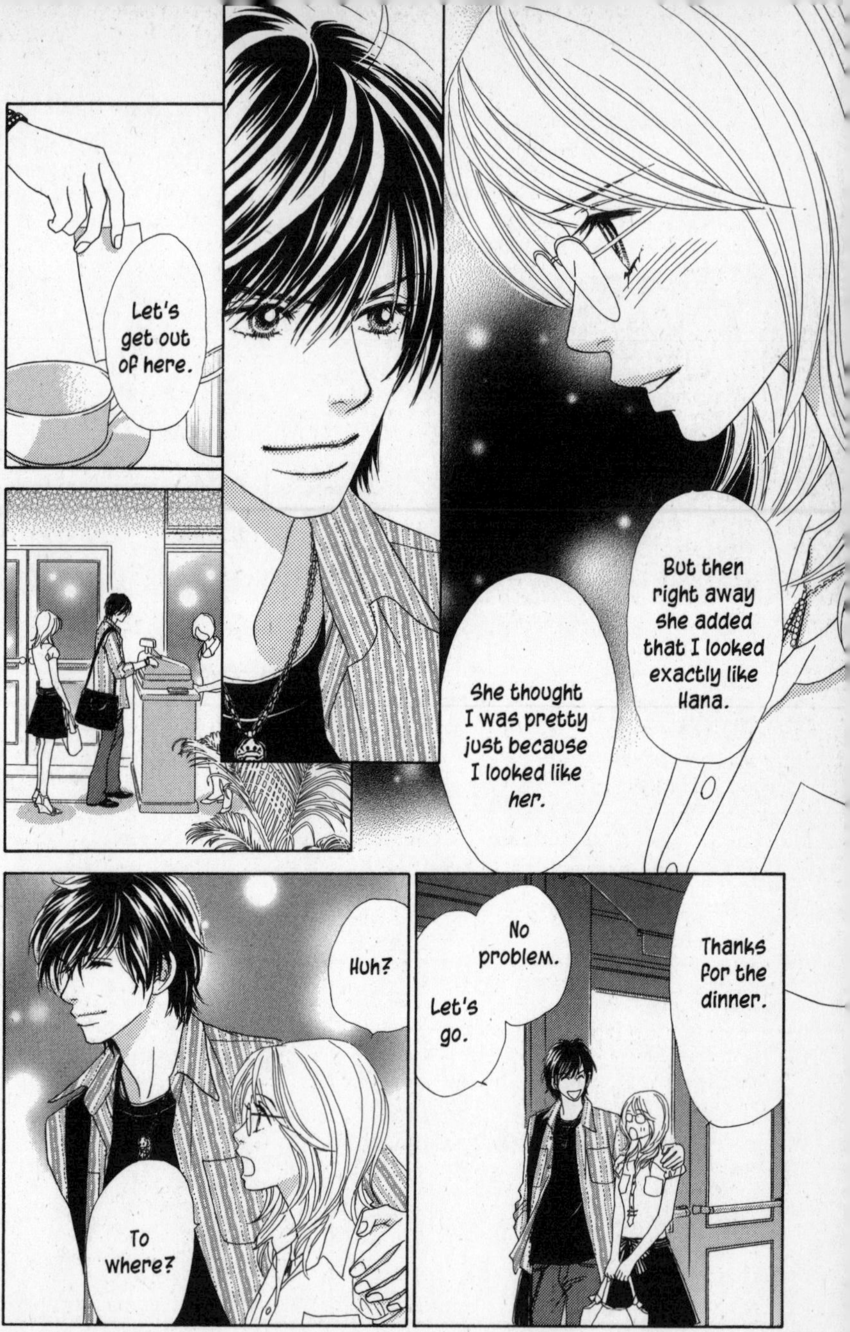
But then right away she added that I looked exactly like Hana.
She thought I was pretty just because I looked like her.
Let's get out of here.
Thanks for the dinner.
No problem.
Let's go.
Huh?
To where?

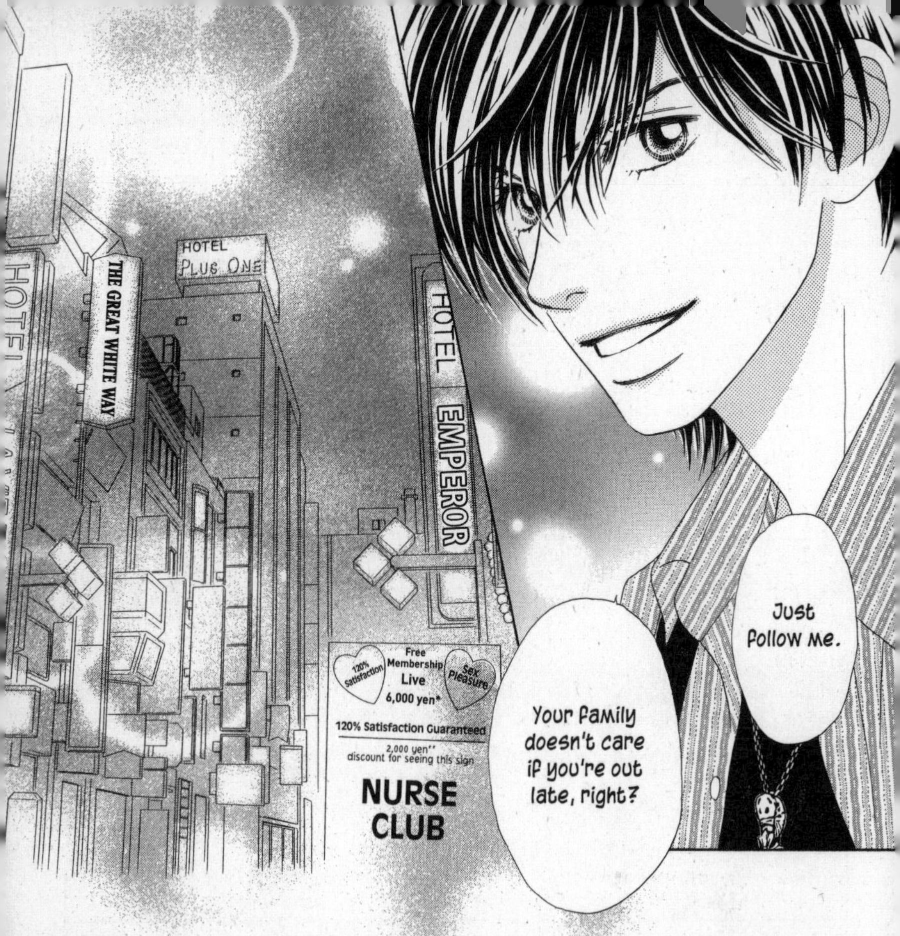
Just follow me.
Your family doesn't care if you're out late, right?
HOTEL EMPEROR
HOTEL PLUS ONE
THE GREAT WHITE WAY
HOTEL
Free Membership Live 6,000 yen*
120% Satisfaction
Sex Pleasure
120% Satisfaction Guaranteed
2,000 yen** discount for seeing this sign
NURSE CLUB

*$60.
**$20.

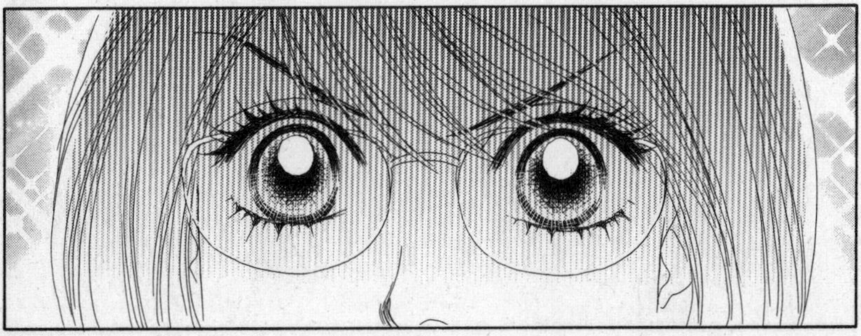

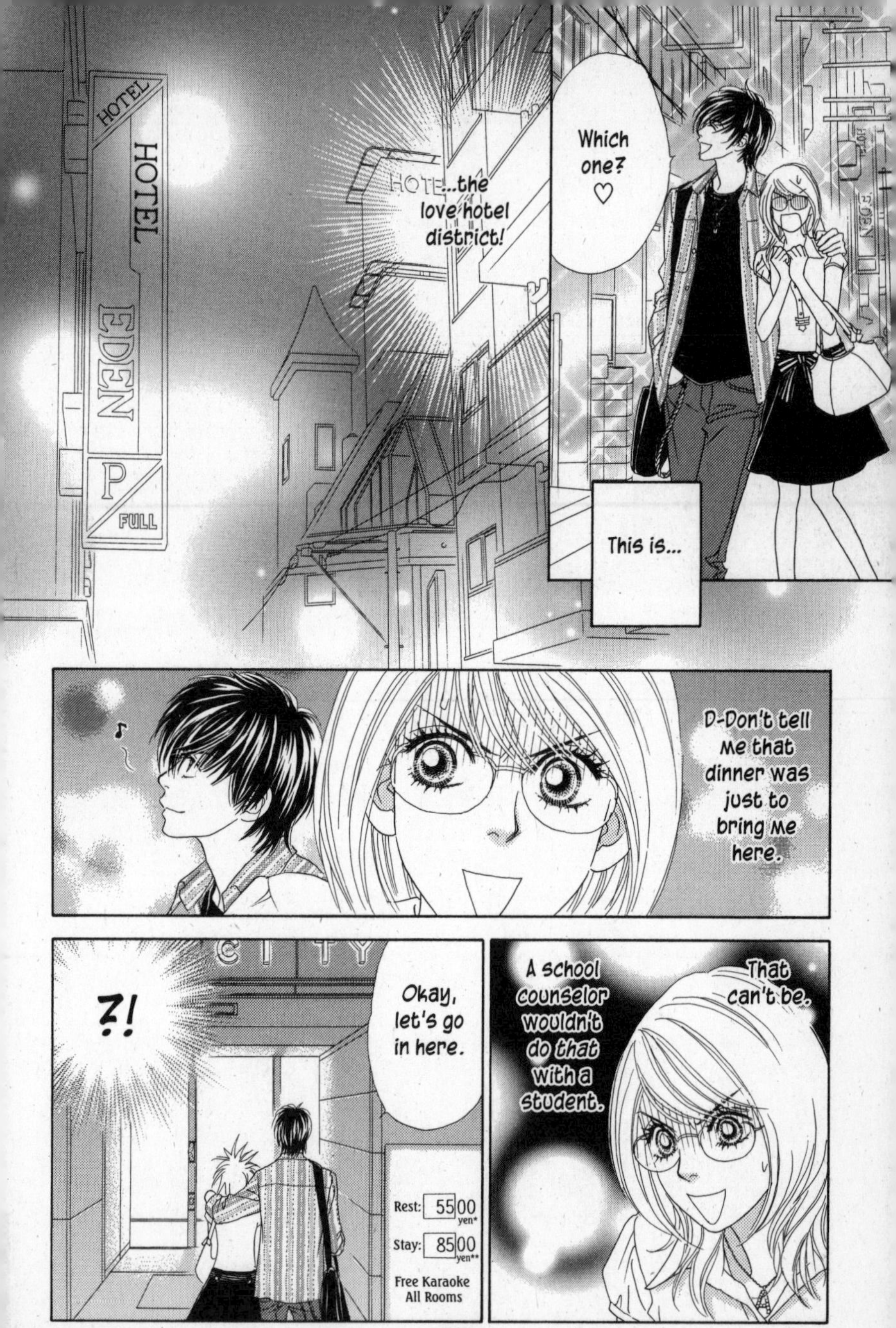
Which one? ♡
This is...
HOTEL
HOTEL
EDEN
P
FULL
HOTE
...the love hotel district!
D-Don't tell me that dinner was just to bring me here.
That can't be.
A school counselor wouldn't do that with a student.
Okay, let's go in here.
?!
CITY
Rest: 5500 yen*
Stay: 8500 yen**
Free Karaoke All Rooms

*$55.
**$85.

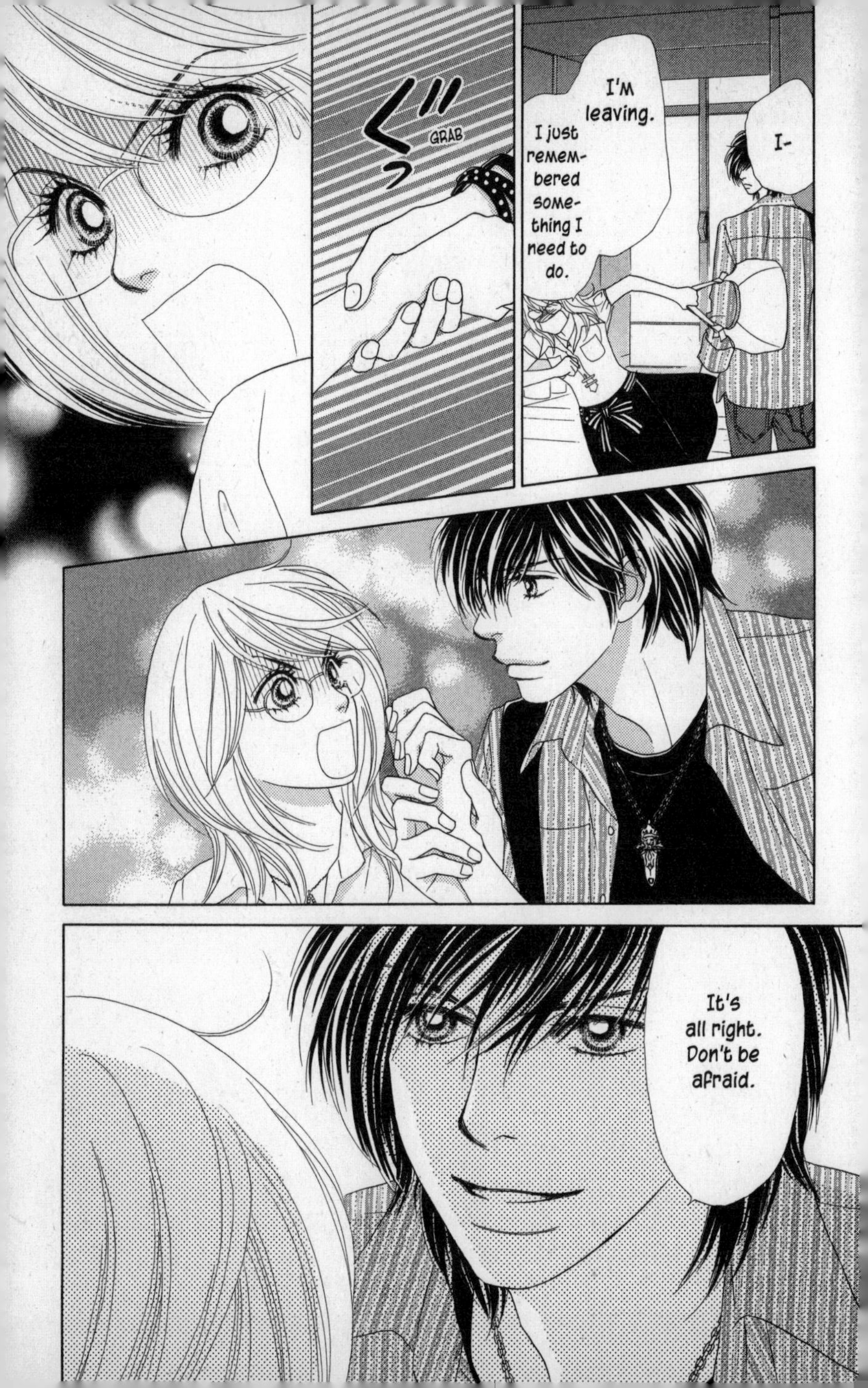
I-
I'M leaving.
I just remembered something I need to do.
GRAB
It's all right. Don't be afraid.

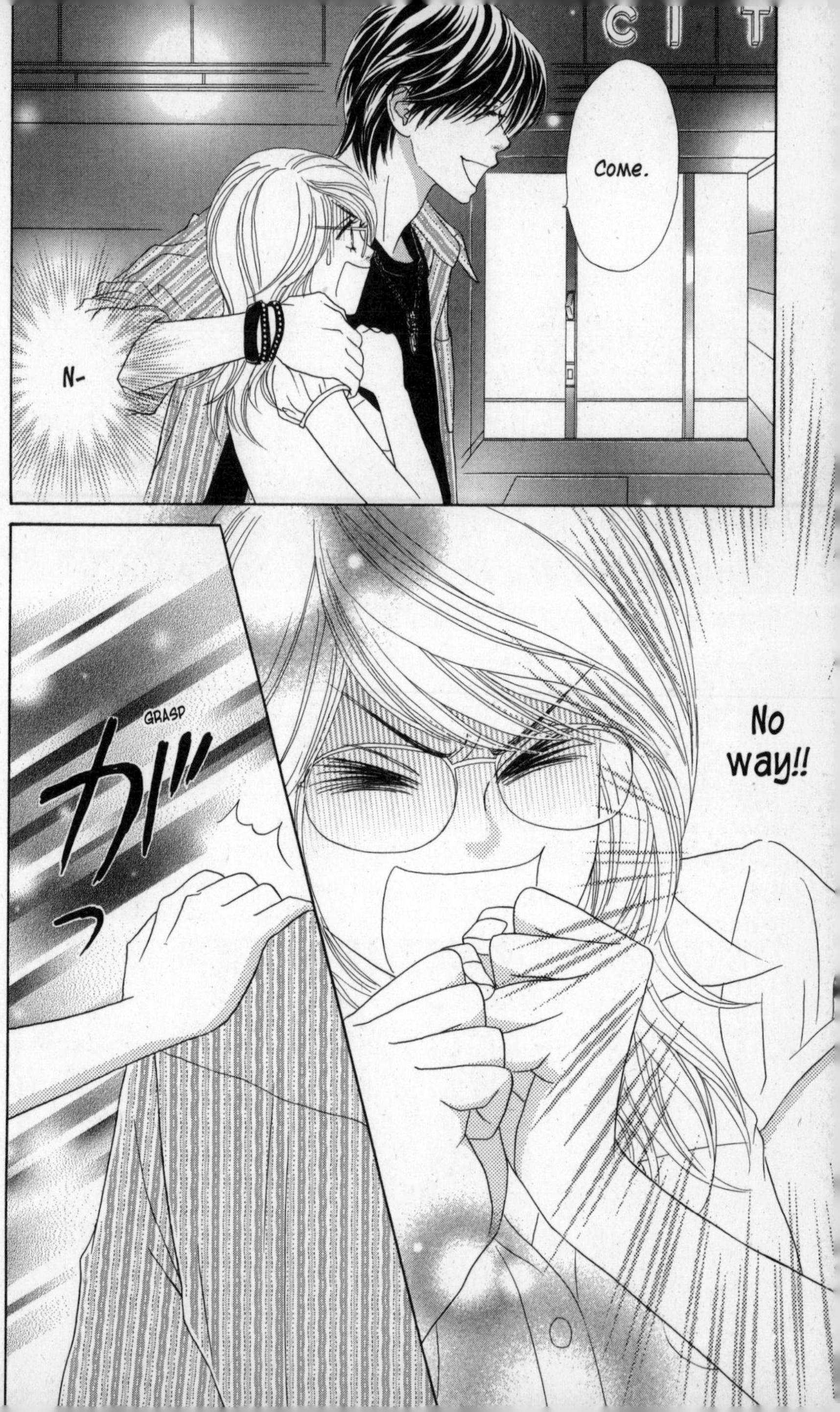
Come.
N-
No way!!
GRASP
ガッ

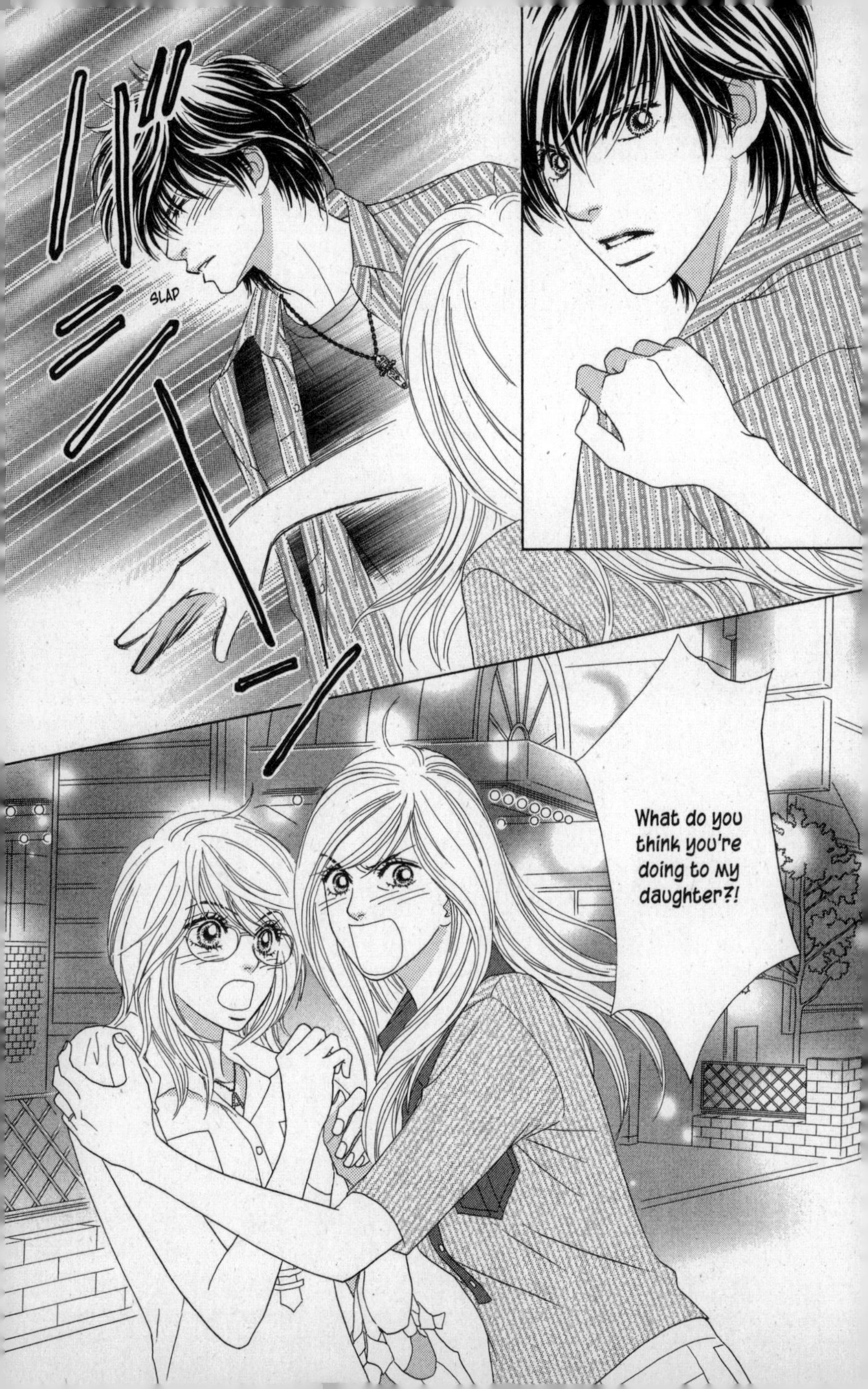
SLAP
What do you think you're doing to my daughter?!

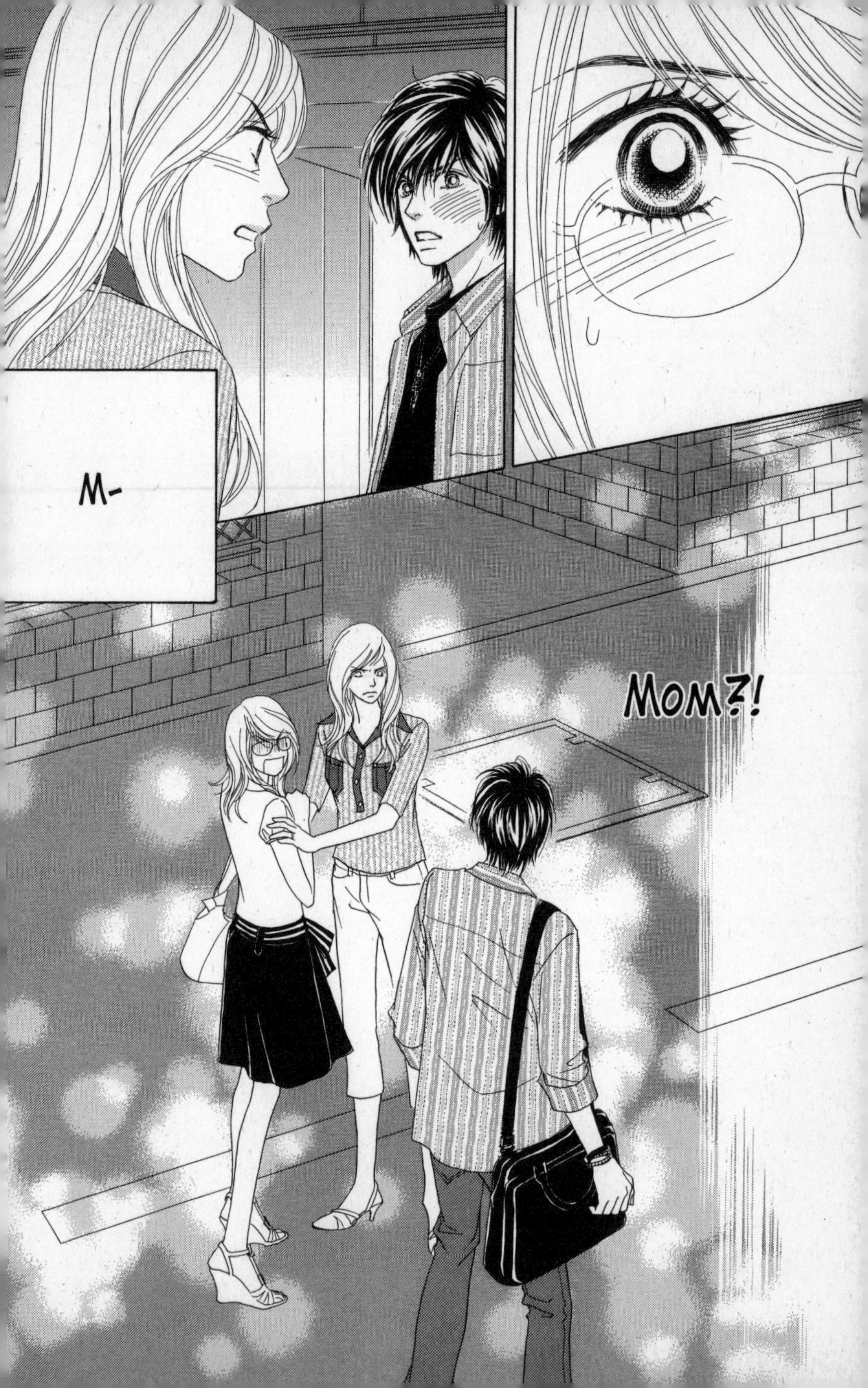
M-
MOM?!

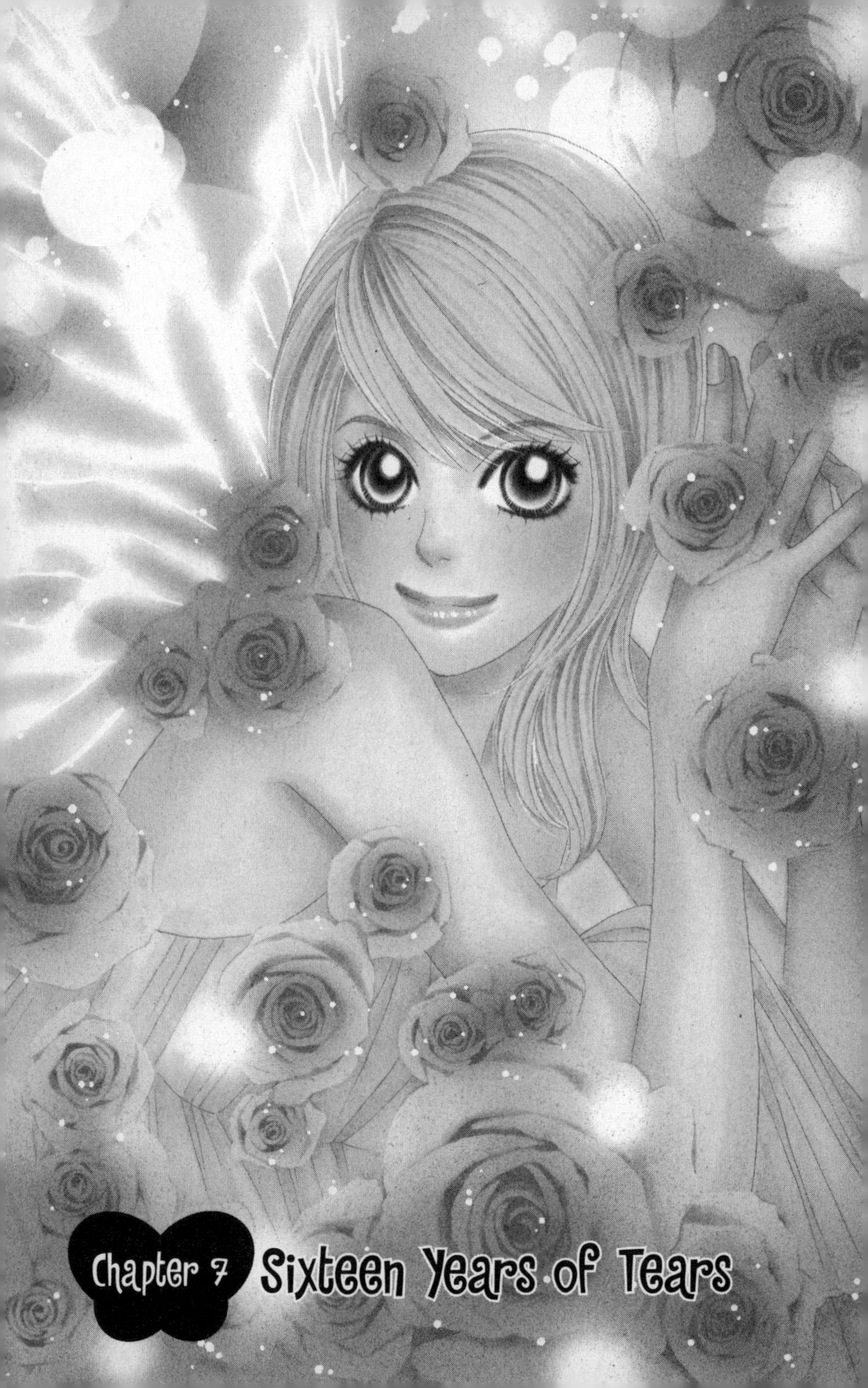
Chapter 7
Sixteen Years of Tears

Papillon

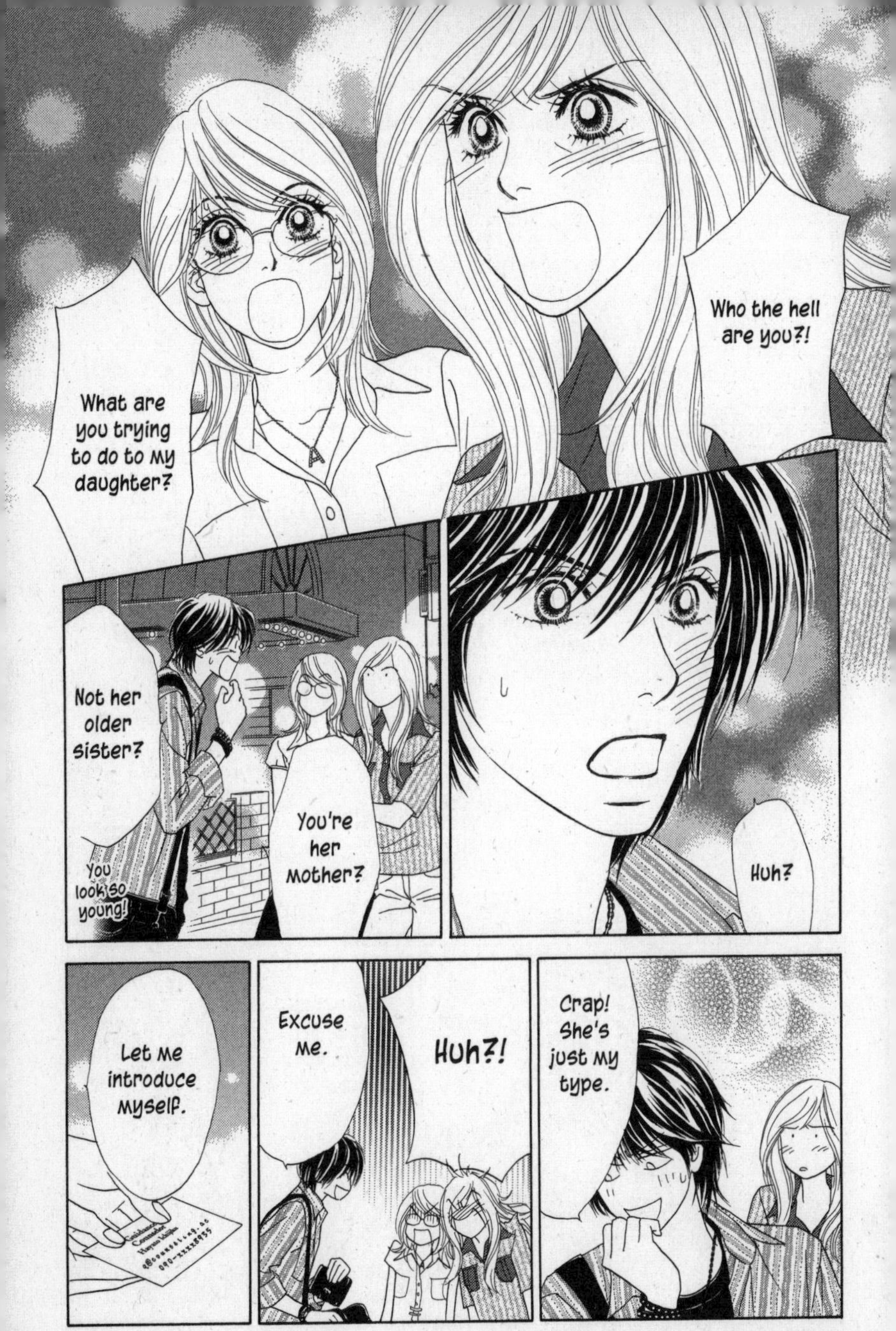
Who the hell are you?!
What are you trying to do to my daughter?
Huh?
You're her mother?
Not her older sister?
You look so young!
Crap! She's just my type.
Huh?!
Excuse me.
Let me introduce myself.

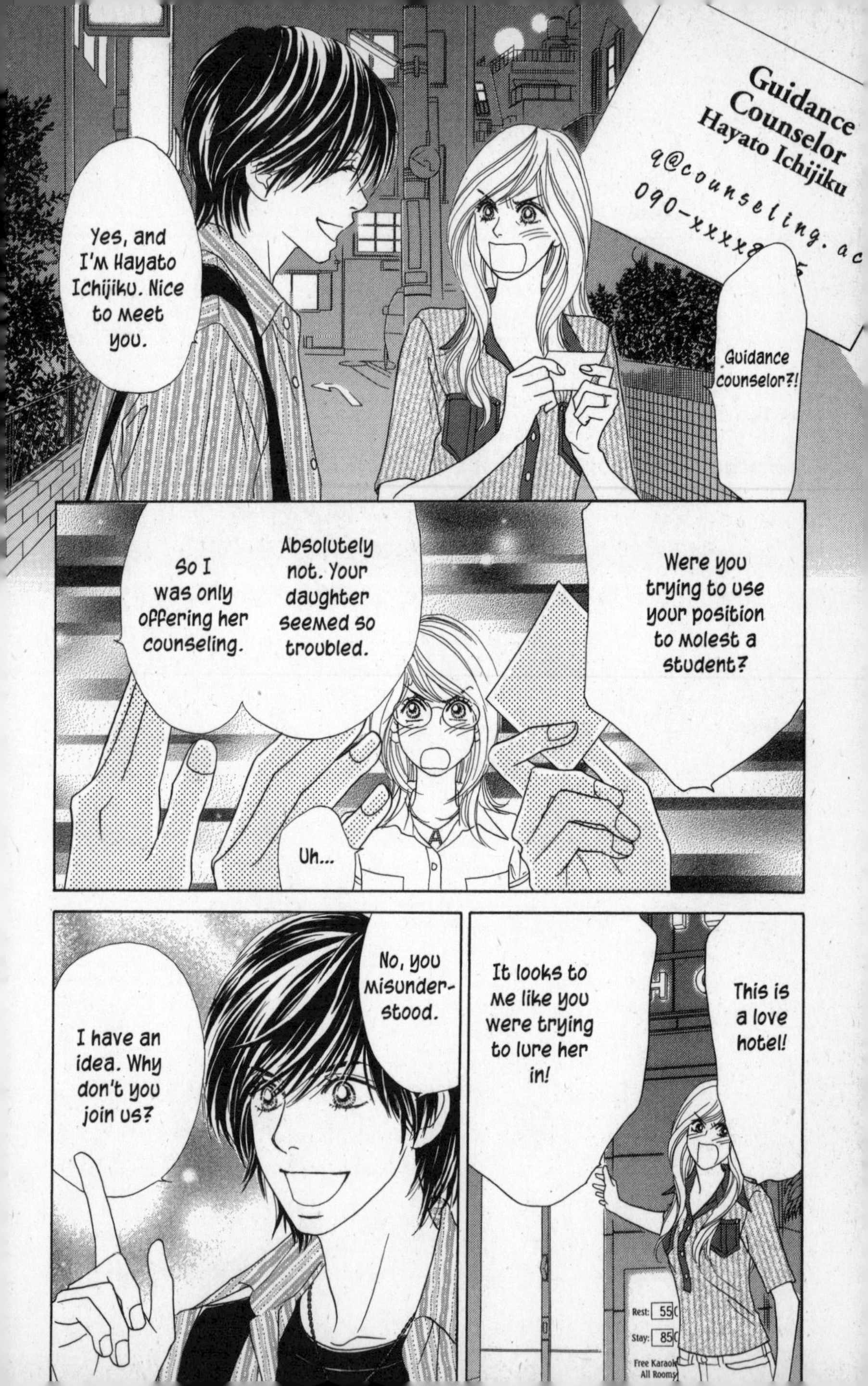

Guidance Counselor
Hayato Ichijiku
q@counseling.ac
090-xxxx8
Guidance counselor?!
Yes, and I'm Hayato Ichijiku. Nice to meet you.
Were you trying to use your position to molest a student?
Absolutely not. Your daughter seemed so troubled.
So I was only offering her counseling.
Uh...
This is a love hotel!
It looks to me like you were trying to lure her in!
Rest: 55
Stay: 85
No, you misunder-stood.
I have an idea. Why don't you join us?

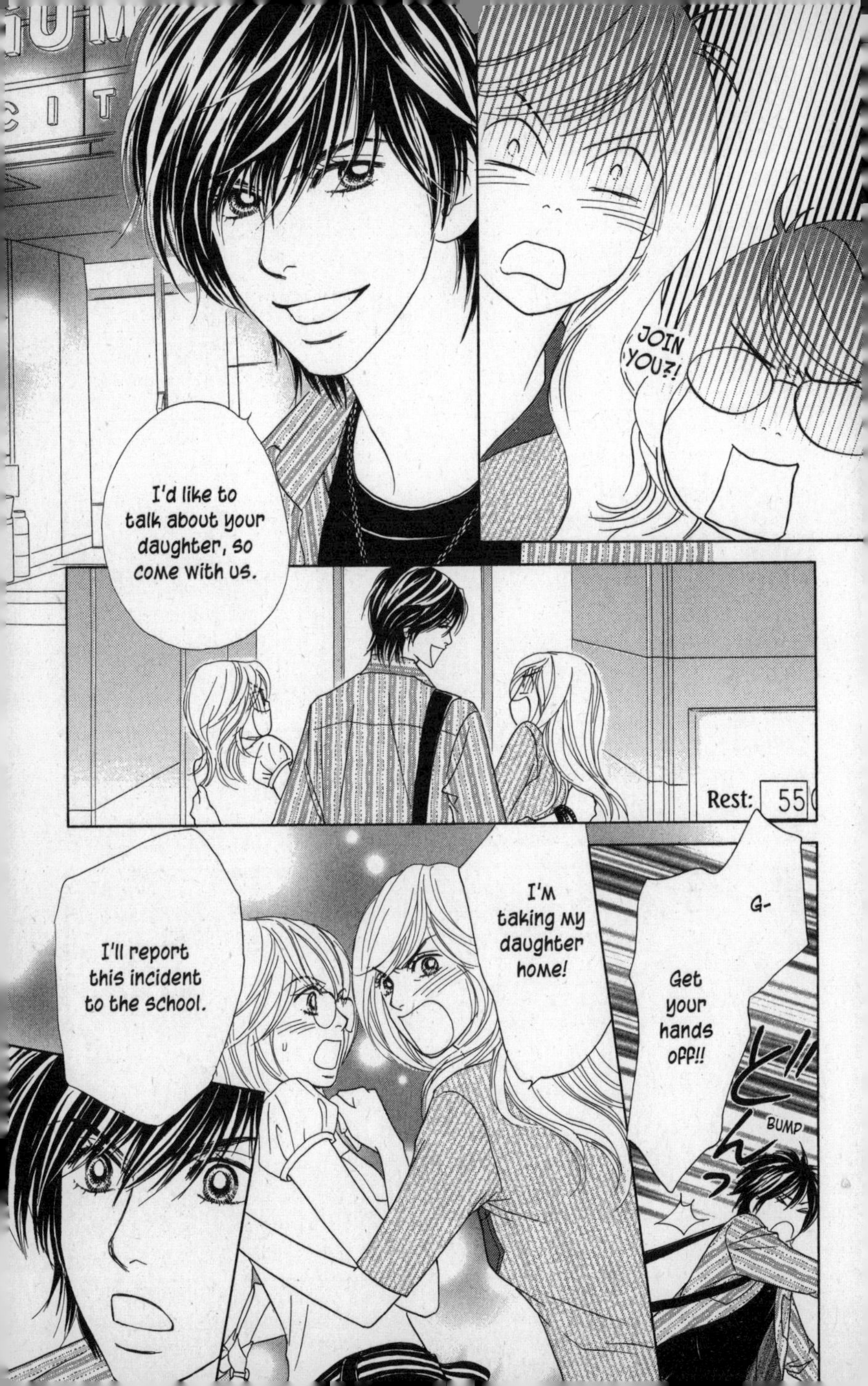
JOIN YOU?!
I'd like to talk about your daughter, so come with us.
Rest: 55
G-
Get your hands off!!
BUMP
I'm taking my daughter home!
I'll report this incident to the school.

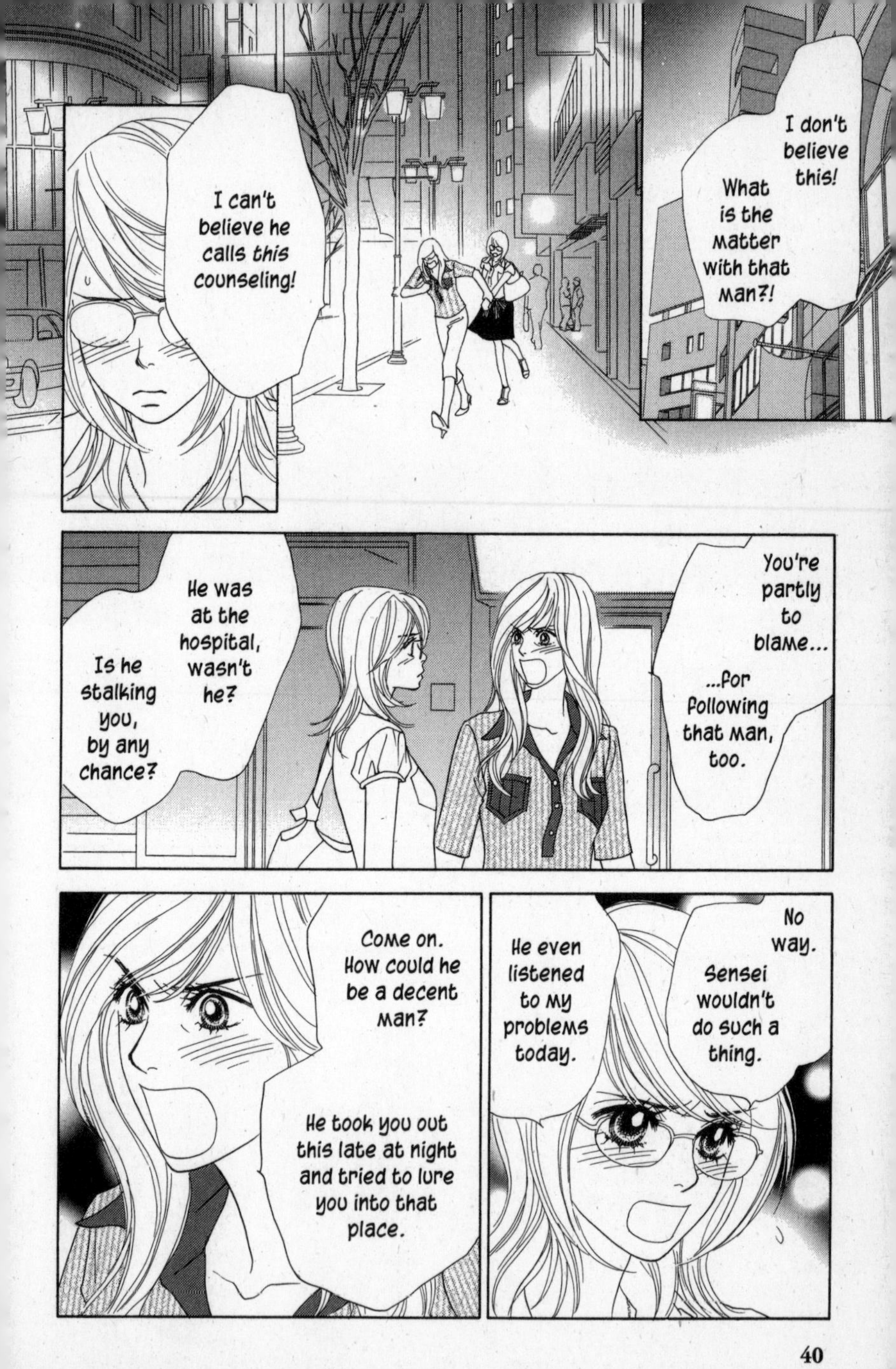
I don't believe this!
What is the matter with that man?!
I can't believe he calls *this* counseling!
You're partly to blame...
...for following that man, too.
He was at the hospital, wasn't he?
Is he stalking you, by any chance?
No way.
Sensei wouldn't do such a thing.
He even listened to my problems today.
Come on. How could he be a decent man?
He took you out this late at night and tried to lure you into that place.

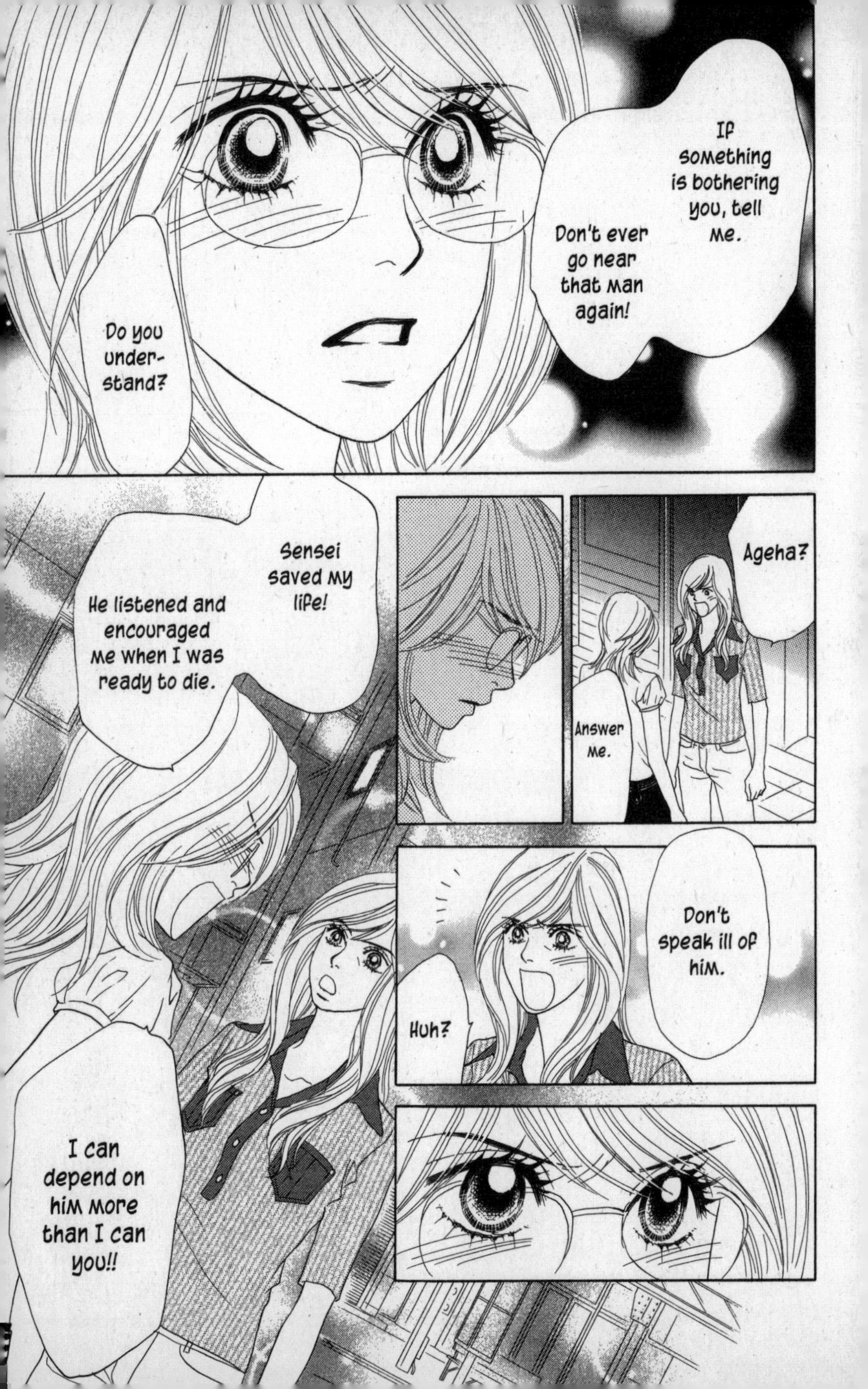

If something is bothering you, tell me.
Don't ever go near that man again!
Do you under-stand?
Ageha?
Answer me.
Don't speak ill of him.
Huh?
Sensei saved my life!
He listened and encouraged me when I was ready to die.
I can depend on him more than I can you!!

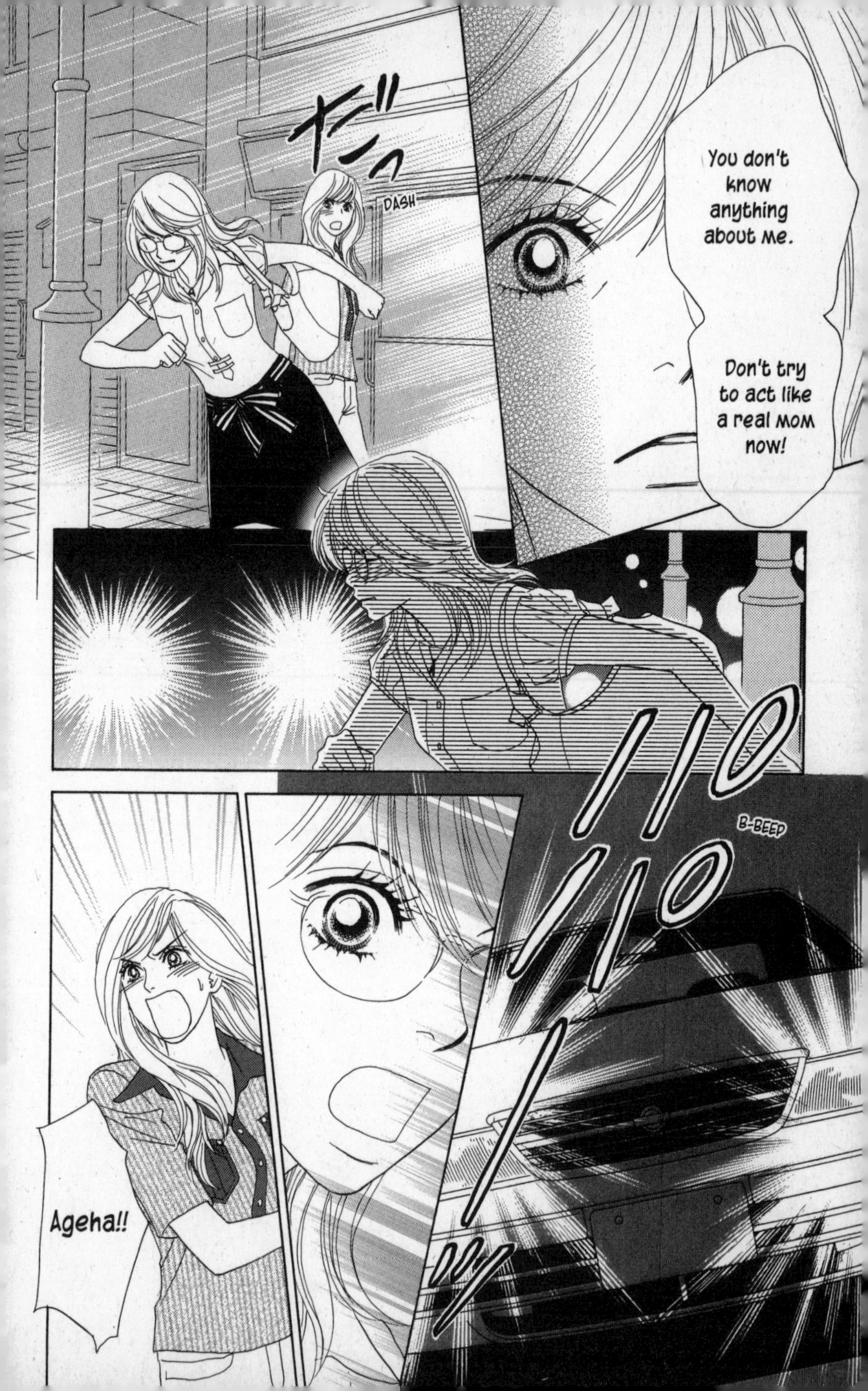
You don't know anything about me.
Don't try to act like a real MOM now!
DASH
B-BEEP
Ageha!!

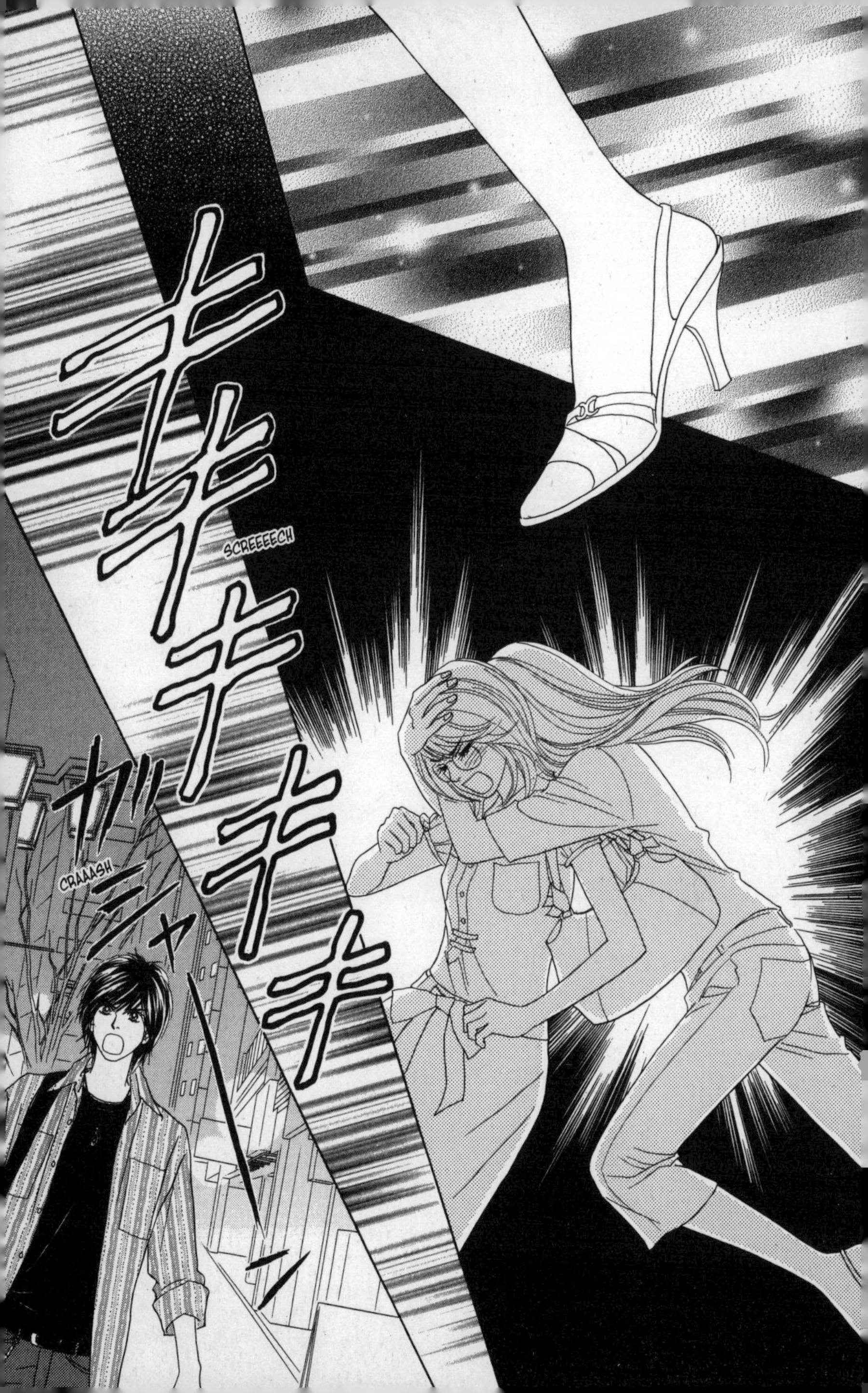
キキキキキ
SCREEEEECH
ガシャーン
CRAAASH

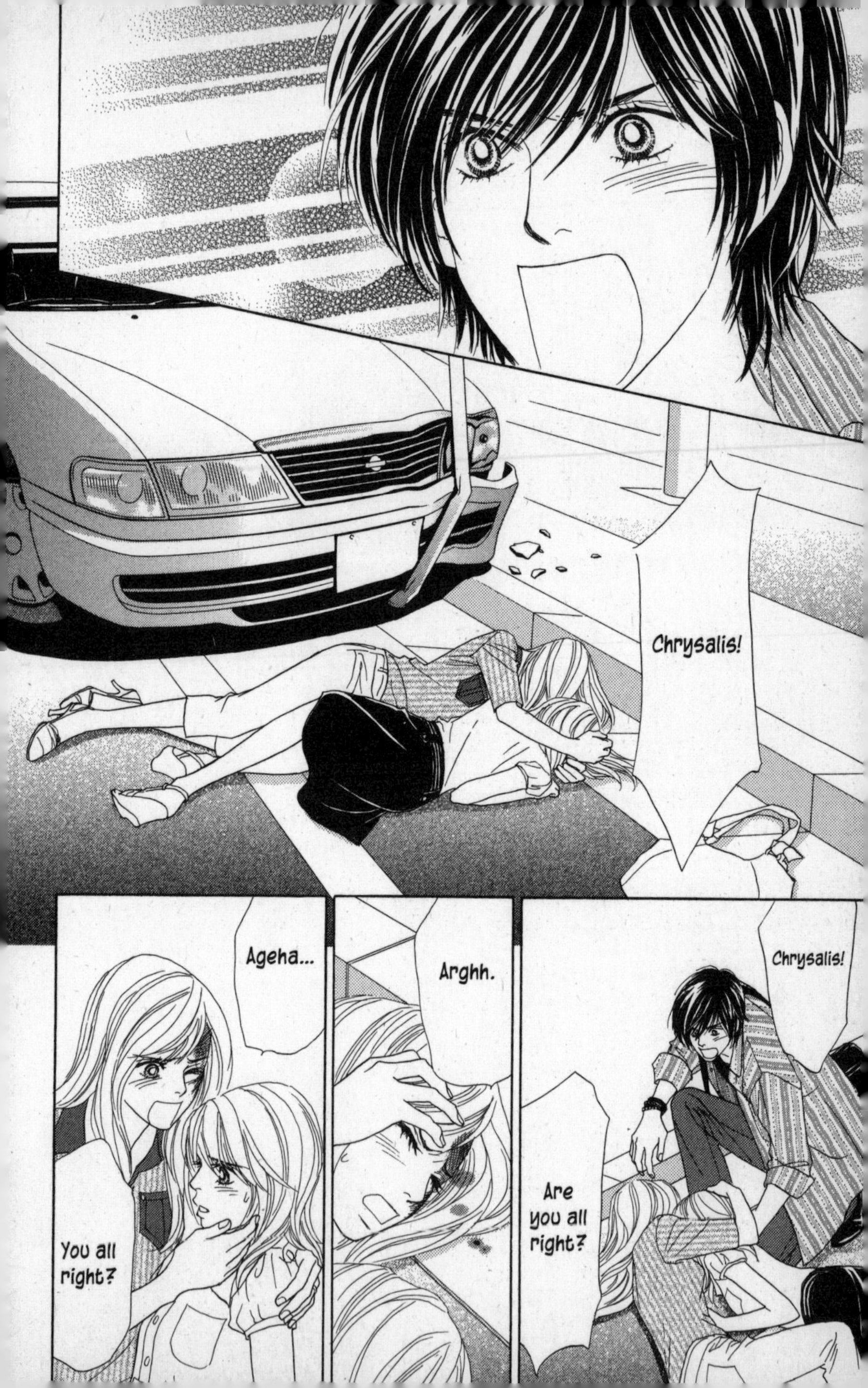
Chrysalis!
Chrysalis!
Arghh.
Are you all right?
Ageha...
You all right?

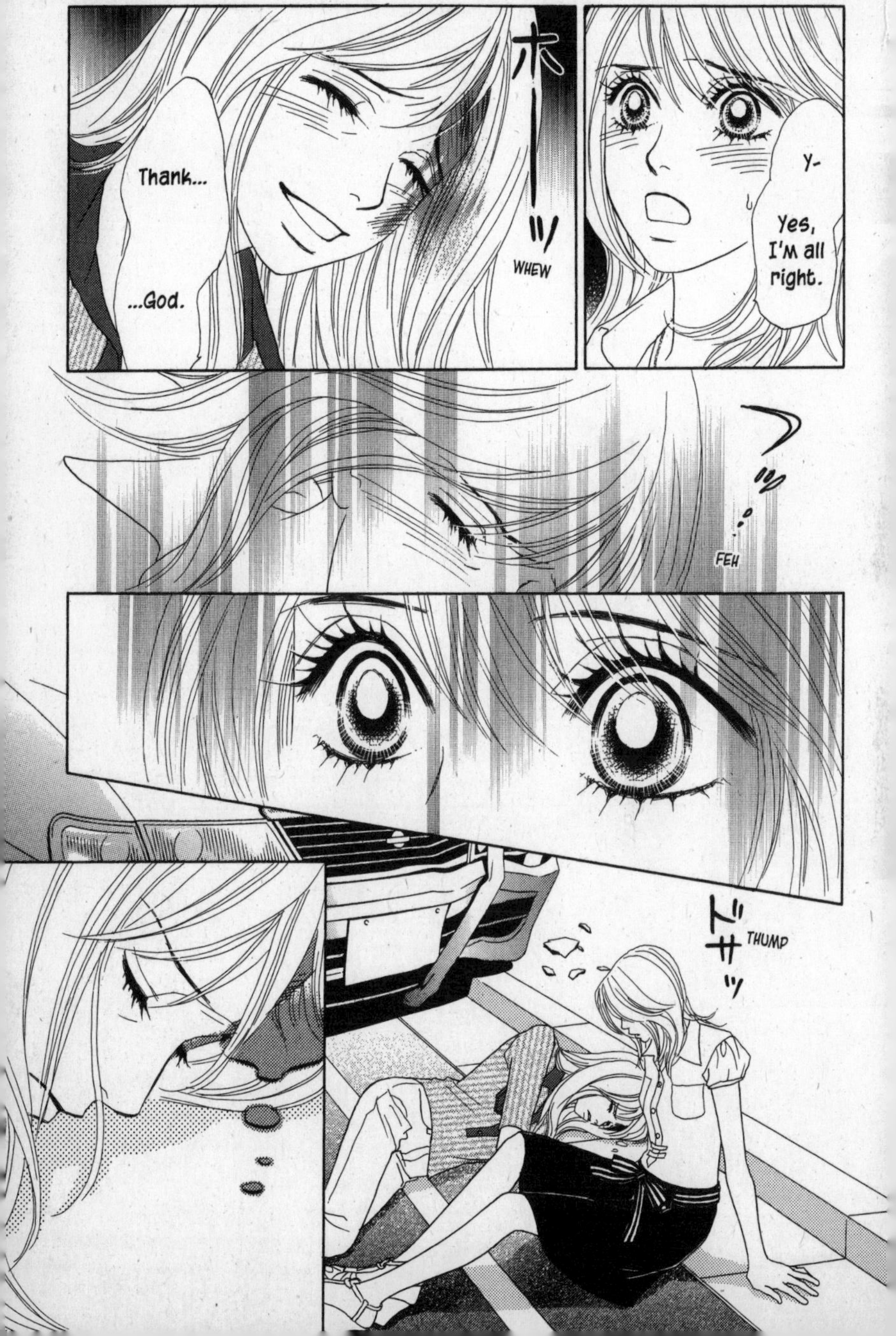
Y-
Yes, I'm all right.
ホーッ
WHEW
Thank...
...God.
フッ
FEH
ドサッ
THUMP

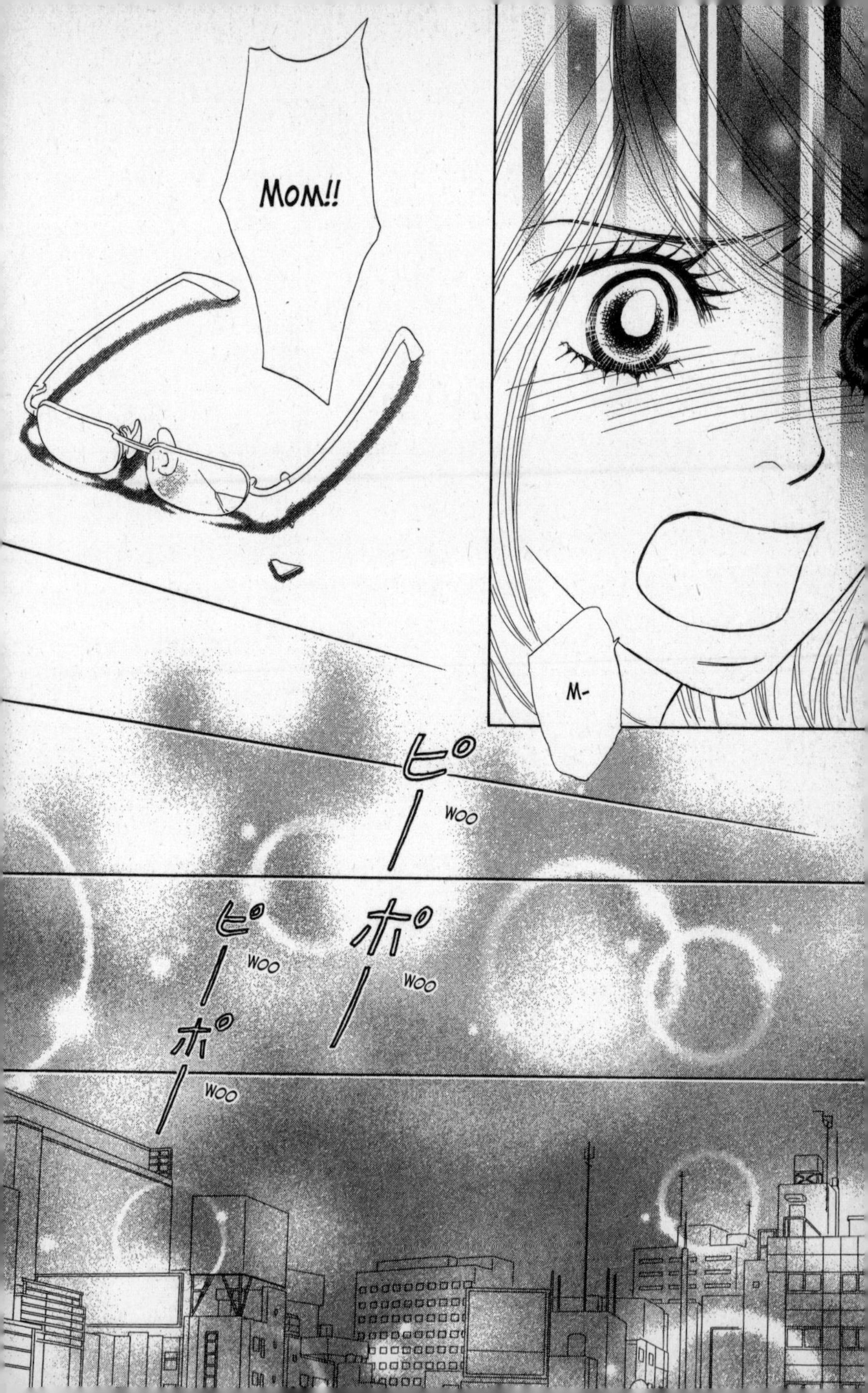
M-
MOM!!
ピーポー
WOO
WOO
ピーポー
WOO
WOO

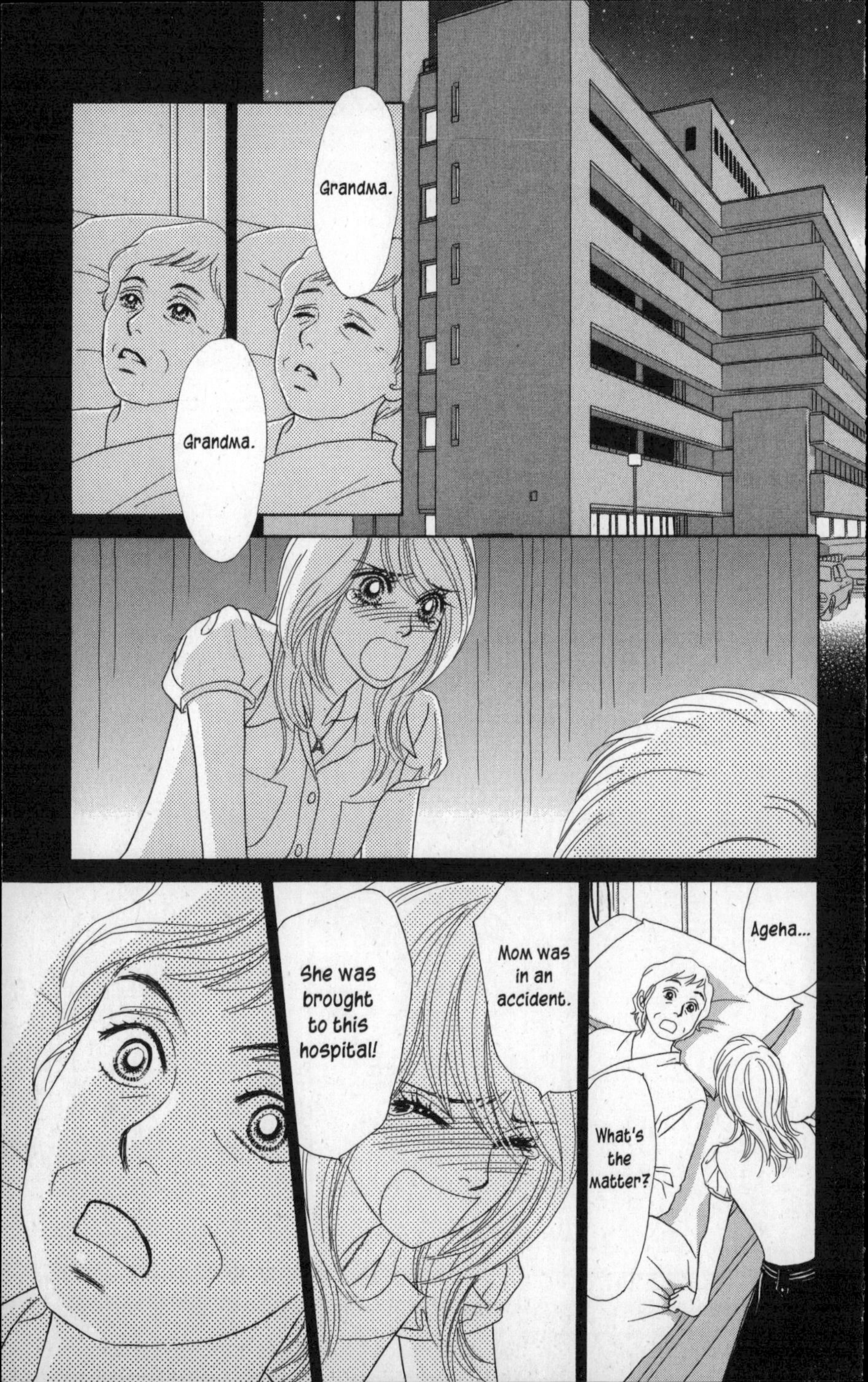
Grandma.
Grandma.
Ageha...
What's the matter?
Mom was in an accident.
She was brought to this hospital!

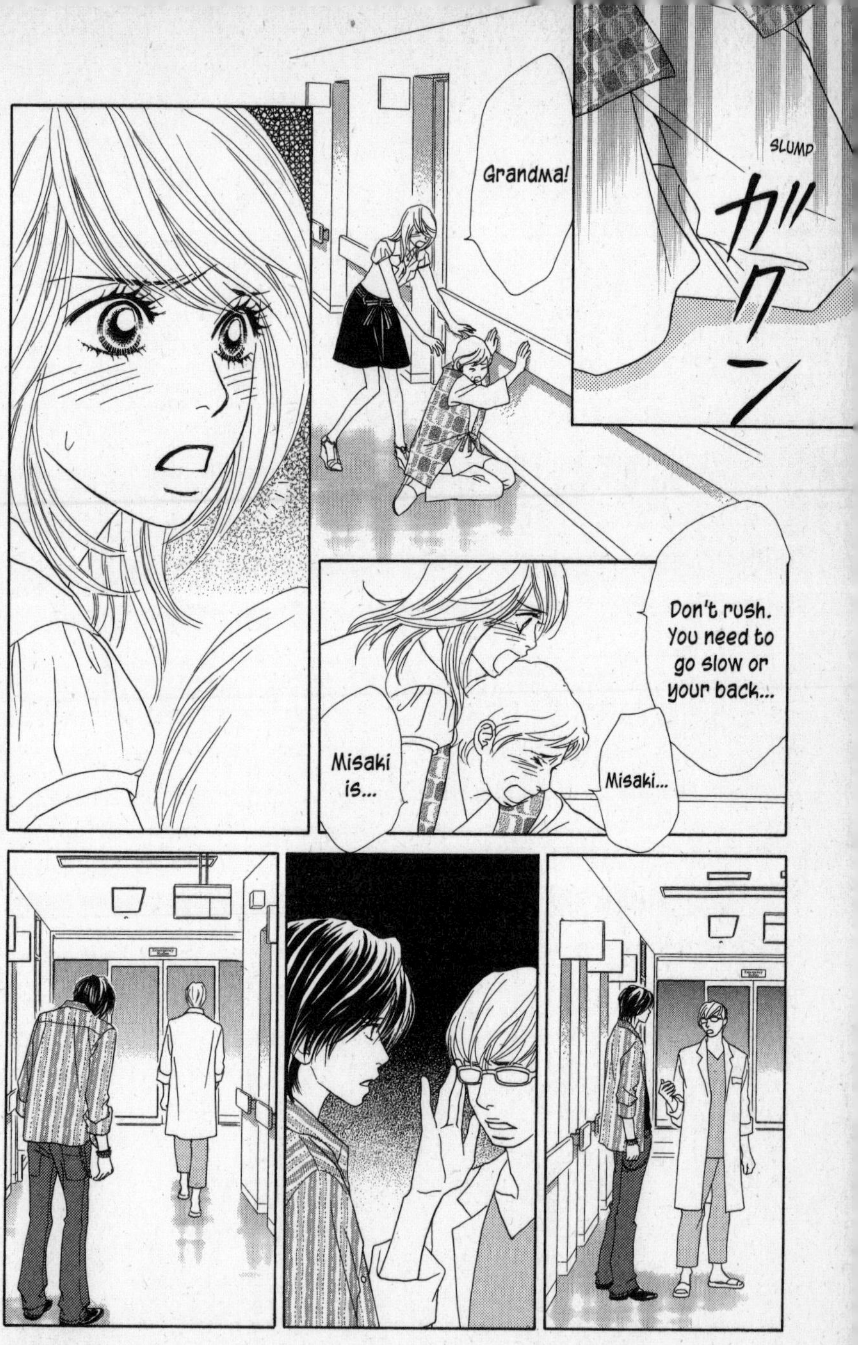
SLUMP
ガクーン
Grandma!
Don't rush. You need to go slow or your back...
Misaki...
Misaki is...

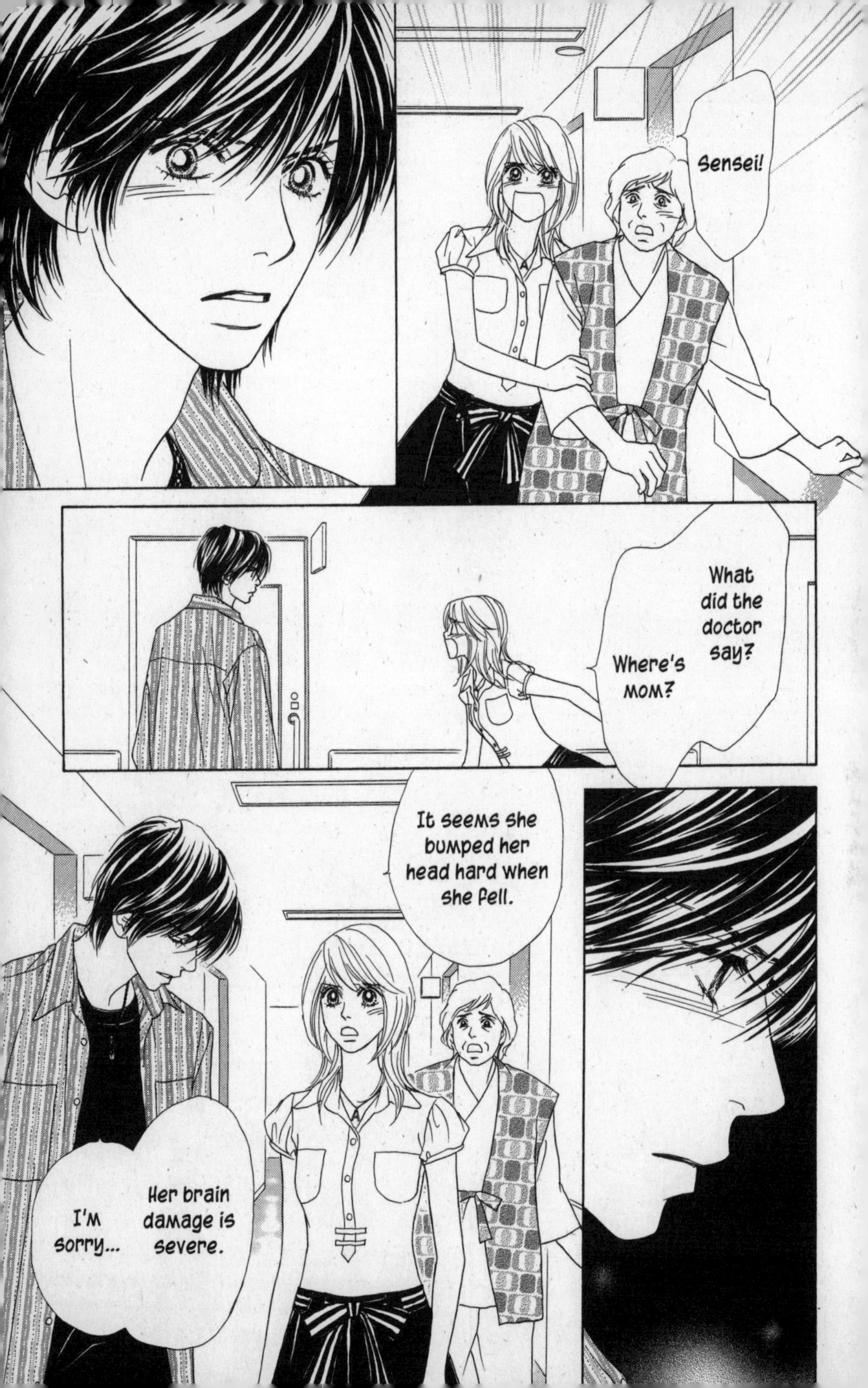
Sensei!
What did the doctor say?
Where's MOM?
It seems she bumped her head hard when she fell.
Her brain damage is severe.
I'm sorry...

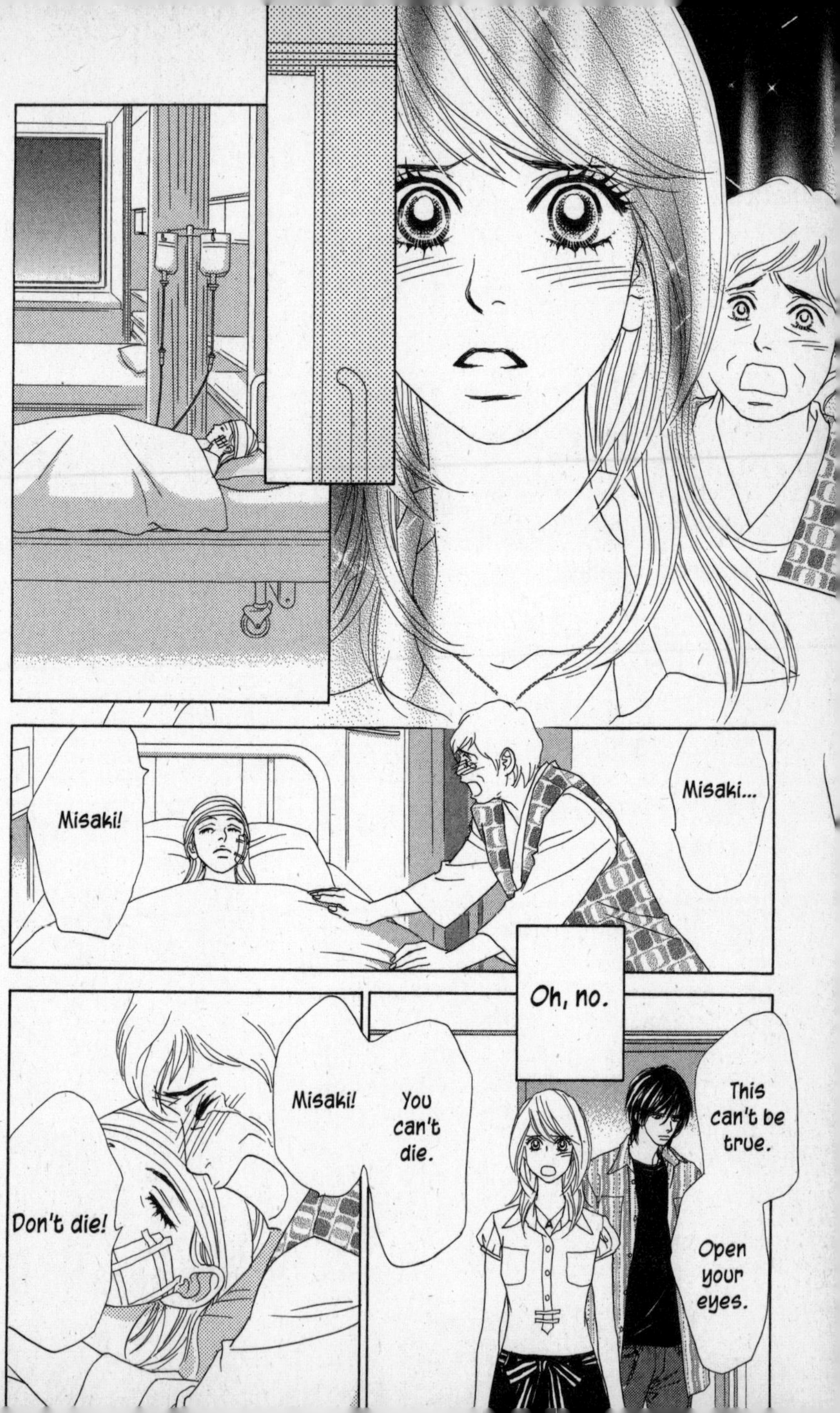
Misaki...
Misaki!
Oh, no.
This can't be true.
Open your eyes.
Misaki! You can't die.
Don't die!

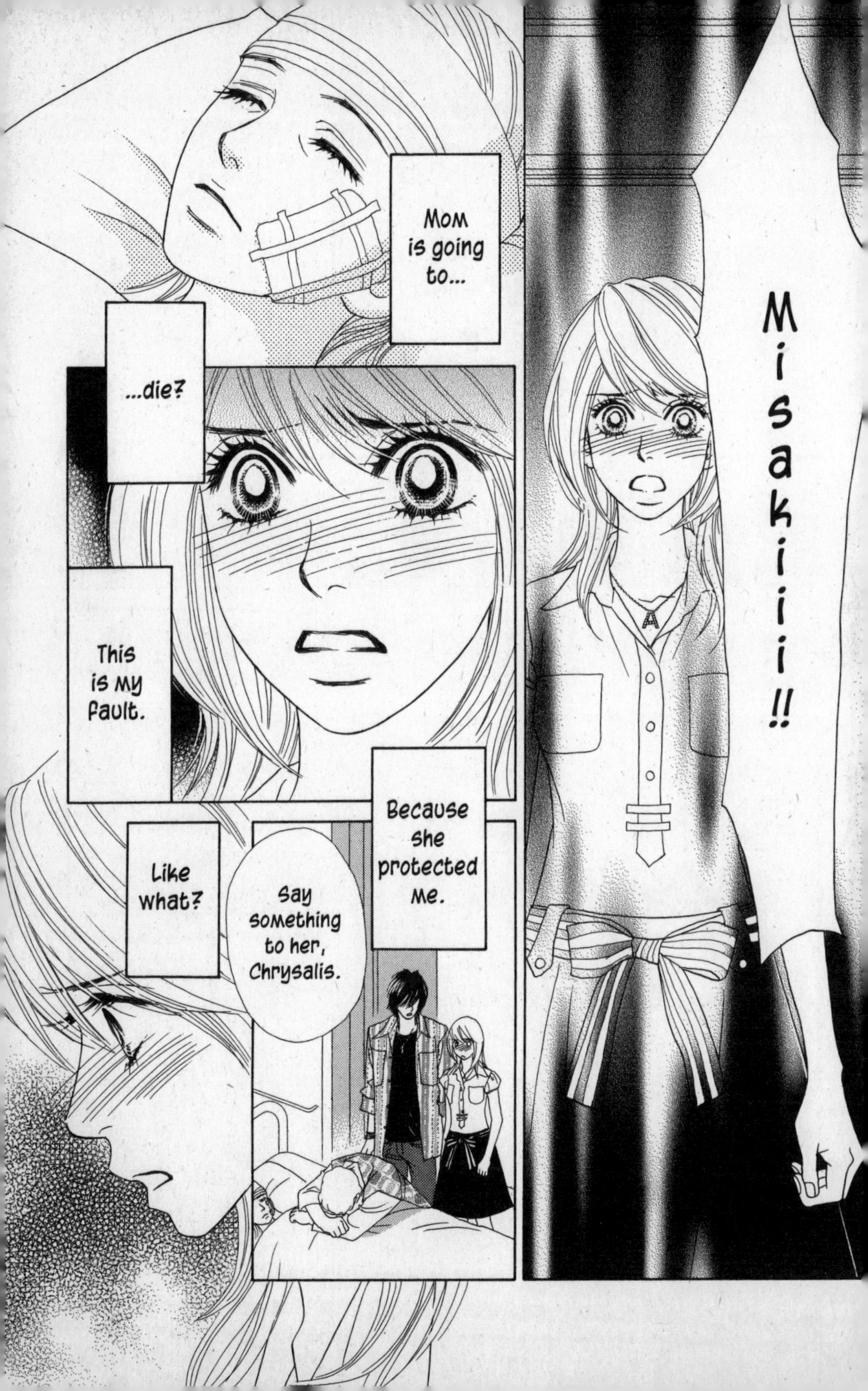
Misakiii!!
Mom is going to...
...die?
This is my fault.
Because she protected me.
Say something to her, Chrysalis.
Like what?

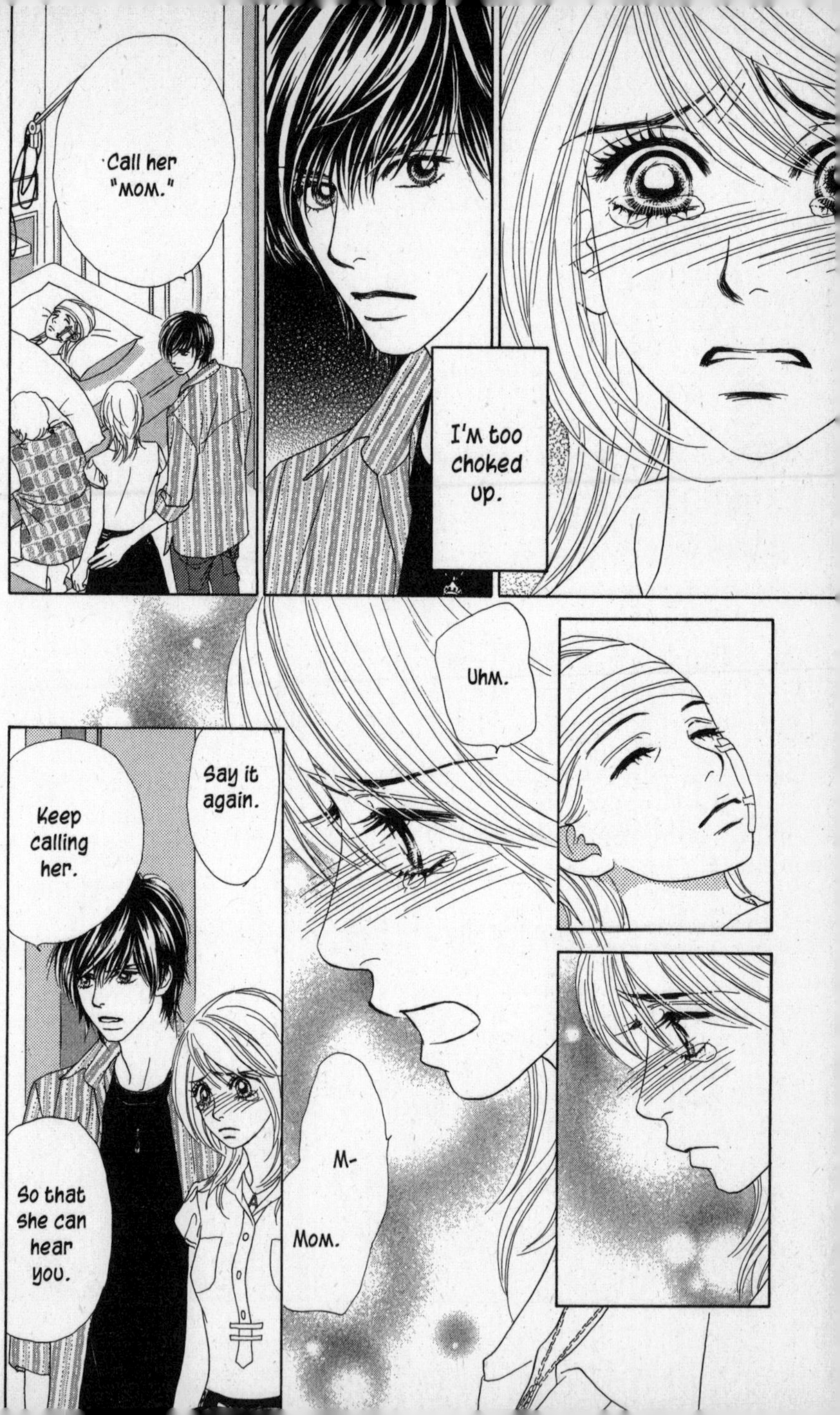
I'm too choked up.
Call her "MOM."
Uhm.
M-
Mom.
Say it again.
Keep calling her.
So that she can hear you.

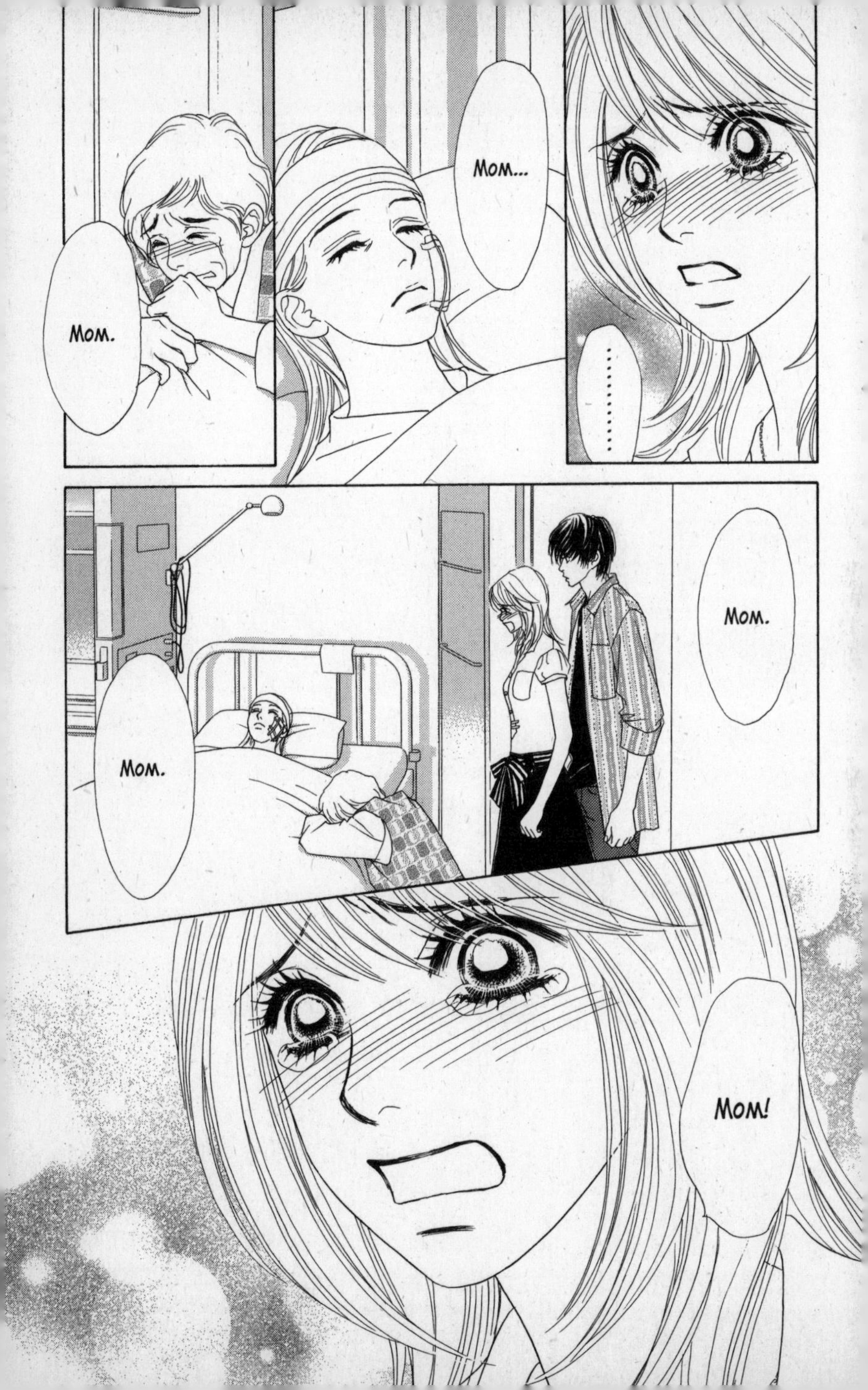
......
Mom...
Mom.
Mom.
Mom.
Mom!

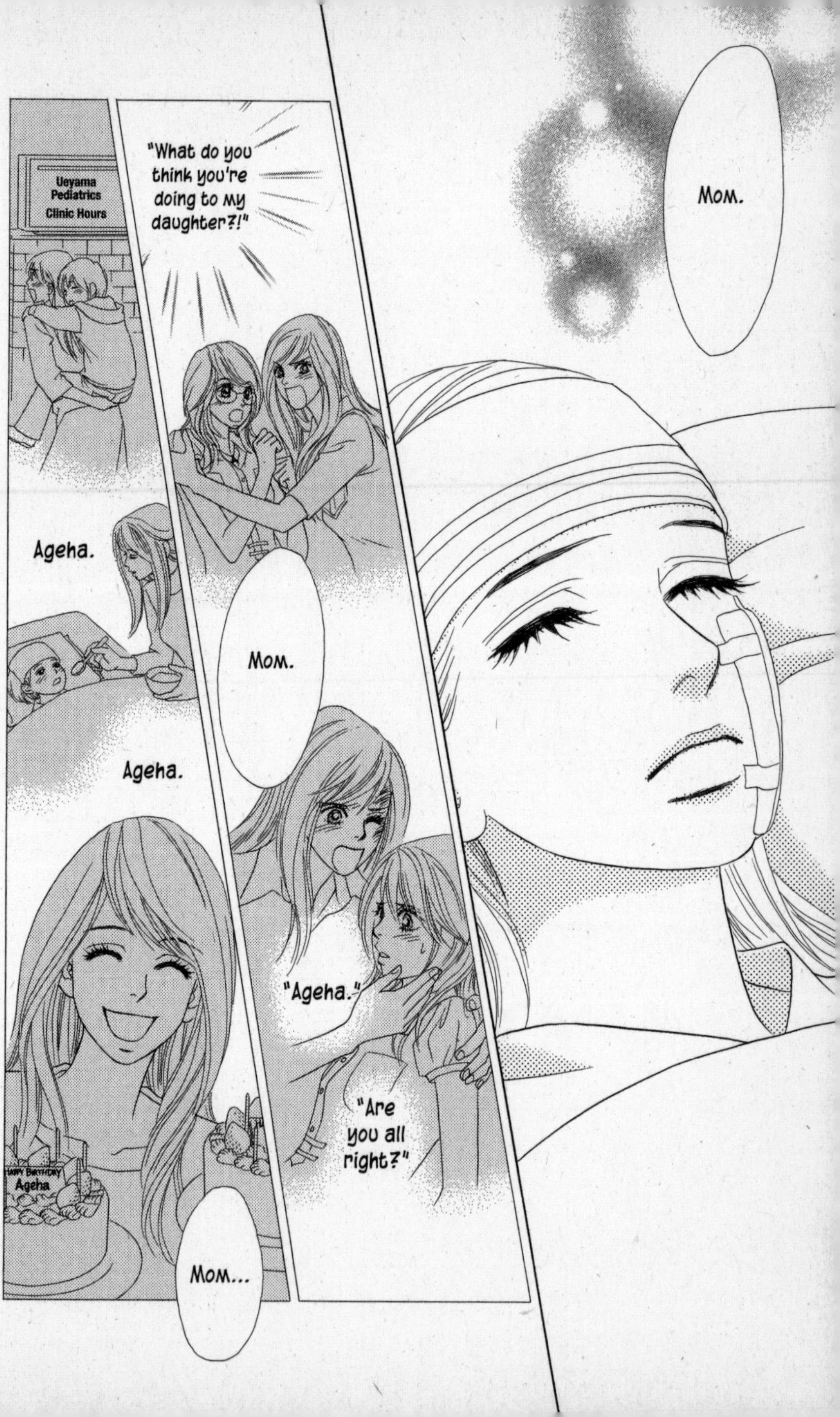

Mom.
"What do you think you're doing to my daughter?!"
Mom.
"Ageha."
"Are you all right?"
Ueyama Pediatrics Clinic Hours
Ageha.
Ageha.
Happy Birthday Ageha
Mom...

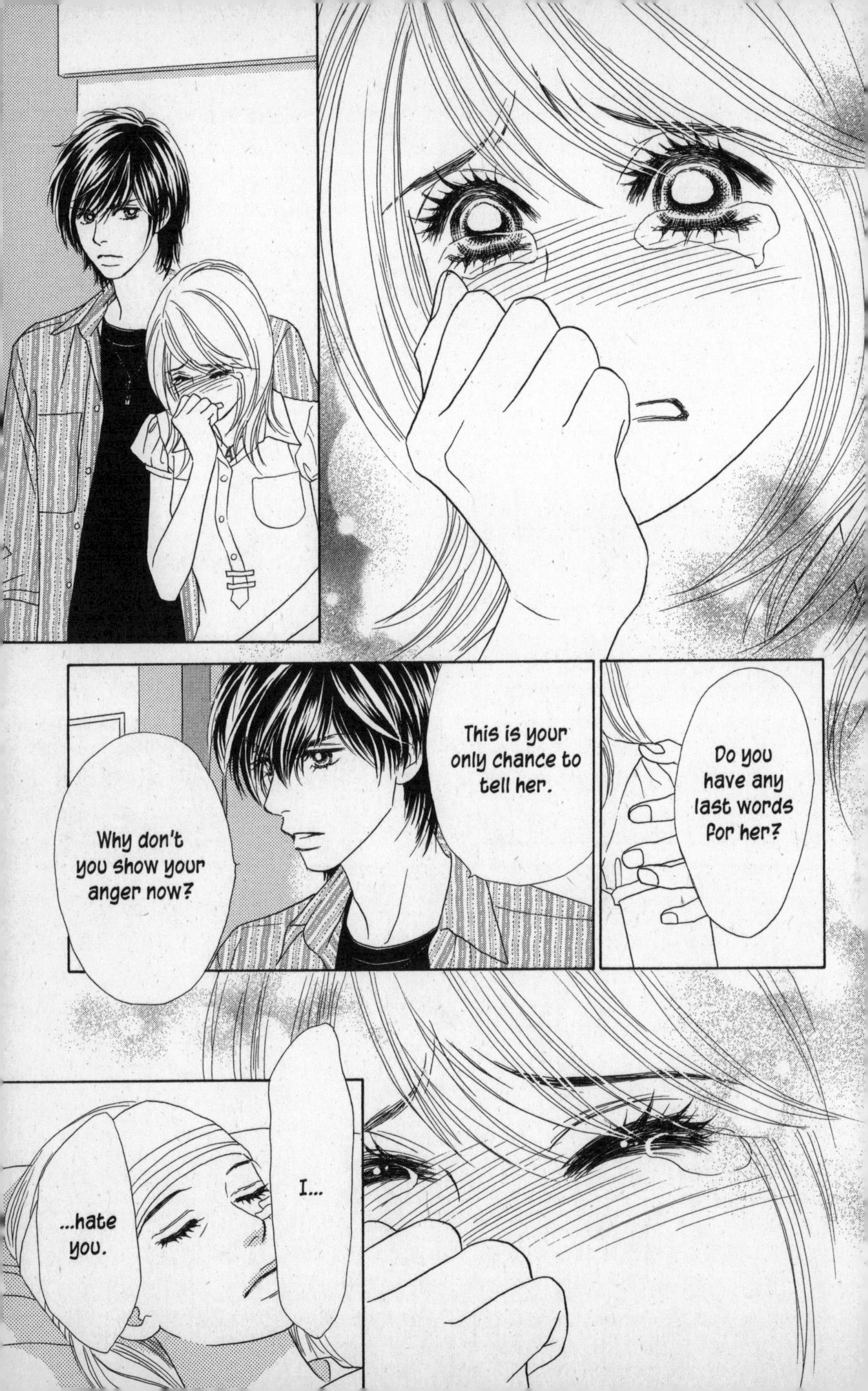
Do you have any last words for her?
This is your only chance to tell her.
Why don't you show your anger now?
I...
...hate you.

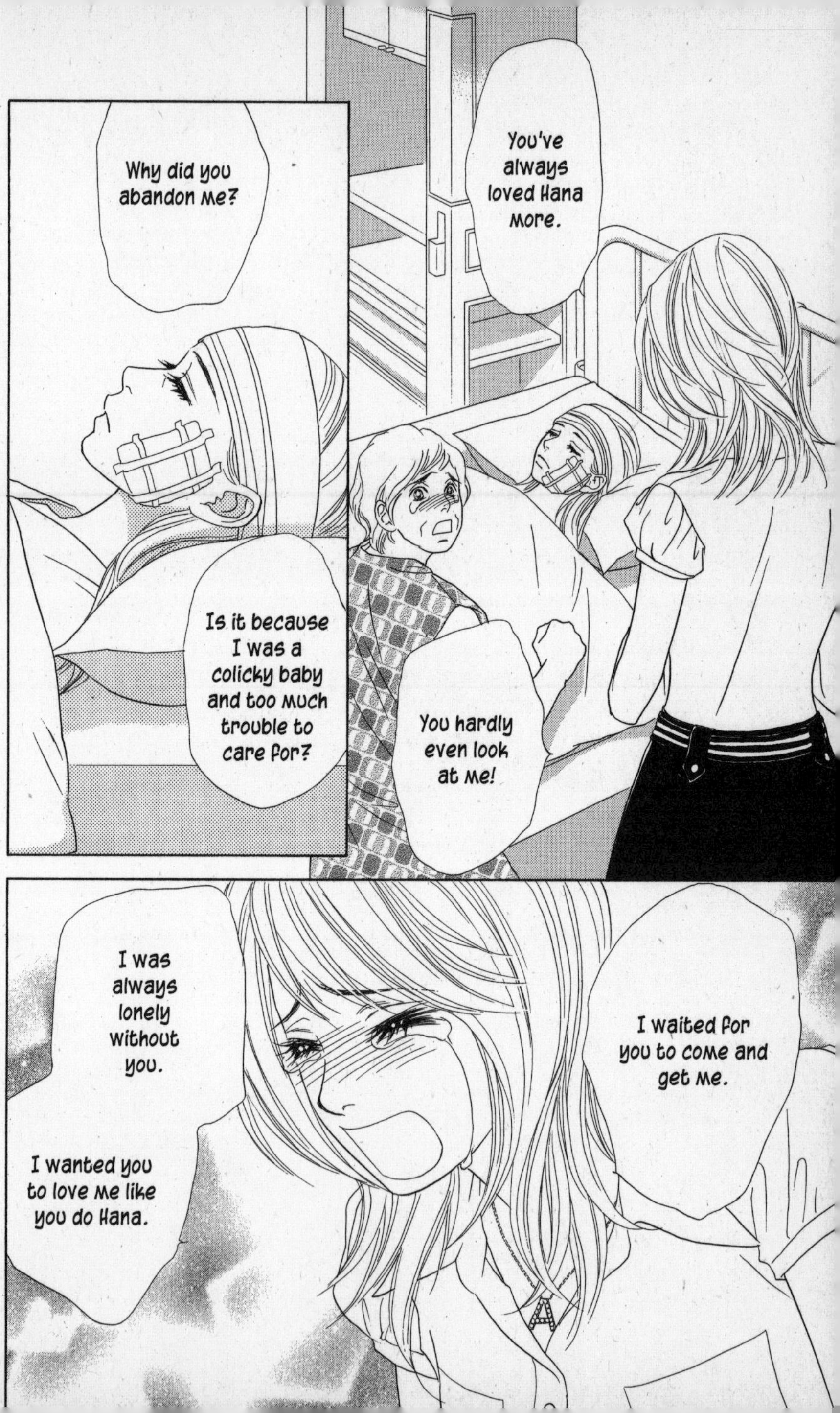
You've always loved Hana more.
You hardly even look at me!
Why did you abandon me?
Is it because I was a colicky baby and too much trouble to care for?
I waited for you to come and get me.
I was always lonely without you.
I wanted you to love me like you do Hana.

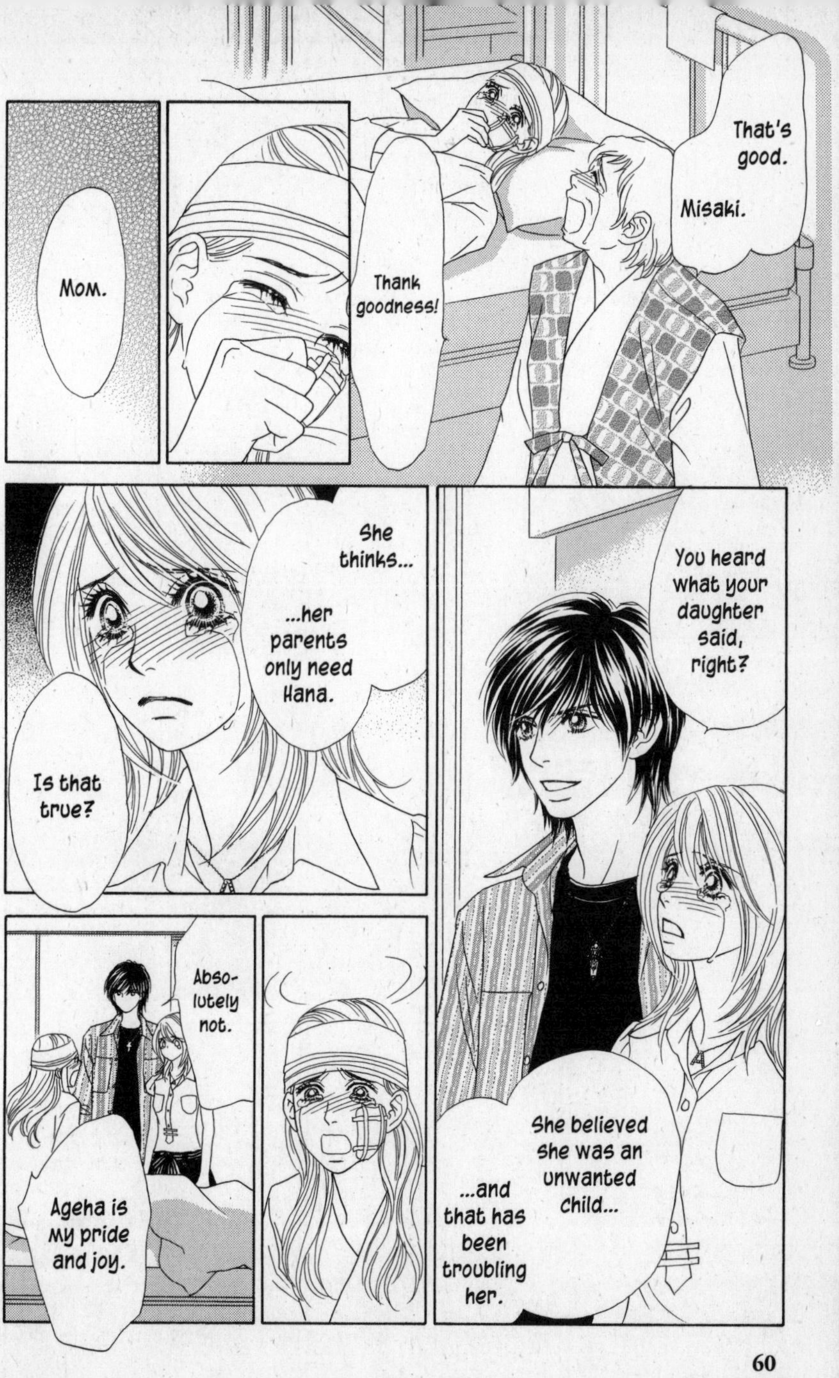
That's good.
Misaki.
Thank goodness!
Mom.
You heard what your daughter said, right?
She believed she was an unwanted child...
...and that has been troubling her.
She thinks...
...her parents only need Hana.
Is that true?
Abso-lutely not.
Ageha is my pride and joy.

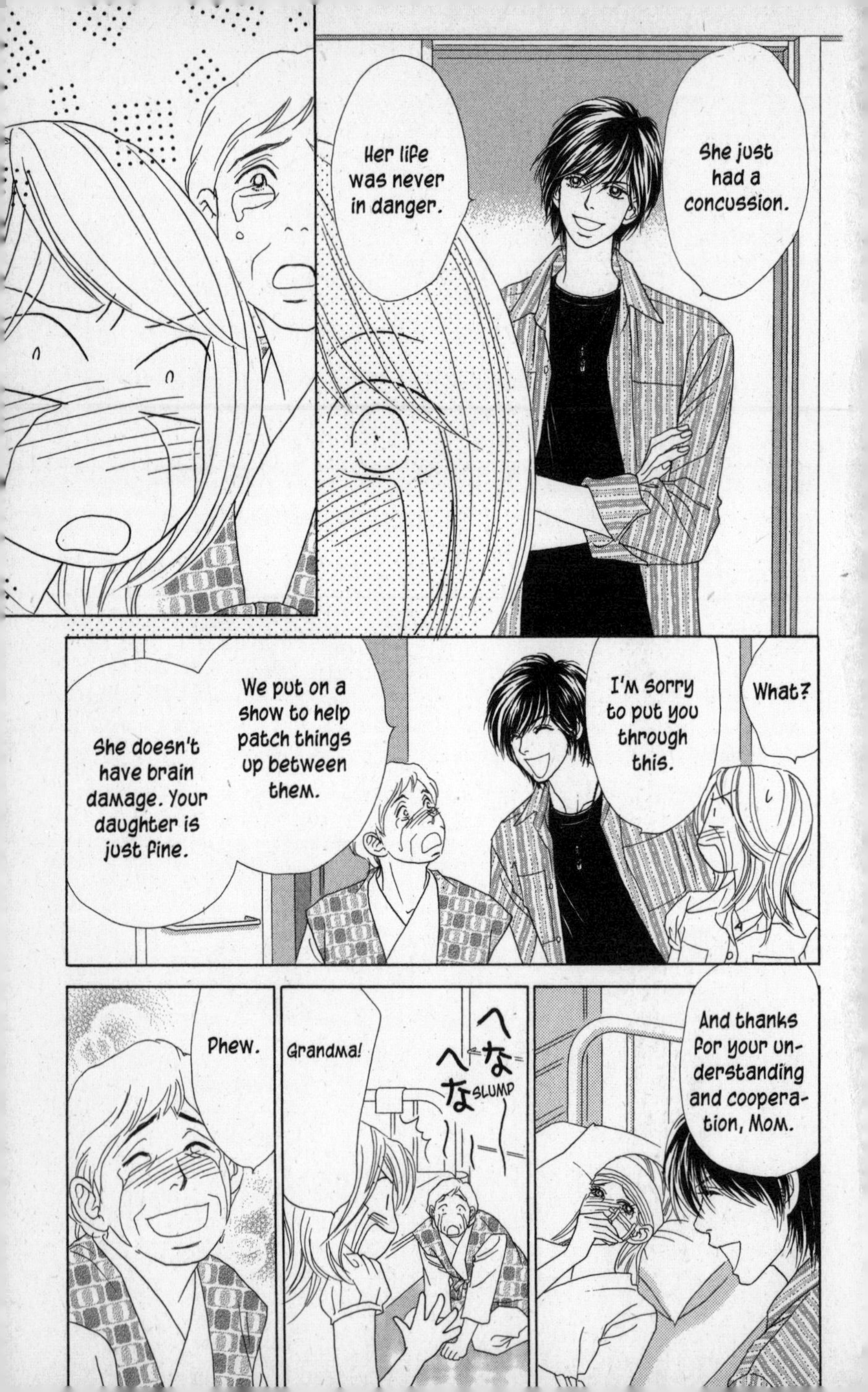
She just had a concussion.
Her life was never in danger.
What?
I'm sorry to put you through this.
We put on a show to help patch things up between them.
She doesn't have brain damage. Your daughter is just fine.
And thanks for your understanding and cooperation, Mom.
へなへな
SLUMP
Grandma!
Phew.

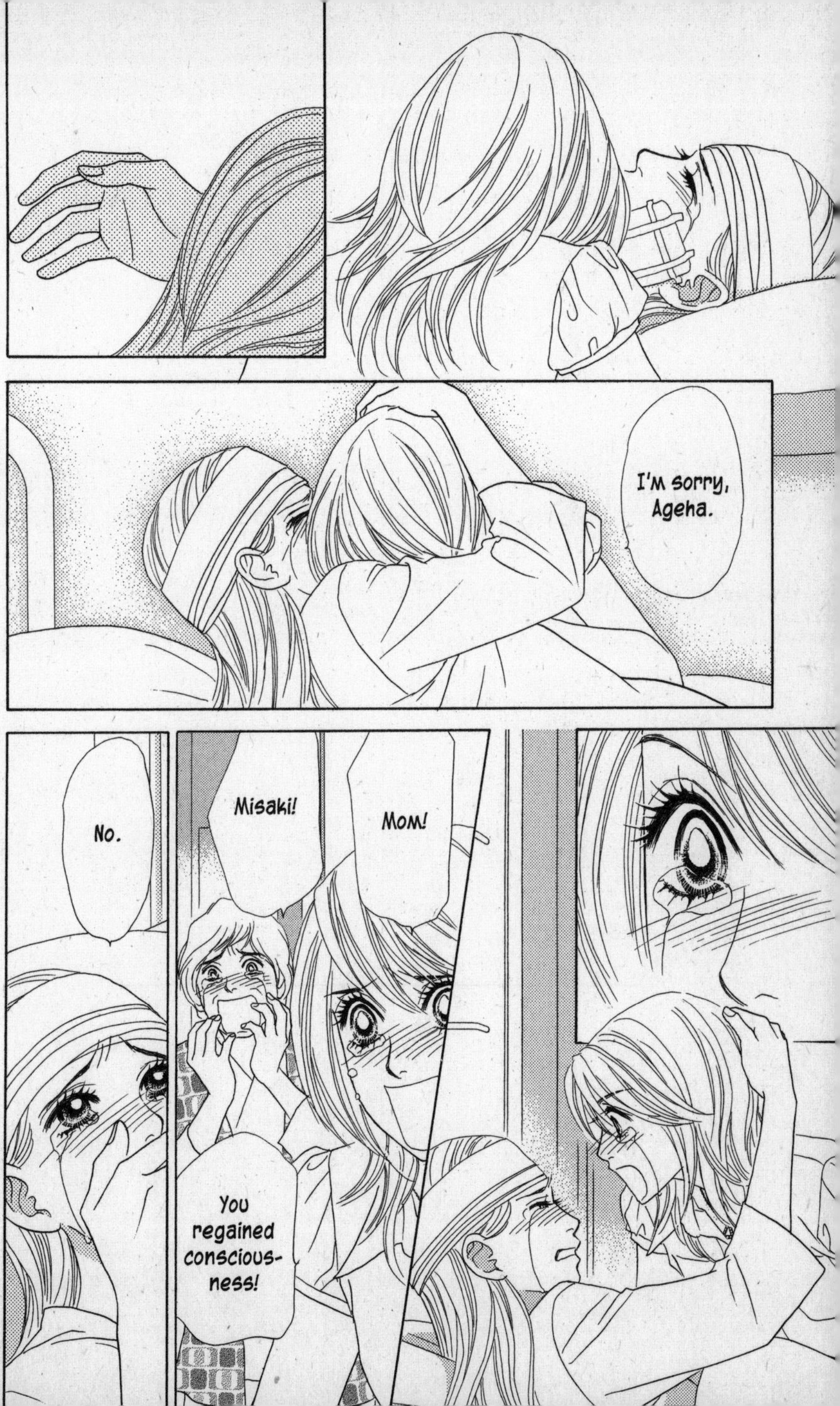
I'm sorry, Ageha.
Mom!
Misaki!
You regained consciousness!
No.

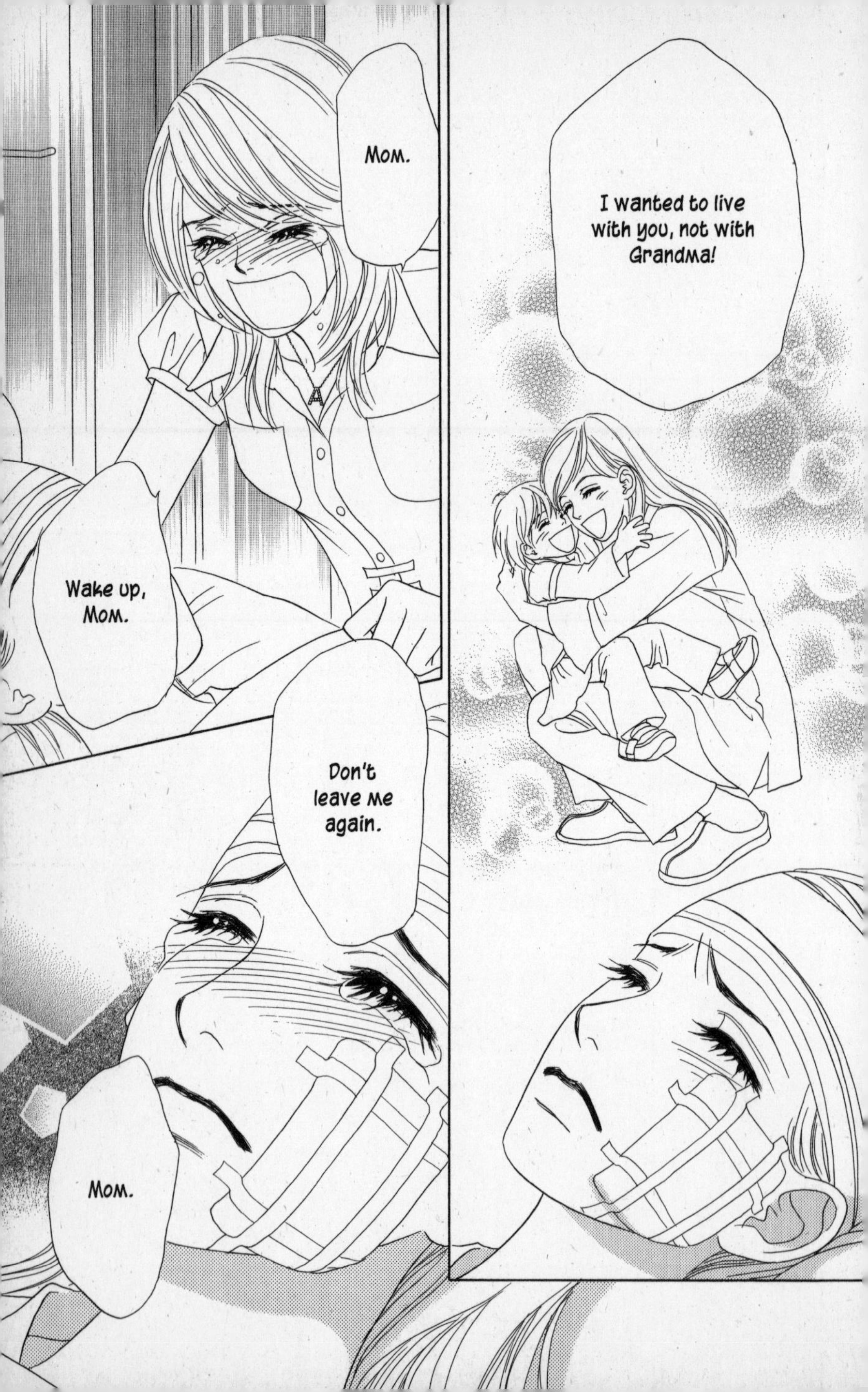
I wanted to live with you, not with Grandma!
Mom.
Wake up, Mom.
Don't leave me again.
Mom.

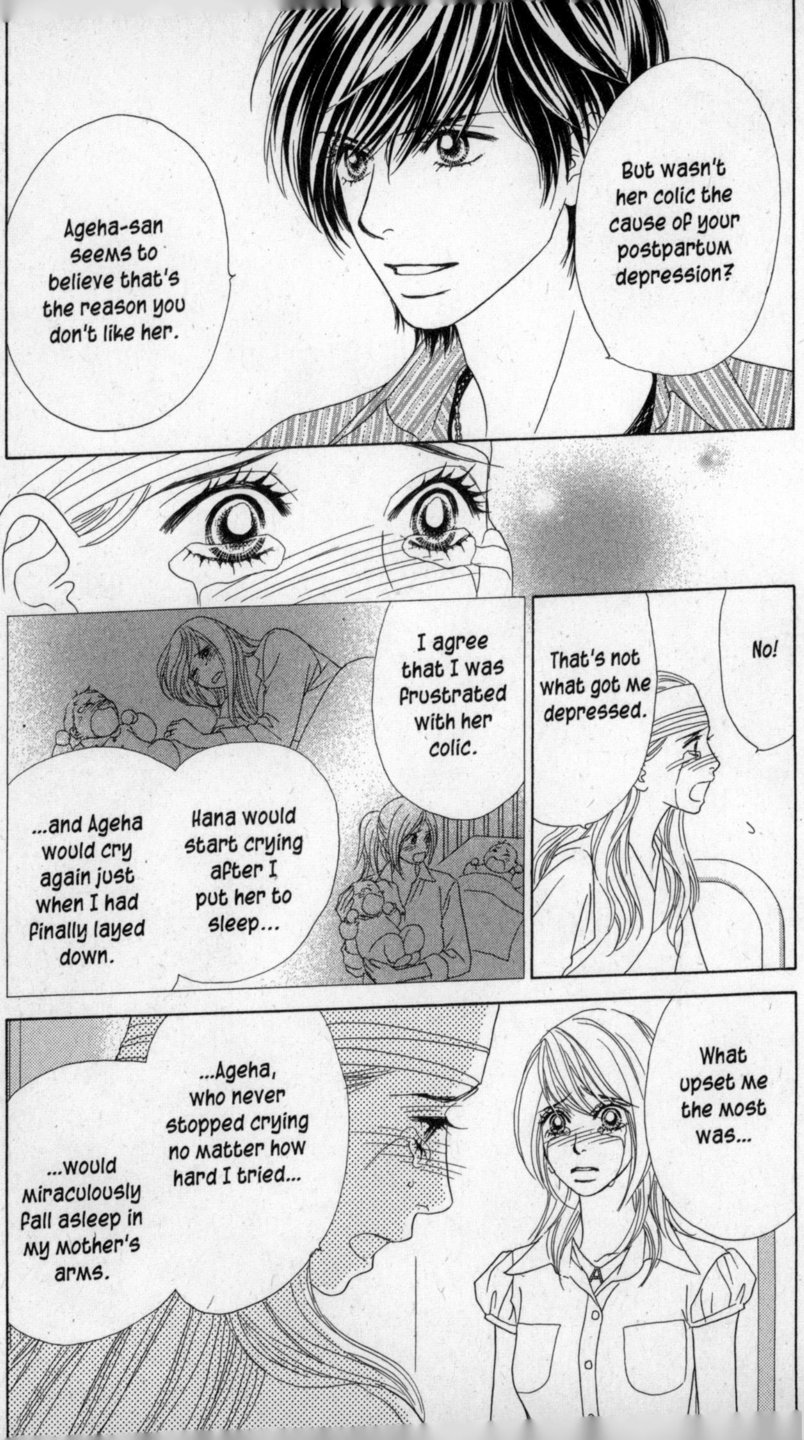
But wasn't her colic the cause of your postpartum depression?
Ageha-san seems to believe that's the reason you don't like her.
No!
That's not what got me depressed.
I agree that I was frustrated with her colic.
Hana would start crying after I put her to sleep...
...and Ageha would cry again just when I had finally layed down.
What upset me the most was...
...Ageha, who never stopped crying no matter how hard I tried...
...would miraculously fall asleep in my mother's arms.

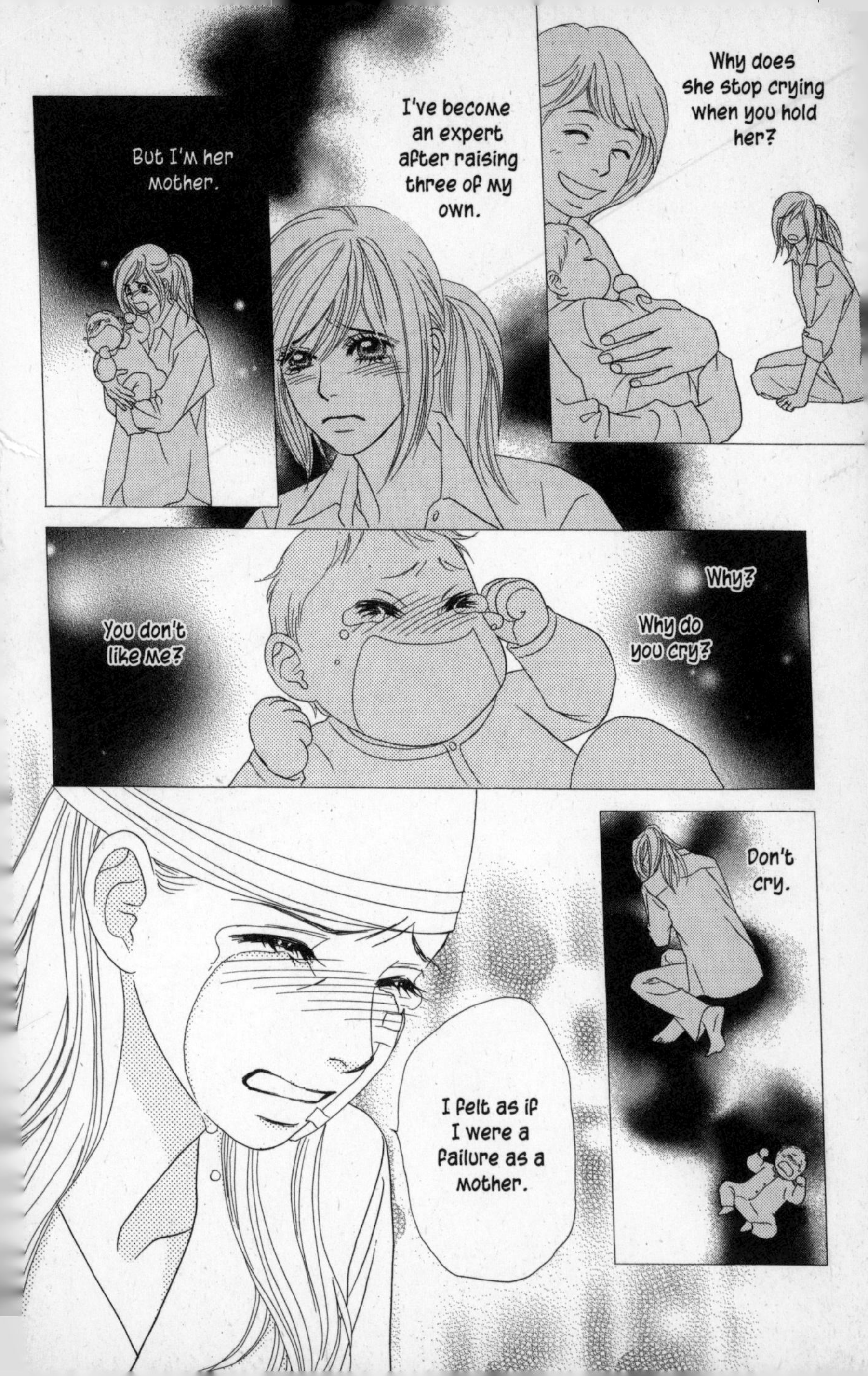
Why does she stop crying when you hold her?
I've become an expert after raising three of my own.
But I'm her mother.
Why?
Why do you cry?
You don't like me?
Don't cry.
I felt as if I were a failure as a mother.

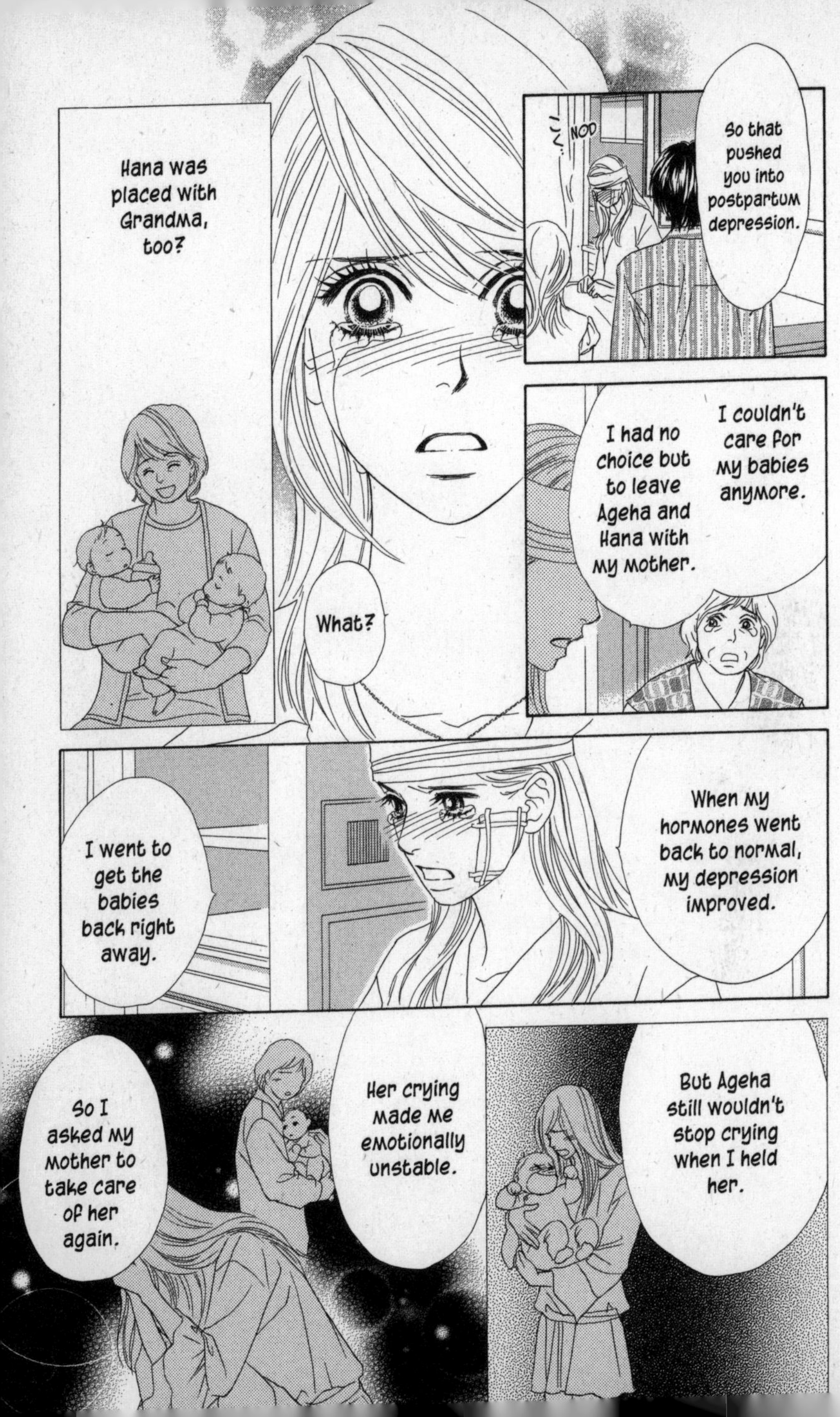

NOD
So that pushed you into postpartum depression.
I couldn't care for my babies anymore.
I had no choice but to leave Ageha and Hana with my mother.
What?
Hana was placed with Grandma, too?
When my hormones went back to normal, my depression improved.
I went to get the babies back right away.
But Ageha still wouldn't stop crying when I held her.
Her crying made me emotionally unstable.
So I asked my mother to take care of her again.

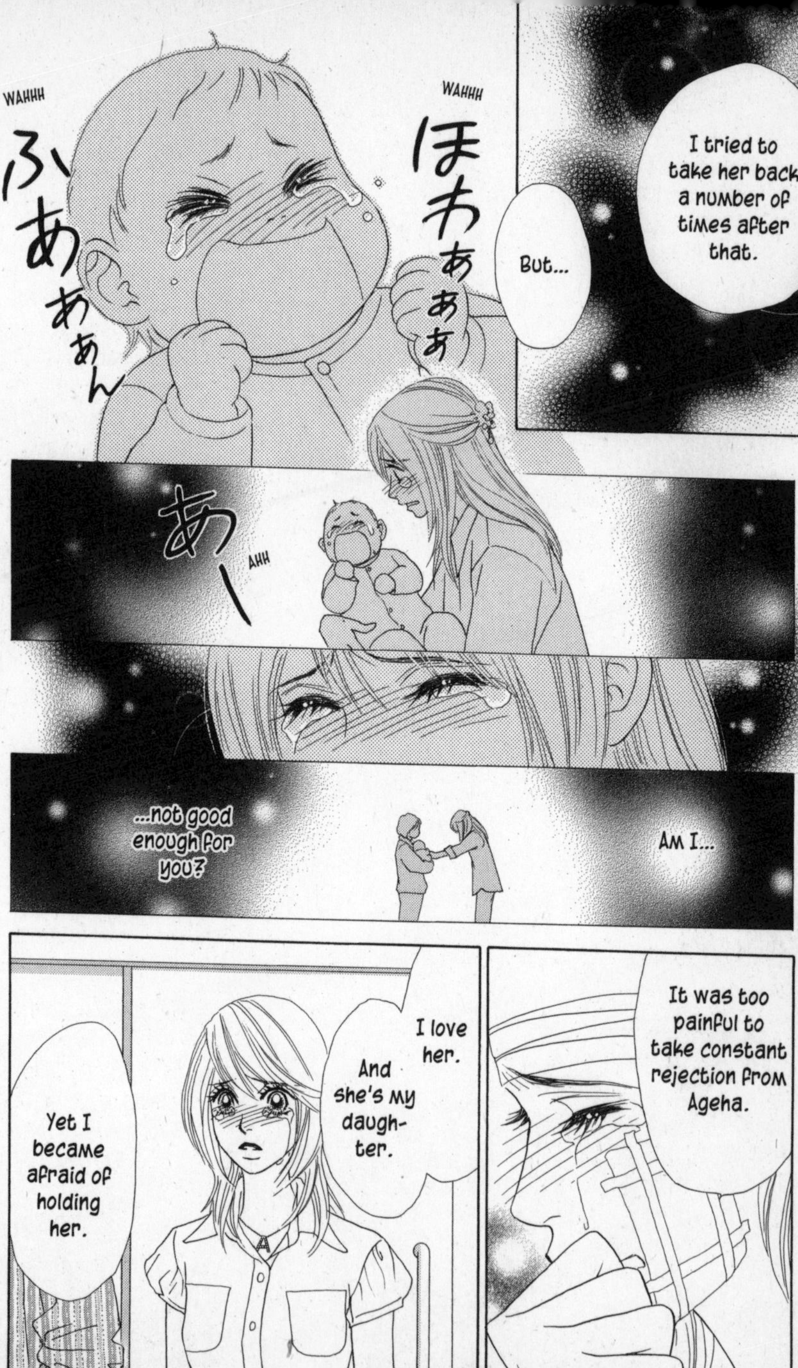
I tried to take her back a number of times after that.
But...
WAHHH
ほわあああ
WAHHH
ふあああん
あー
AHH
Am I...
...not good enough for you?
It was too painful to take constant rejection from Ageha.
I love her.
And she's my daughter.
Yet I became afraid of holding her.

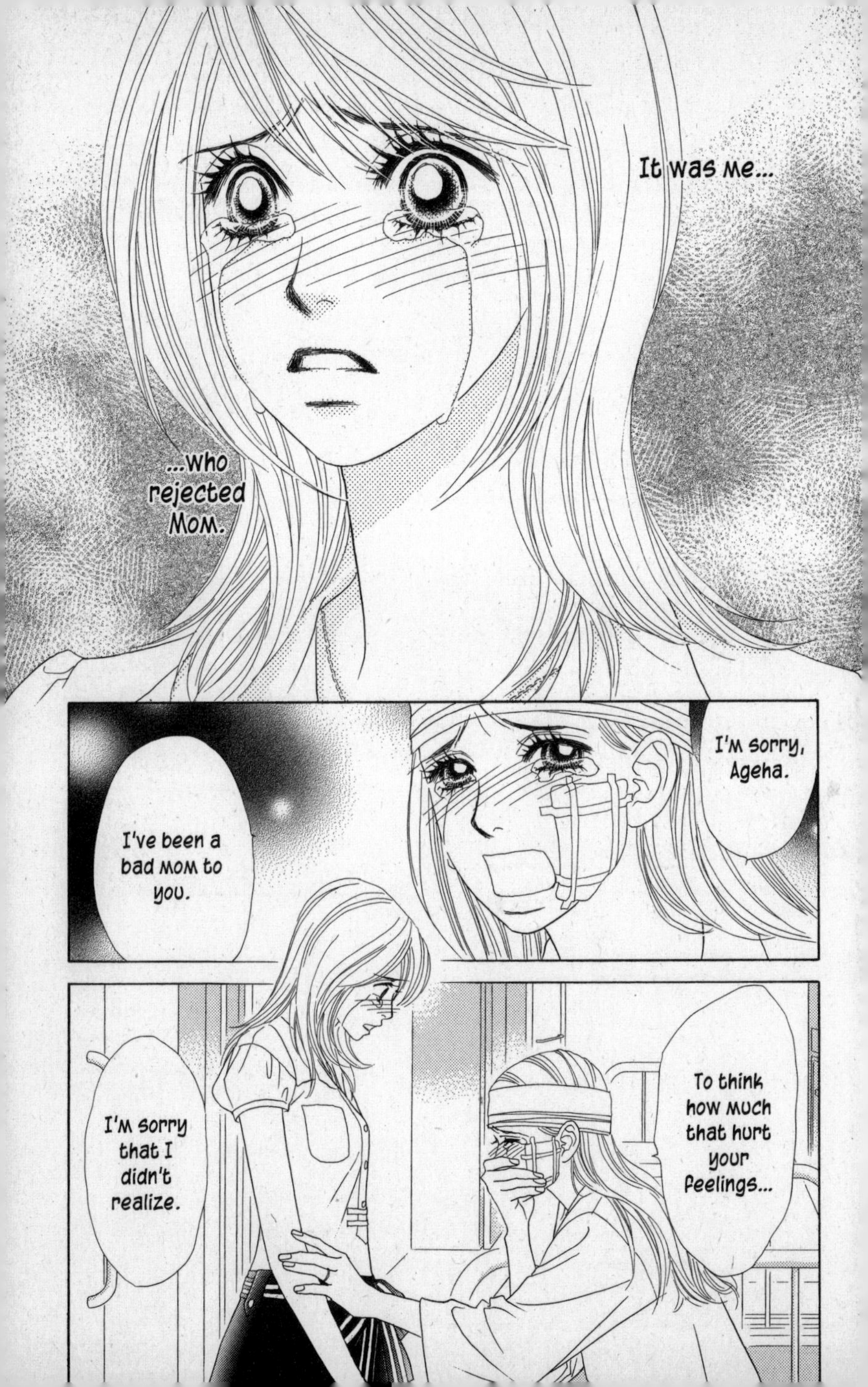
It was me...
...who rejected Mom.
I'm sorry, Ageha.
I've been a bad mom to you.
To think how much that hurt your feelings...
I'm sorry that I didn't realize.

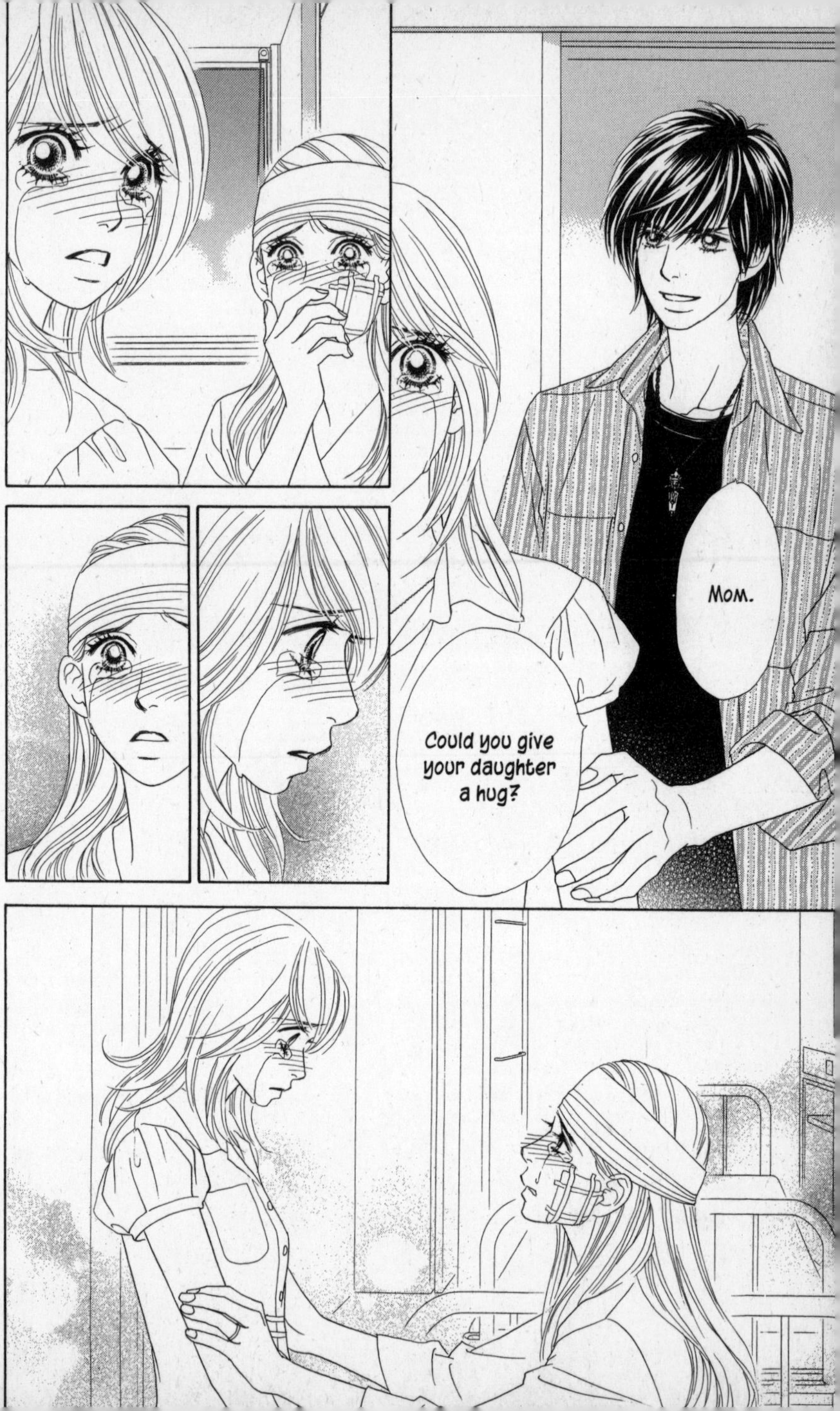
Mom.
Could you give your daughter a hug?

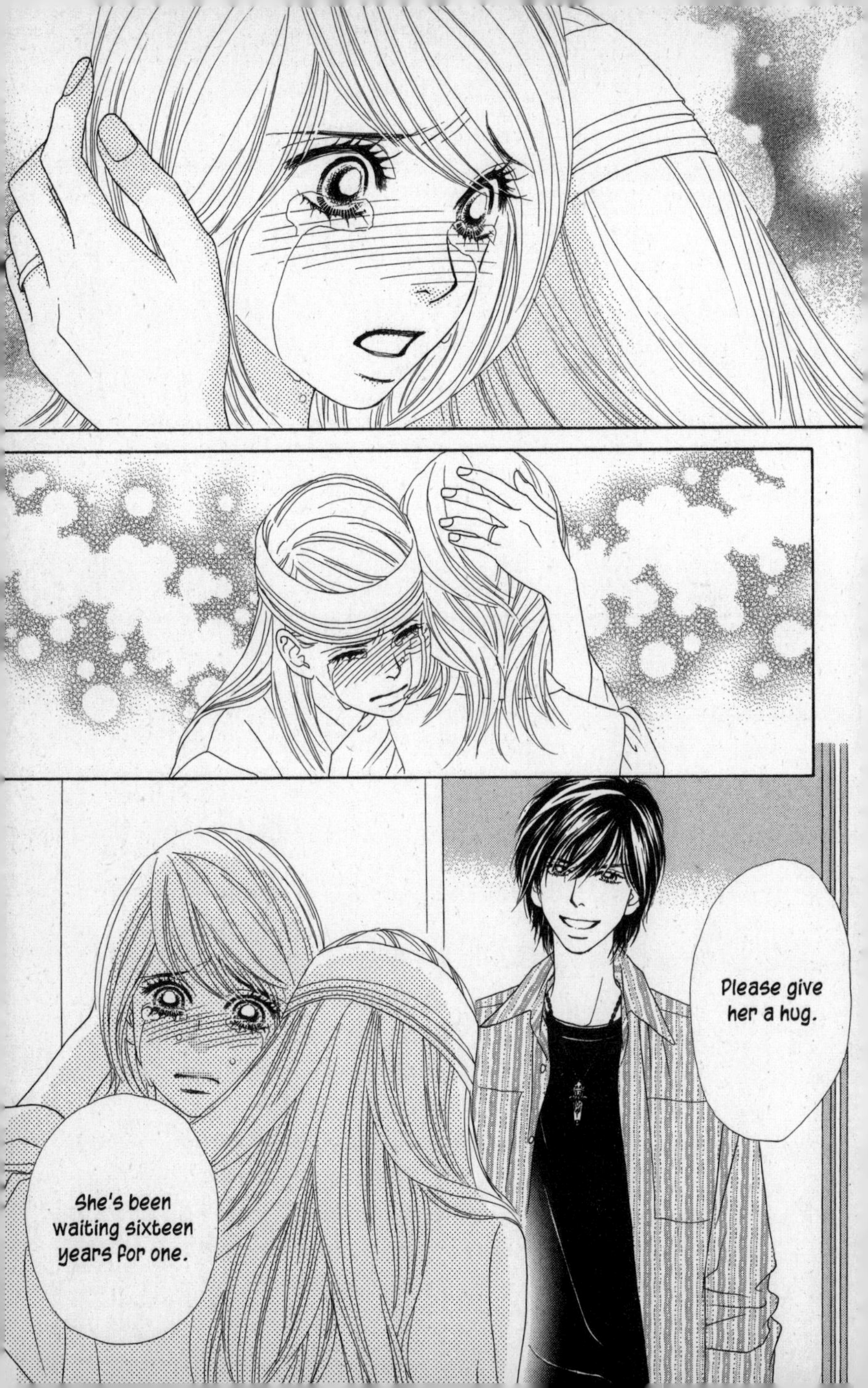
Please give her a hug.
She's been waiting sixteen years for one.

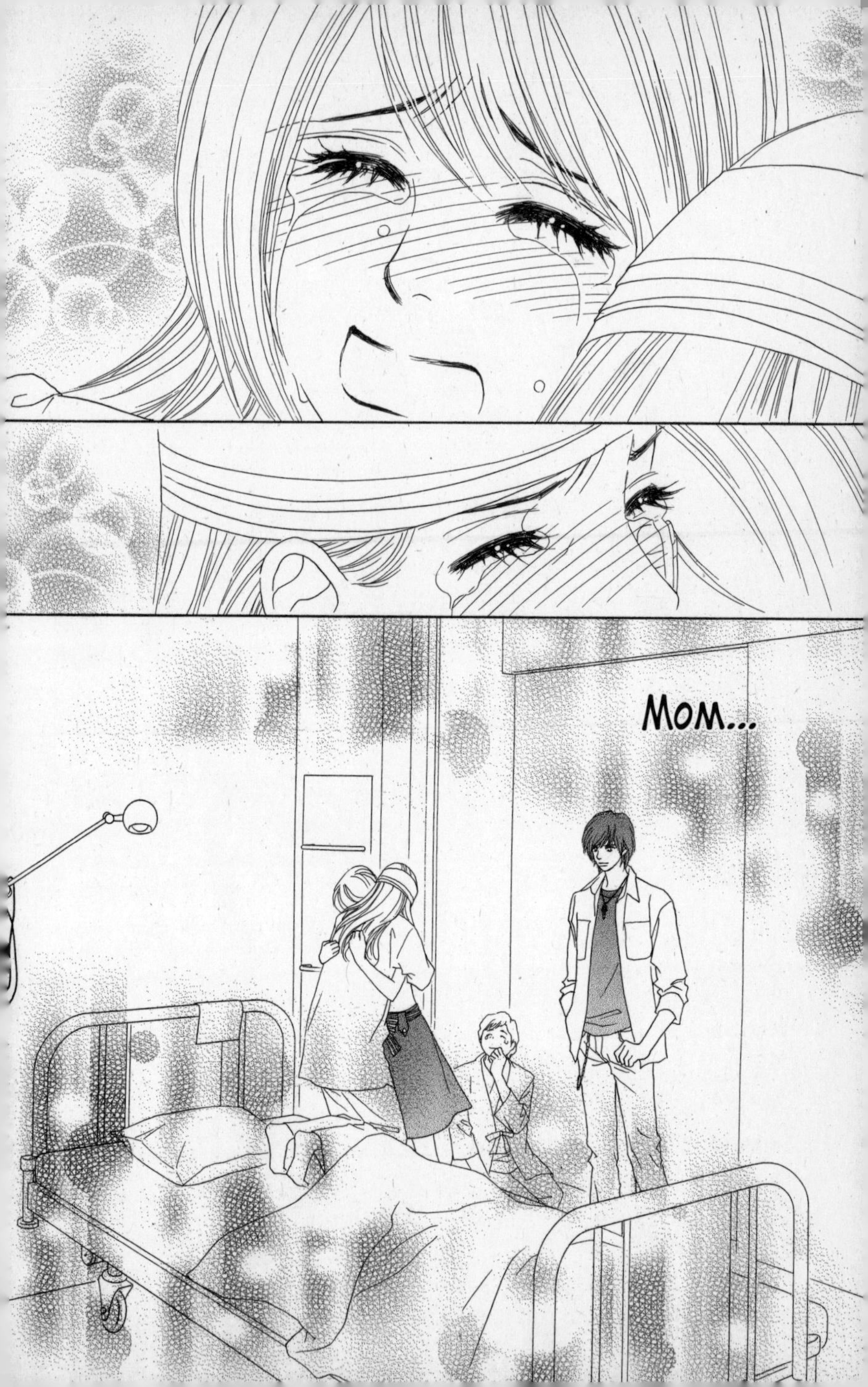
MOM...

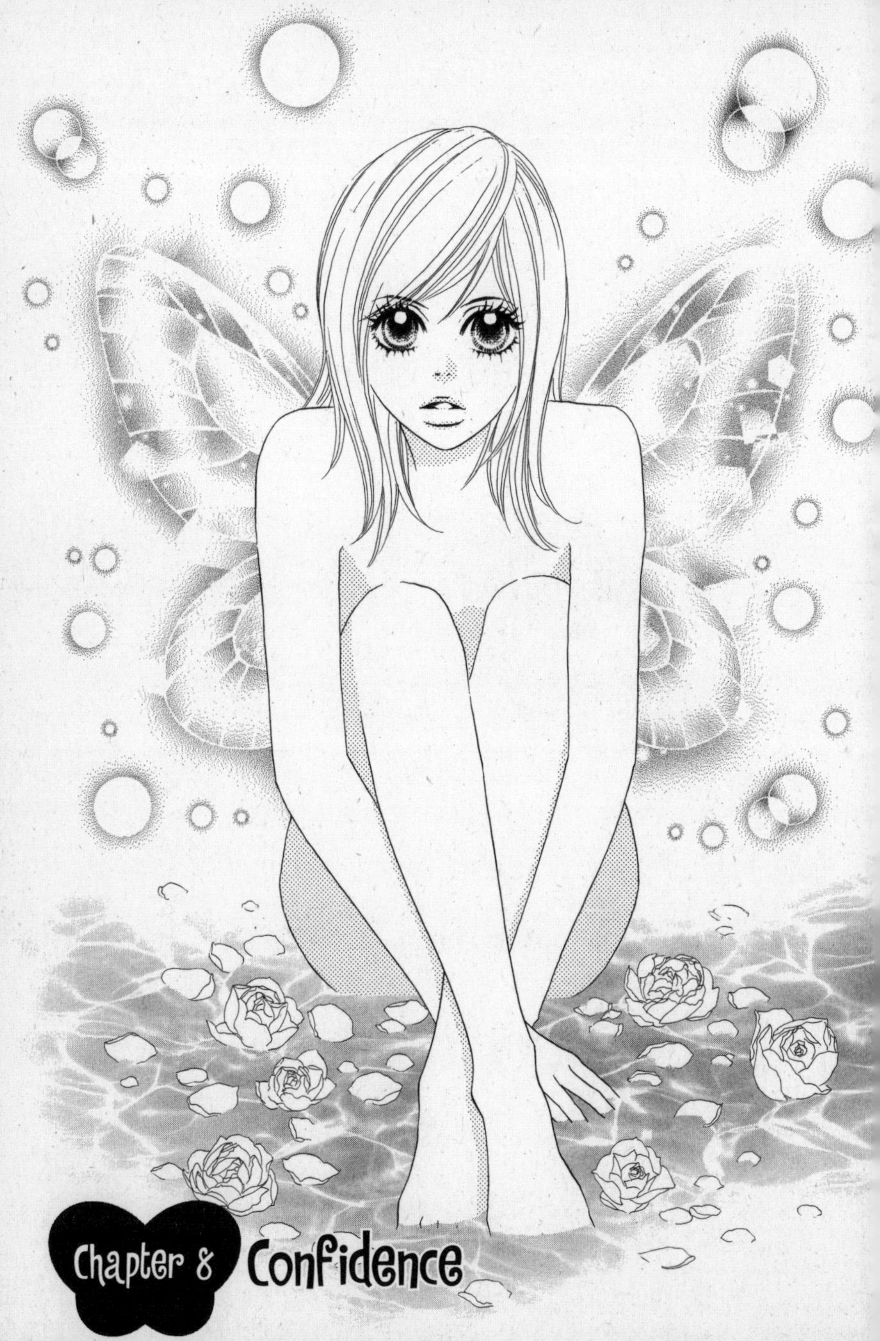
Chapter 8
Confidence

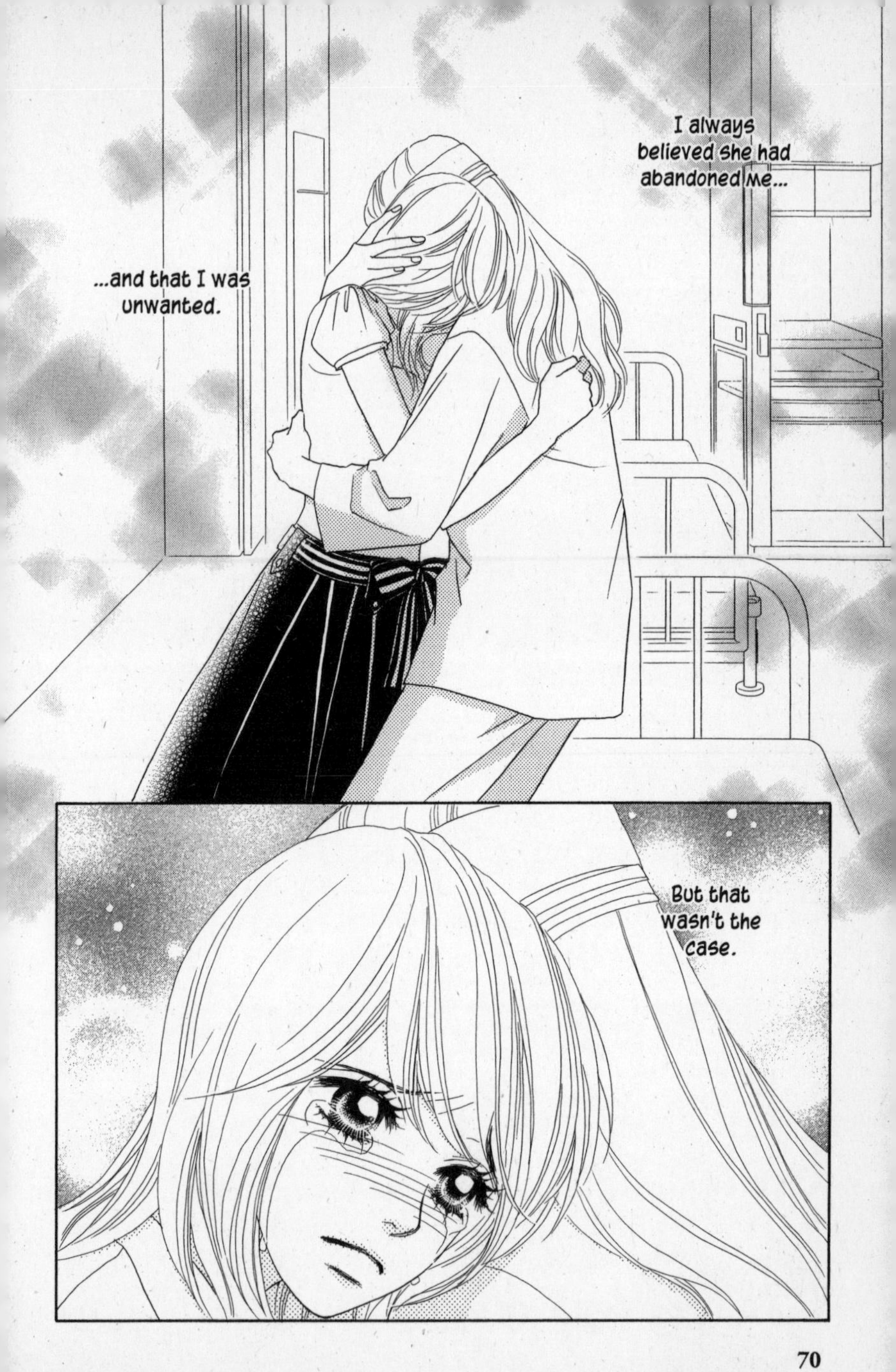
I always believed she had abandoned me...
...and that I was unwanted.
But that wasn't the case.

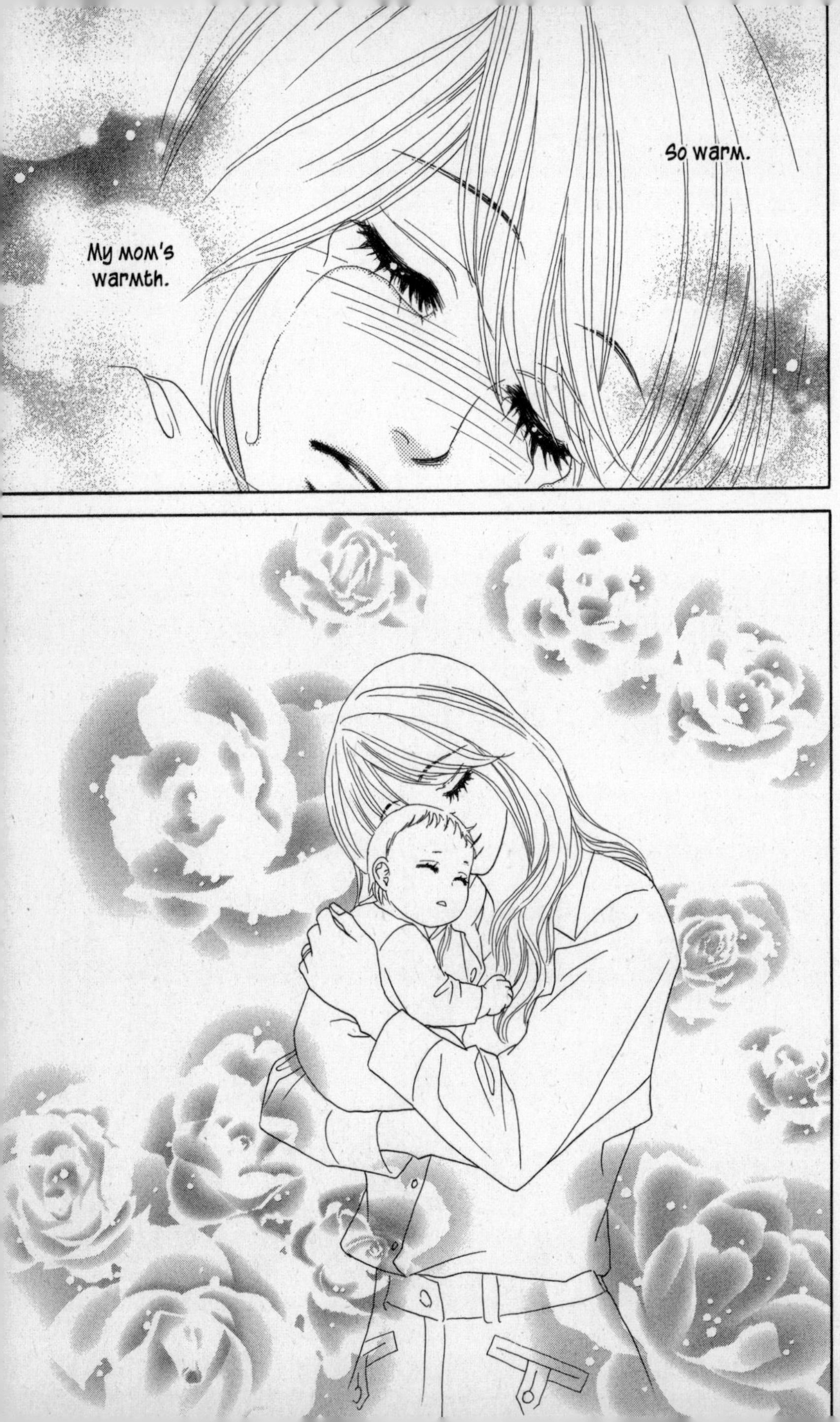
So warm.
My mom's warmth.

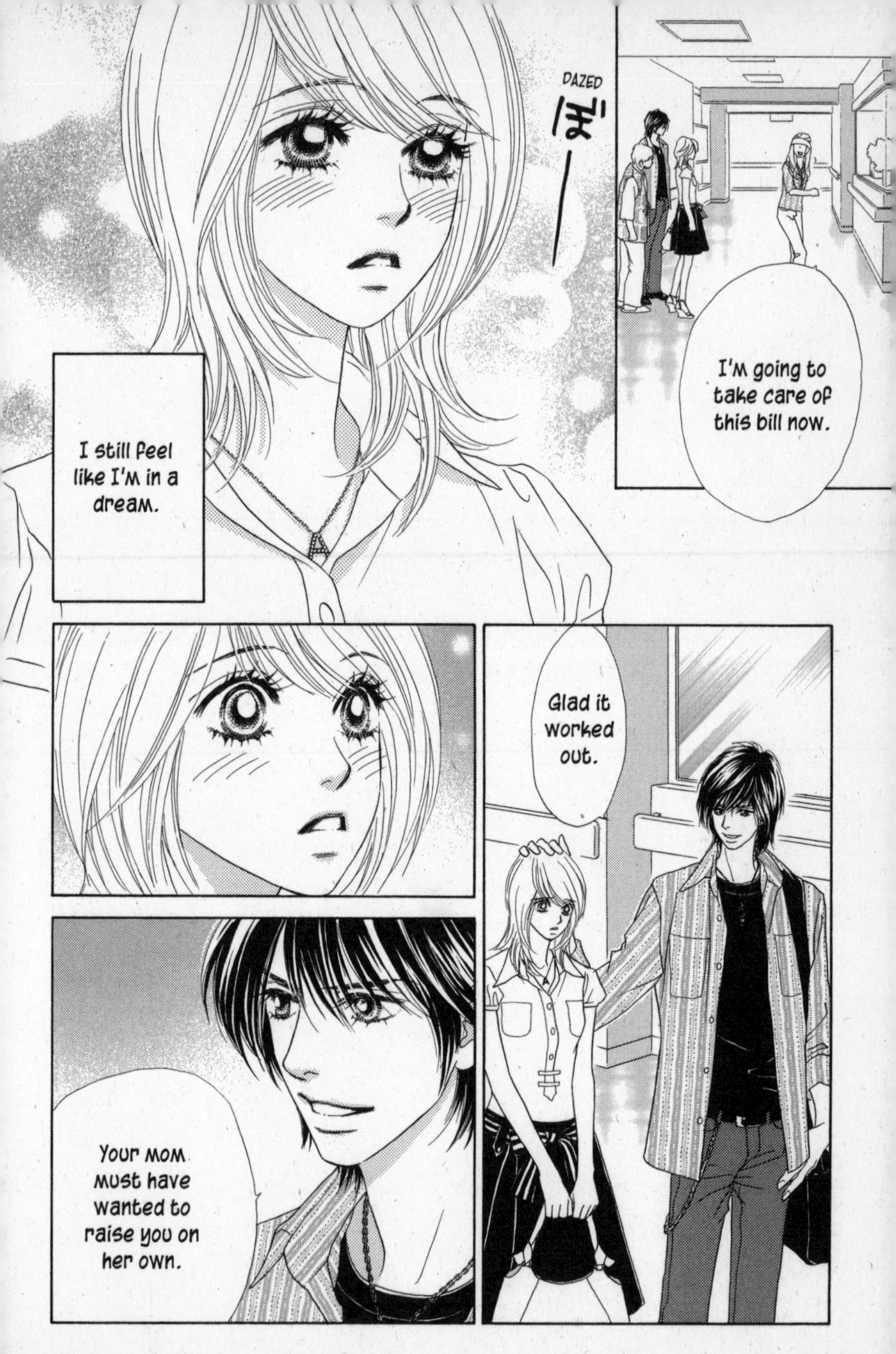
I'm going to take care of this bill now.
DAZED
ぼー
I still feel like I'm in a dream.
Glad it worked out.
Your mom must have wanted to raise you on her own.

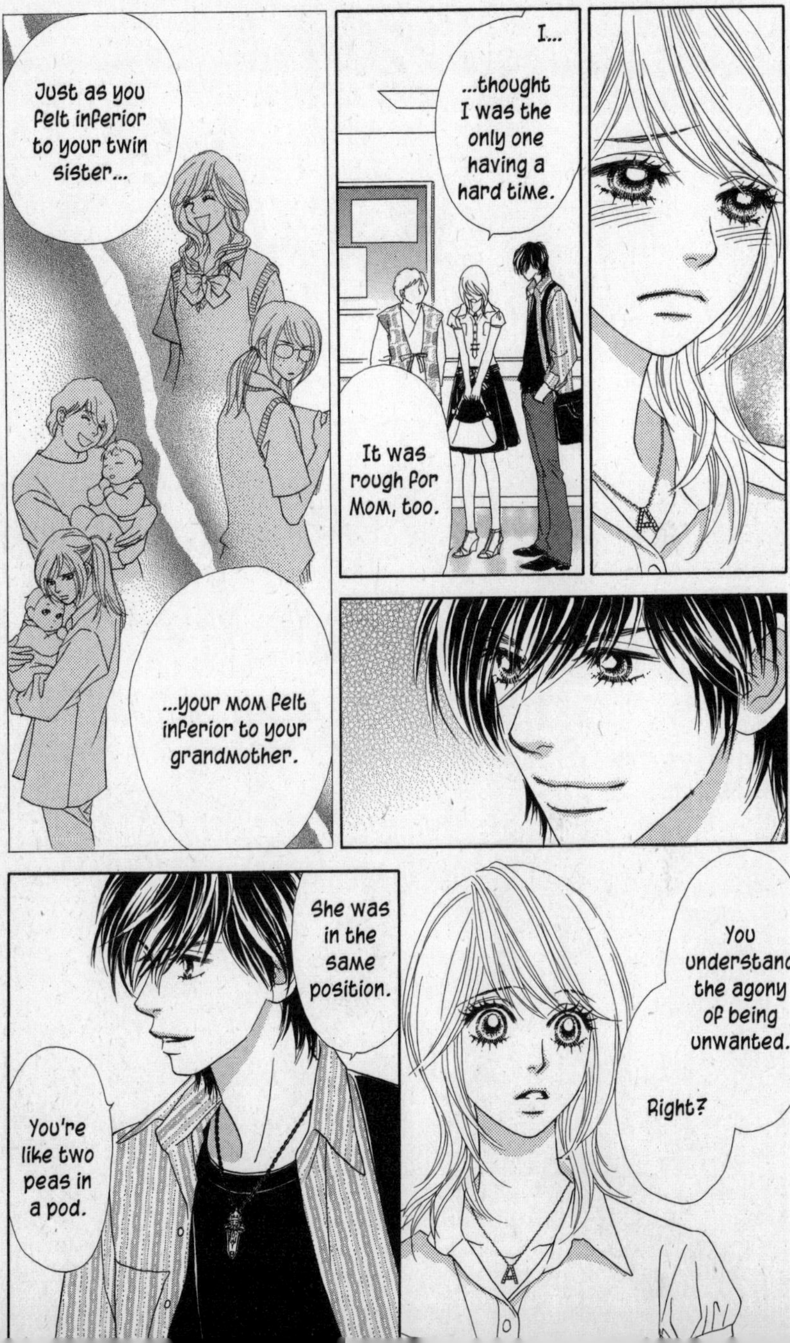
I...
...thought I was the only one having a hard time.
It was rough for Mom, too.
Just as you felt inferior to your twin sister...
...your mom felt inferior to your grandmother.
You understand the agony of being unwanted.
Right?
She was in the same position.
You're like two peas in a pod.

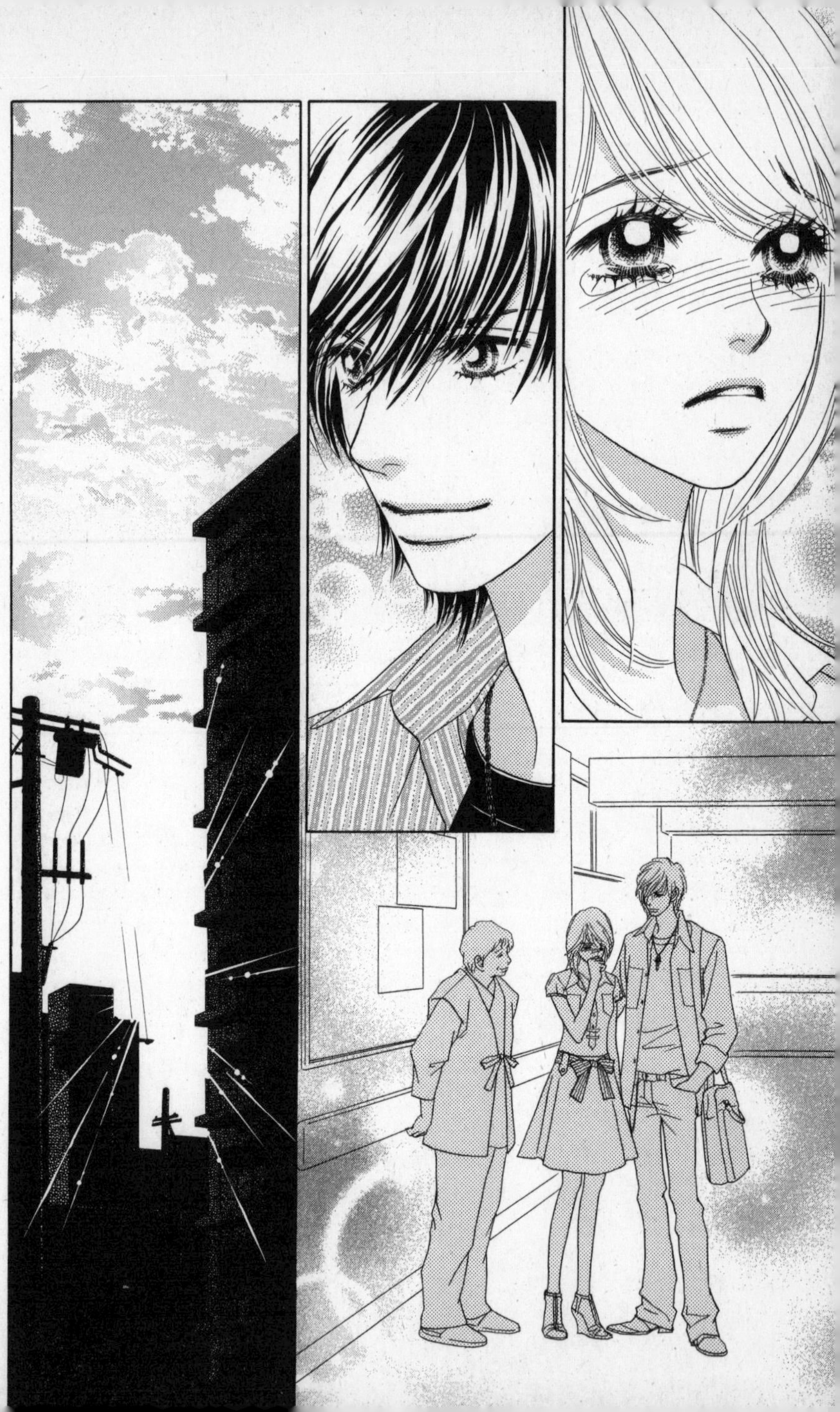

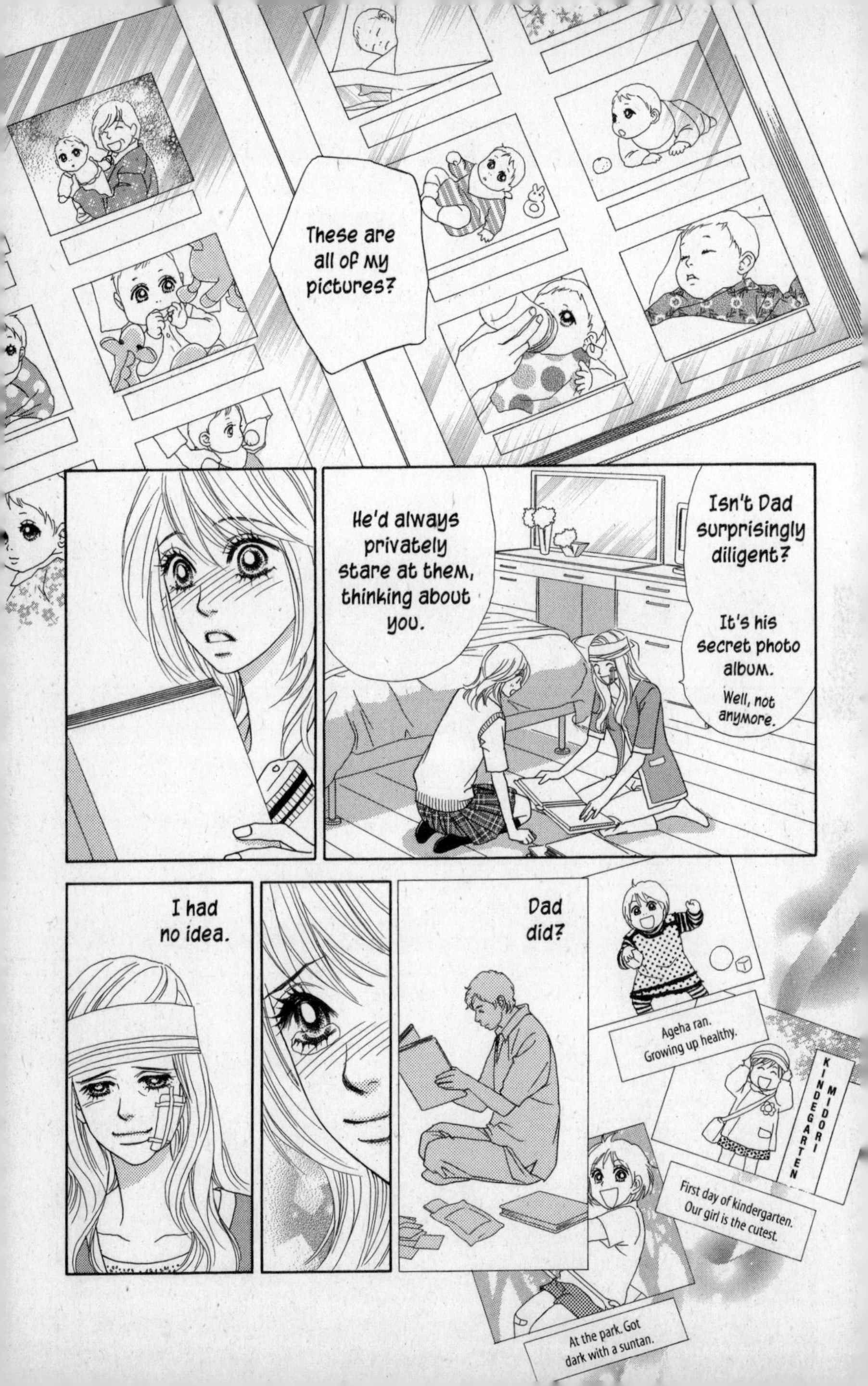
These are all of my pictures?
Isn't Dad surprisingly diligent?
It's his secret photo album.
Well, not anymore.
He'd always privately stare at them, thinking about you.
Ageha ran. Growing up healthy.
MIDORI KINDEGARTEN
First day of kindergarten. Our girl is the cutest.
At the park. Got dark with a suntan.
Dad did?
I had no idea.

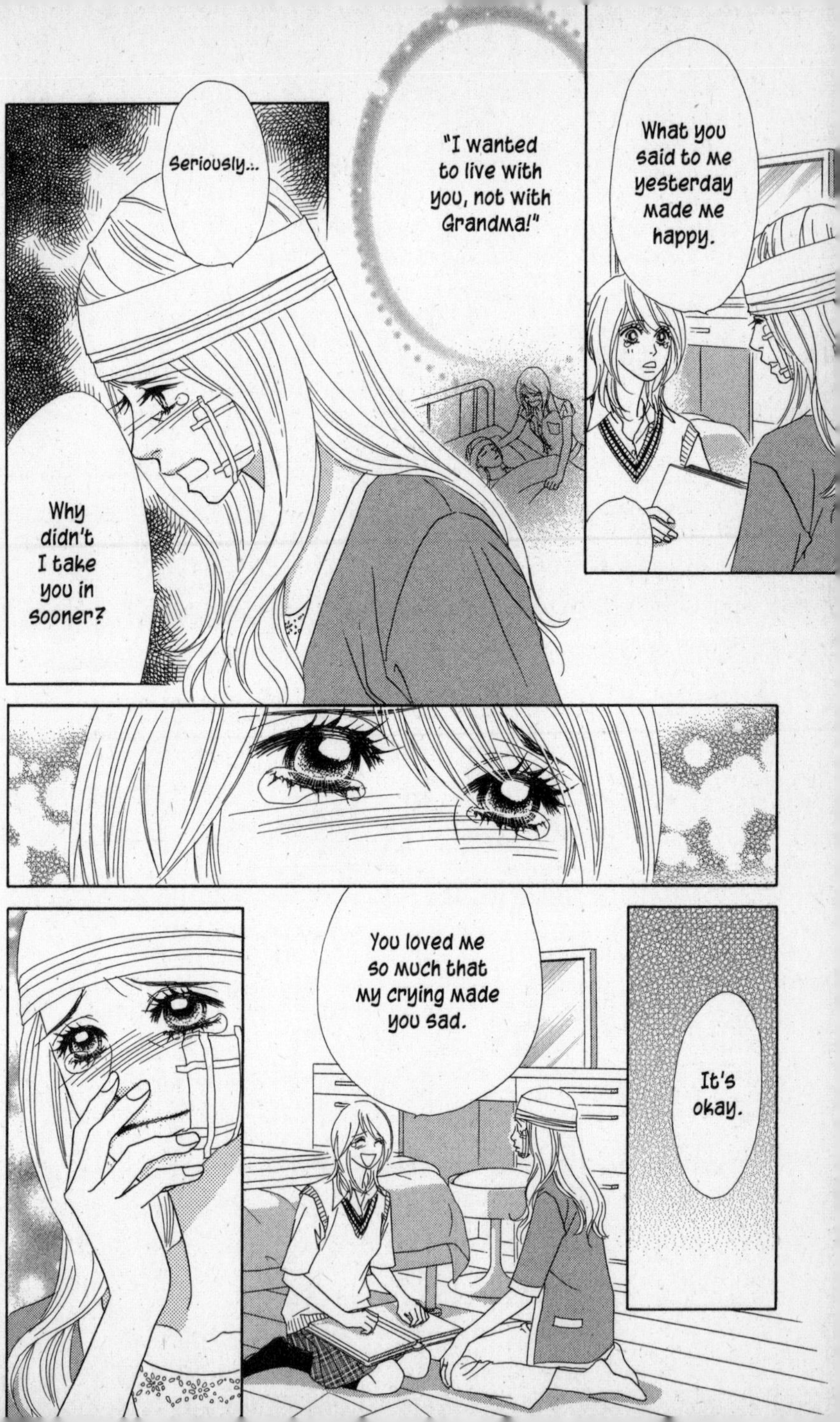
What you said to me yesterday made me happy.
"I wanted to live with you, not with Grandma!"
Seriously...
Why didn't I take you in sooner?
It's okay.
You loved me so much that my crying made you sad.

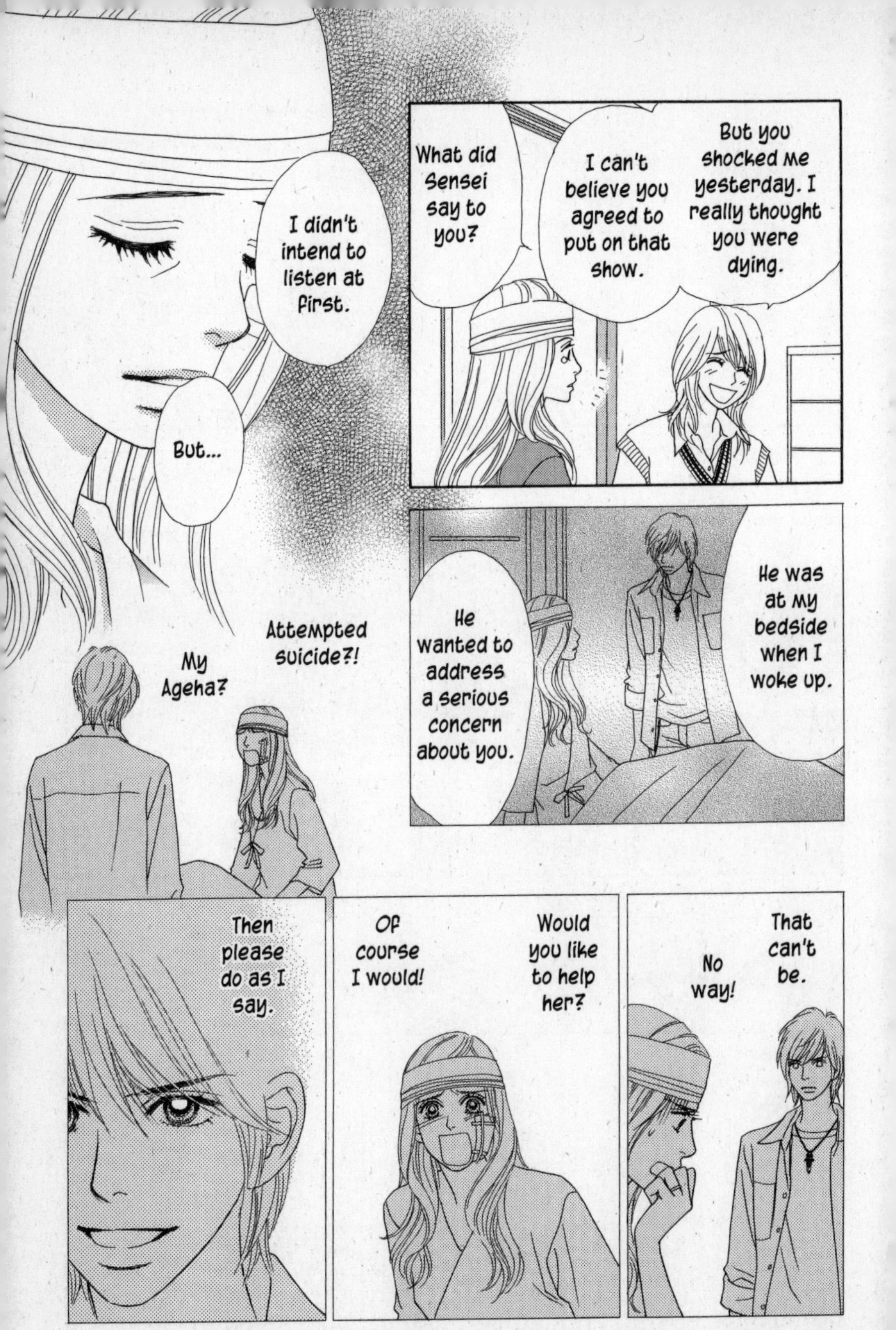
But you shocked me yesterday. I really thought you were dying.
I can't believe you agreed to put on that show.
What did Sensei say to you?
He was at my bedside when I woke up.
He wanted to address a serious concern about you.
I didn't intend to listen at first.
But...
Attempted suicide?!
My Ageha?
That can't be.
No way!
Would you like to help her?
Of course I would!
Then please do as I say.

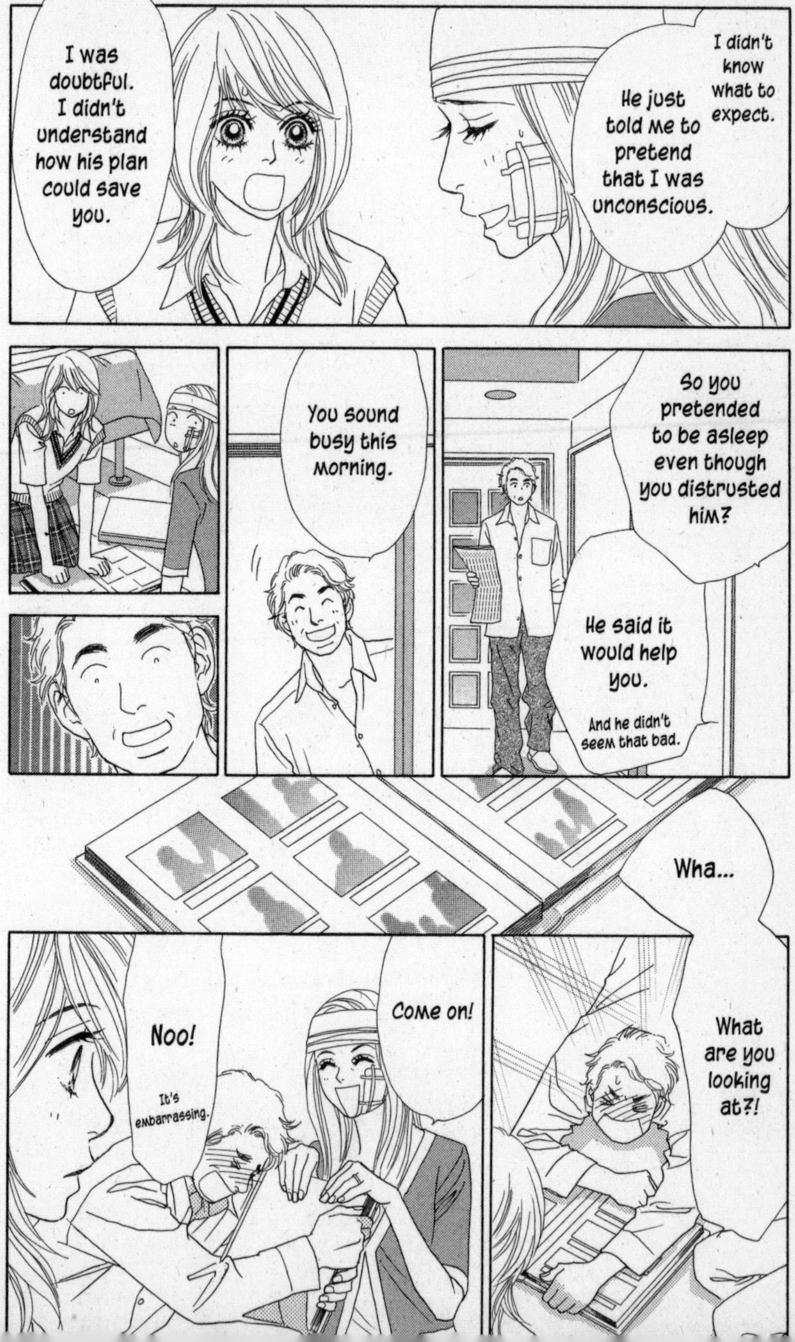
I didn't know what to expect.
He just told me to pretend that I was unconscious.
I was doubtful. I didn't understand how his plan could save you.
So you pretended to be asleep even though you distrusted him?
He said it would help you.
And he didn't seem that bad.
You sound busy this morning.
Wha...
What are you looking at?!
Come on!
Noo!
It's embarrassing.

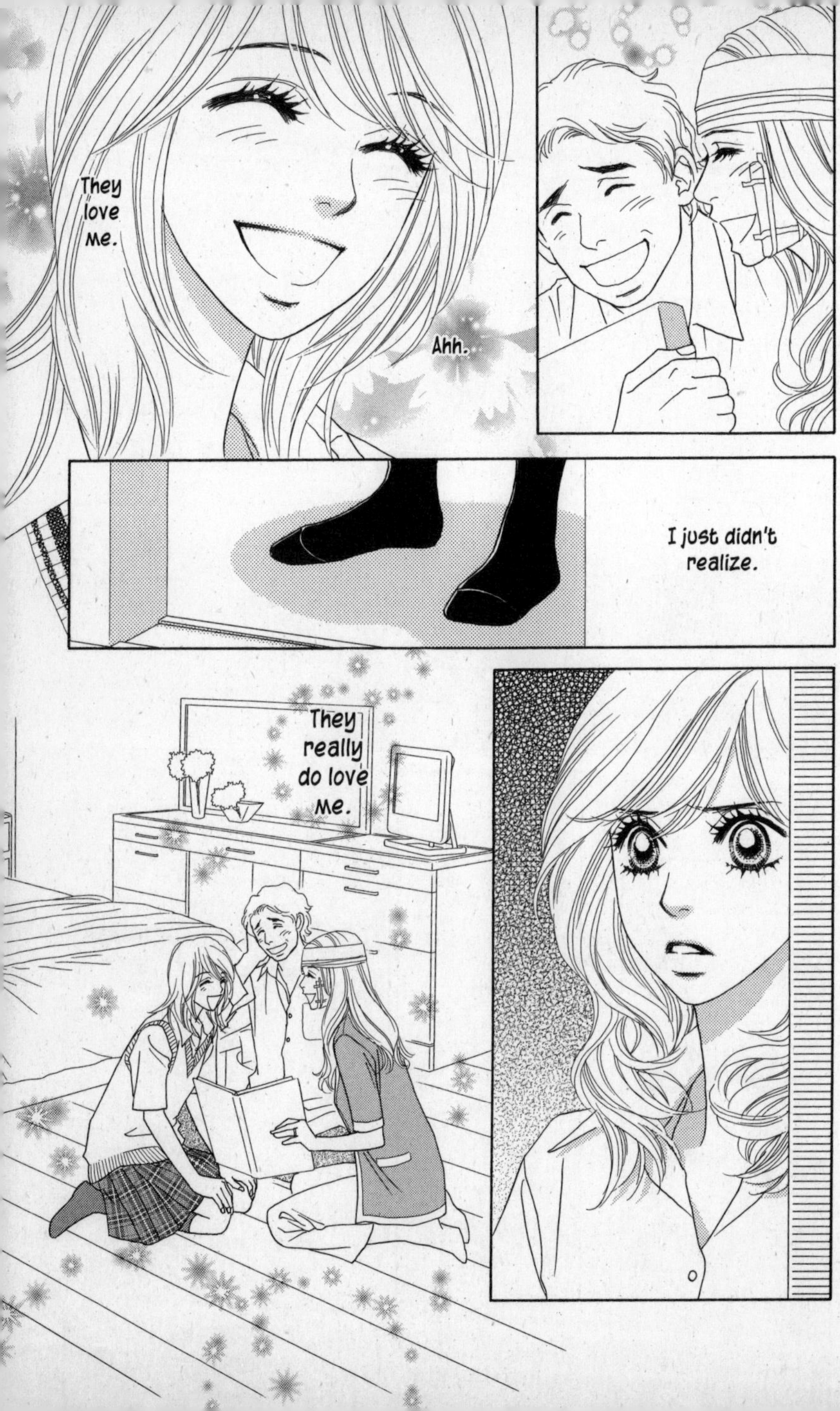
They love me.
Ahh.
I just didn't realize.
They really do love me.

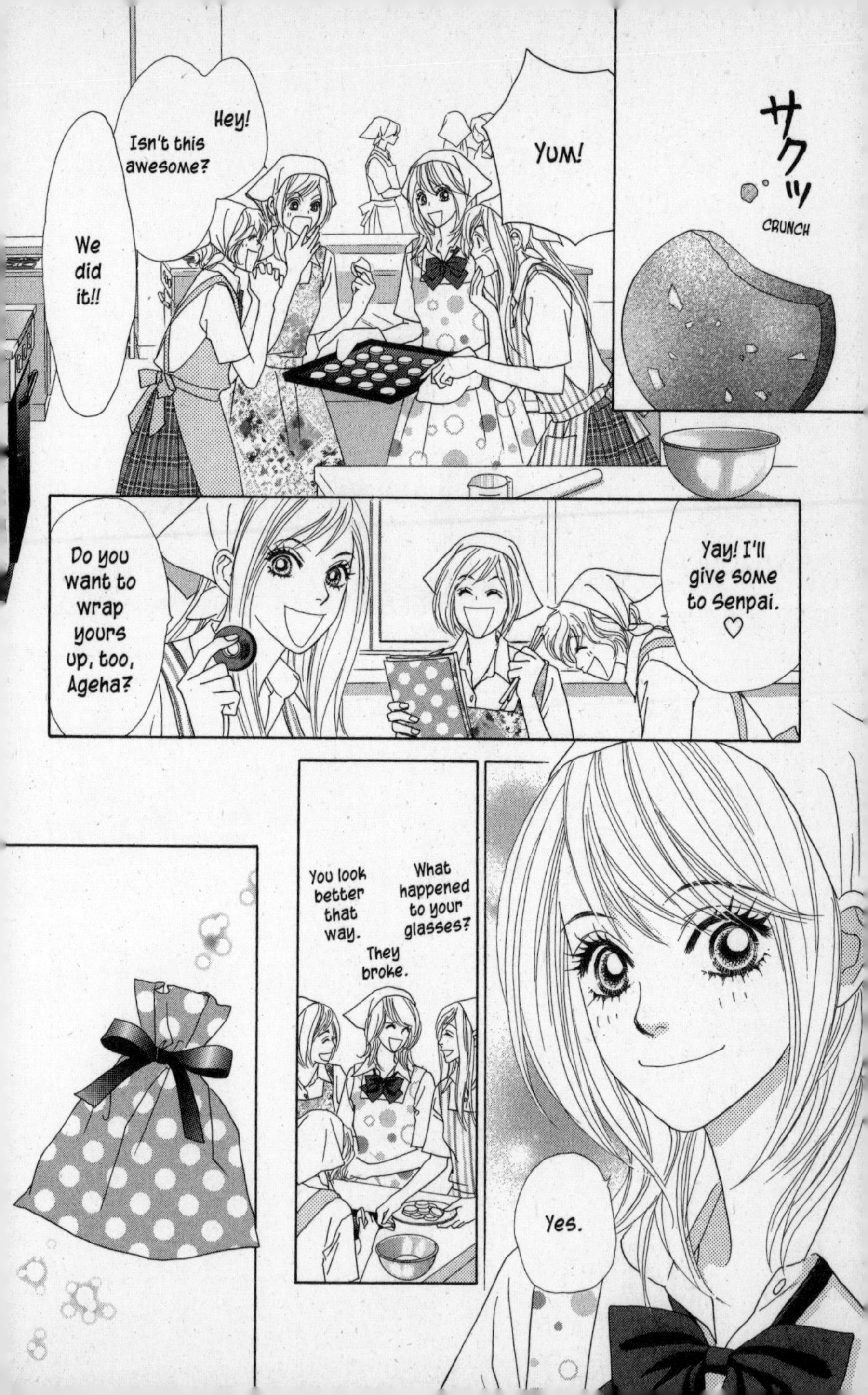
サクッ
CRUNCH
YUM!
Hey! Isn't this awesome?
We did it!!
Yay! I'll give some to Senpai. ♡
Do you want to wrap yours up, too, Ageha?
Yes.
What happened to your glasses?
You look better that way.
They broke.

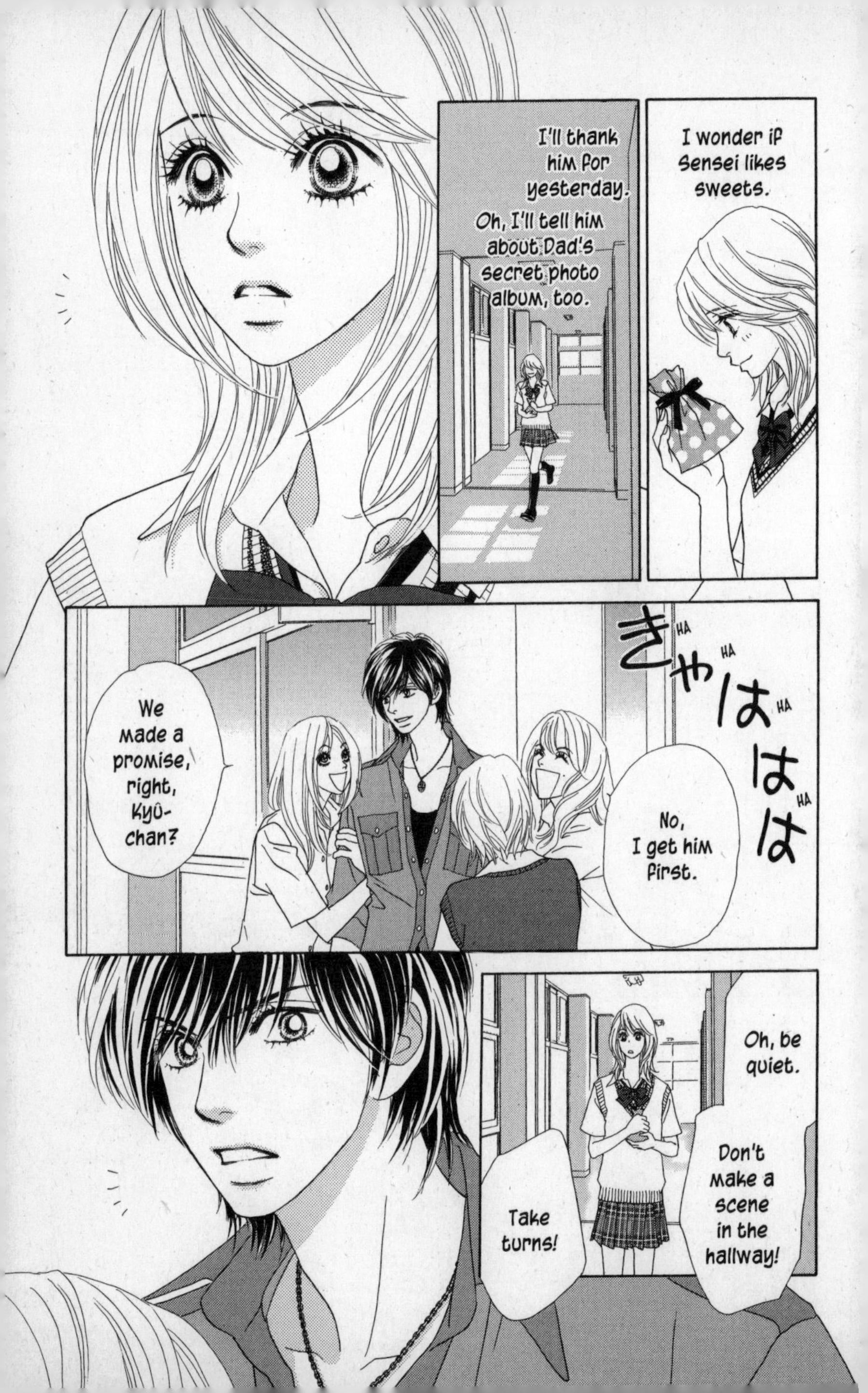
I wonder if Sensei likes sweets.
I'll thank him for yesterday.
Oh, I'll tell him about Dad's secret photo album, too.
きゃははは
HA HA HA HA
No, I get him first.
We made a promise, right, Kyû-chan?
Oh, be quiet.
Don't make a scene in the hallway!
Take turns!

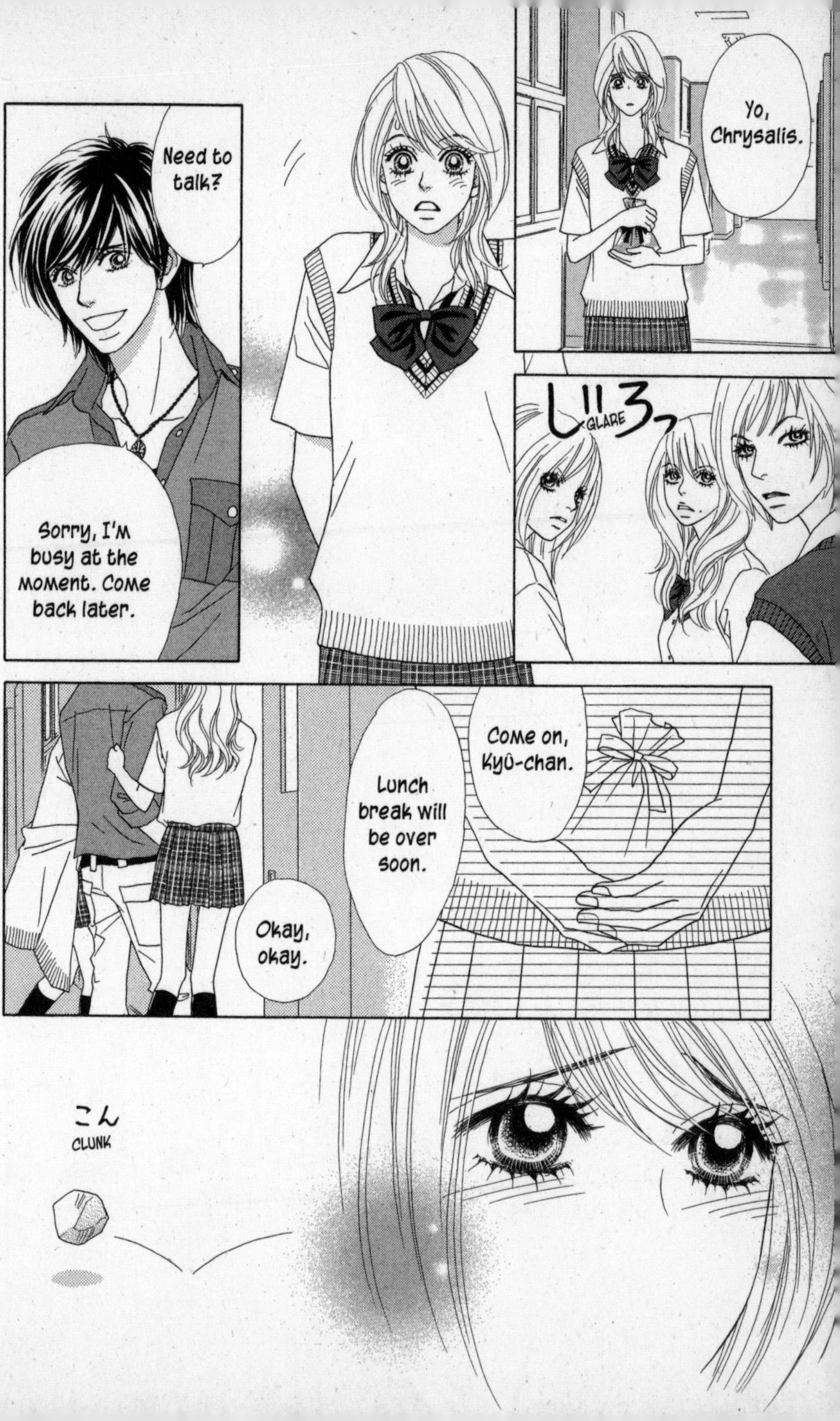
Yo, Chrysalis.
GLARE
Need to talk?
Sorry, I'm busy at the moment. Come back later.
Come on, Kyû-chan.
Lunch break will be over soon.
Okay, okay.
こん
CLUNK

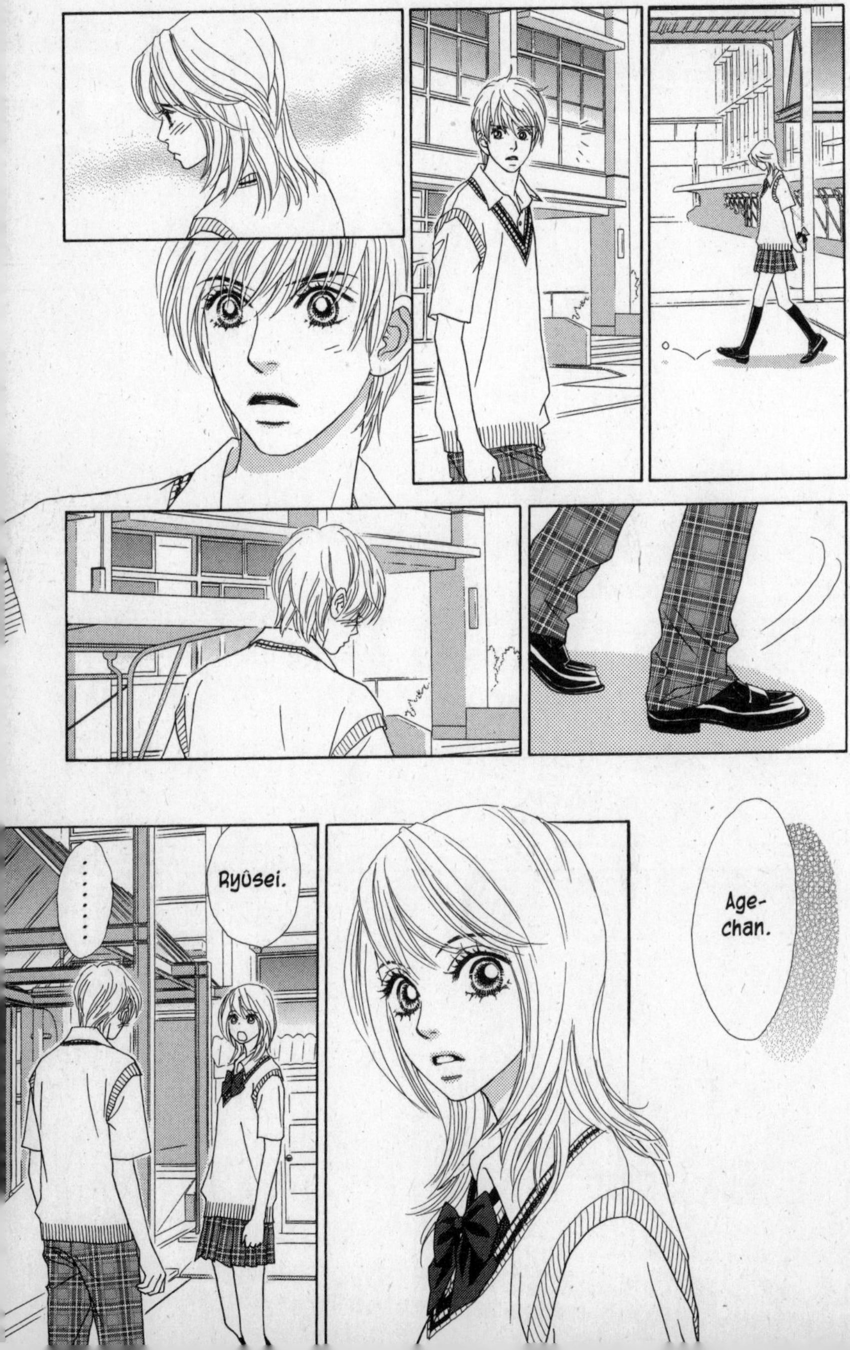
Age-chan.
Ryûsei.
......

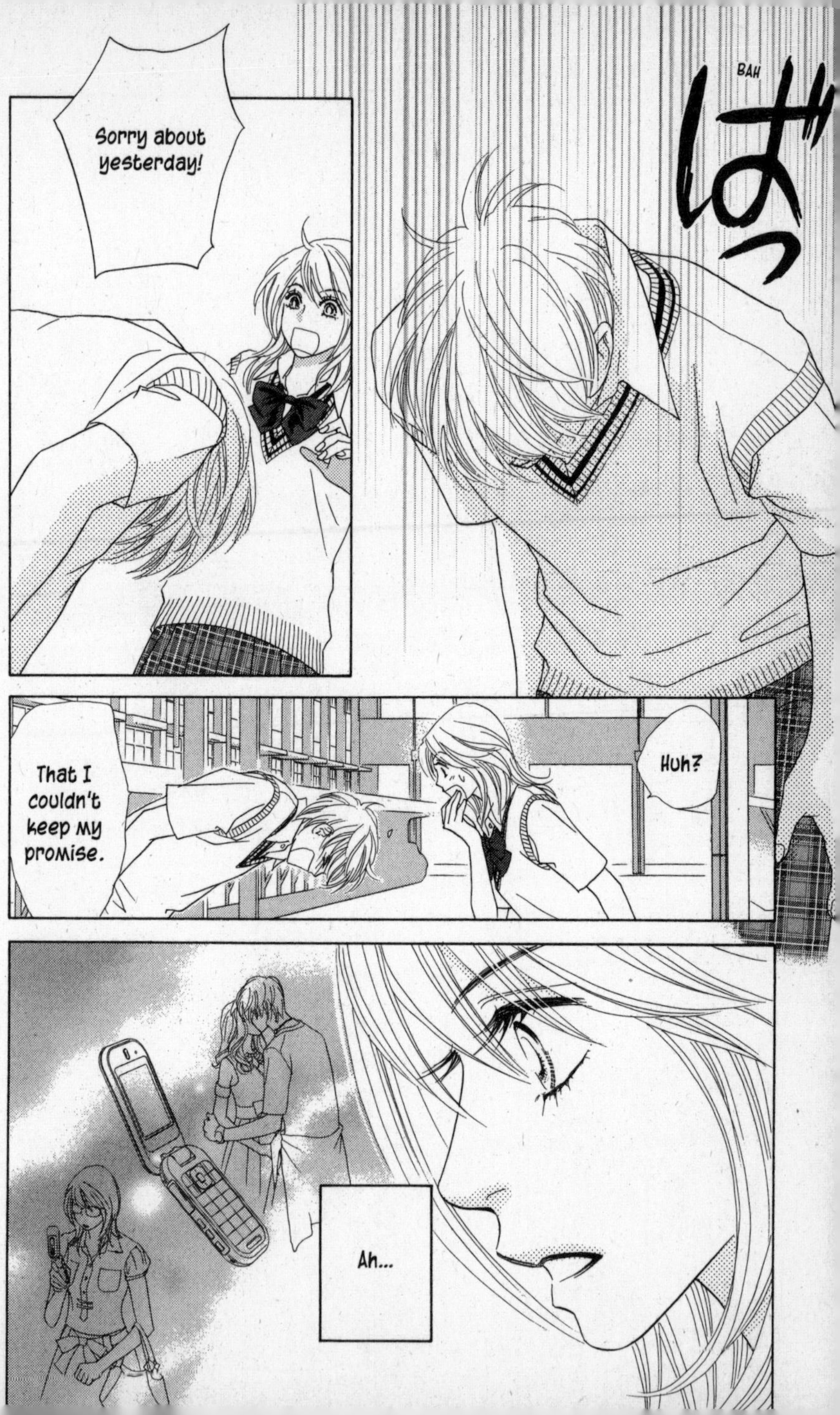
BAH
ばっ
Sorry about yesterday!
Huh?
That I couldn't keep my promise.
Ah...

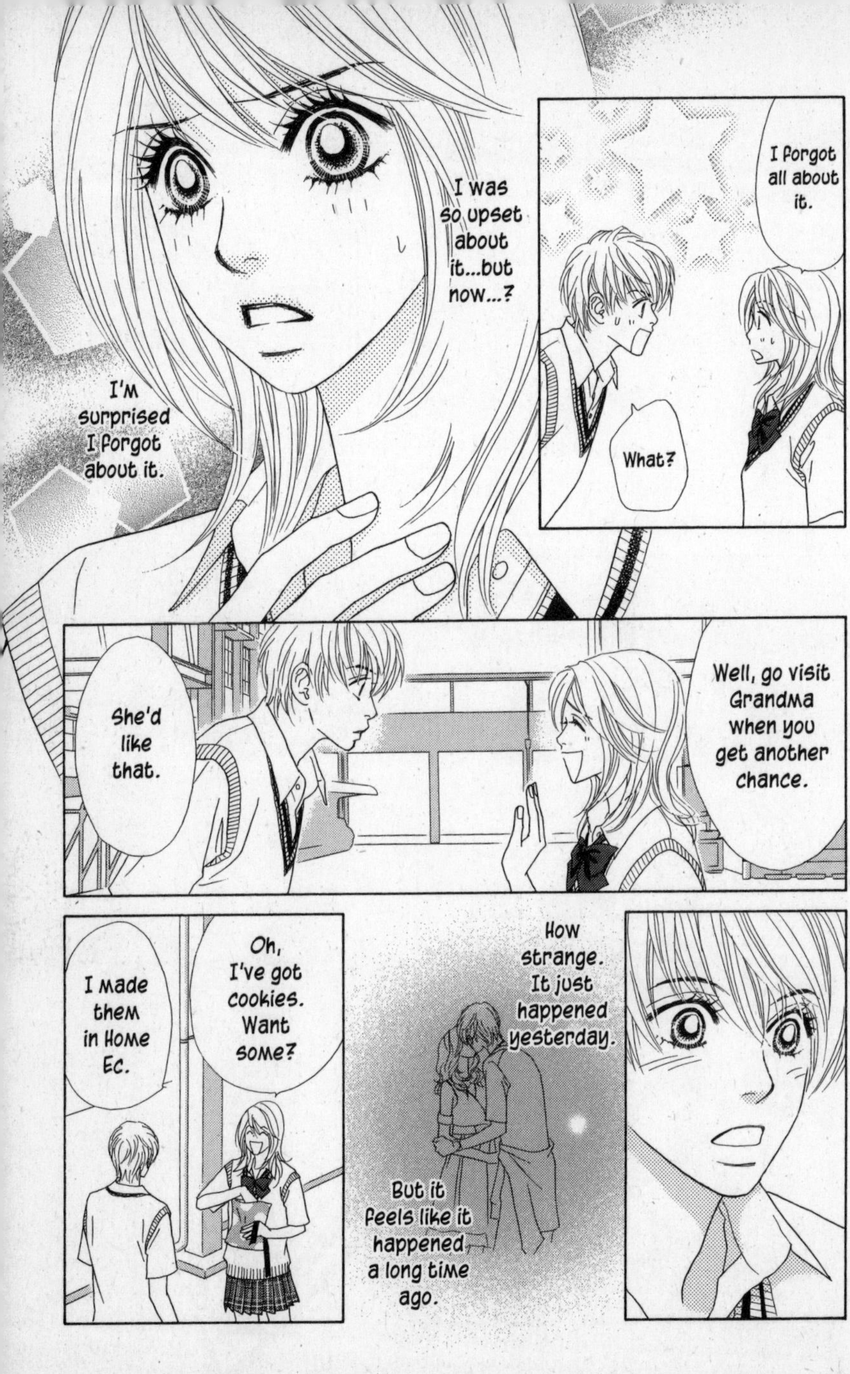
I forgot all about it.
What?
I was so upset about it...but now...?
I'm surprised I forgot about it.
Well, go visit Grandma when you get another chance.
She'd like that.
How strange. It just happened yesterday.
But it feels like it happened a long time ago.
Oh, I've got cookies. Want some?
I made them in Home Ec.

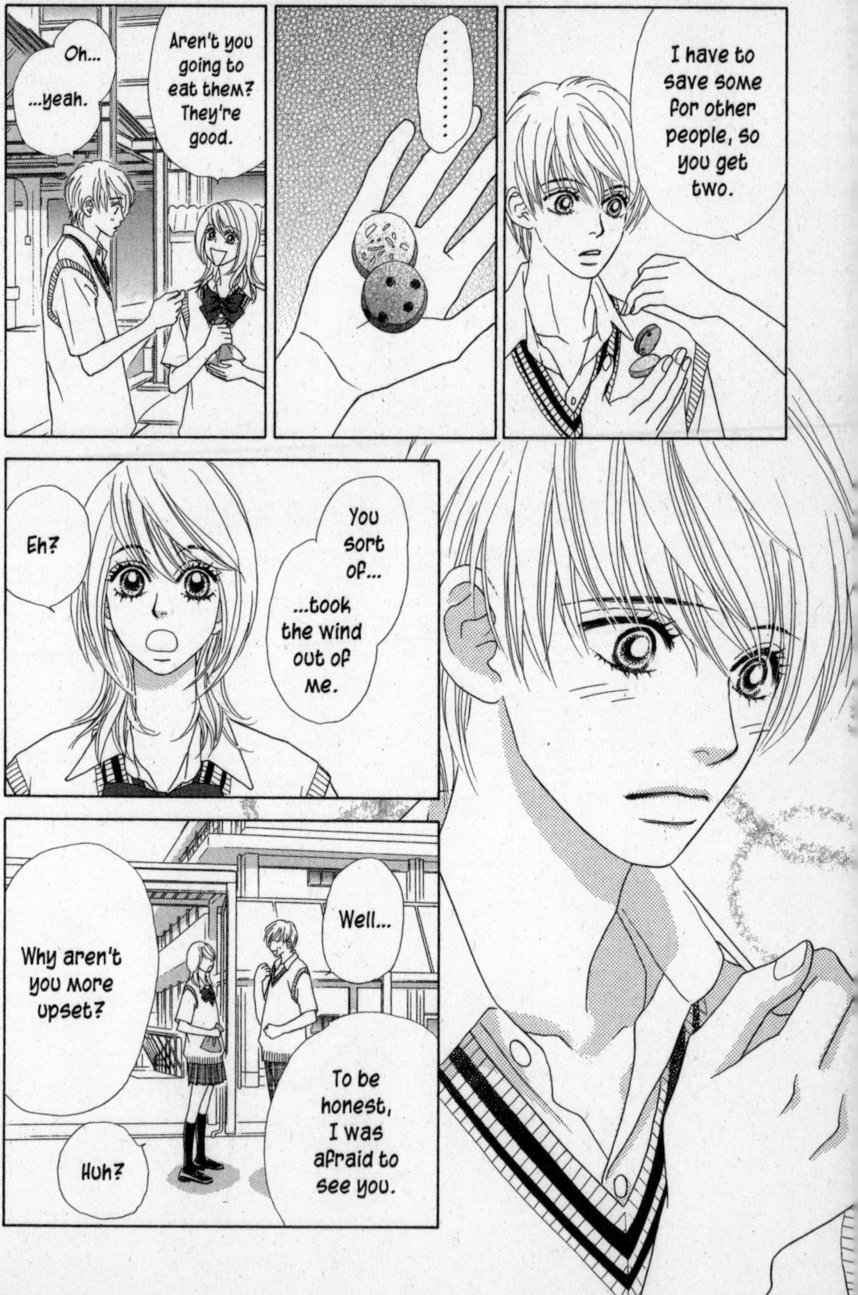
I have to save some for other people, so you get two.
......
Aren't you going to eat them? They're good.
Oh... ...yeah.
You sort of... ...took the wind out of me.
Eh?
Well...
Why aren't you more upset?
To be honest, I was afraid to see you.
Huh?

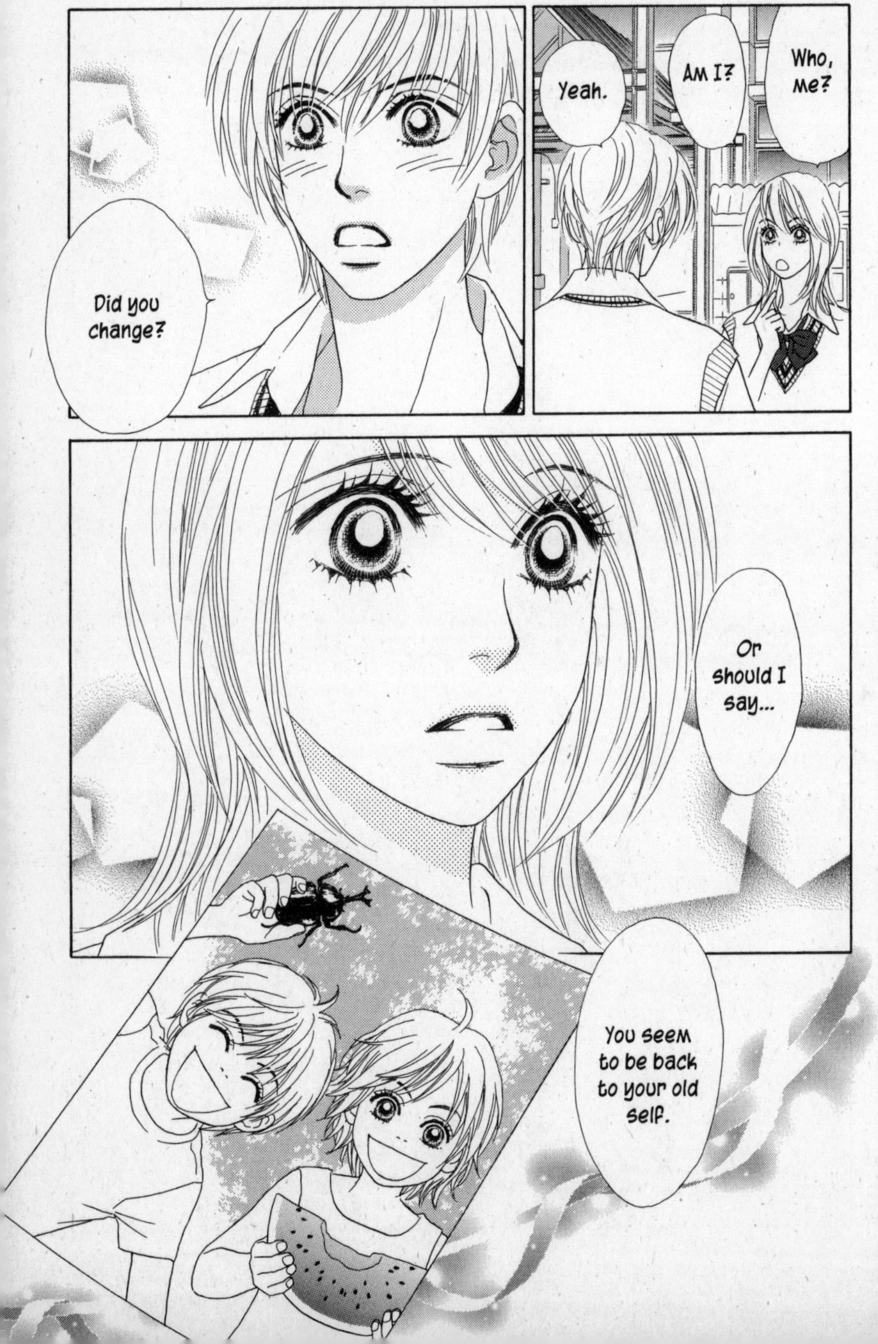
Who, me?
Am I?
Yeah.
Did you change?
Or should I say...
You seem to be back to your old self.

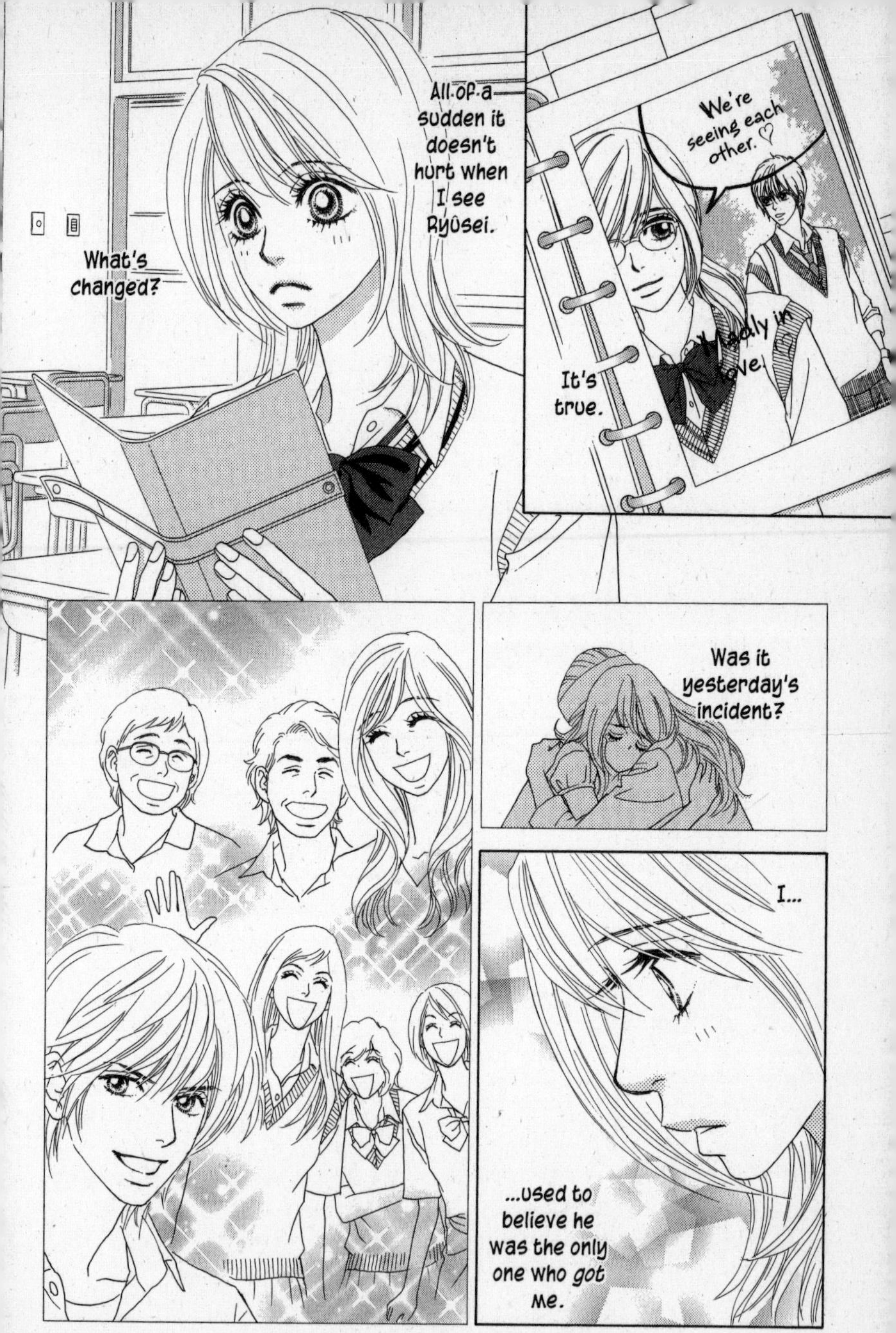
We're seeing each other. ♡
It's true.
All of a sudden it doesn't hurt when I see Ryûsei.
What's changed?
Was it yesterday's incident?
I...
...used to believe he was the only one who got me.

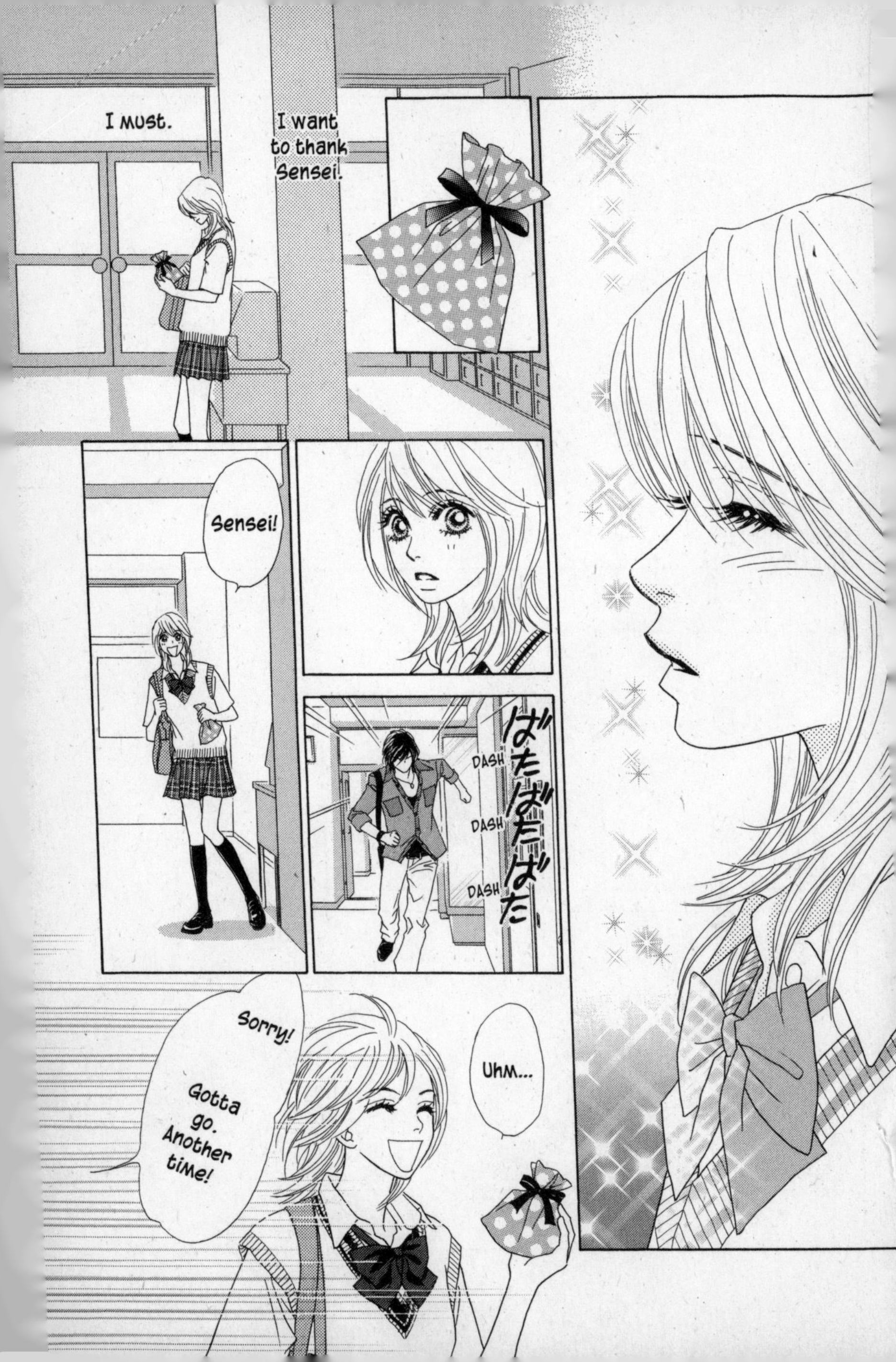
I want to thank Sensei.
I must.
ばたばた
DASH
DASH
DASH
Sensei!
Uhm...
Sorry!
Gotta go. Another time!

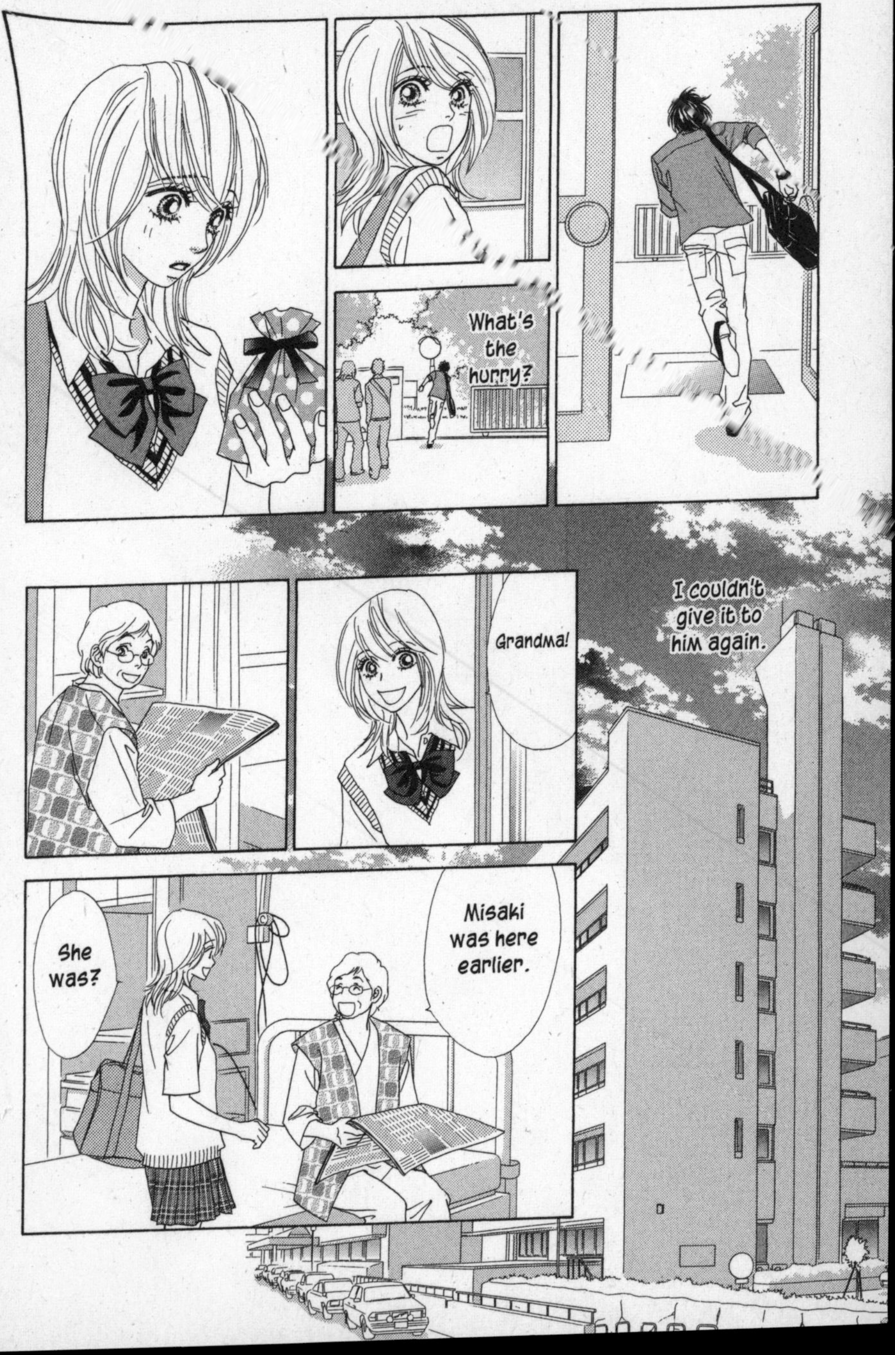
What's the hurry?
I couldn't give it to him again.
Grandma!
Misaki was here earlier.
She was?

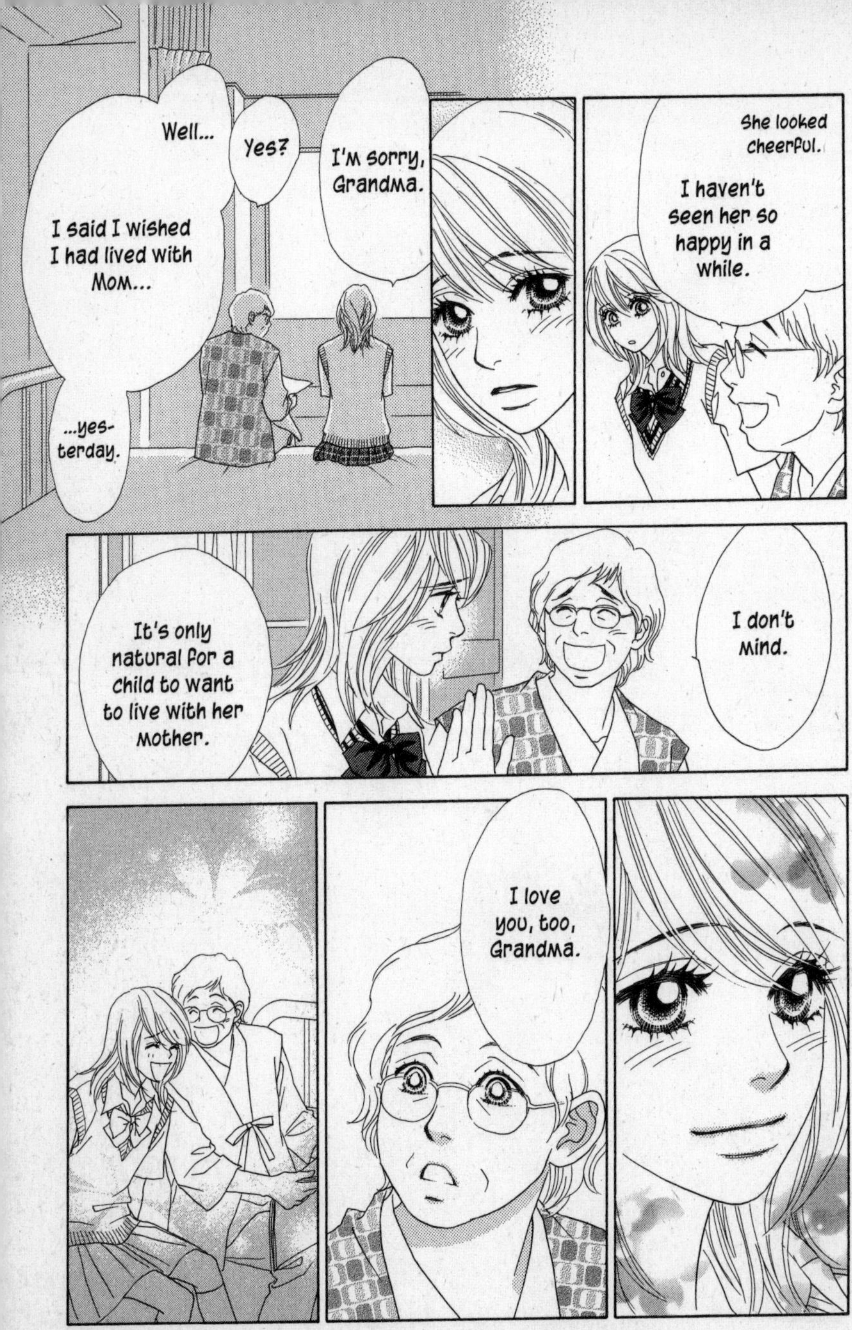
She looked cheerful.
I haven't seen her so happy in a while.
I'm sorry, Grandma.
Yes?
Well...
I said I wished I had lived with Mom...
...yes-terday.
I don't mind.
It's only natural for a child to want to live with her mother.
I love you, too, Grandma.

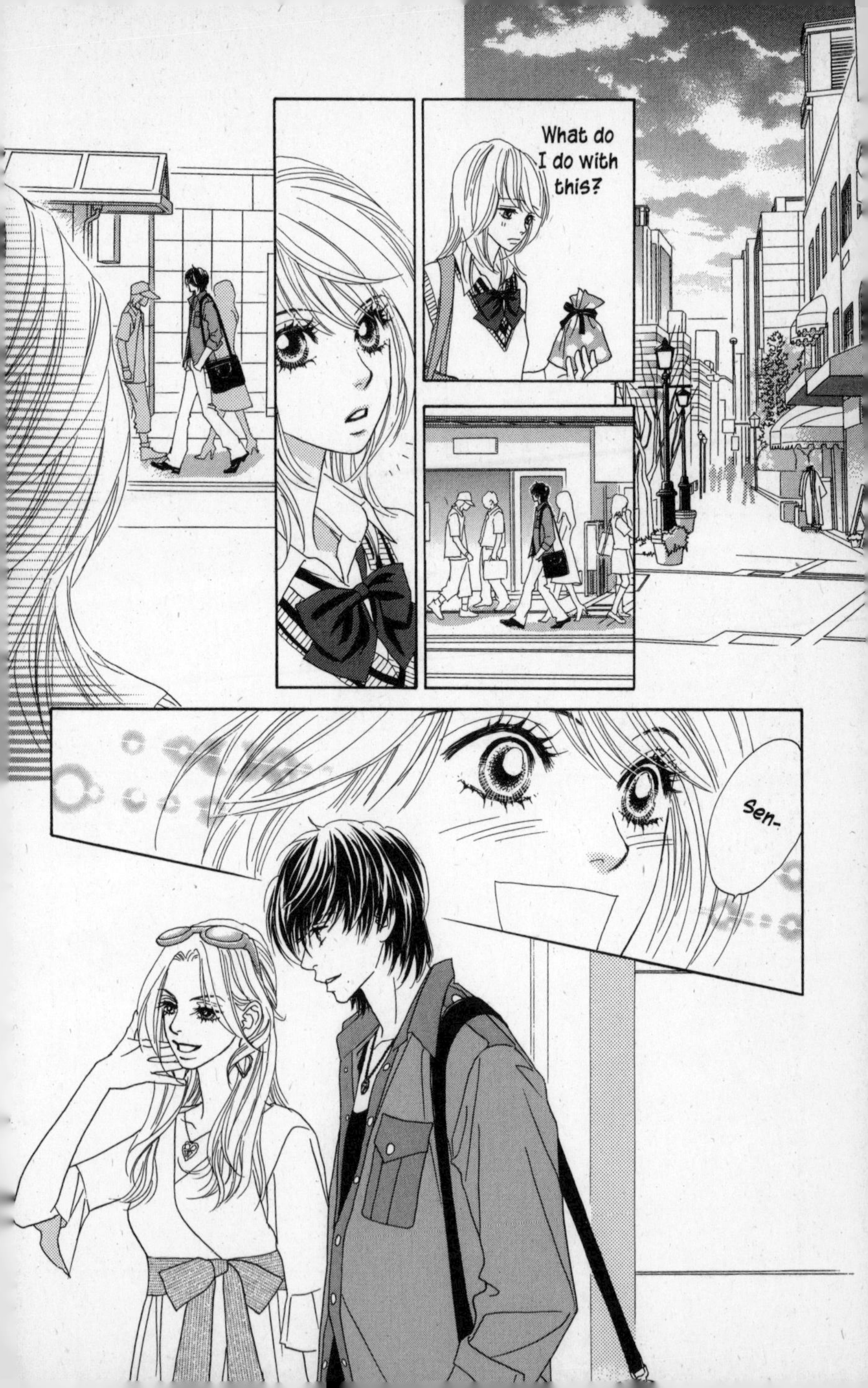
What do I do with this?
Sen-

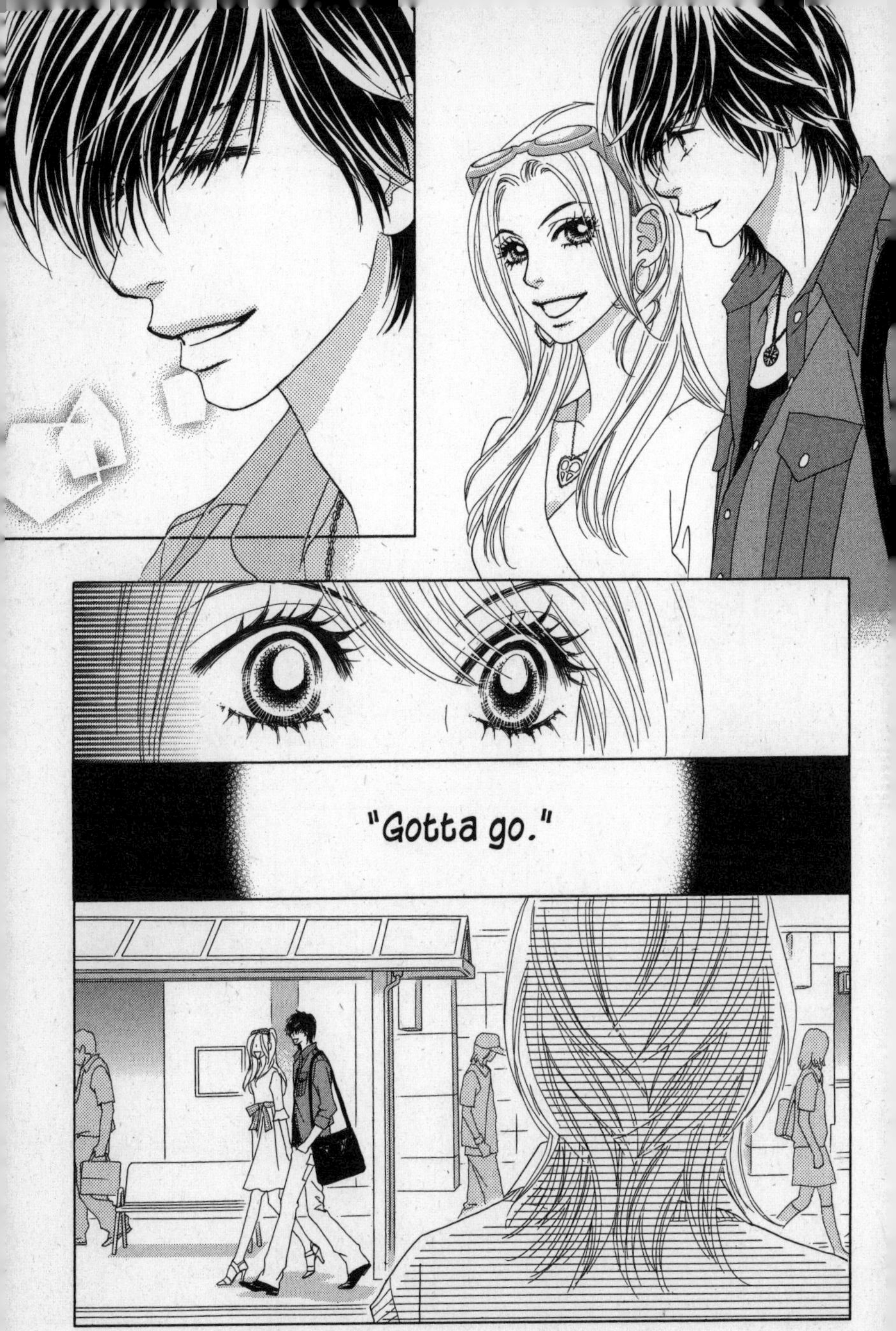
"Gotta go."

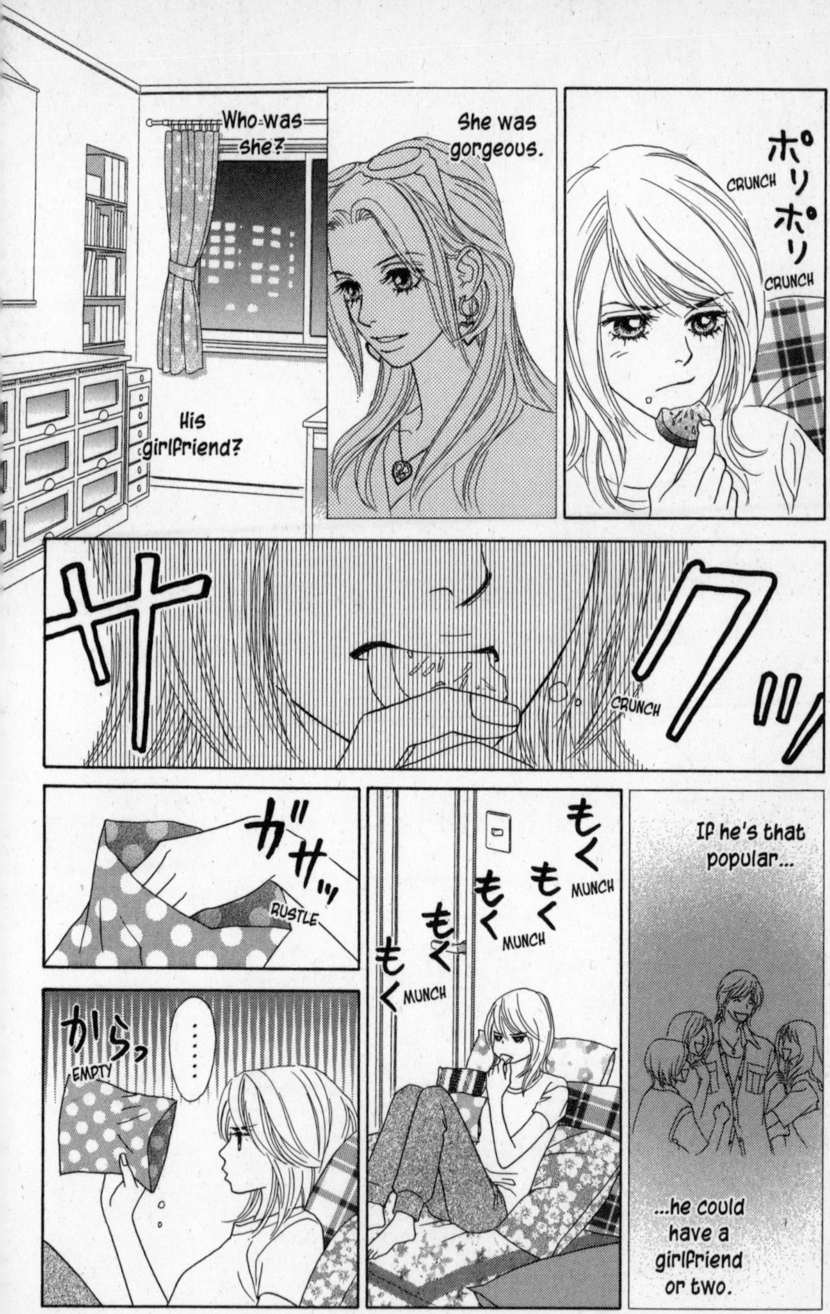
ポリポリ
CRUNCH
CRUNCH
She was gorgeous.
Who was she?
His girlfriend?
ザクッ
CRUNCH
If he's that popular...
...he could have a girlfriend or two.
もくもくもくもく
MUNCH
MUNCH
MUNCH
ガサッ
RUSTLE
からっ
EMPTY
......

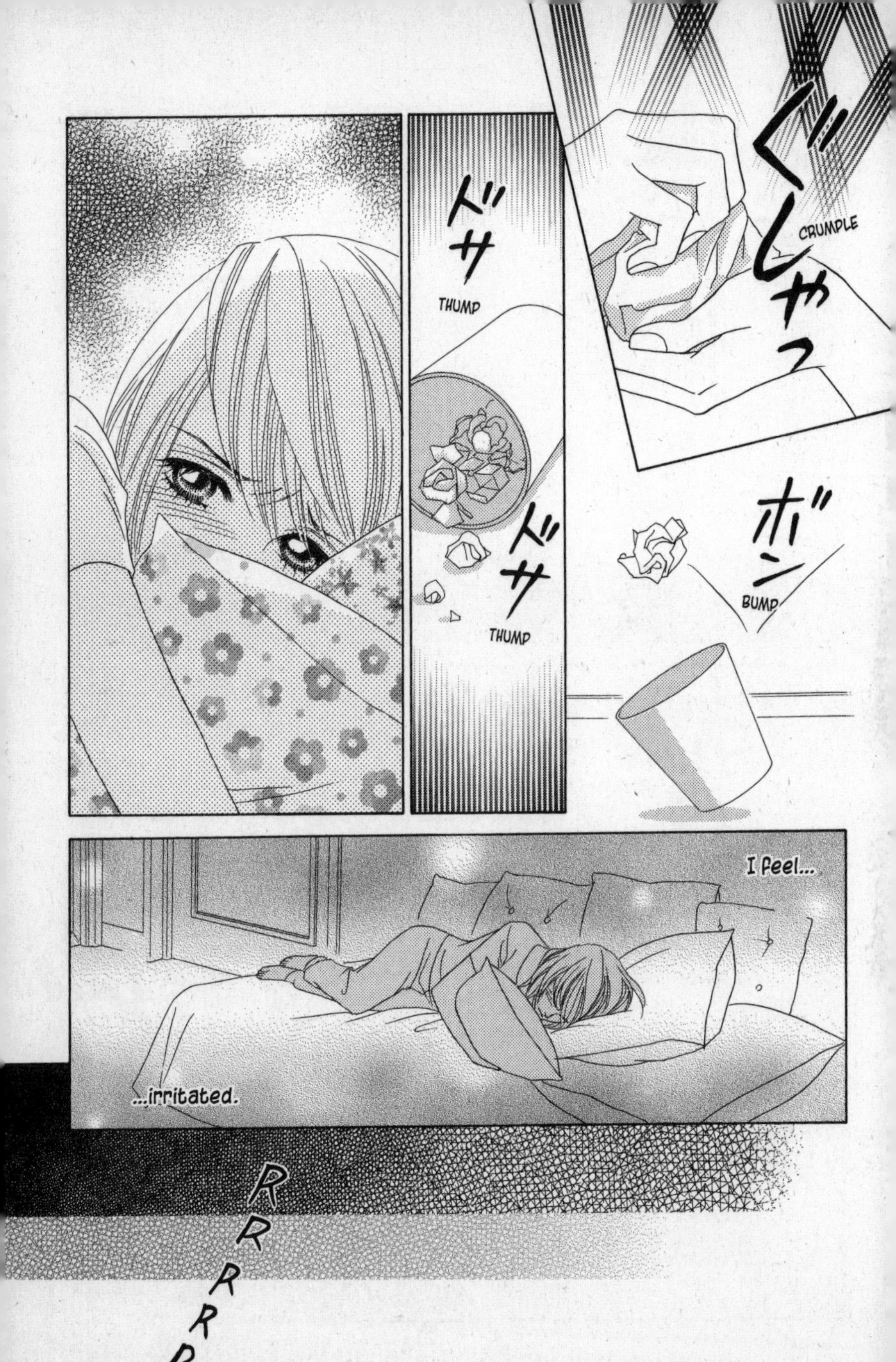
ぐしゃっ
CRUMPLE
ボン
BUMP
ドサ
THUMP
ドサ
THUMP
I feel...
...irritated.
RRRRR

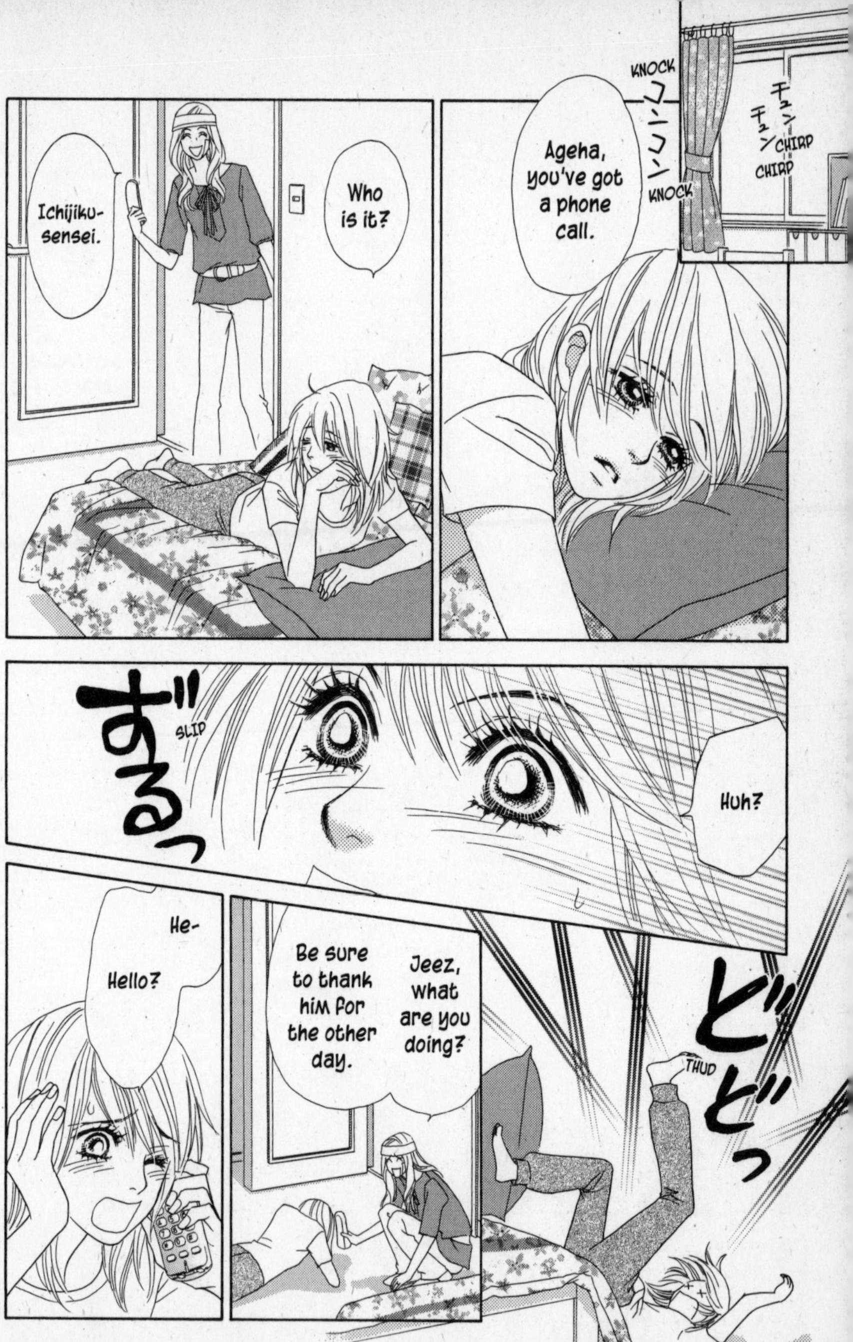
チュンチュン
CHIRP CHIRP
コンコン
KNOCK KNOCK
Ageha, you've got a phone call.
Who is it?
Ichijiku-sensei.
Huh?
するっ
SLIP
どどっ
THUD
Jeez, what are you doing?
Be sure to thank him for the other day.
He-
Hello?

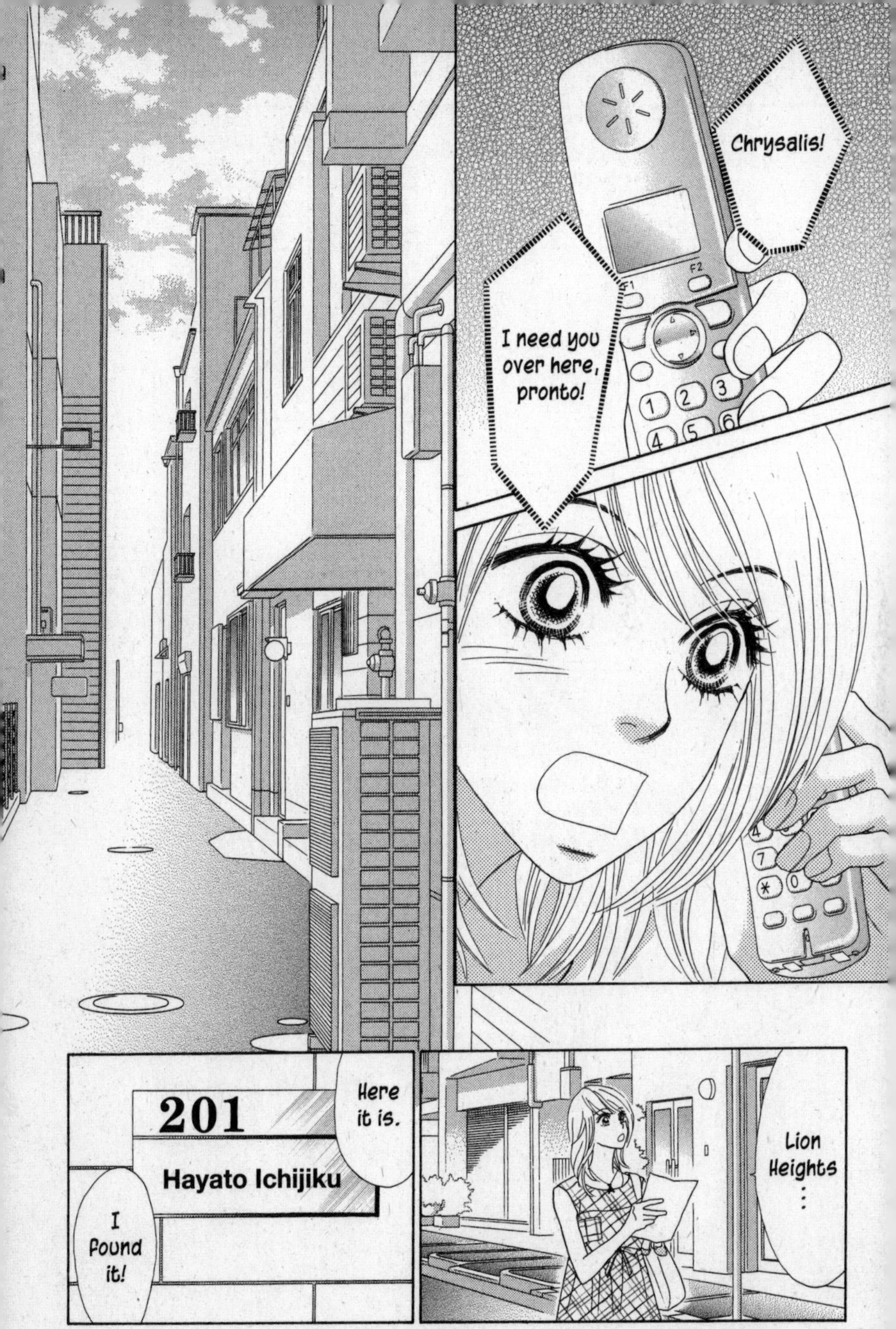
Chrysalis!
I need you over here, pronto!
Lion Heights...
Here it is.
201
Hayato Ichijiku
I found it!

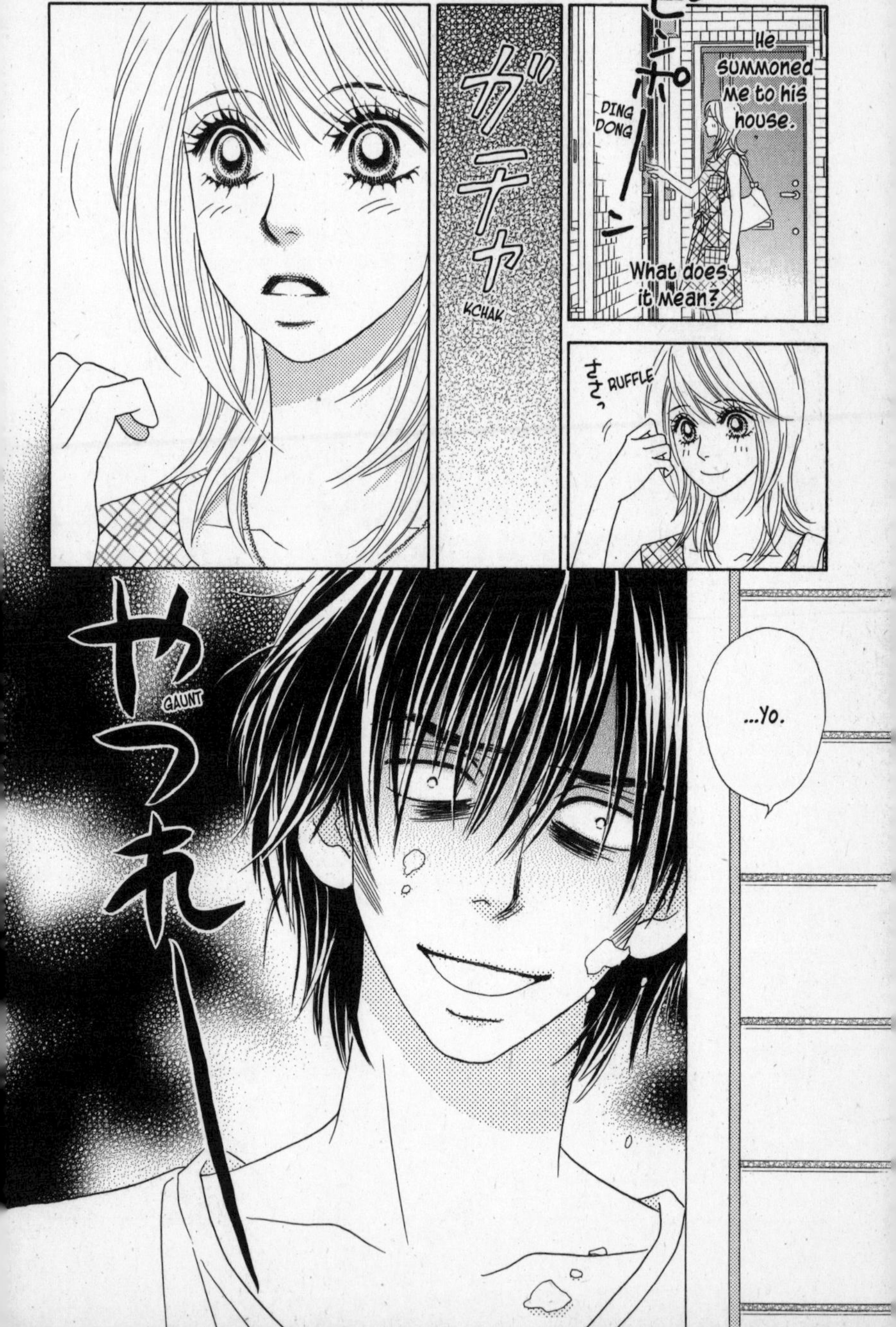
He summoned me to his house.
ピンポーン
DING DONG
What does it mean?
ささっ
RUFFLE
ガチャ
KCHAK
...Yo.
やつれ
GAUNT

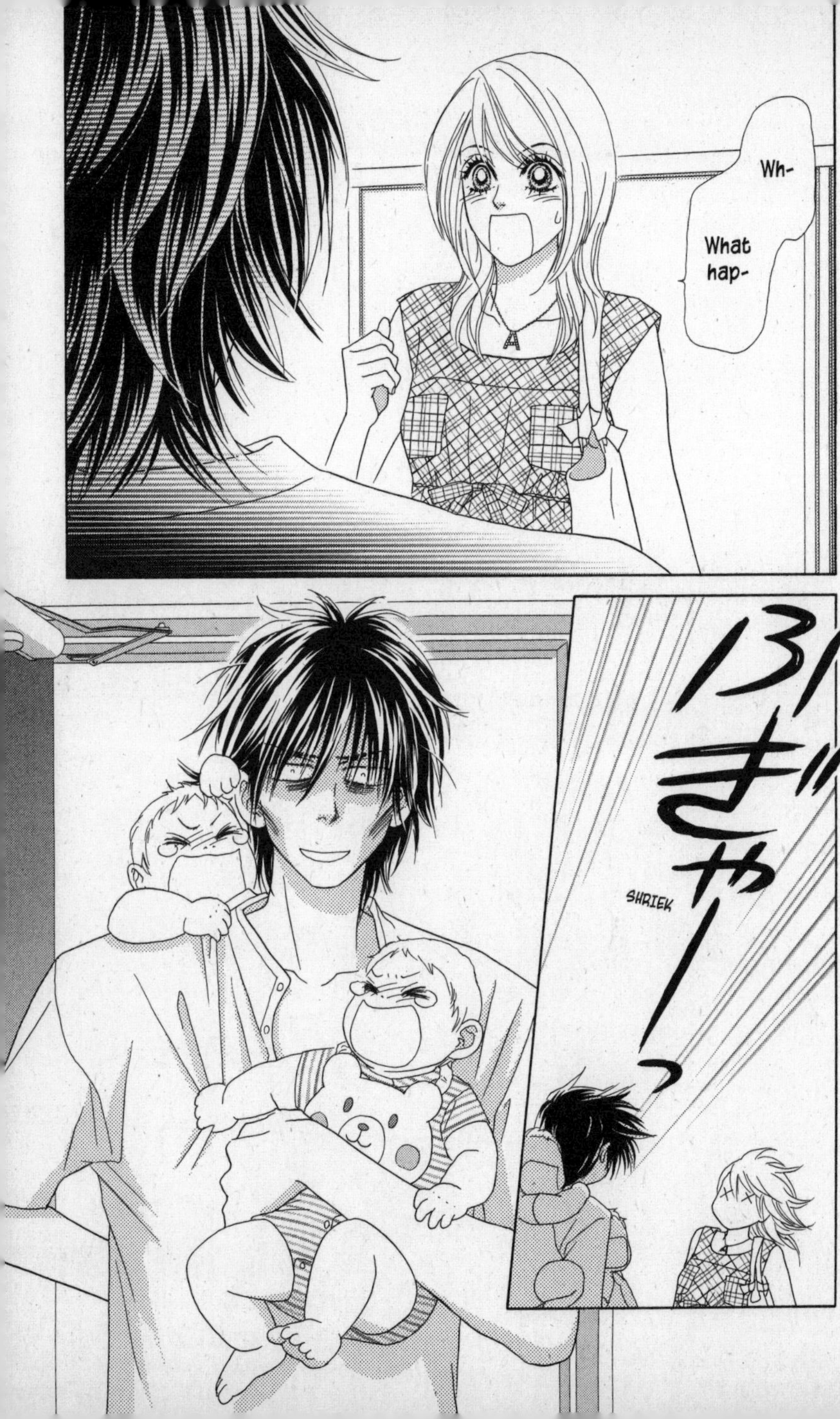
Wh-
What hap-
ふぎゃーっ
SHRIEK

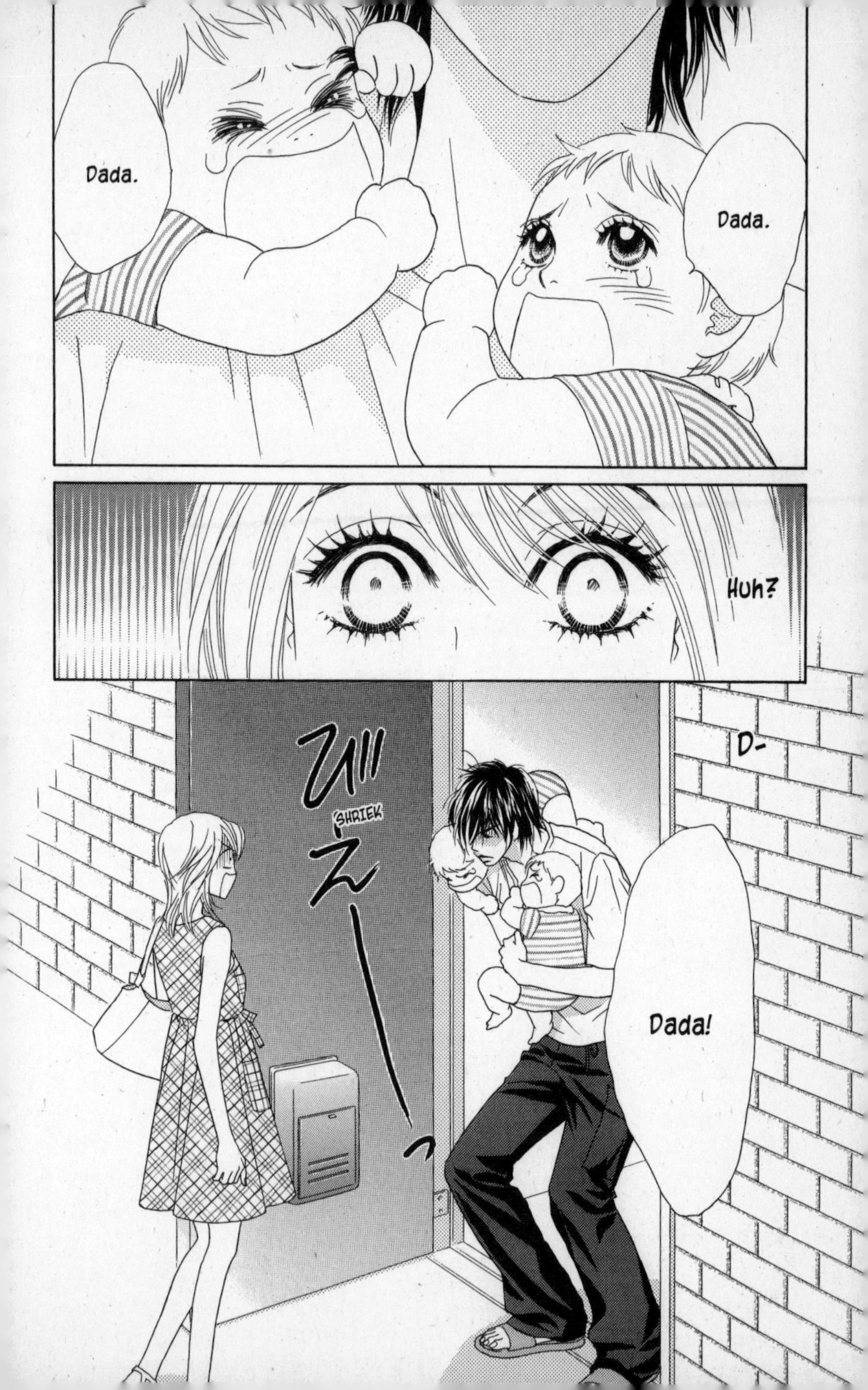

Dada.
Dada.
Huh?
D-
Dada!
びえーっ
SHRIEK

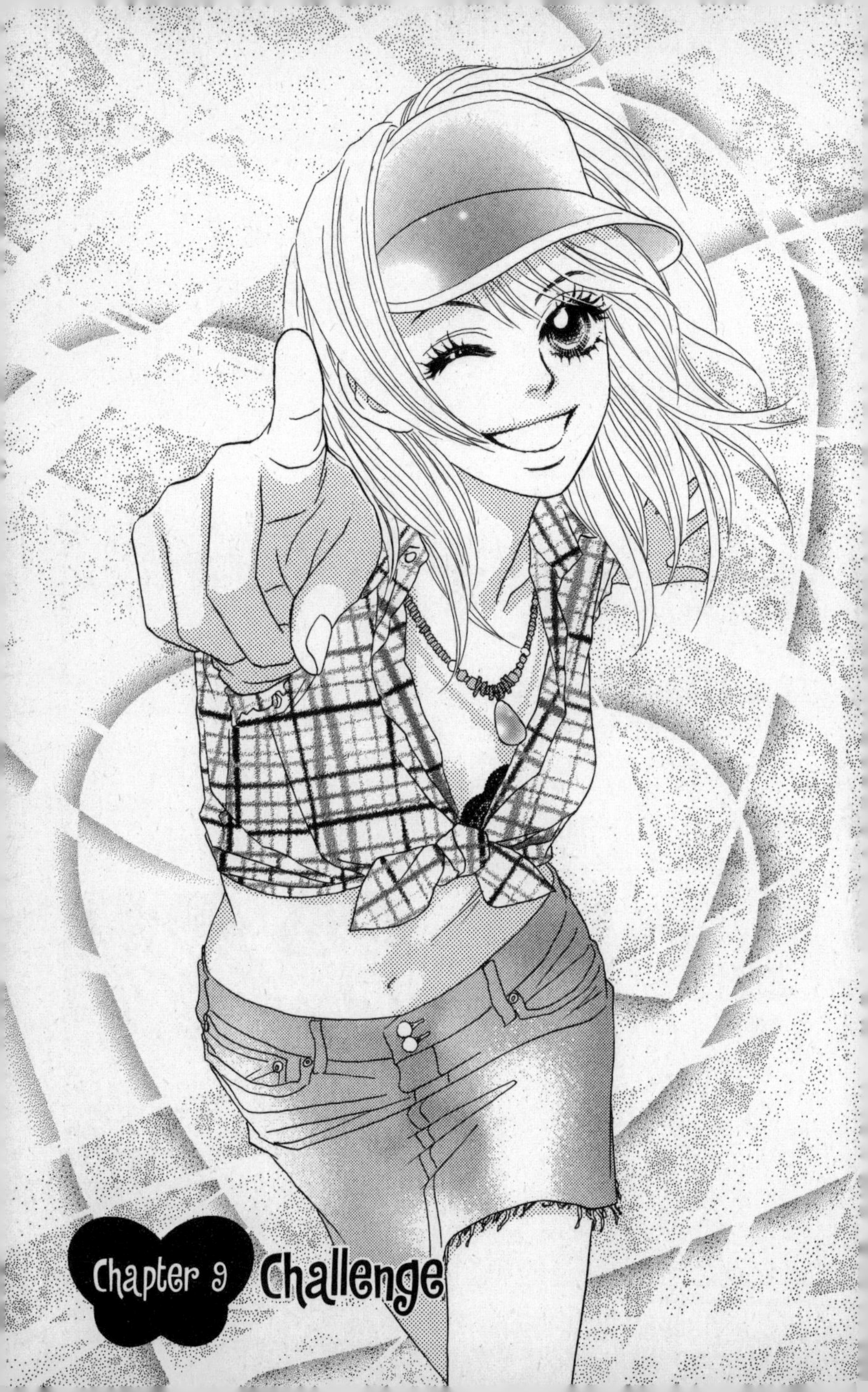
Chapter 9
Challenge

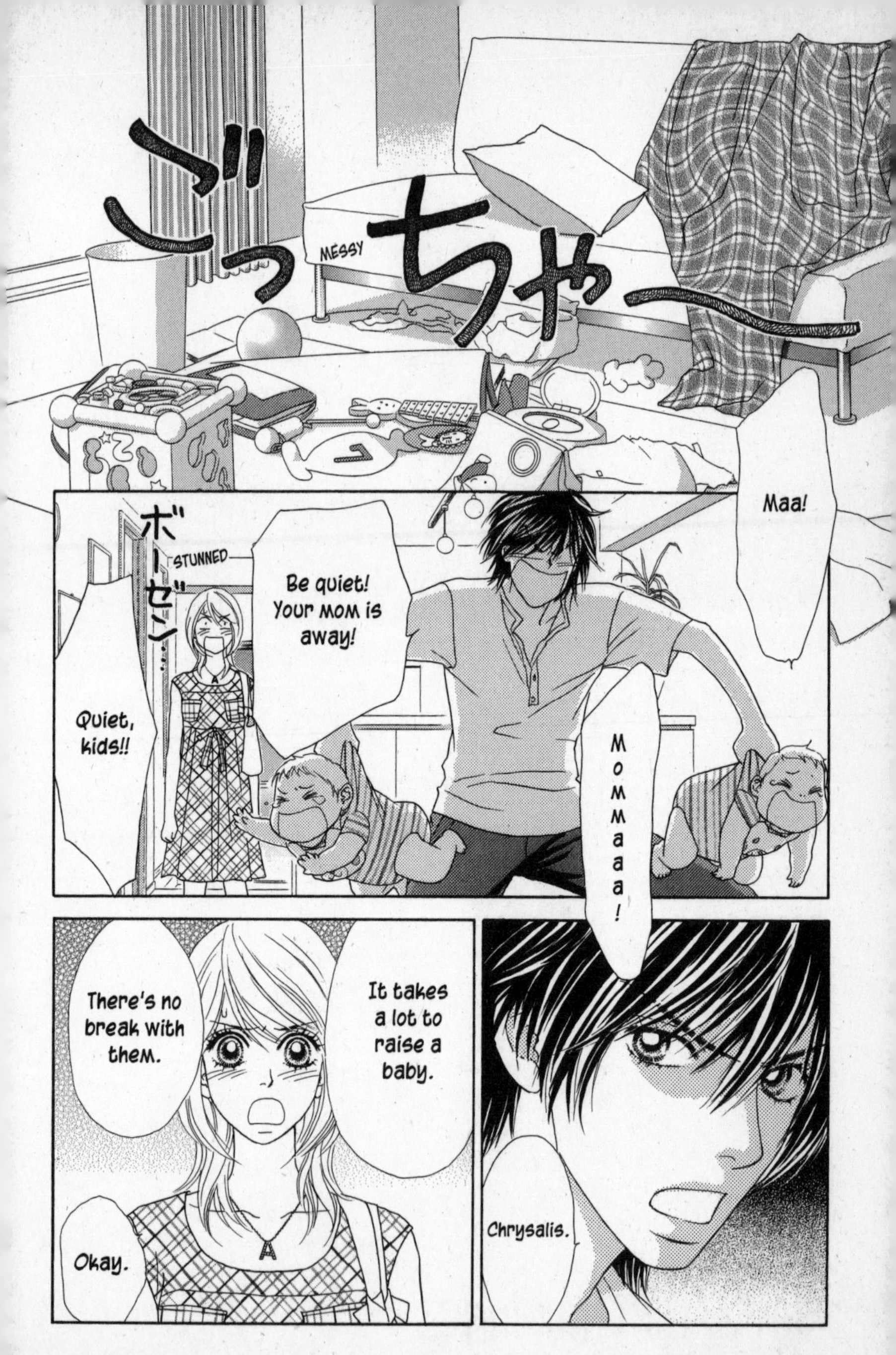
ごっちゃ〜
MESSY
Maa!
Mommaaa!
Be quiet! Your mom is away!
ボーゼン…
STUNNED
Quiet, kids!!
Chrysalis.
It takes a lot to raise a baby.
There's no break with them.
Okay.

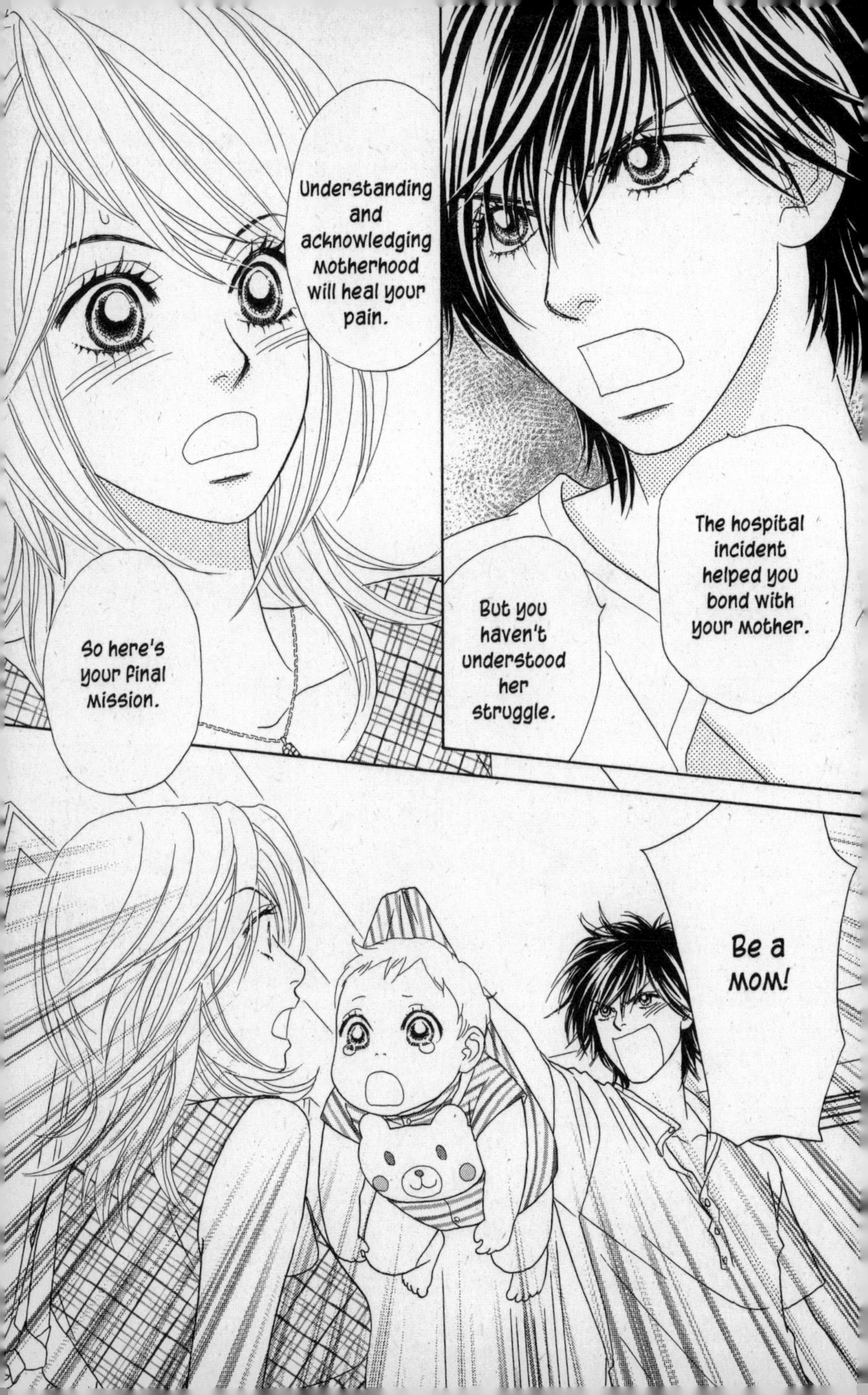
The hospital incident helped you bond with your mother.
But you haven't understood her struggle.
Understanding and acknowledging motherhood will heal your pain.
So here's your final mission.
Be a MOM!

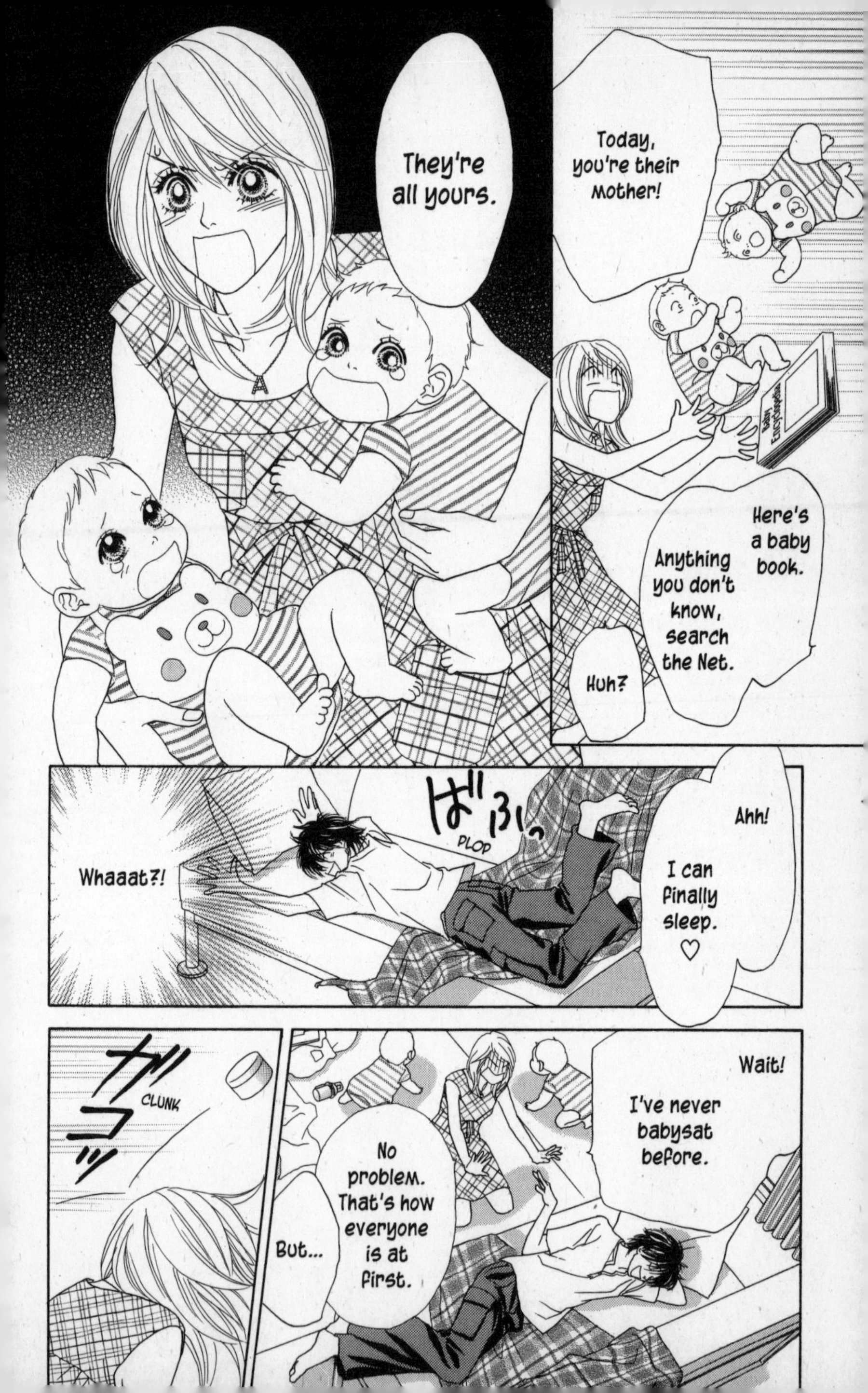

Today, you're their mother!
Baby Encyclopedia
Here's a baby book.
Anything you don't know, search the Net.
Huh?
They're all yours.
Ahh!
I can finally sleep. ♡
ぱふ
PLOP
Whaaat?!
Wait!
I've never babysat before.
No problem. That's how everyone is at first.
But...
ガコッ
CLUNK

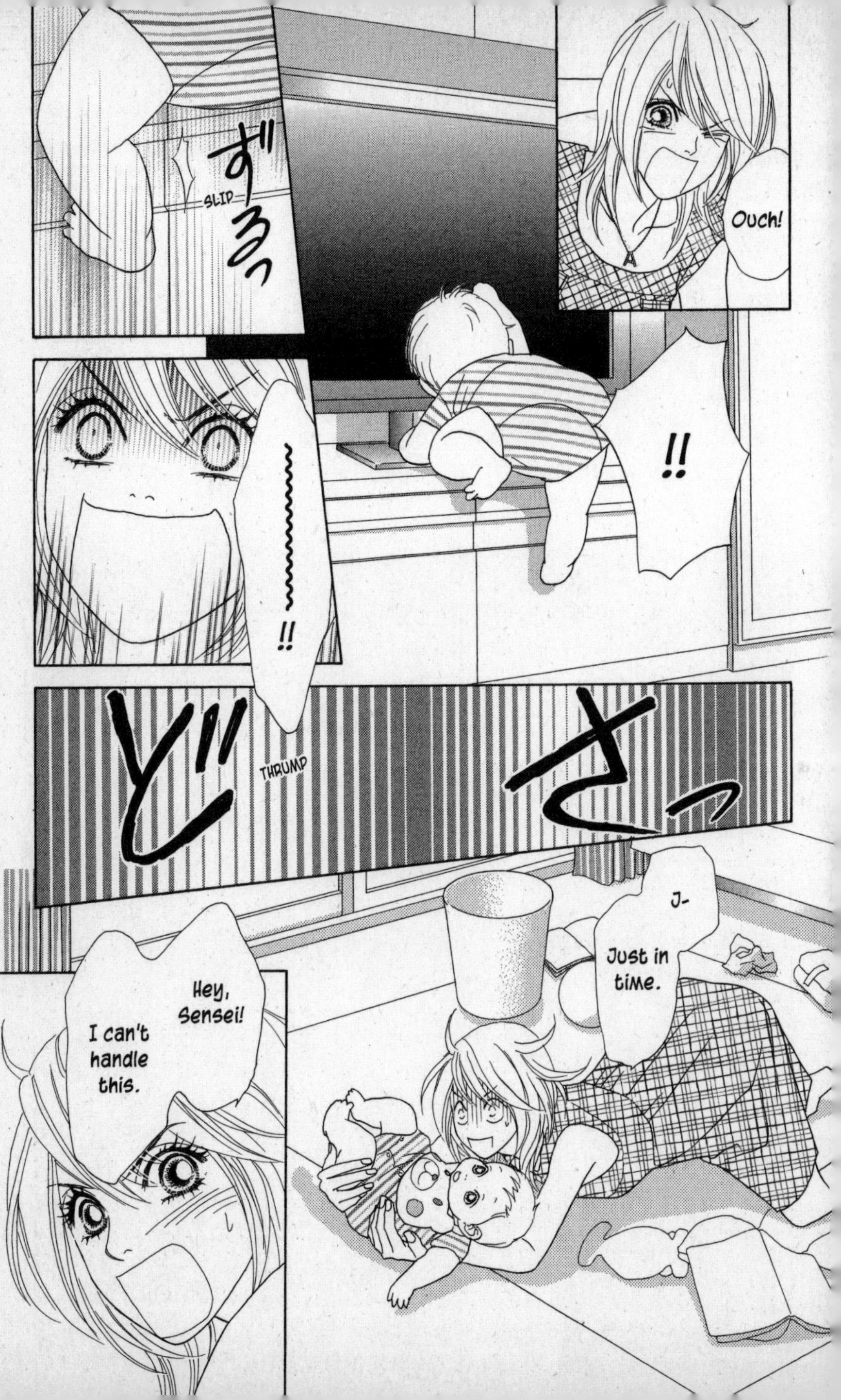

Ouch!
ずるっ
SLIP
!!
!!
どさっ
THRUMP
J-
Just in time.
Hey, Sensei!
I can't handle this.

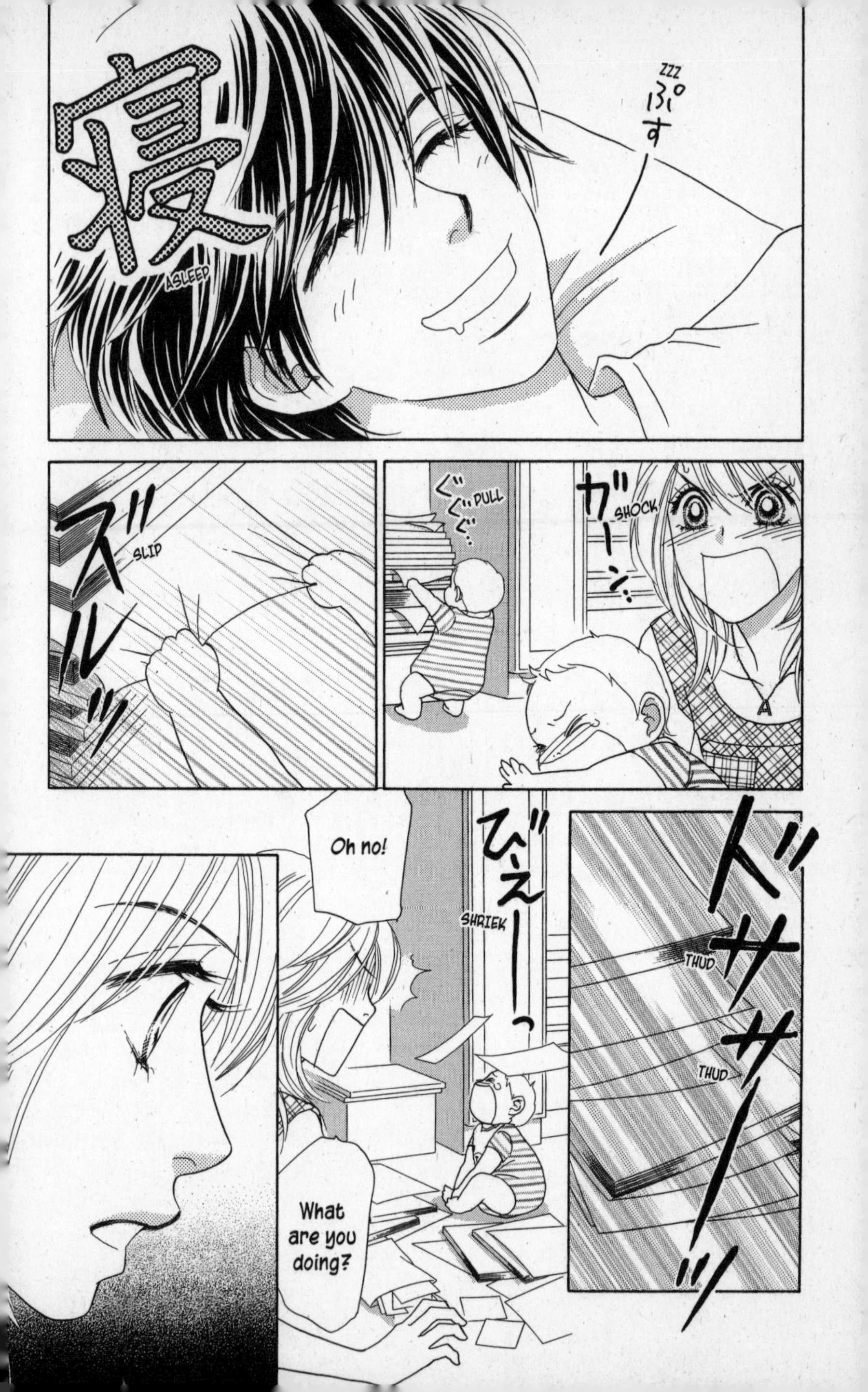
ZZZ
ぷすー
寝
ASLEEP
ガーン
SHOCK
ぐぐぐ
PULL
ズルッ
SLIP
ドサササーッ
THUD
THUD
びえーっ
SHRIEK
Oh no!
What are you doing?

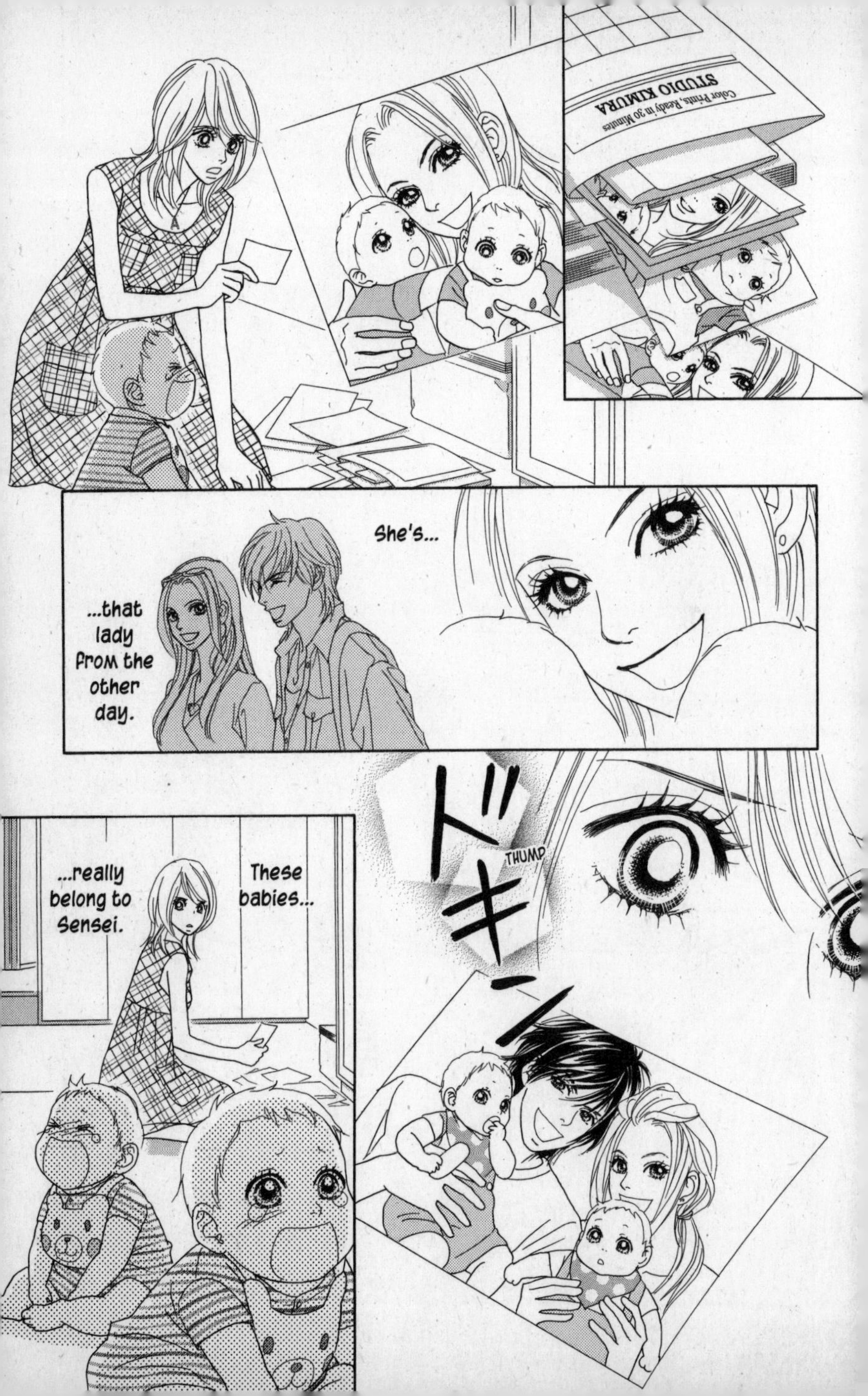
STUDIO KIMURA
Color Prints, Ready in 30 Minutes
She's...
...that lady from the other day.
ドキー
THUMP
These babies...
...really belong to Sensei.

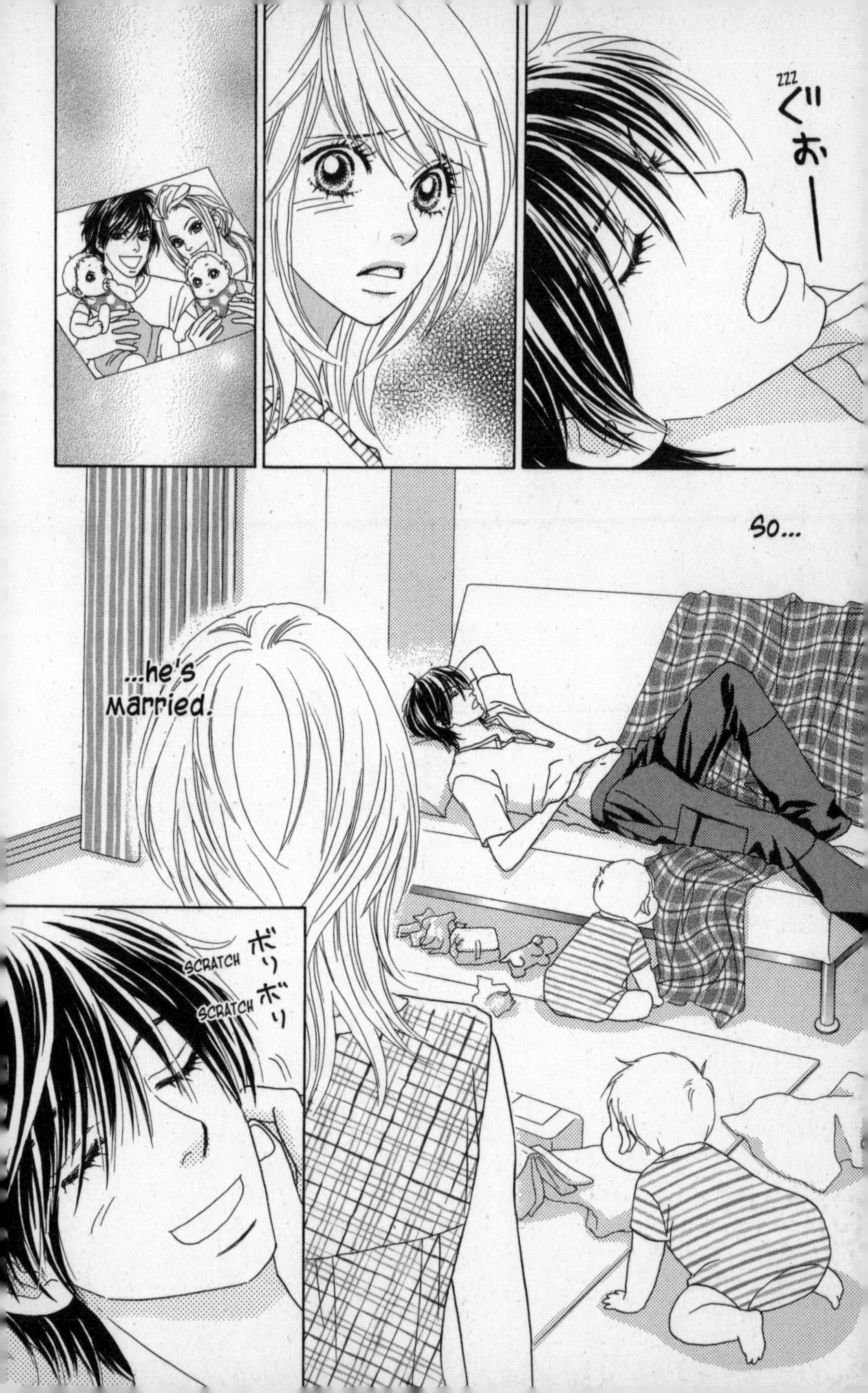
zzz
ぐぉーー
So...
...he's married.
SCRATCH ボリ
SCRATCH ボリ

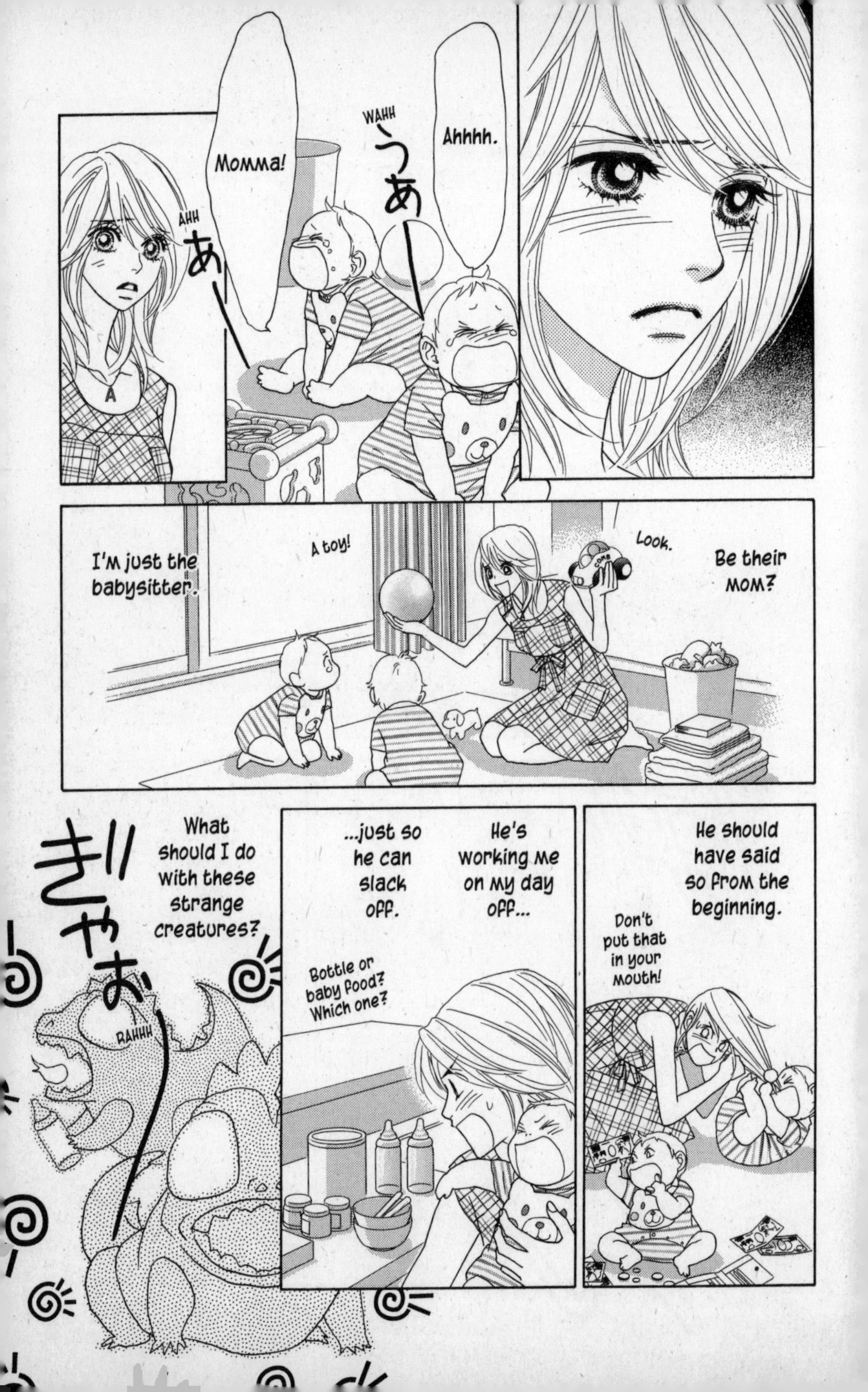
Ahhhh.
WAHH
うあー
Momma!
AHH
あー
Be their MOM?
Look.
A toy!
I'm just the babysitter.
He should have said so from the beginning.
Don't put that in your mouth!
He's working me on my day off...
...just so he can slack off.
Bottle or baby food? Which one?
What should I do with these strange creatures?
ぎゃお
RAHHH

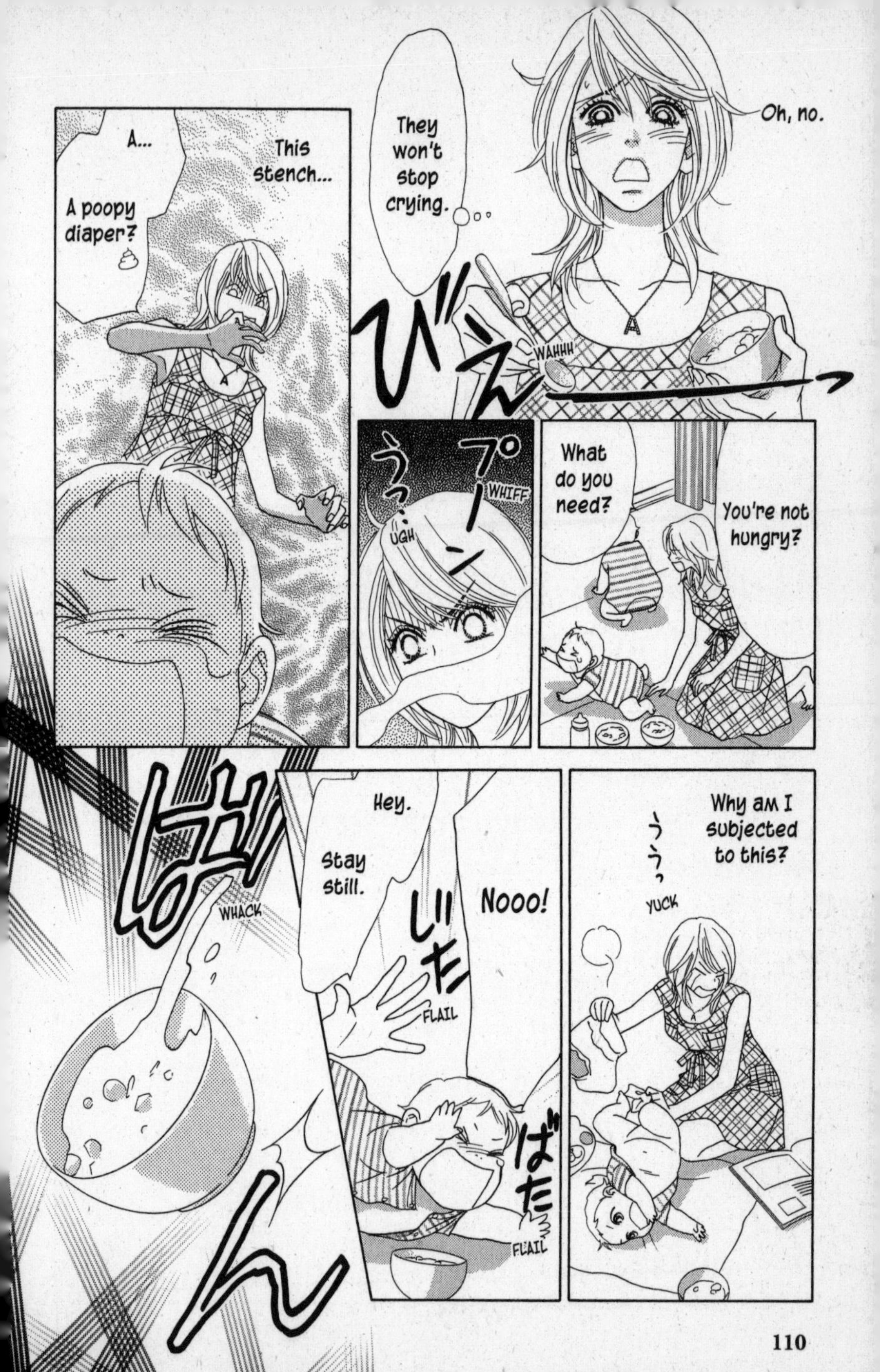
Oh, no.
They won't stop crying.
びえ～ん
WAHHH
You're not hungry?
What do you need?
プーン
WHIFF
うっ
UGH
This stench...
A...
A poopy diaper?
Why am I subjected to this?
うぅっ
YUCK
Nooo!
Hey.
Stay still.
じたばた
FLAIL
FLAIL
ばん
WHACK

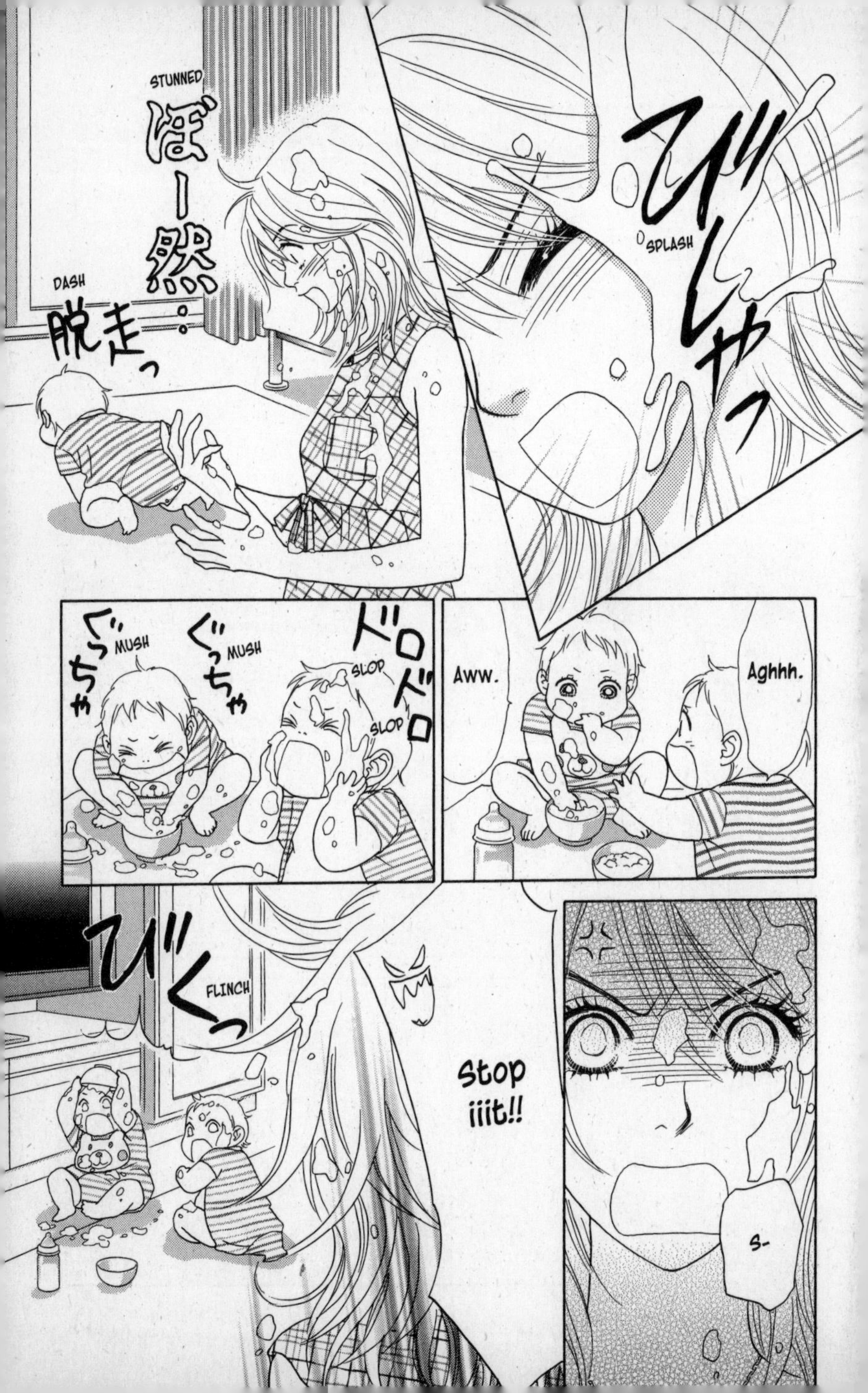

びしゃっ
SPLASH
ぼー然。
STUNNED
脱走っ
DASH
Aww.
Aghhh.
ドロドロ
SLOP
SLOP
ぐっちゃ
MUSH
ぐっちゃ
MUSH
S-
Stop iiit!!
びくっ
FLINCH

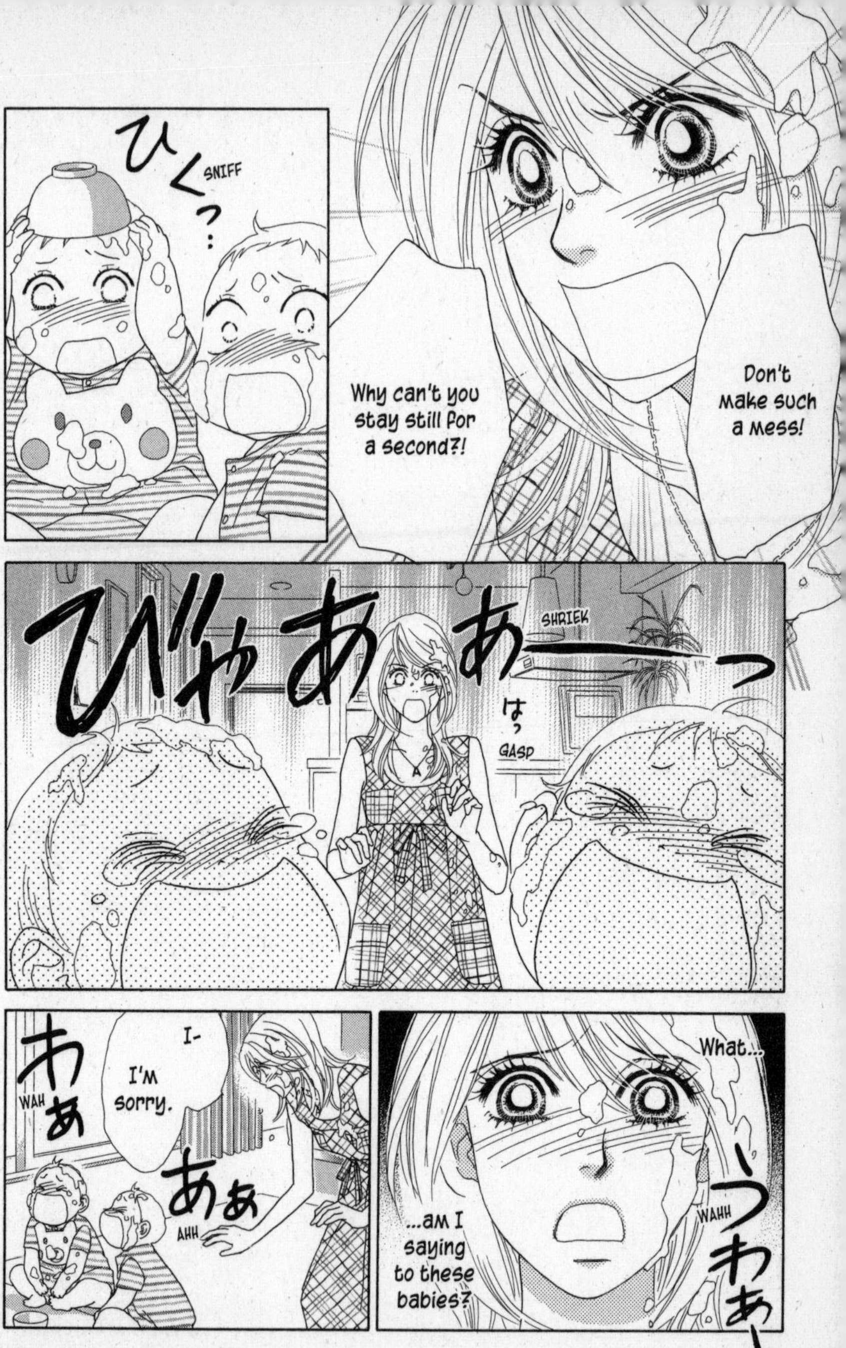
Don't make such a mess!
Why can't you stay still for a second?!
ひくっ..
SNIFF
ひゃあああーーっ
SHRIEK
はっ
GASP
What...
...am I saying to these babies?
うわあー
WAHH
I-
I'm sorry.
わあ
WAH
ああ
AHH

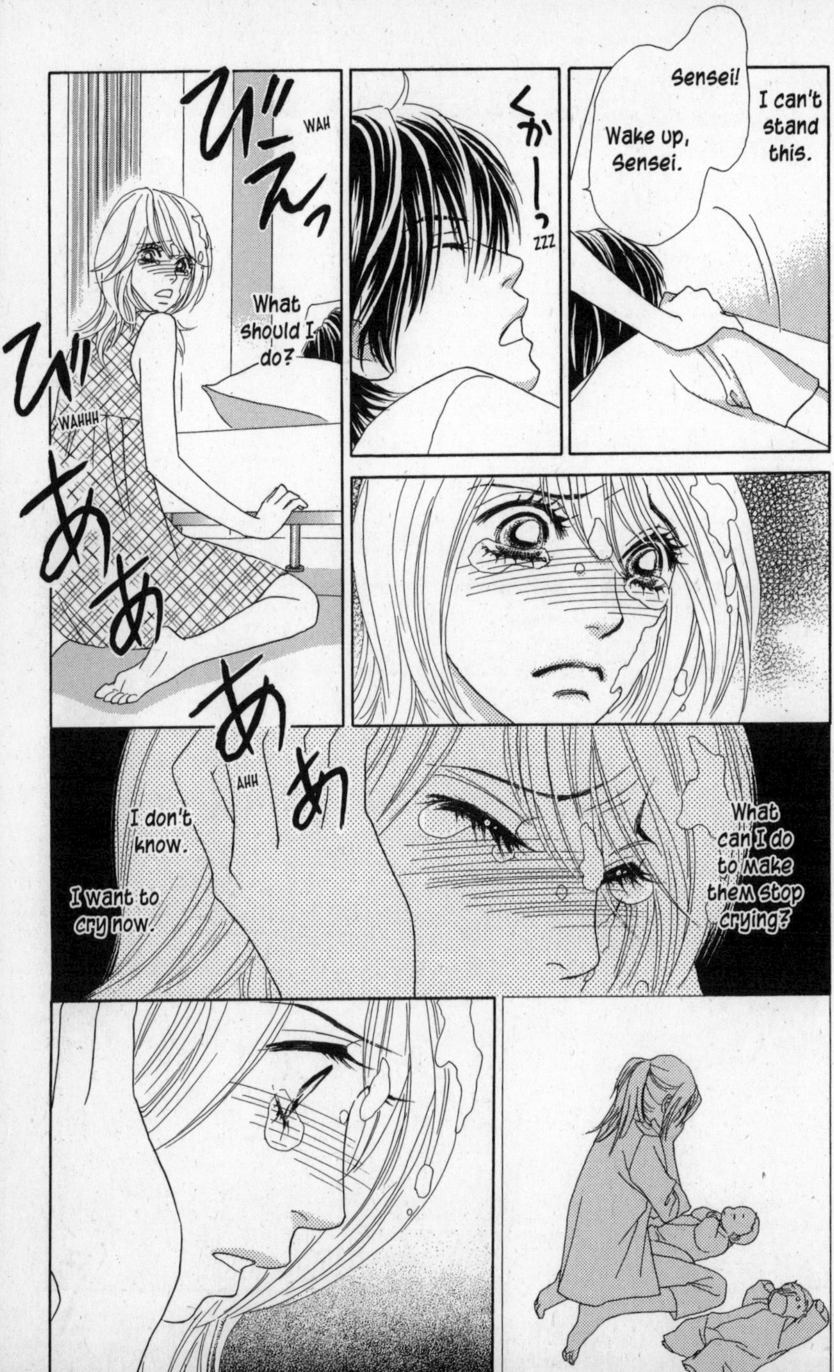
I can't stand this.
Sensei! Wake up, Sensei.
くかーっ
ZZZ
びえんっ
WAH
What should I do?
びあああ
WAHHH
What can I do to make them stop crying?
ああ
AHH
I don't know.
I want to cry now.

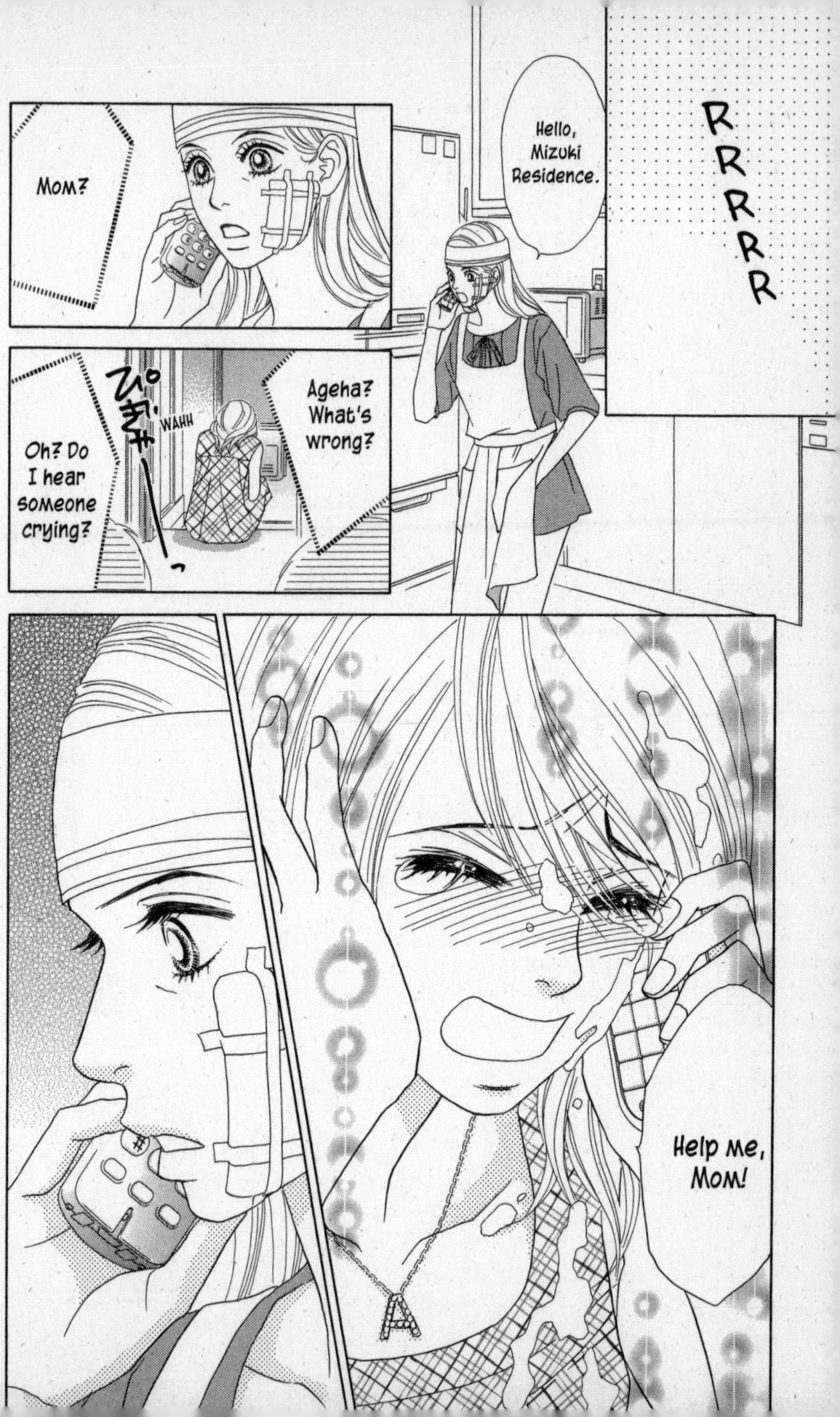
RRRRR
Hello, Mizuki Residence.
Mom?
Ageha? What's wrong?
WAHH
Oh? Do I hear someone crying?
Help me, Mom!

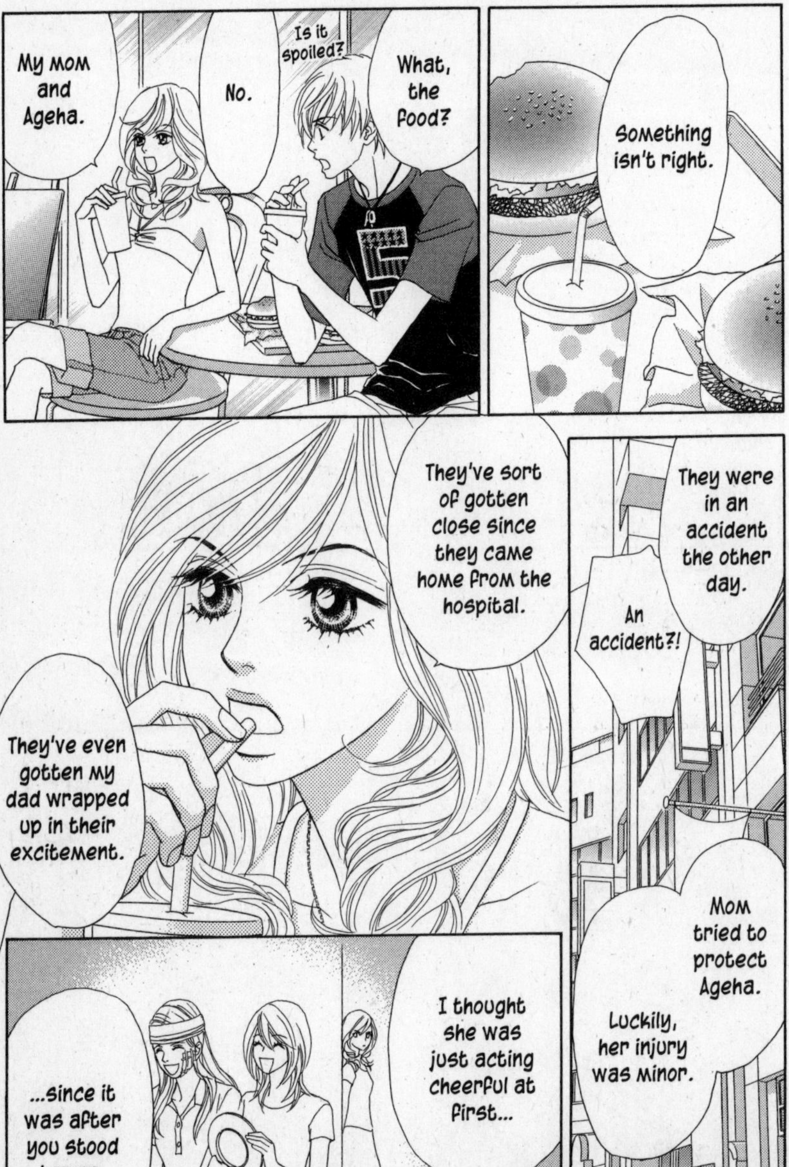
Something isn't right.
What, the food?
Is it spoiled?
No.
My mom and Ageha.
They were in an accident the other day.
An accident?!
Mom tried to protect Ageha.
Luckily, her injury was minor.
They've sort of gotten close since they came home from the hospital.
They've even gotten my dad wrapped up in their excitement.
I thought she was just acting cheerful at first...
...since it was after you stood her up.

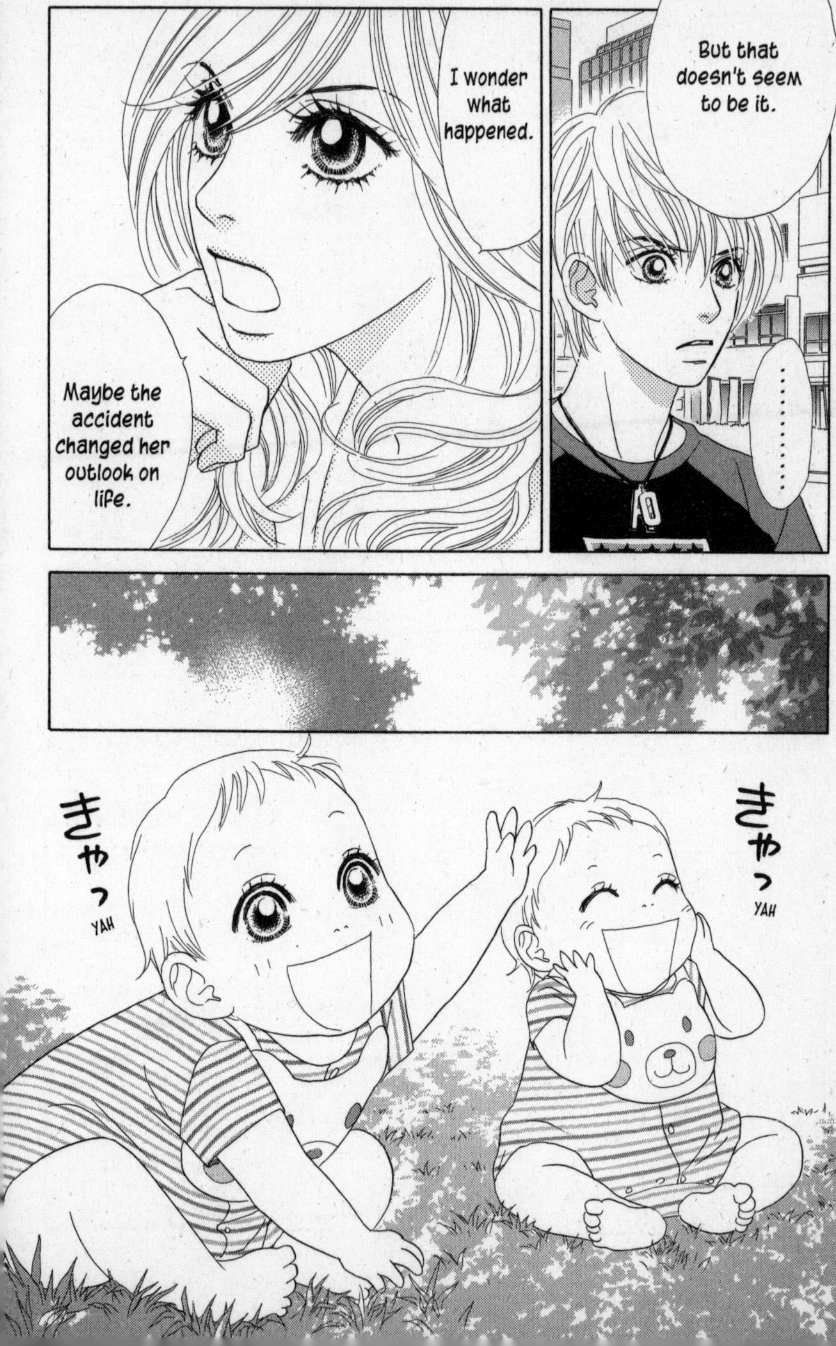
But that doesn't seem to be it.
......
I wonder what happened.
Maybe the accident changed her outlook on life.
きゃっ
YAH
きゃっ
YAH

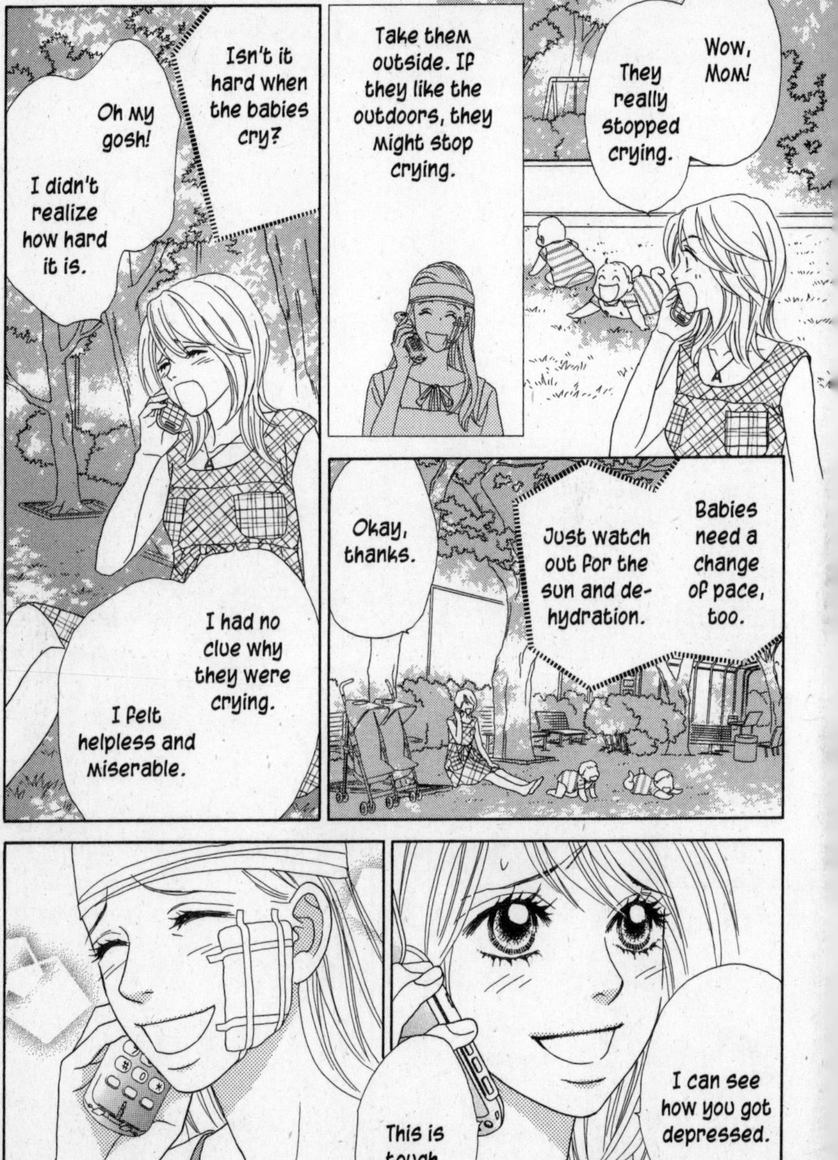
Wow, Mom!
They really stopped crying.
Take them outside. If they like the outdoors, they might stop crying.
Babies need a change of pace, too.
Just watch out for the sun and de-hydration.
Okay, thanks.
Isn't it hard when the babies cry?
Oh my gosh!
I didn't realize how hard it is.
I had no clue why they were crying.
I felt helpless and miserable.
I can see how you got depressed.
This is tough.

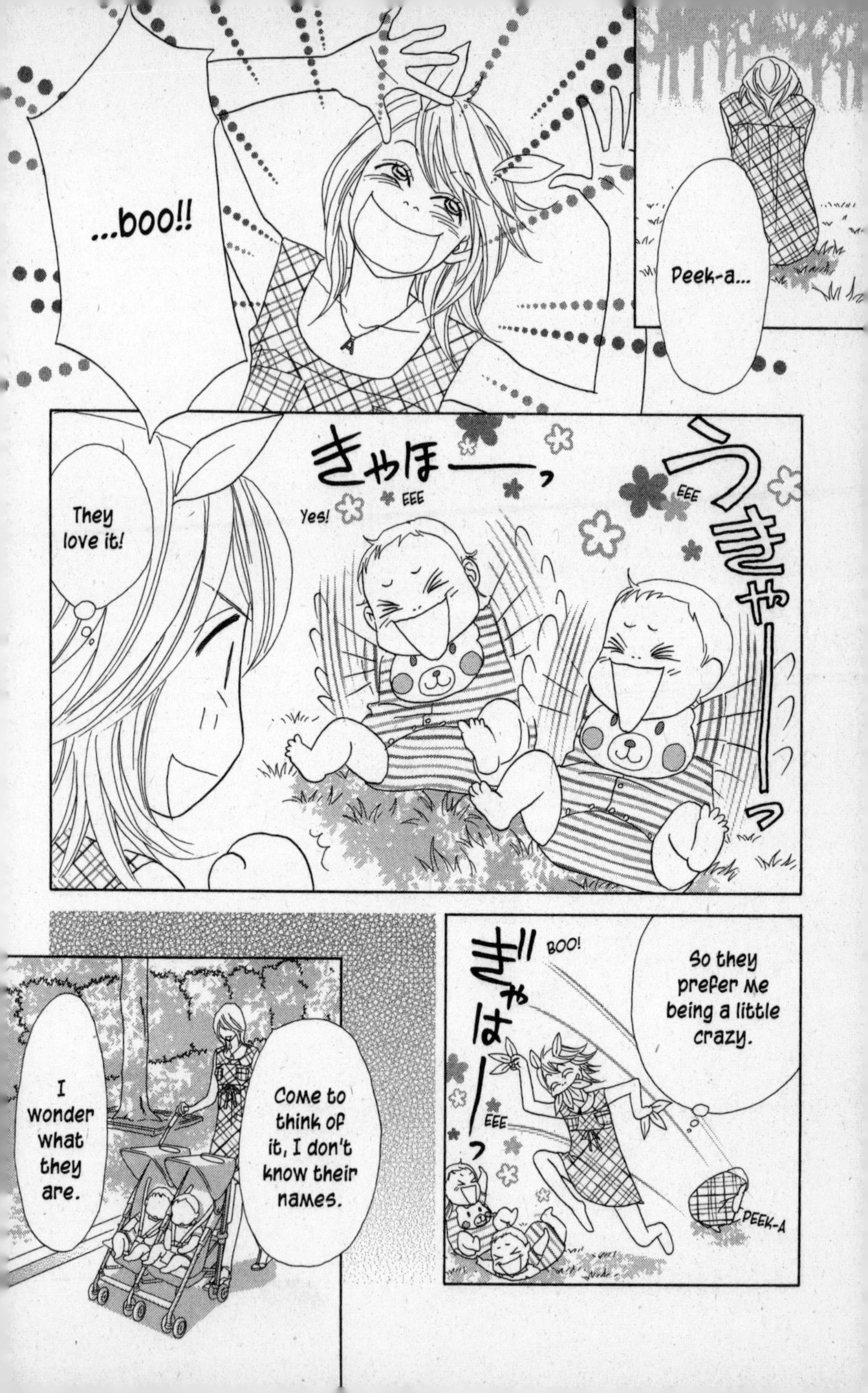
Peek-a...
...boo!!
うきゃーーっ
EEE
きゃほーっ
EEE
Yes!
They love it!
So they prefer me being a little crazy.
ぎゃはーっ
BOO!
EEE
PEEK-A
Come to think of it, I don't know their names.
I wonder what they are.

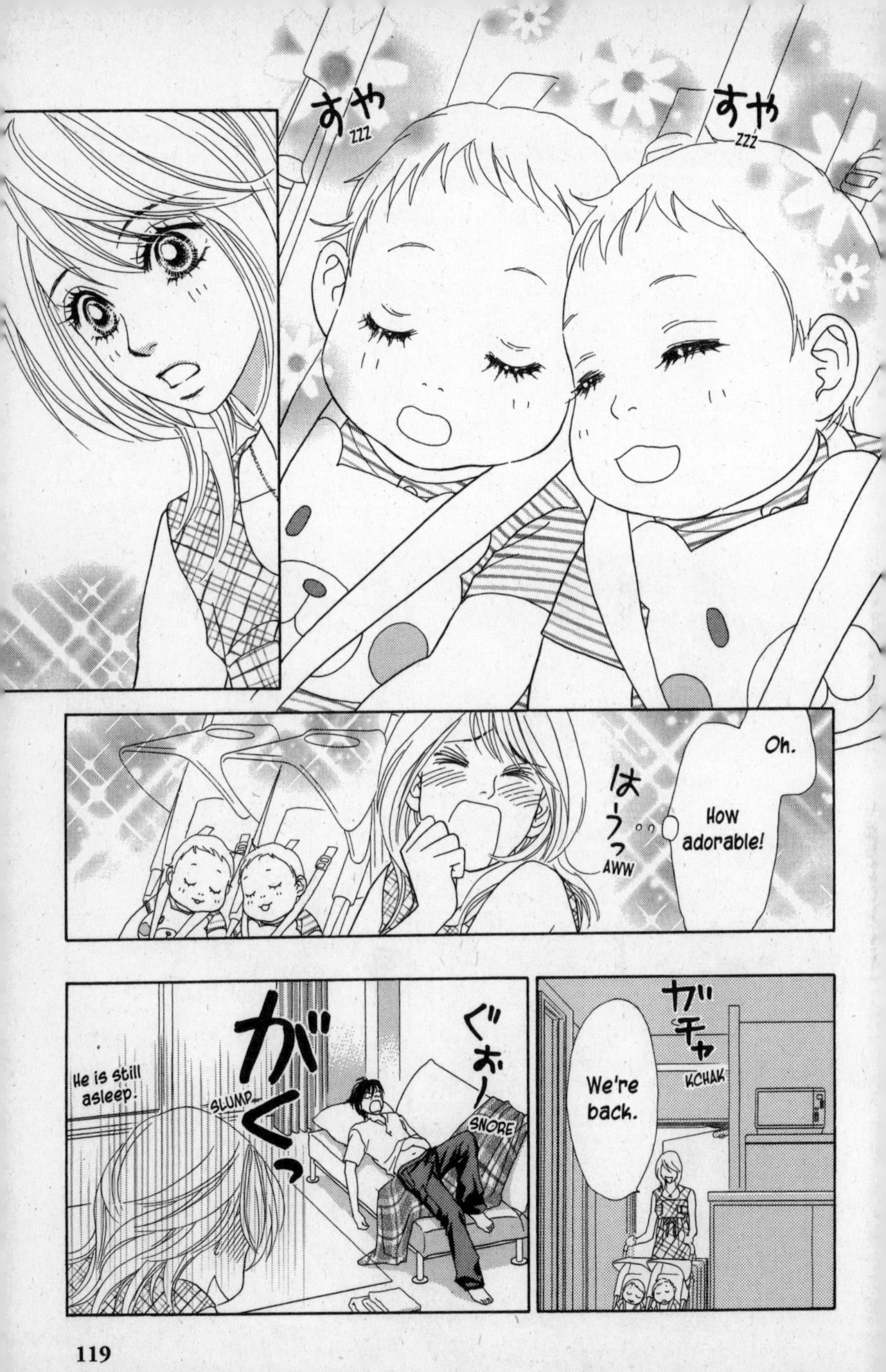
すや
ZZZ
すや
ZZZ
Oh.
How adorable!
はうっ
AWW
ガチャ
KCHAK
We're back.
ぐぉー
SNORE
がくっ
SLUMP
He is still asleep.

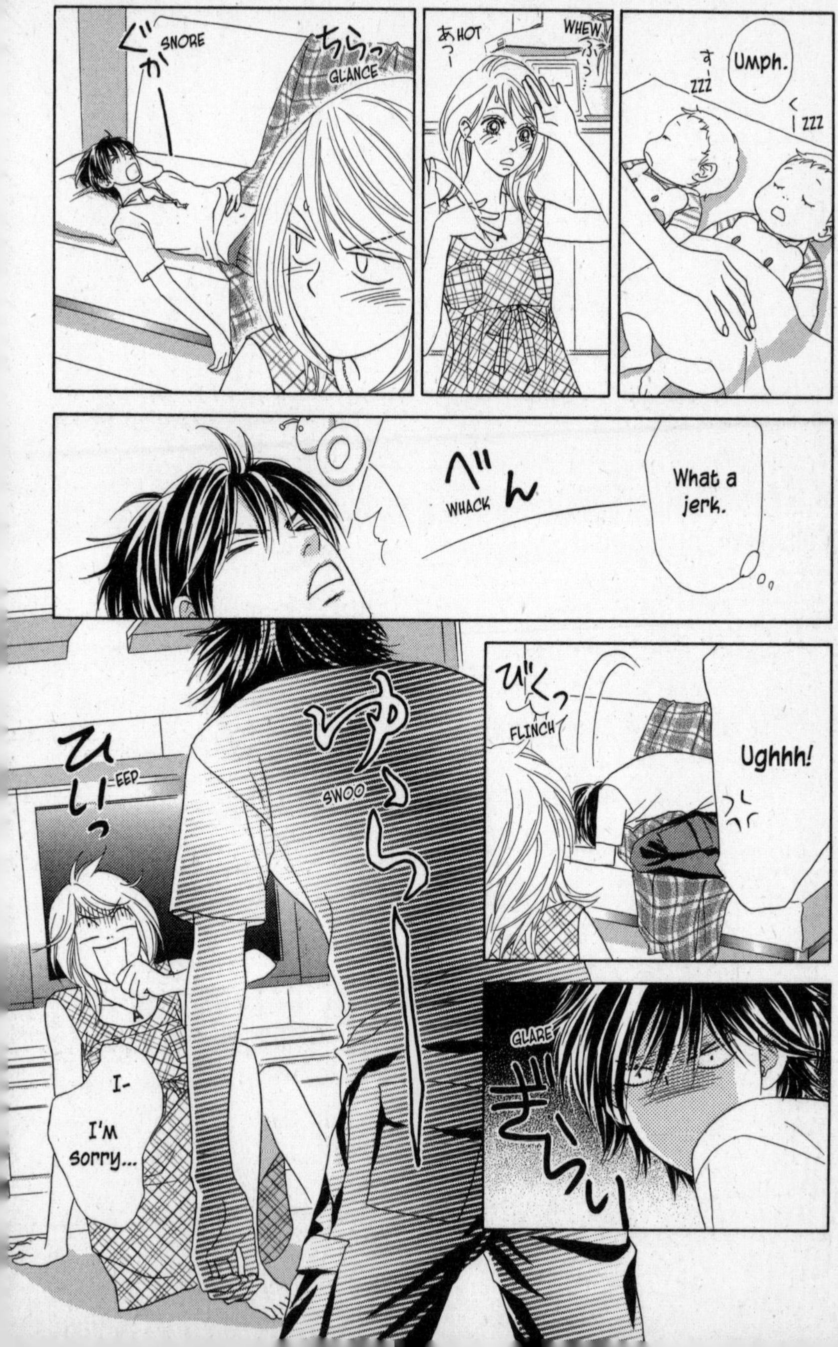

すー ZZZ
Umph.
くー ZZZ
あつー HOT
WHEW ふぅ…
ちらっ GLANCE
ぐがー SNORE
What a jerk.
べん WHACK
びくっ FLINCH
Ughhh!
GLARE
ゆらー SWOO
ひぃっ EEP
I- I'm sorry...

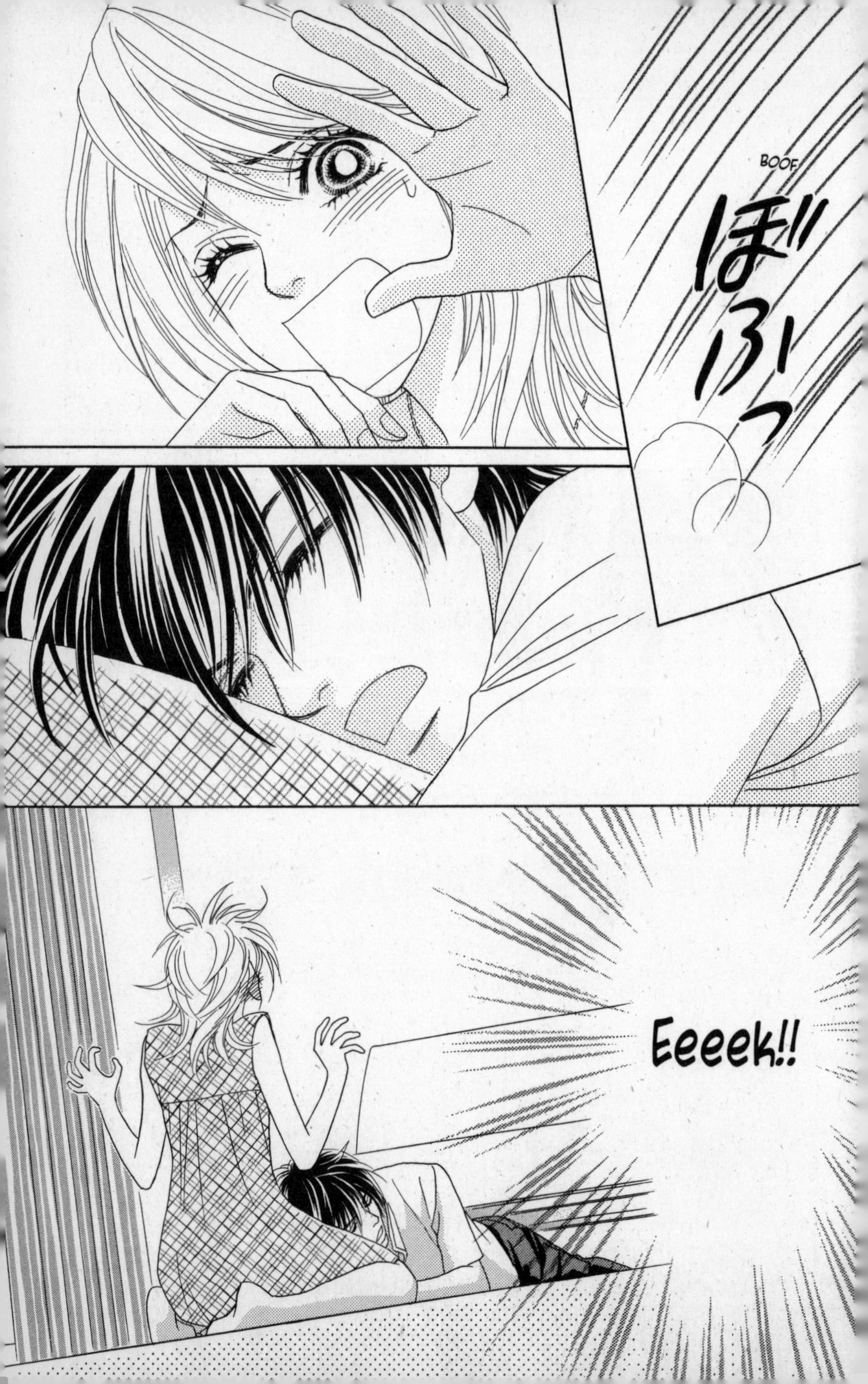
BOOF
ぼふっ
Eeeek!!

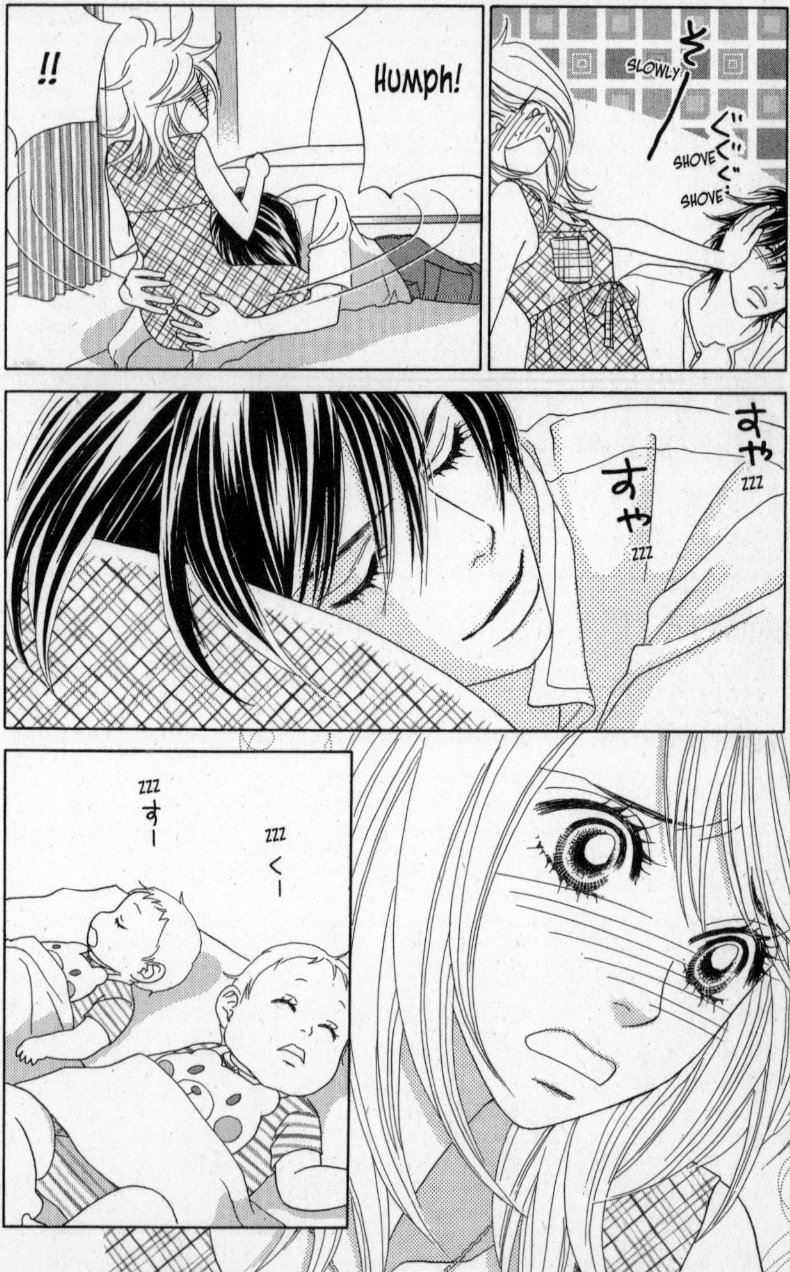

そ
SLOWLY
ぐぐぐ
SHOVE
SHOVE
Humph!
!!
すや
ZZZ
すや
ZZZ
ZZZ
くー
ZZZ
すー

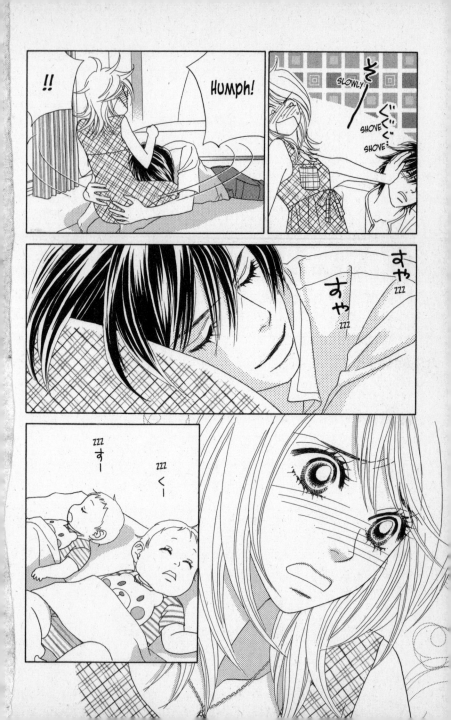

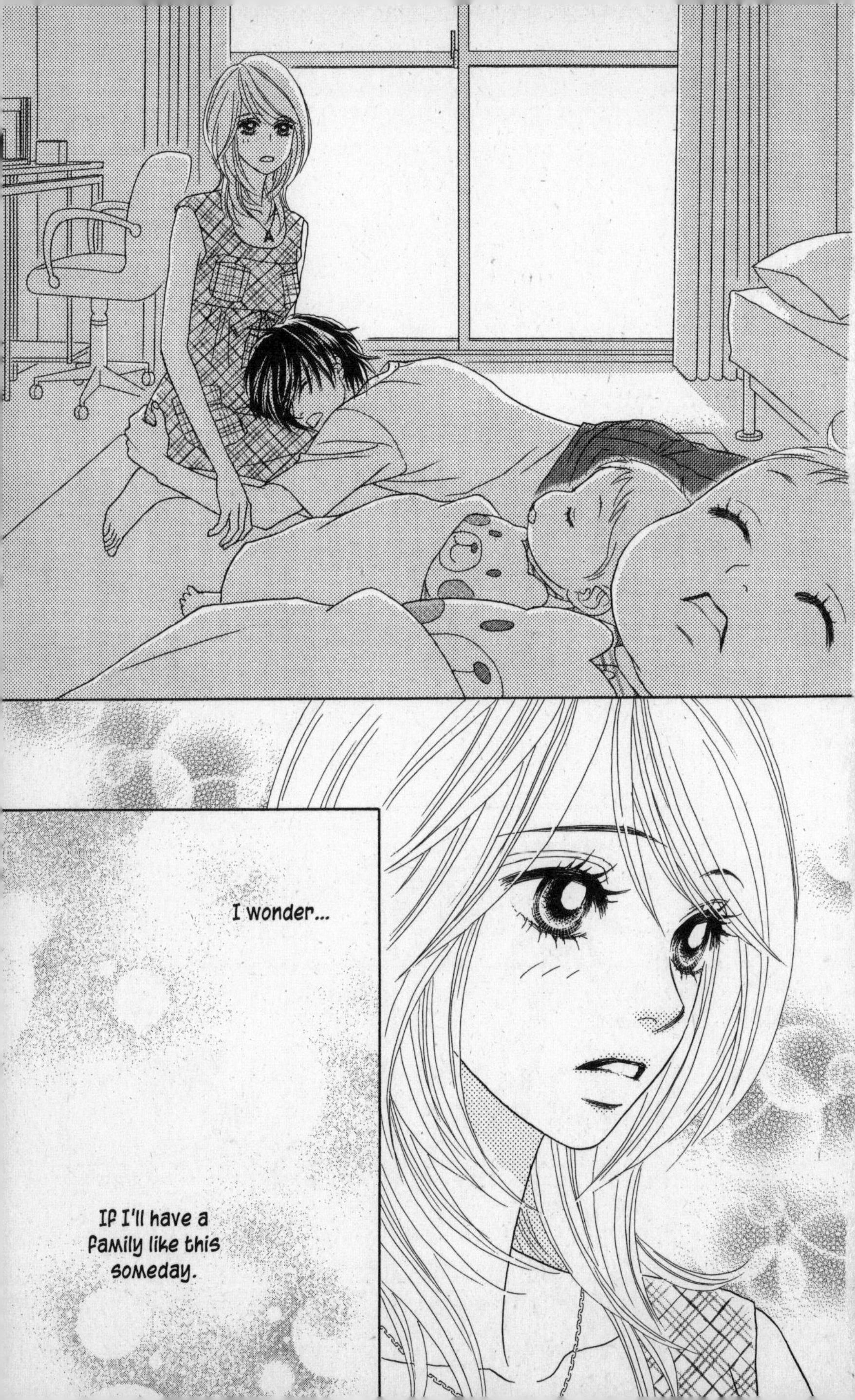
I wonder...
If I'll have a family like this someday.

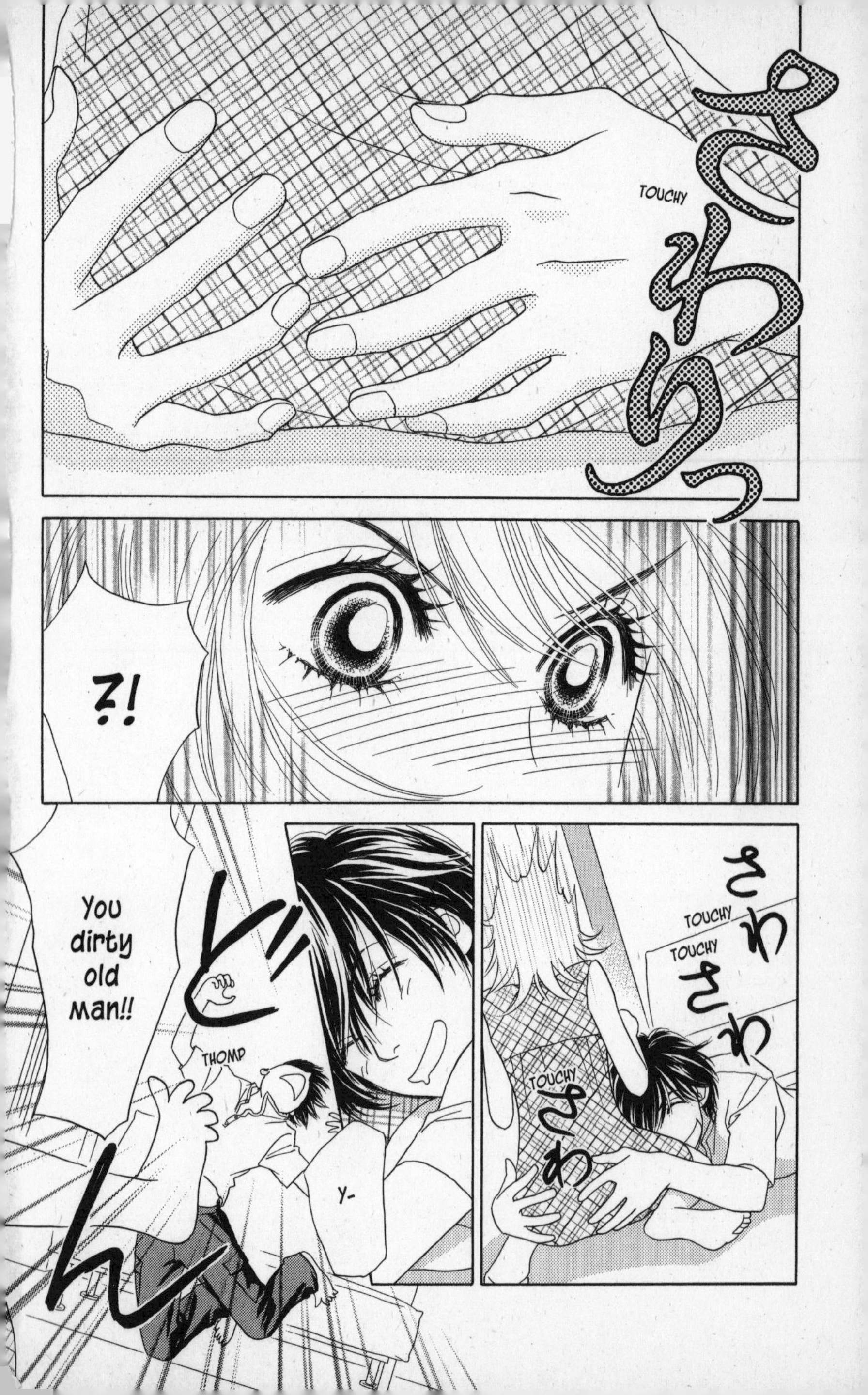

TOUCHY
?!
TOUCHY
TOUCHY
TOUCHY
Y-
THOMP
You dirty old man!!

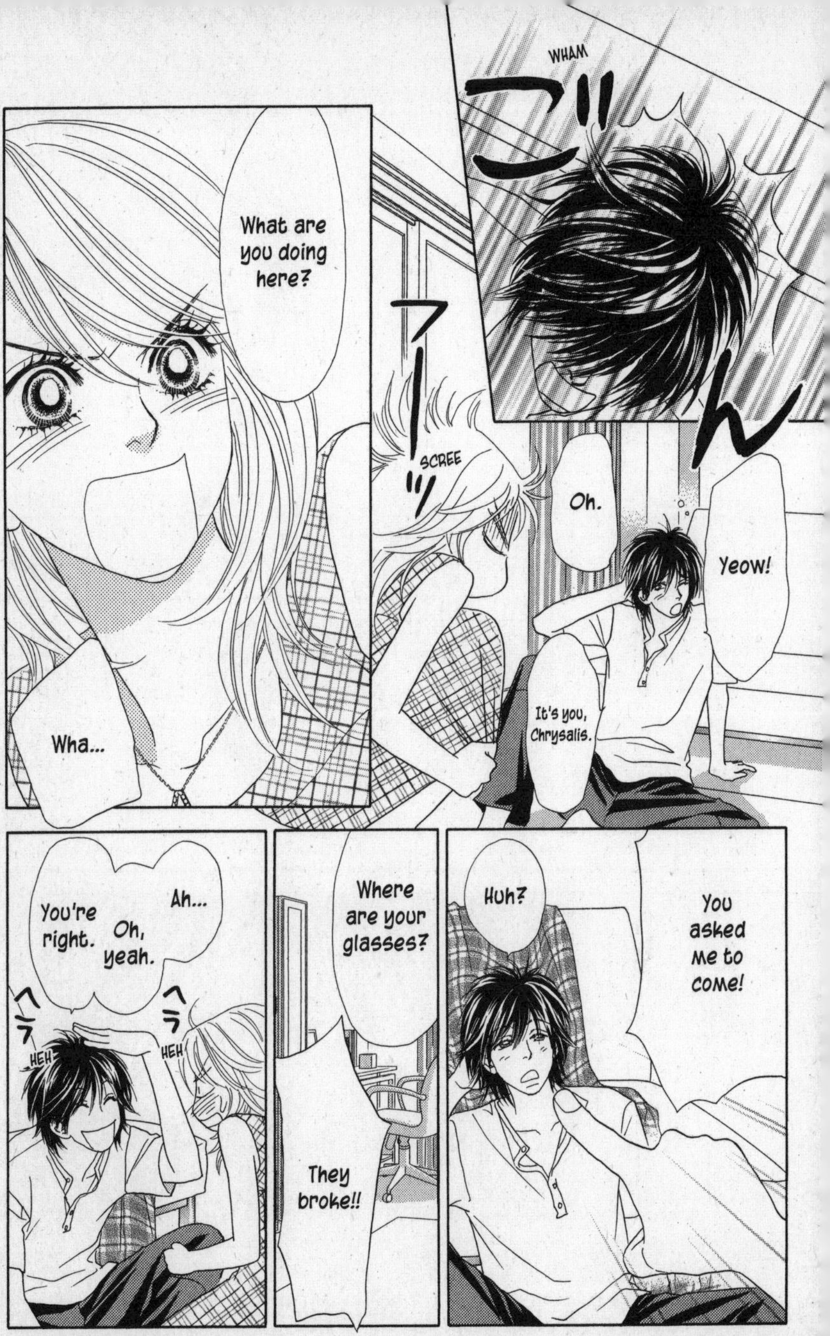
WHAM
Yeow!
Oh.
It's you, Chrysalis.
SCREE
What are you doing here?
Wha...
You asked me to come!
Huh?
Where are your glasses?
They broke!!
Ah...
Oh, yeah.
You're right.
HEH
HEH

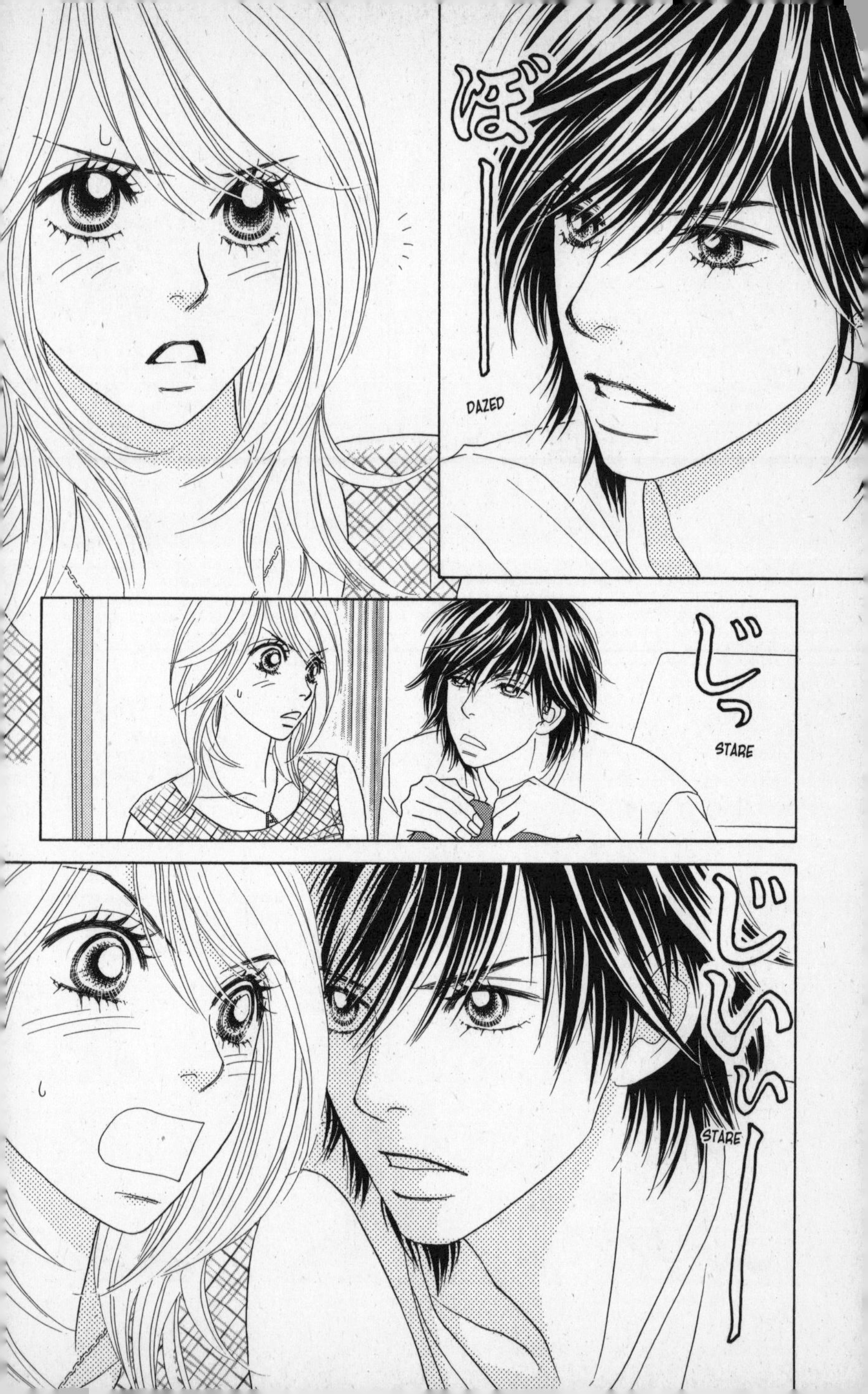
ぼー
DAZED
じっ
STARE
じぃぃー
STARE

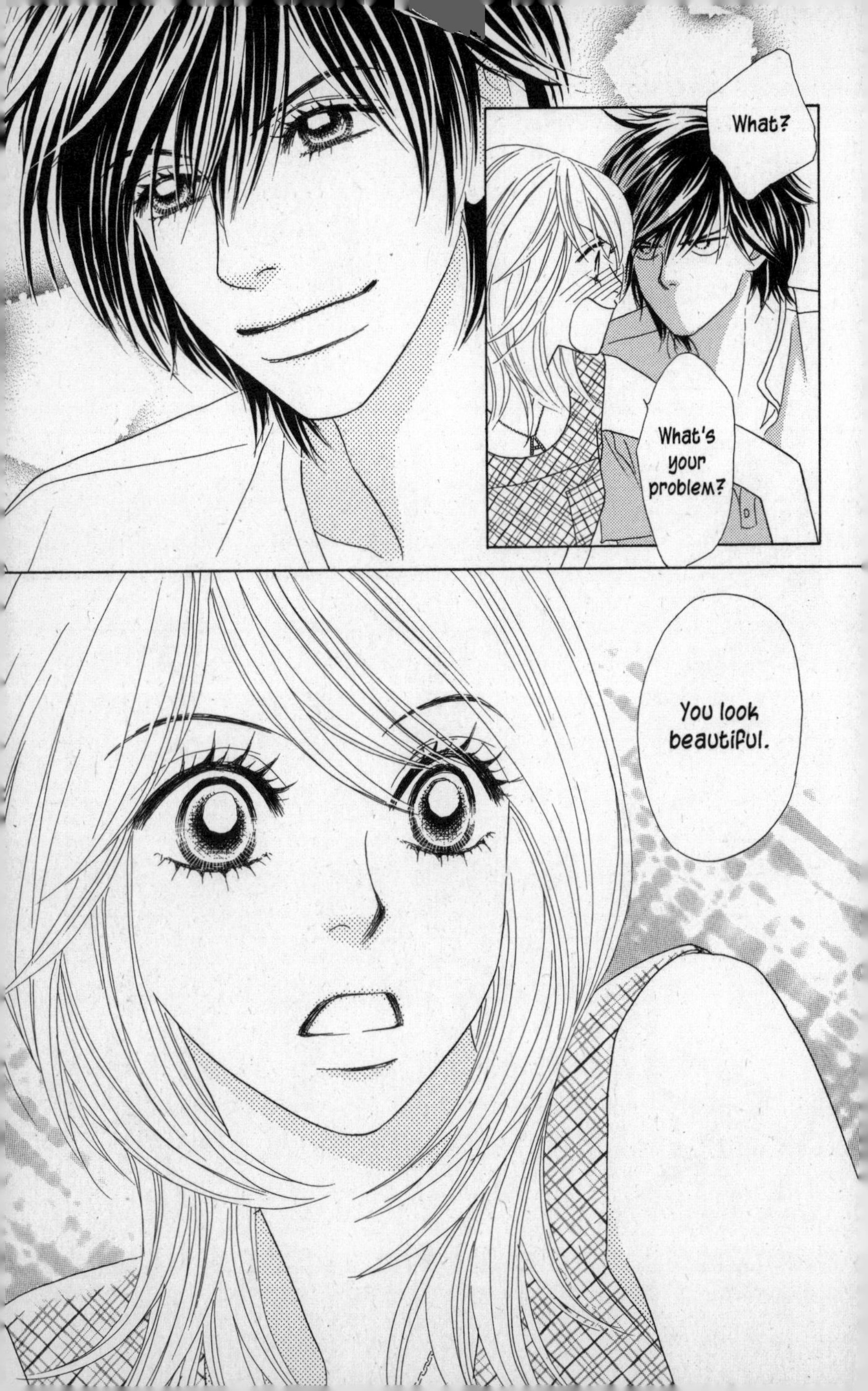
What?
What's your problem?
You look beautiful.

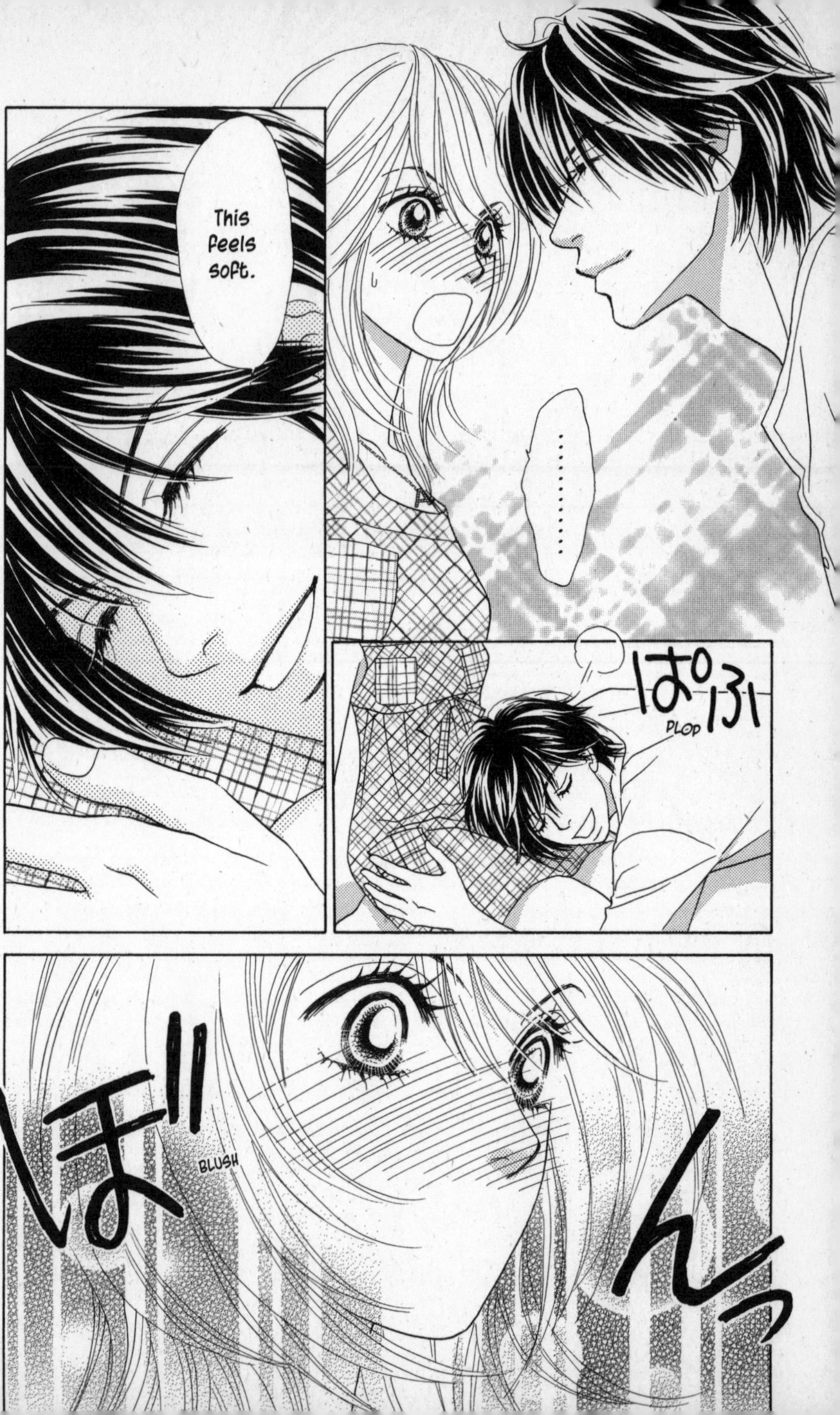
......
ぱふ
PLOP
This feels soft.
ぼんっ
BLUSH

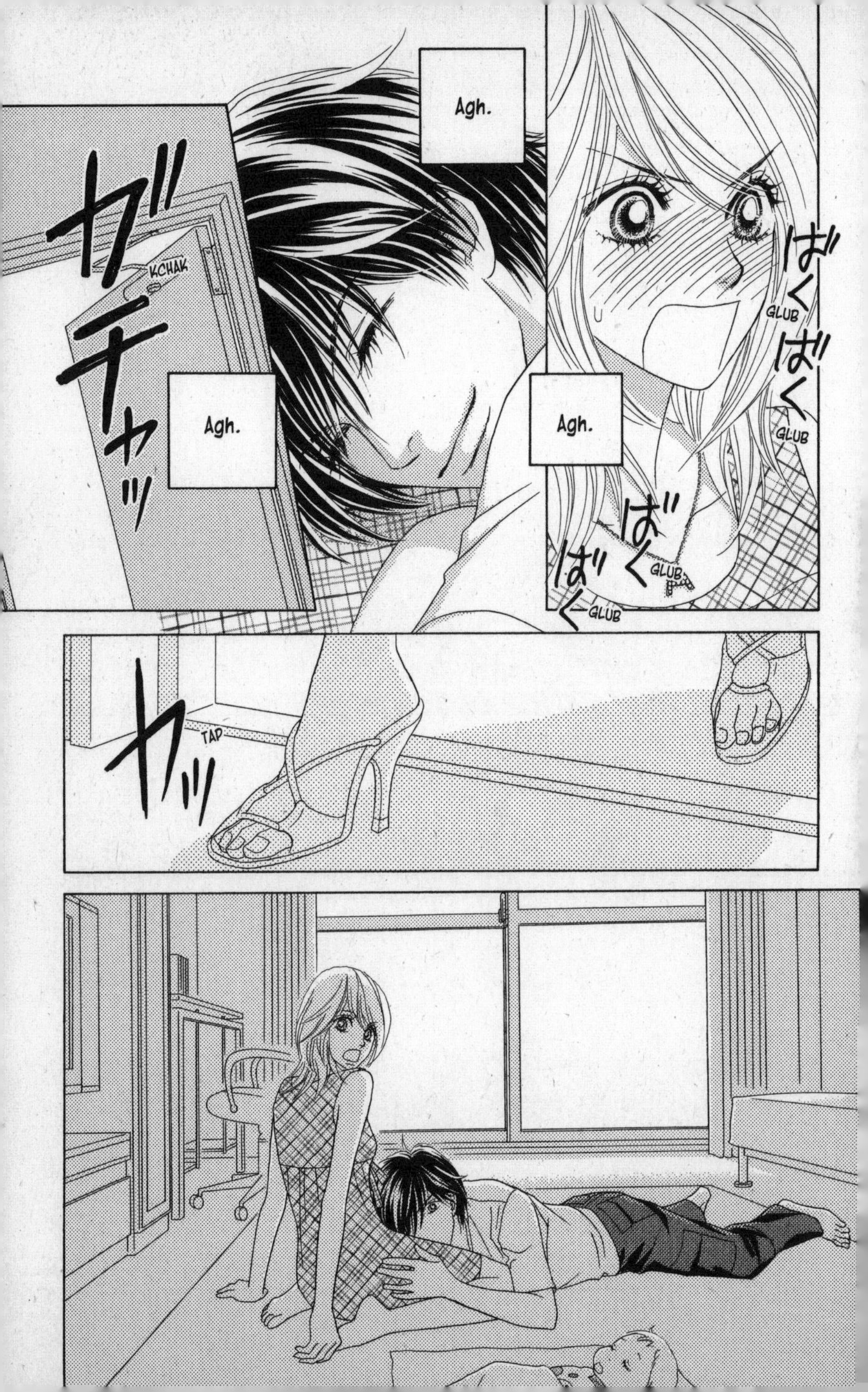
ばくばく
GLUB
GLUB
Agh.
ばくばく
GLUB
GLUB
Agh.
Agh.
ガチャッ
KCHAK
ヤッ
TAP

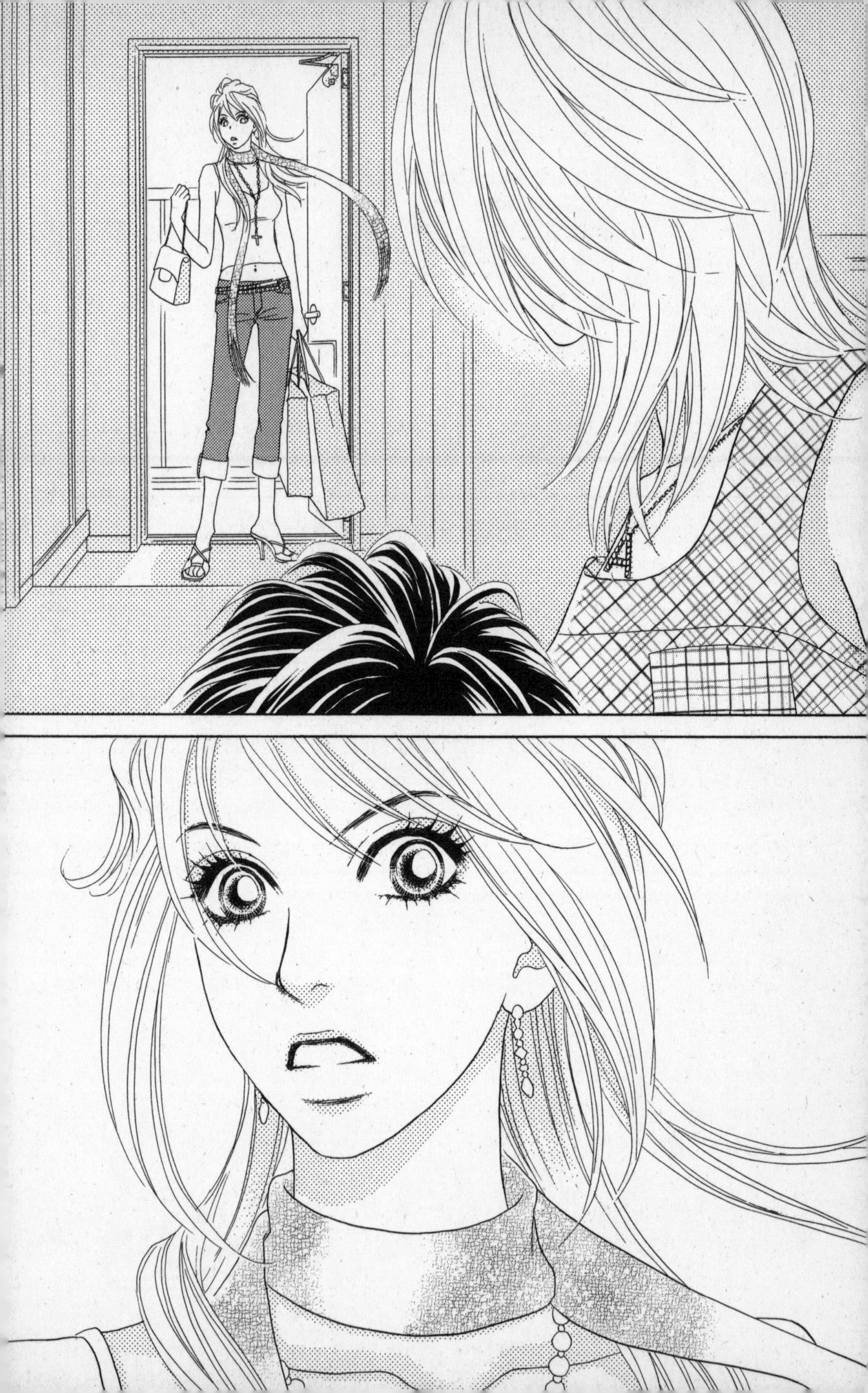

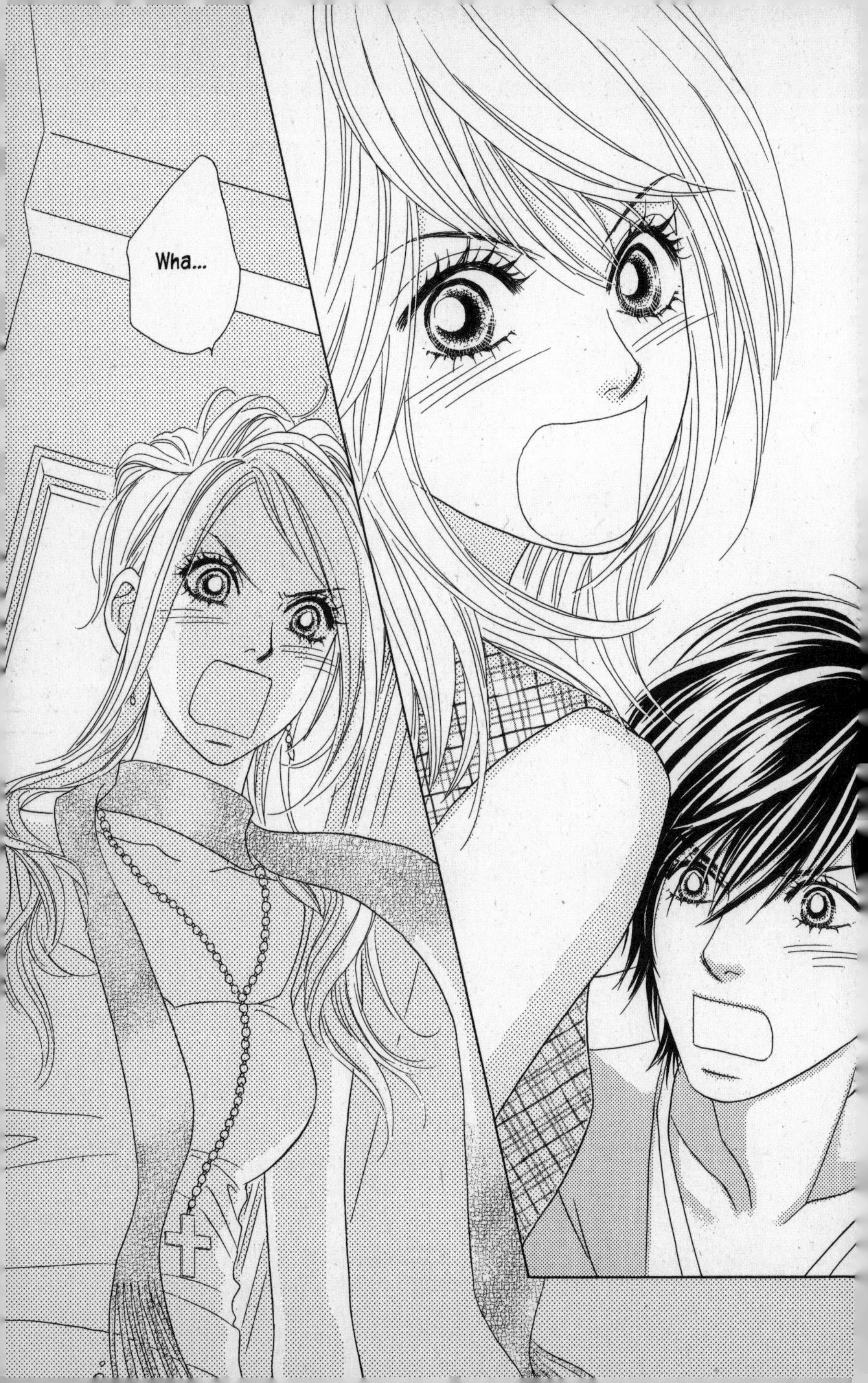
Wha...

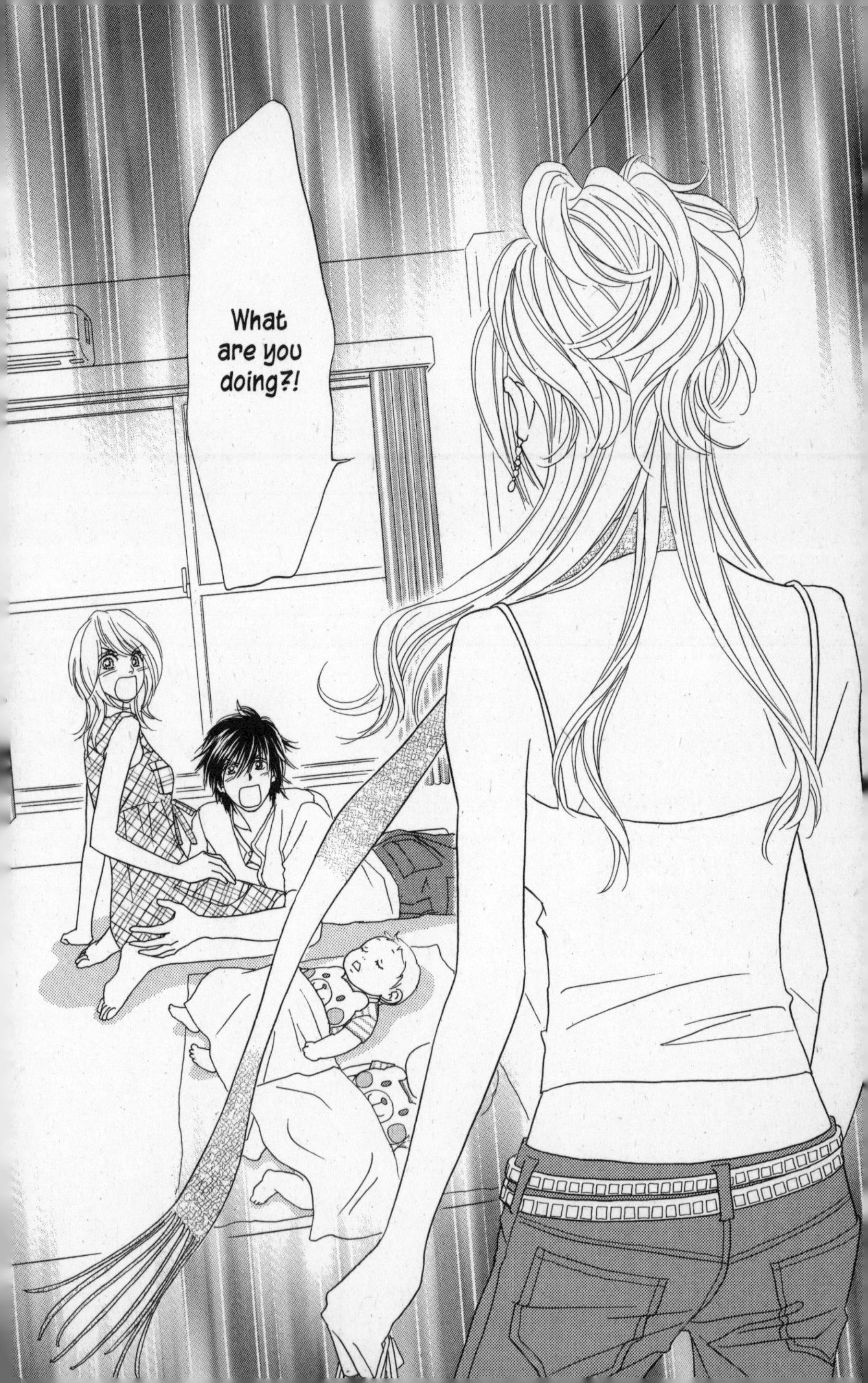
What are you doing?!

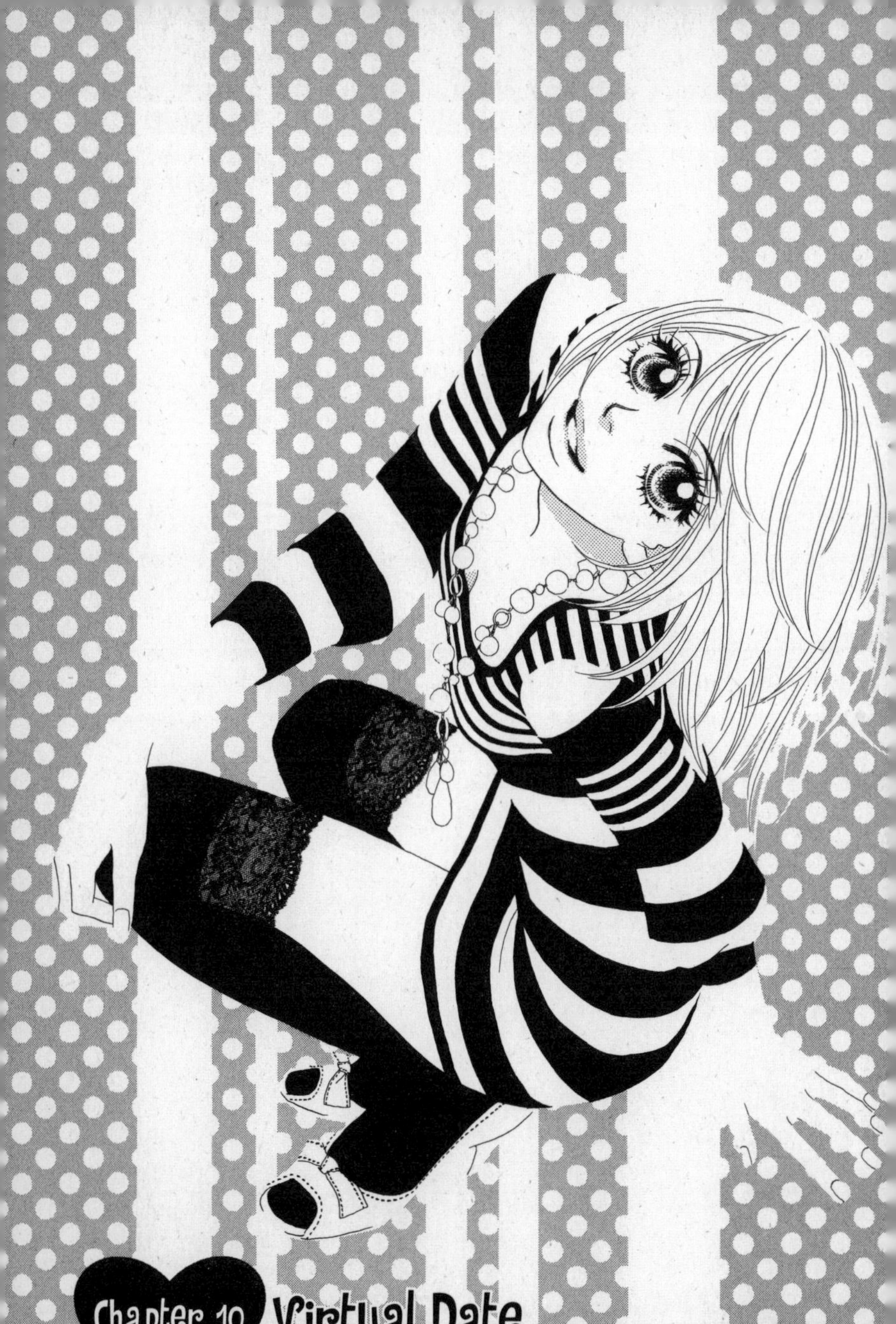

Chapter 10 Virtual Date

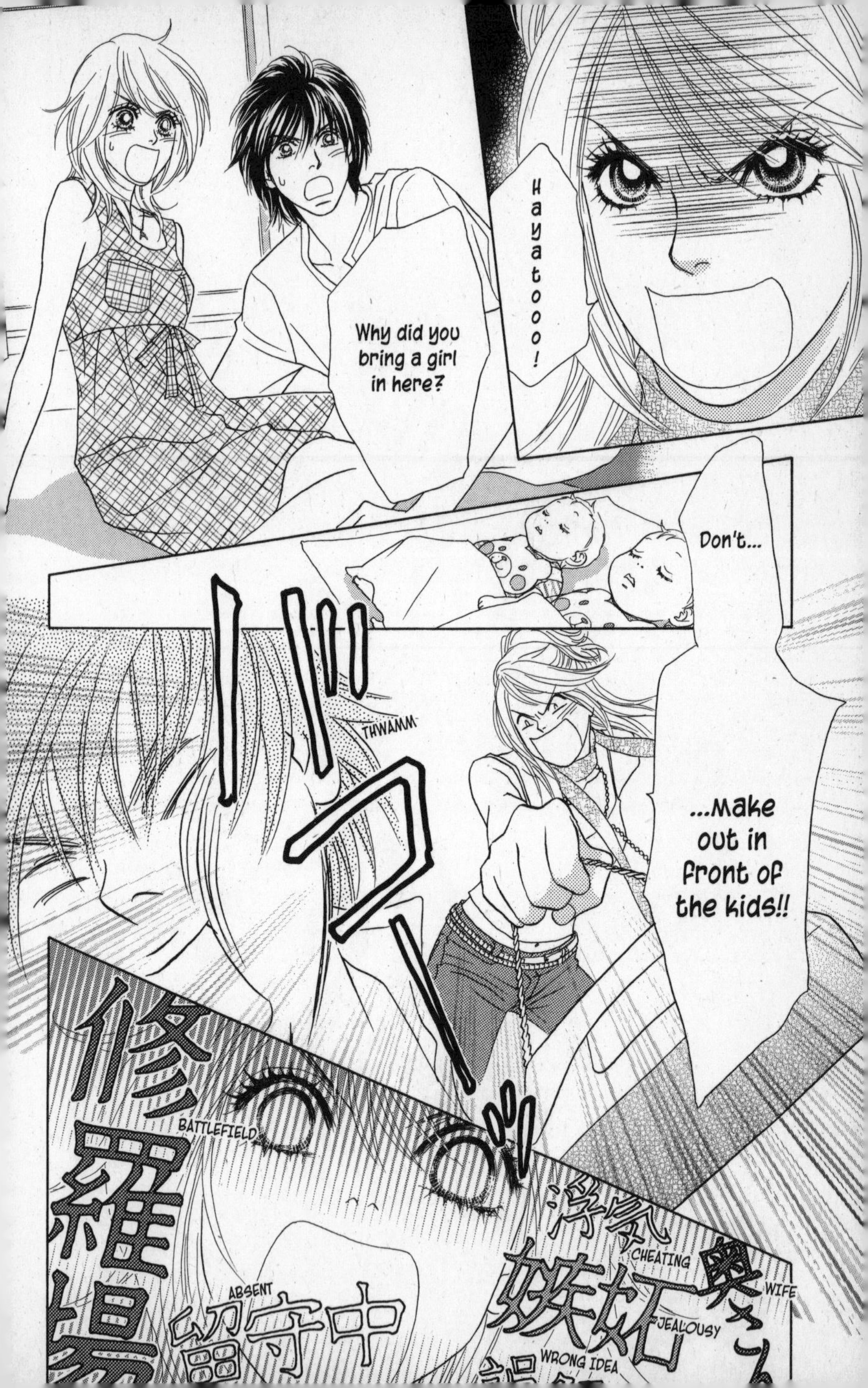
Hayatoooo!
Why did you bring a girl in here?
Don't...
THWAMM
...make out in front of the kids!!
修羅場
BATTLEFIELD
浮気
CHEATING
奥さん
WIFE
嫉妬
JEALOUSY
留守中
ABSENT
WRONG IDEA

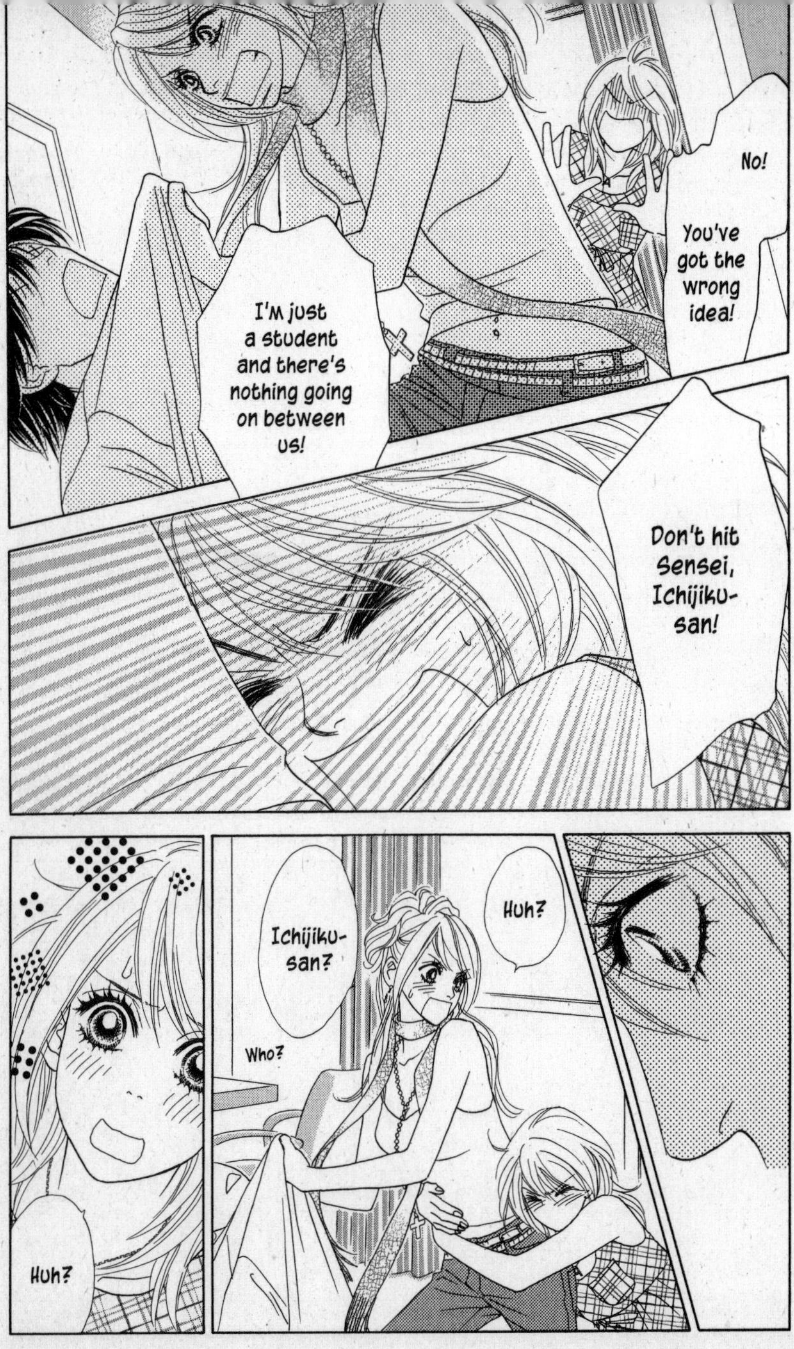
No!
You've got the wrong idea!
I'm just a student and there's nothing going on between us!
Don't hit Sensei, Ichijiku-san!
Huh?
Ichijiku-san?
Who?
Huh?

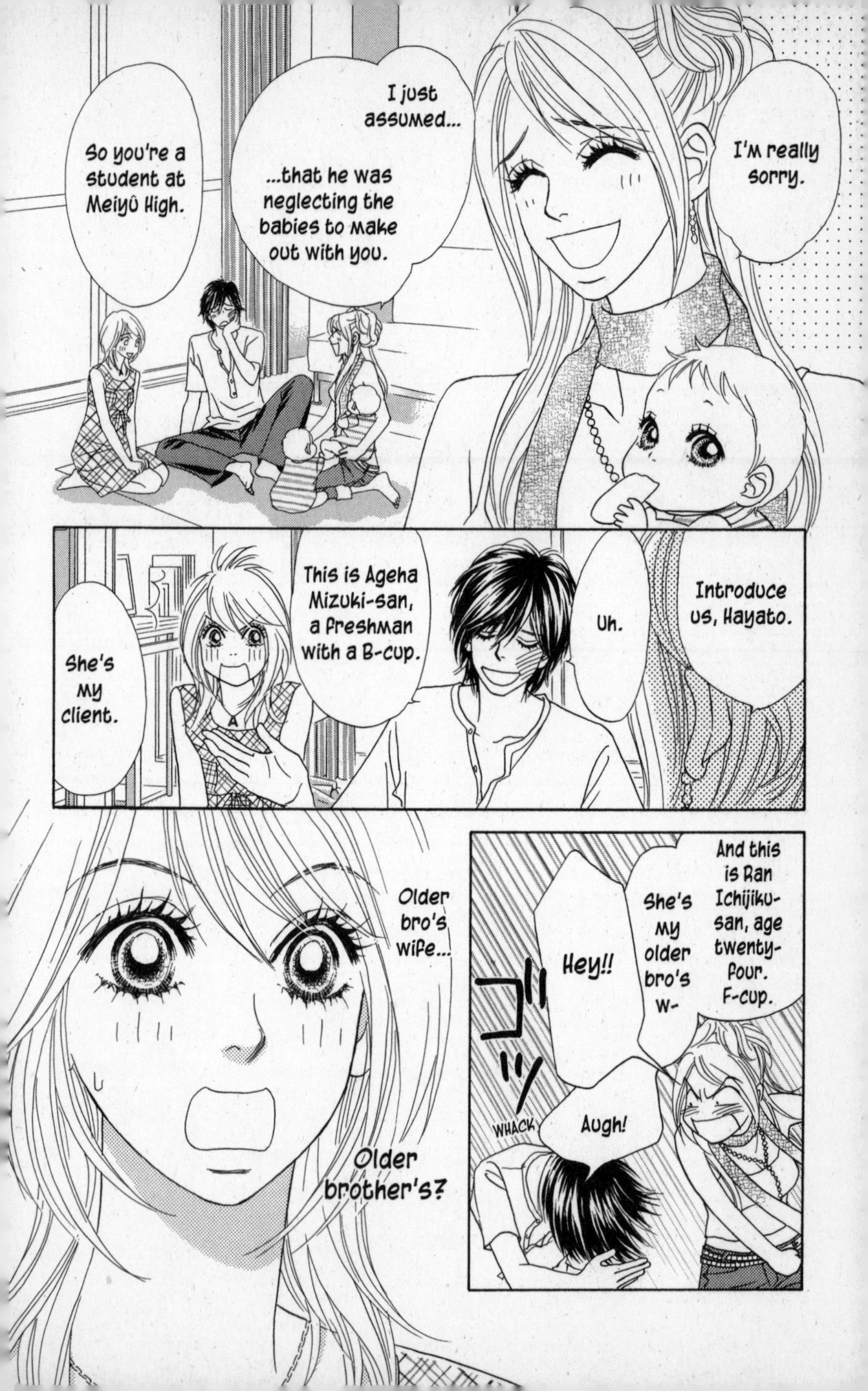
I'm really sorry.
I just assumed...
...that he was neglecting the babies to make out with you.
So you're a student at Meiyû High.
Introduce us, Hayato.
Uh.
This is Ageha Mizuki-san, a freshman with a B-cup.
She's my client.
And this is Ran Ichijiku-san, age twenty-four. F-cup.
She's my older bro's w-
Hey!!
ゴッ
WHACK
Augh!
Older bro's wife...
Older brother's?

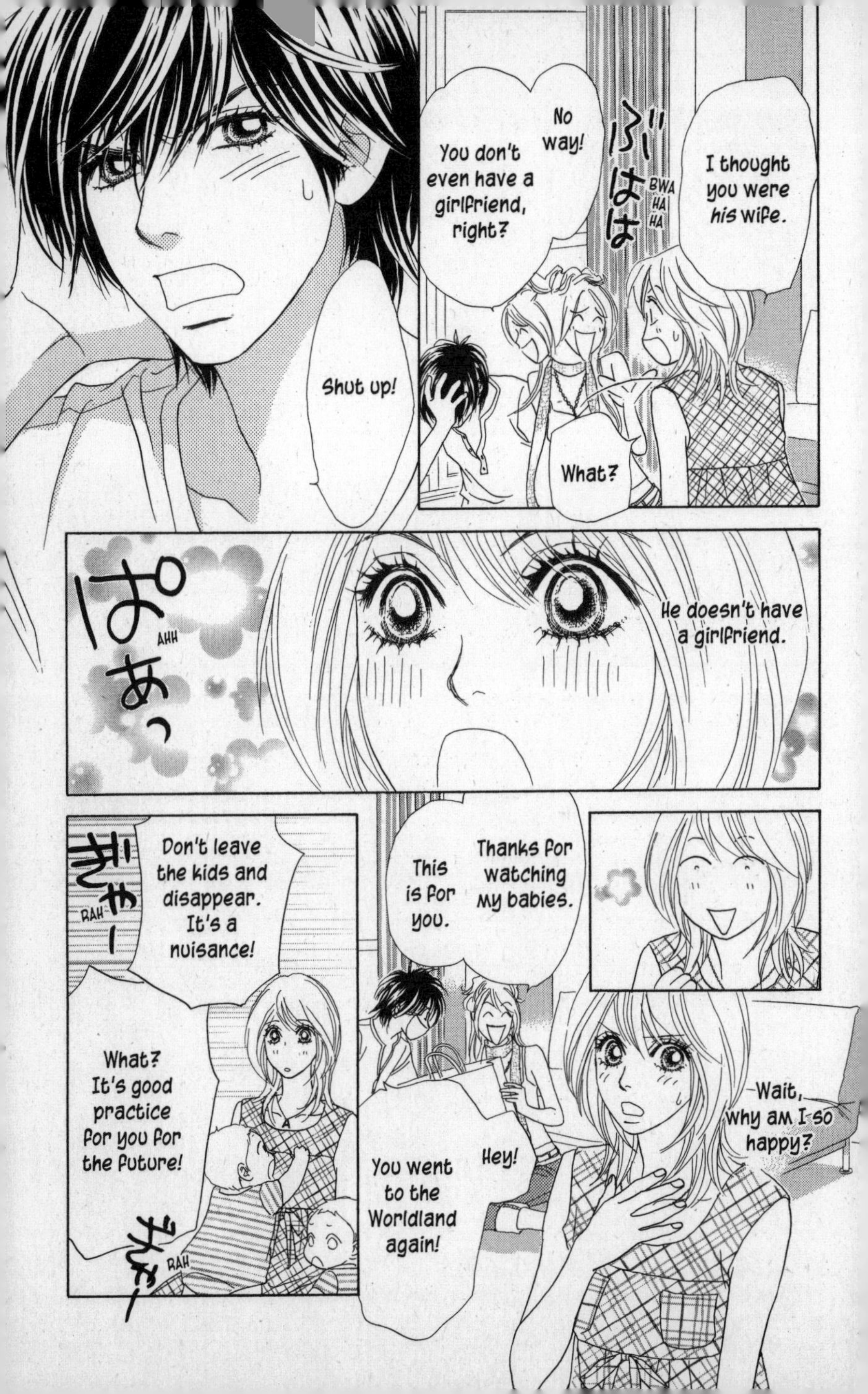
I thought you were his wife.
ぶはは
BWA HA HA
No way!
You don't even have a girlfriend, right?
What?
Shut up!
He doesn't have a girlfriend.
ぱあっ
AHH
Thanks for watching my babies.
This is for you.
Hey!
You went to the Worldland again!
Wait, why am I so happy?
ぎゃー
RAH
Don't leave the kids and disappear. It's a nuisance!
What? It's good practice for you for the future!
RAH

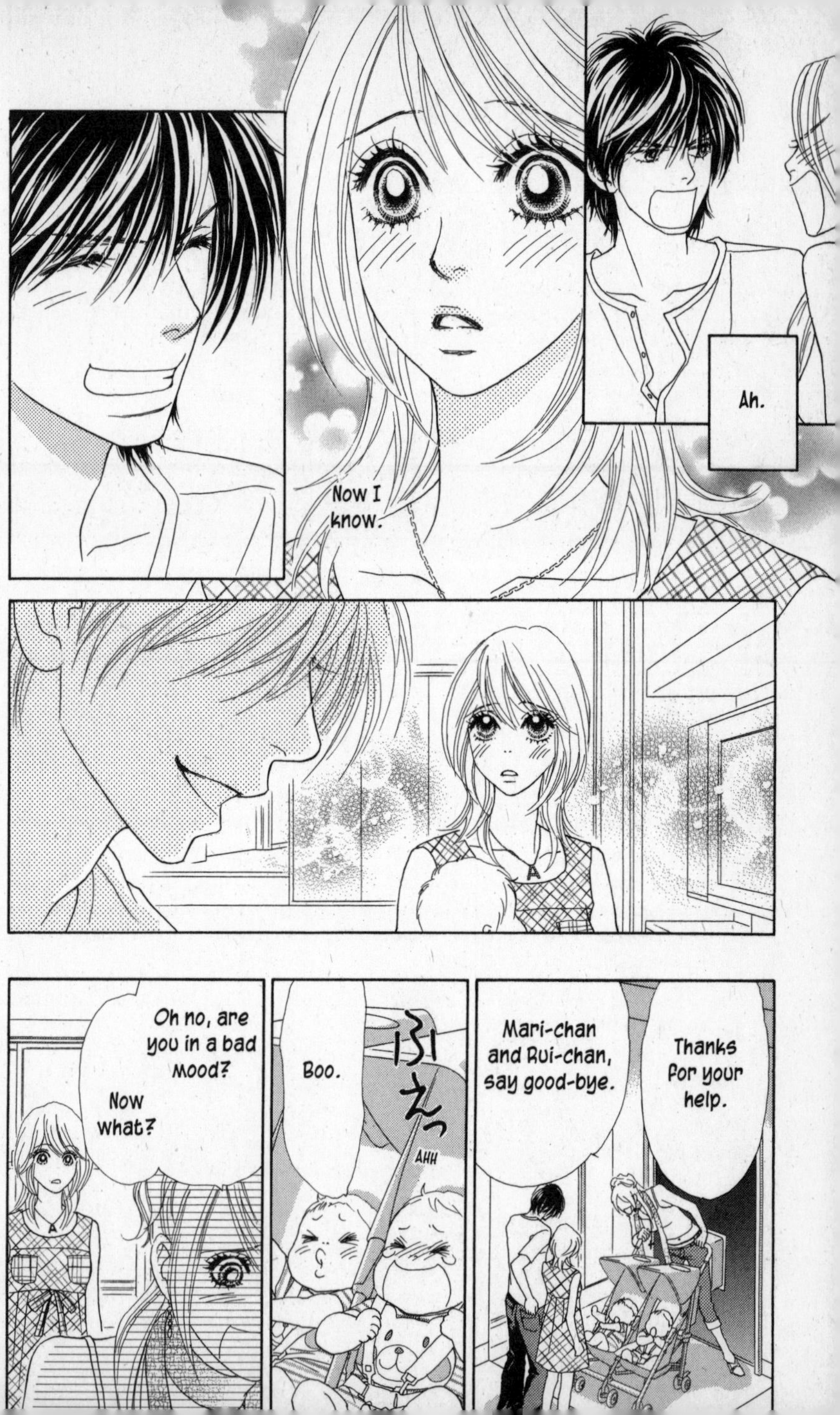
Ah.
Now I know.
Thanks for your help.
Mari-chan and Rui-chan, say good-bye.
ふえっ
AHH
Boo.
Oh no, are you in a bad mood?
Now what?

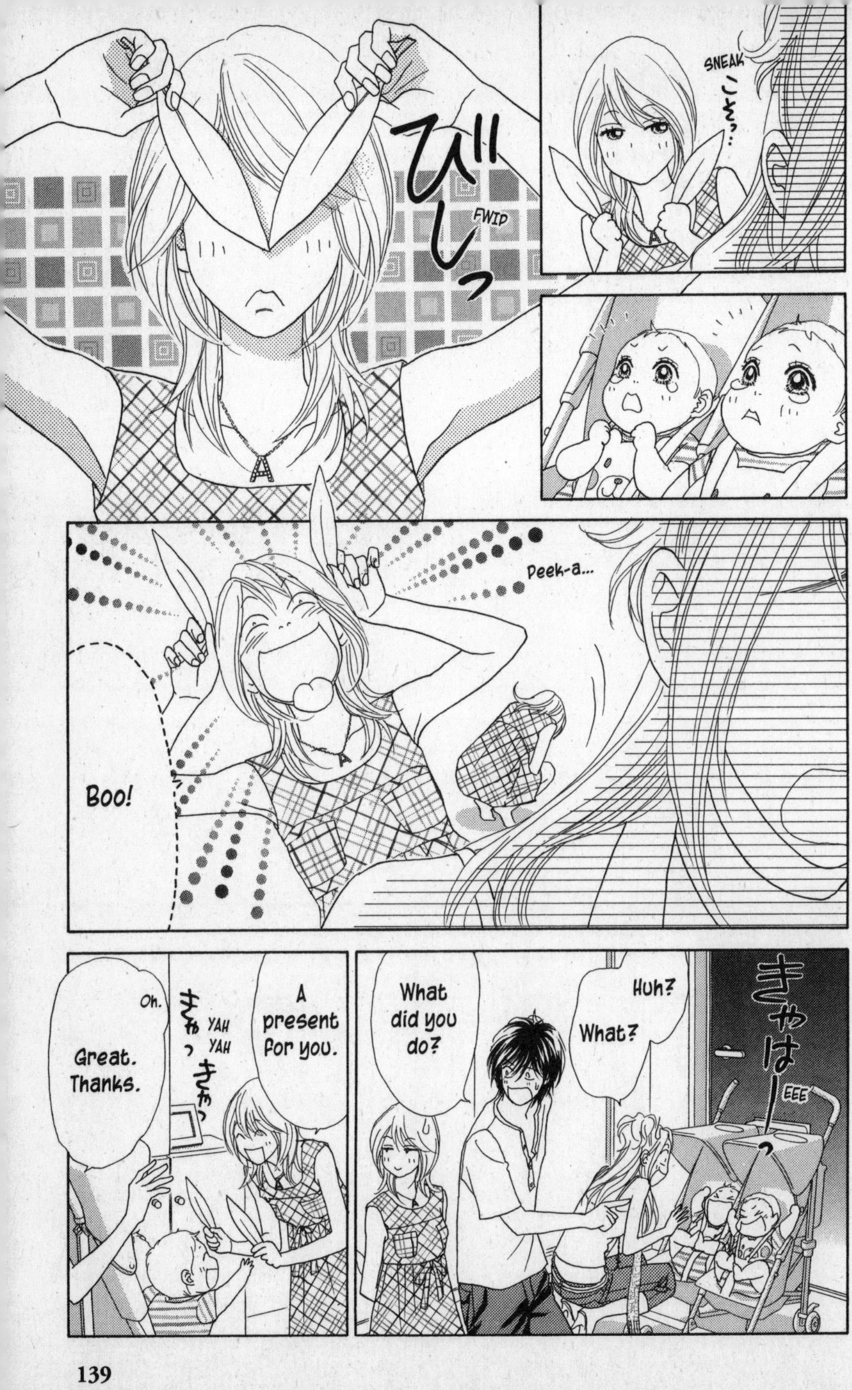
SNEAK
こそっ…
びしっ
FWIP
Peek-a...
Boo!
きゃはーっ
EEE
Huh?
What?
What did you do?
A present for you.
きゃっ きゃっ
YAH YAH
Oh.
Great. Thanks.

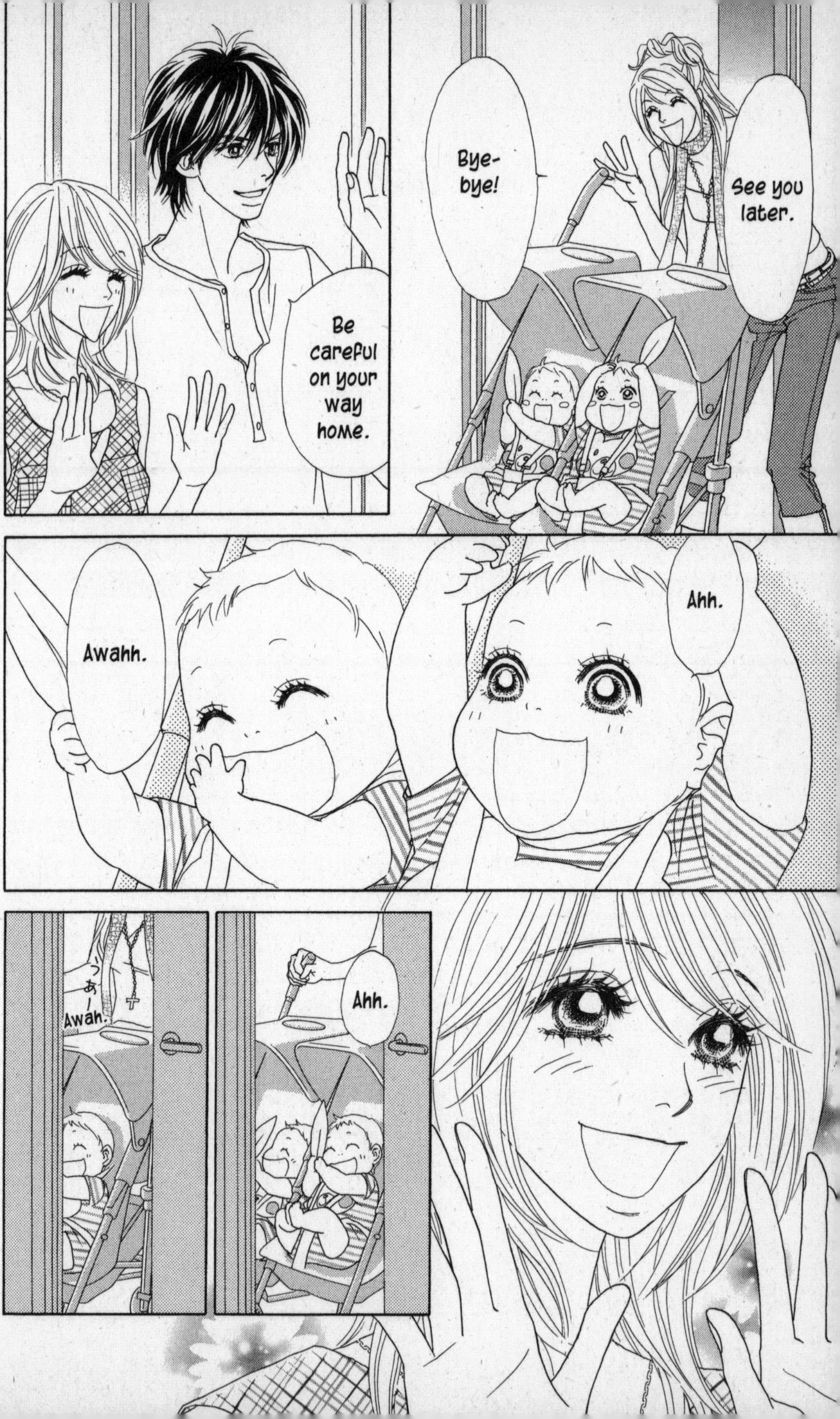
See you later.
Bye-bye!
Be careful on your way home.
Ahh.
Awahh.
Ahh.
Awah.

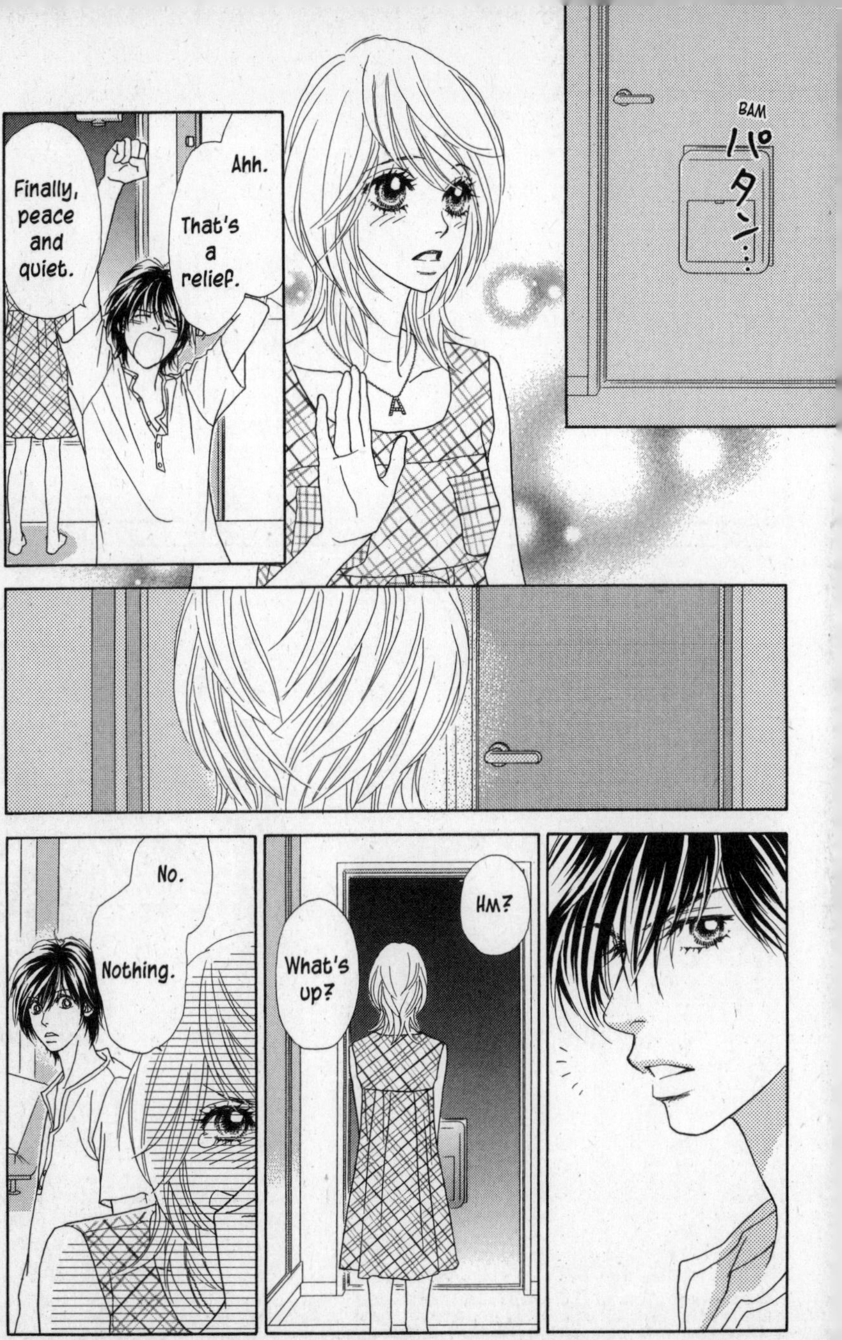
BAM
パタン…
Ahh.
That's a relief.
Finally, peace and quiet.
Hm?
What's up?
No.
Nothing.

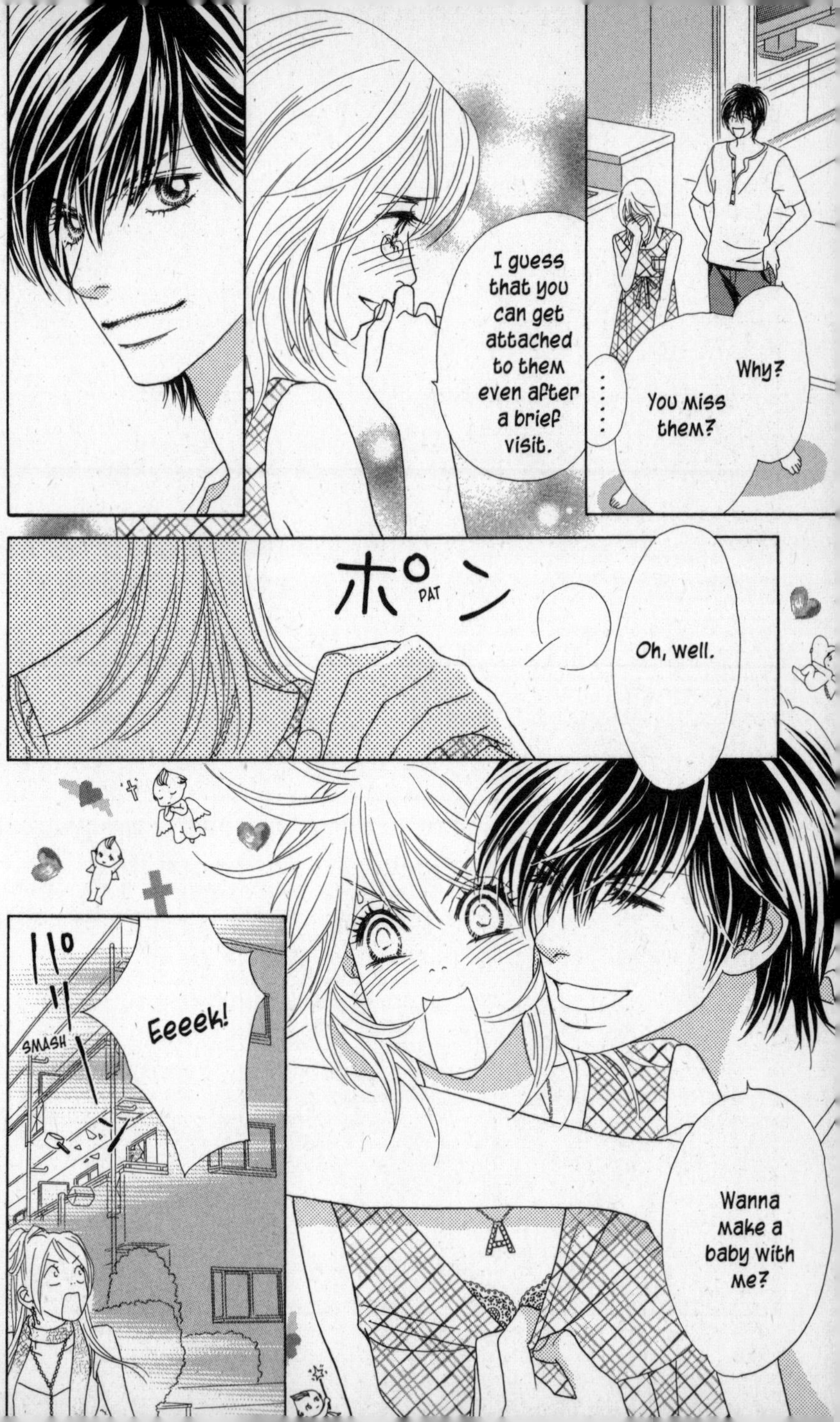
Why?
You miss them?
......
I guess that you can get attached to them even after a brief visit.
ポン
PAT
Oh, well.
Wanna make a baby with me?
Eeeek!
SMASH

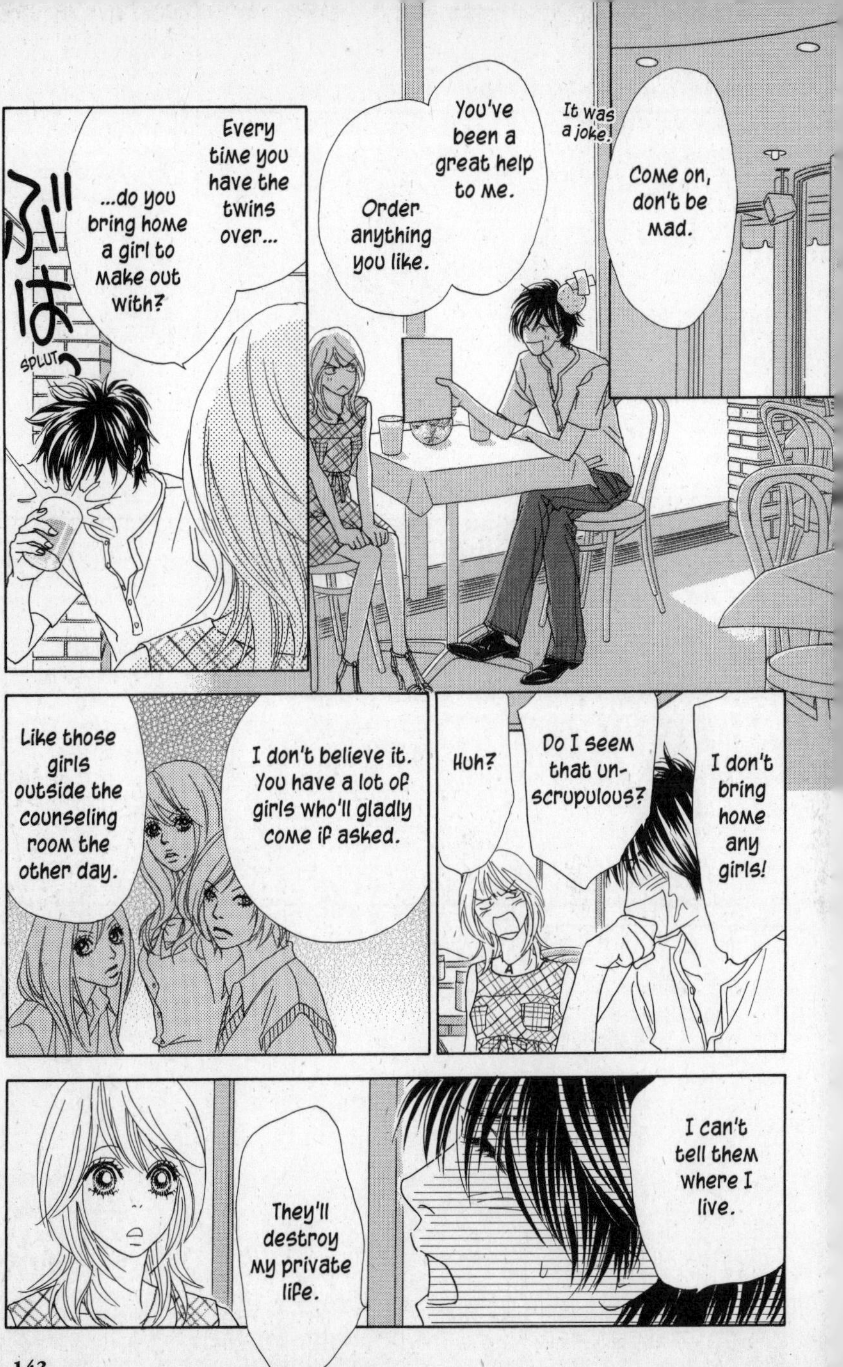
Come on, don't be mad.
It was a joke!
You've been a great help to me.
Order anything you like.
Every time you have the twins over...
...do you bring home a girl to make out with?
ぶはっ
SPLUT
I don't bring home any girls!
Do I seem that un-scrupulous?
Huh?
I don't believe it. You have a lot of girls who'll gladly come if asked.
Like those girls outside the counseling room the other day.
I can't tell them where I live.
They'll destroy my private life.

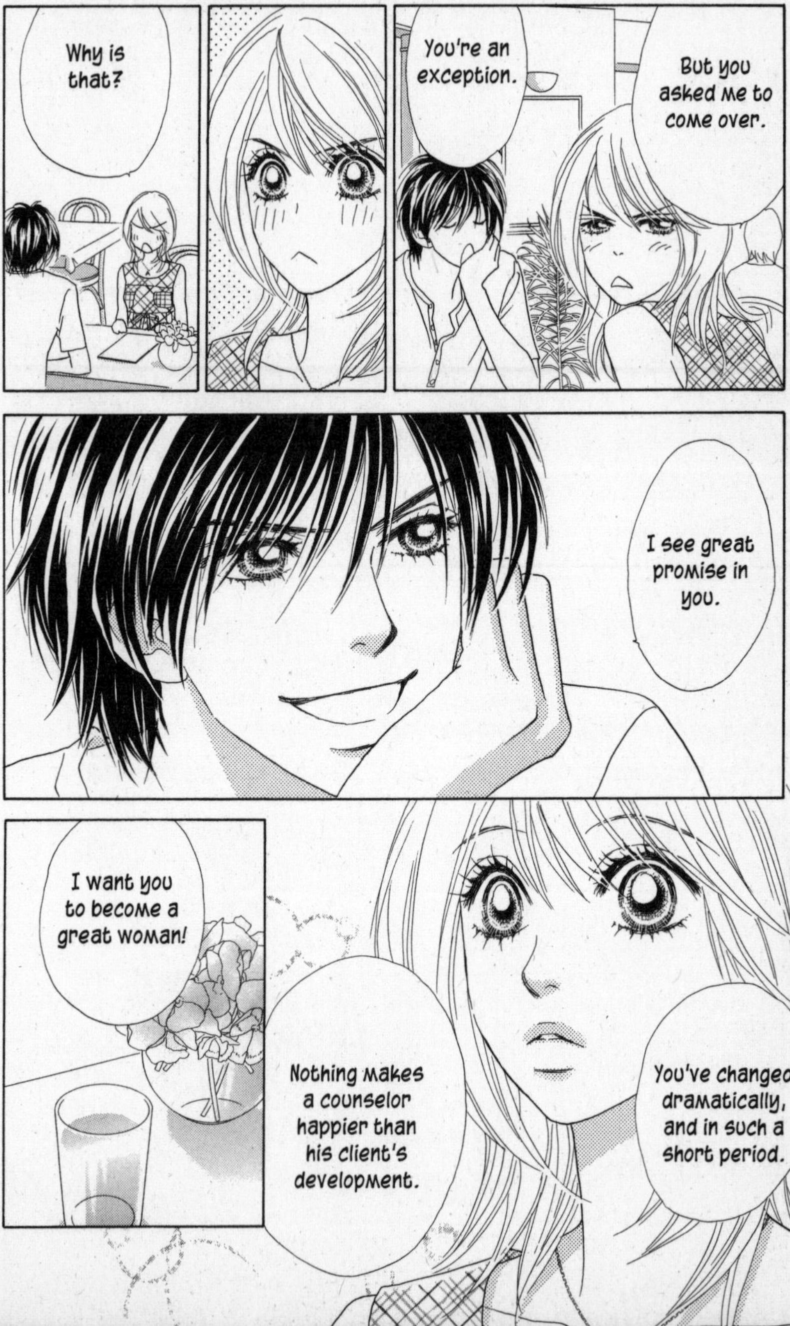

But you asked me to come over.
You're an exception.
Why is that?
I see great promise in you.
You've changed dramatically, and in such a short period.
Nothing makes a counselor happier than his client's development.
I want you to become a great woman!

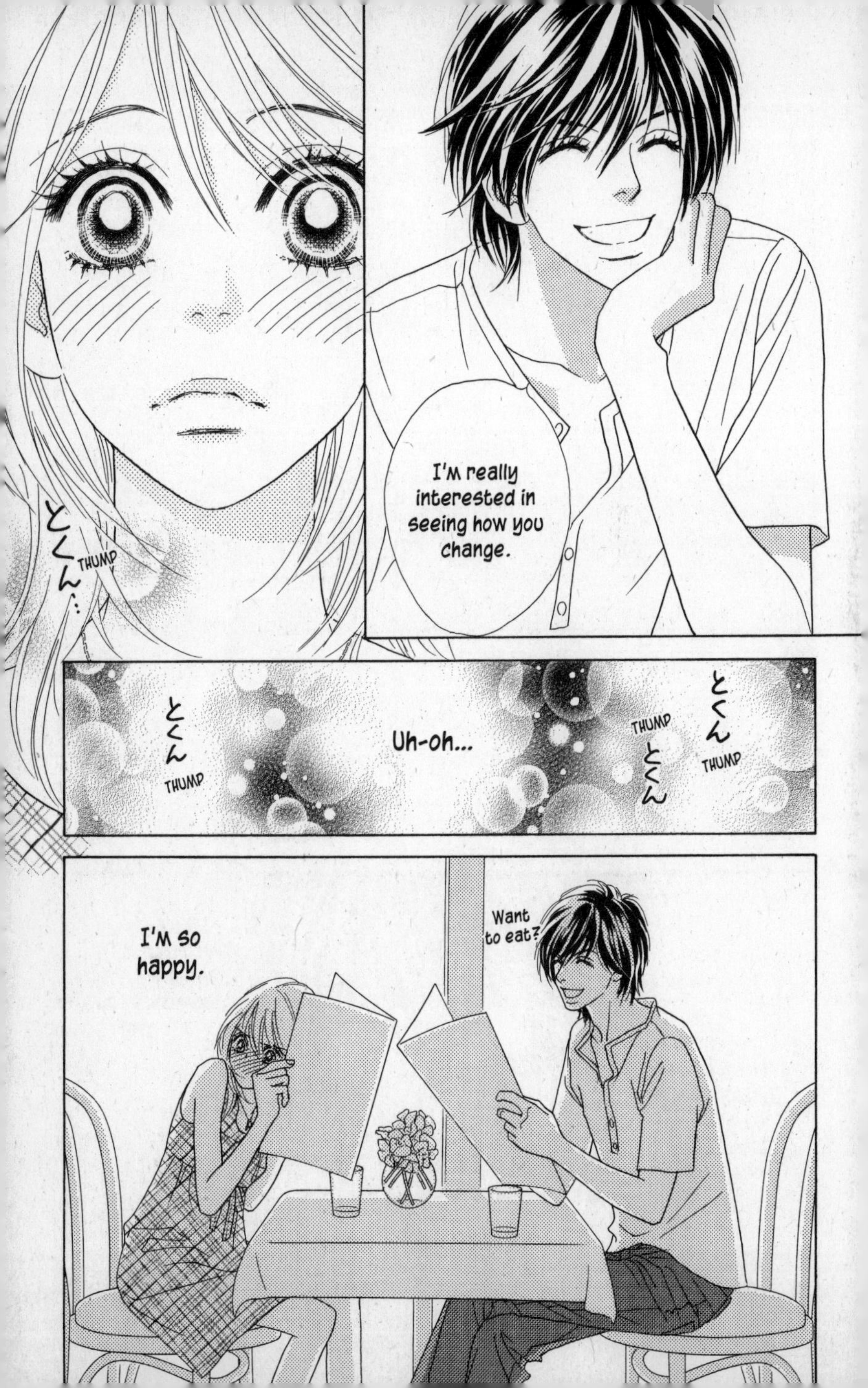
I'm really interested in seeing how you change.
とくん... THUMP
とくん THUMP
THUMP とくん
Uh-oh...
とくん THUMP
Want to eat?
I'm so happy.

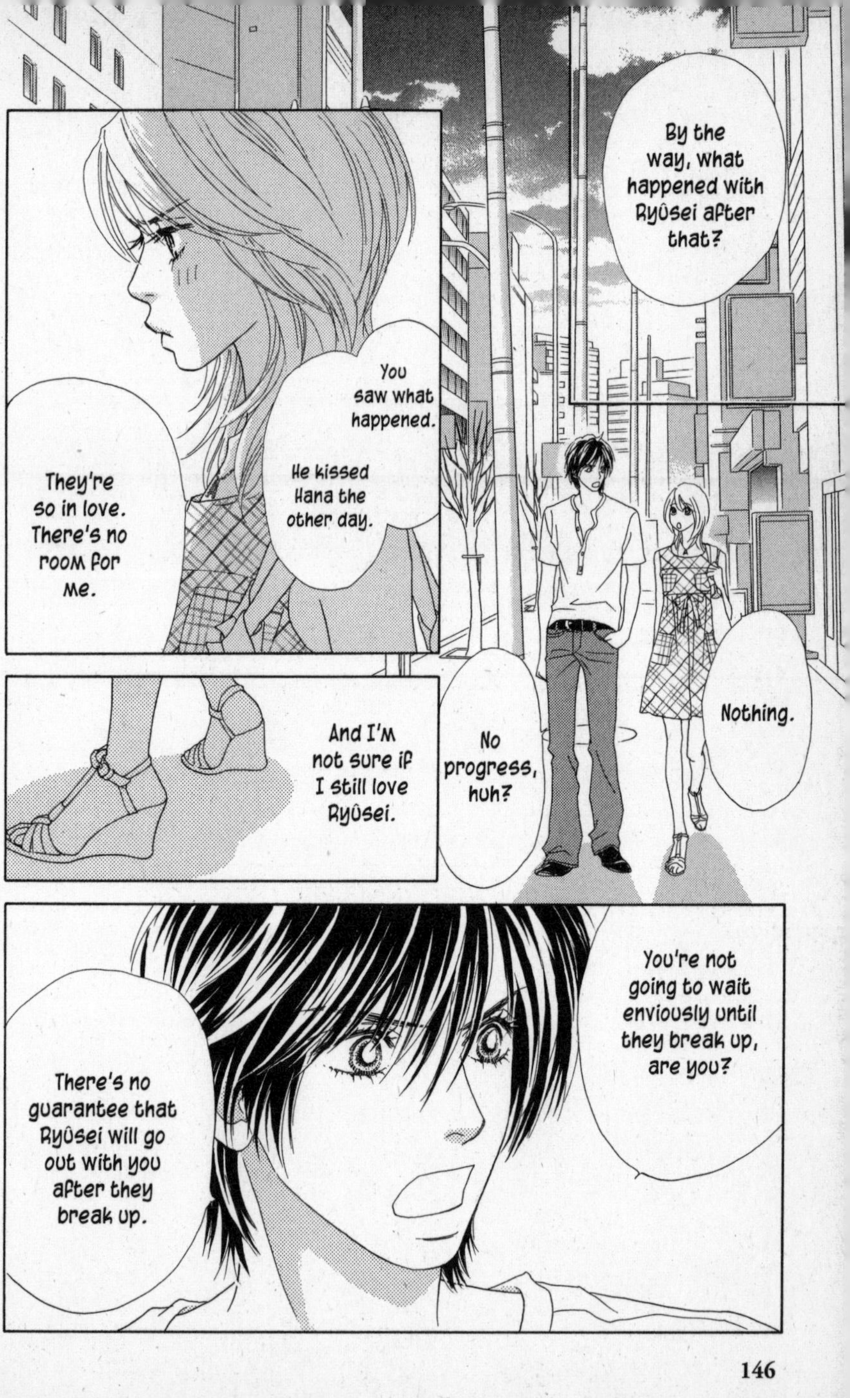
By the way, what happened with Ryûsei after that?
Nothing.
No progress, huh?
You saw what happened.
He kissed Hana the other day.
They're so in love. There's no room for me.
And I'm not sure if I still love Ryûsei.
You're not going to wait enviously until they break up, are you?
There's no guarantee that Ryûsei will go out with you after they break up.

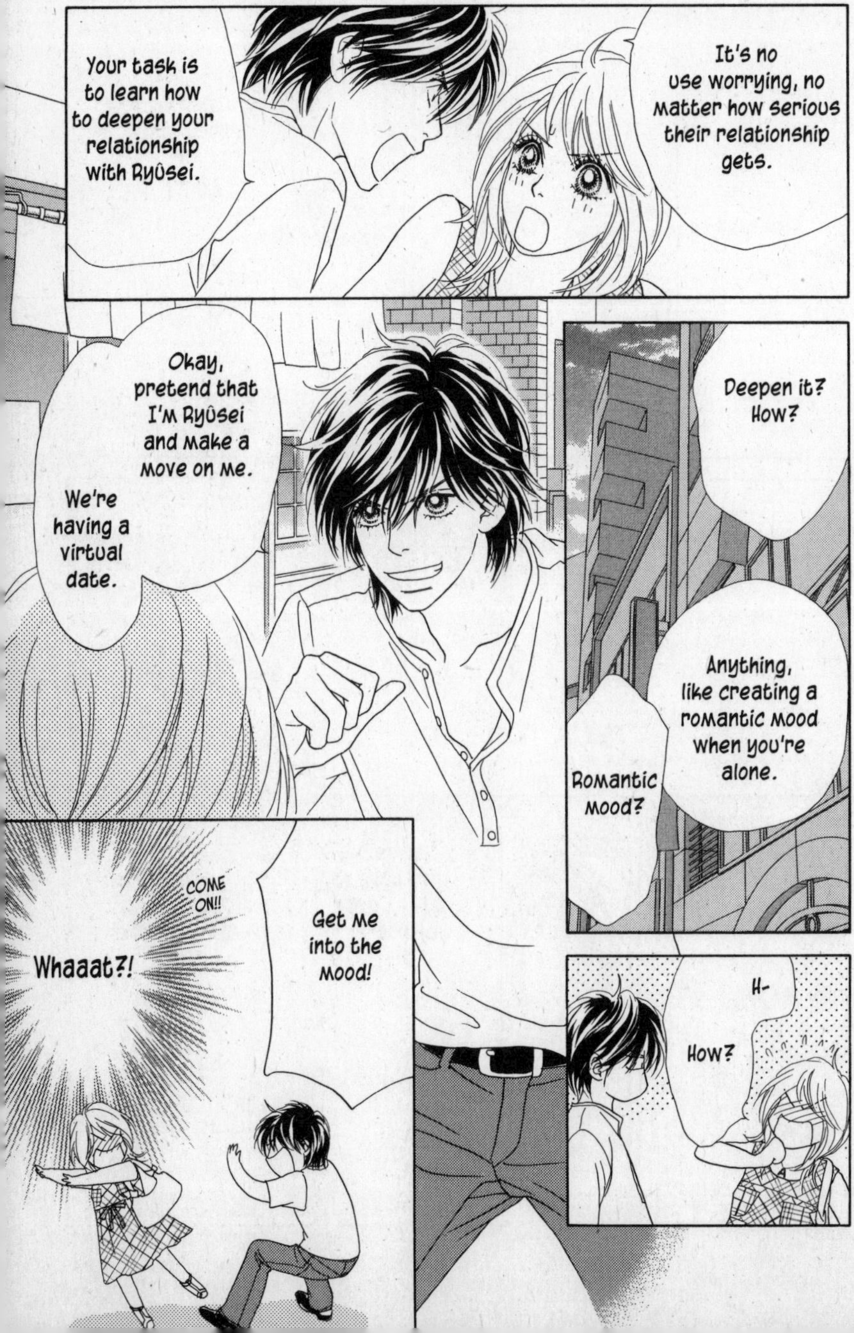
It's no use worrying, no matter how serious their relationship gets.
Your task is to learn how to deepen your relationship with Ryûsei.
Deepen it? How?
Anything, like creating a romantic mood when you're alone.
Romantic mood?
H-
How?
Okay, pretend that I'm Ryûsei and make a move on me.
We're having a virtual date.
Get me into the mood!
COME ON!!
Whaaat?!

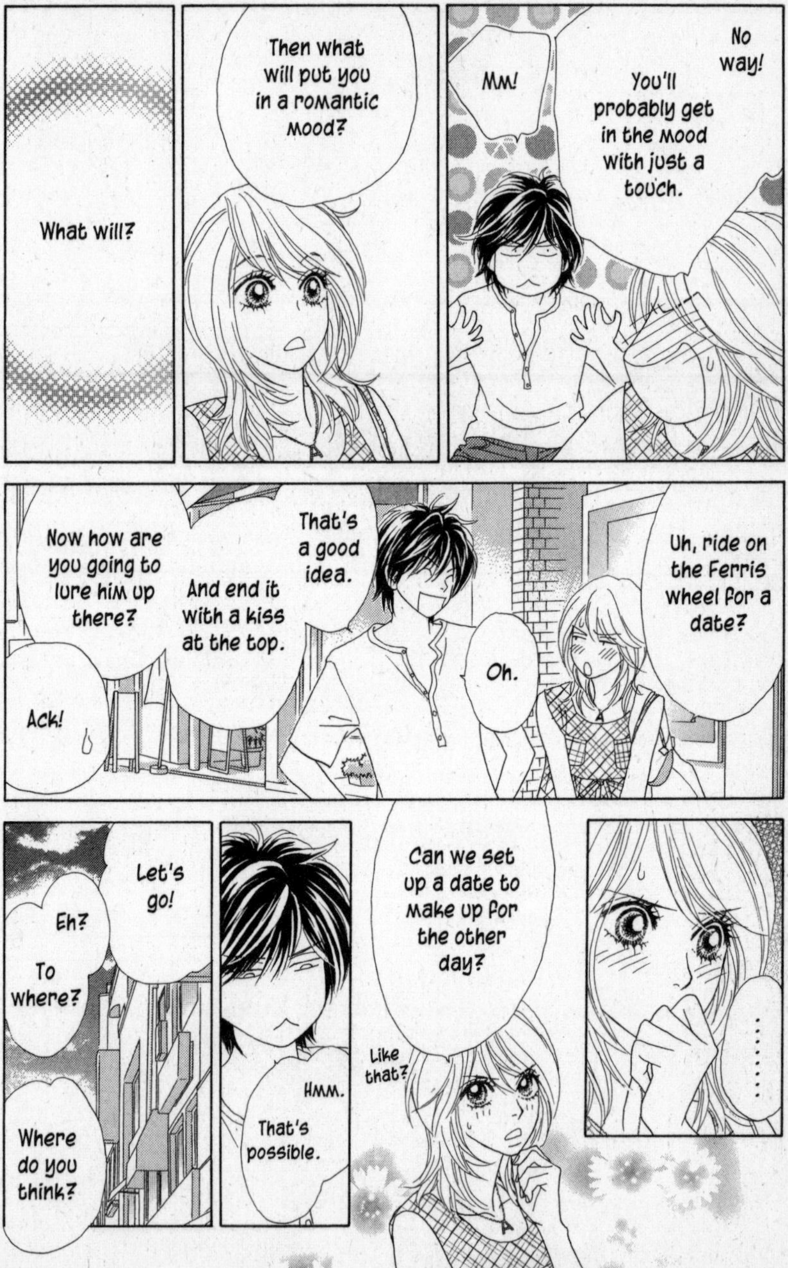
No way!
You'll probably get in the mood with just a touch.
Mm!
Then what will put you in a romantic mood?
What will?
Uh, ride on the Ferris wheel for a date?
Oh.
That's a good idea.
And end it with a kiss at the top.
Now how are you going to lure him up there?
Ack!
......
Can we set up a date to make up for the other day?
Like that?
Hmm.
That's possible.
Let's go!
Eh?
To where?
Where do you think?

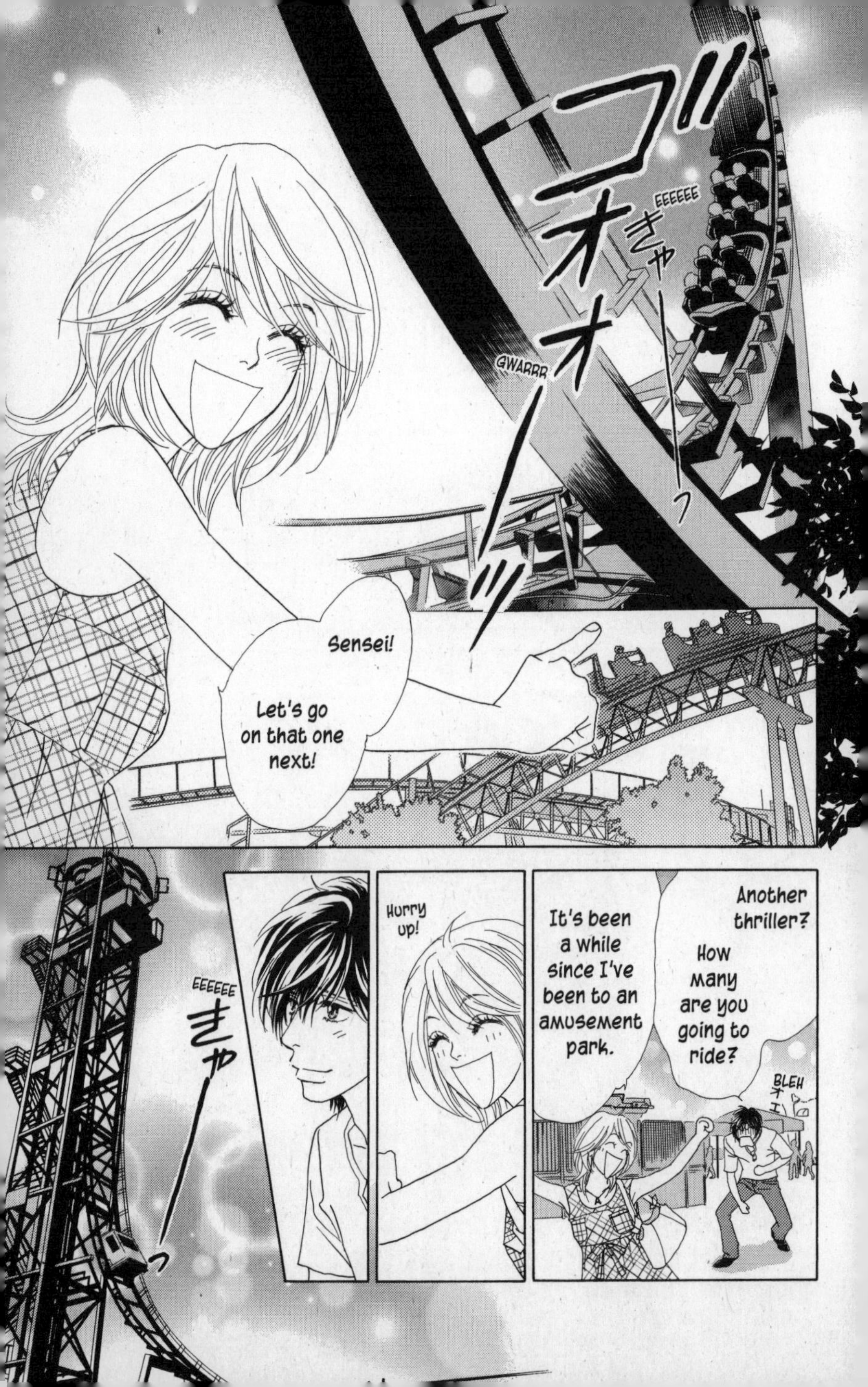
ゴオオーッ
GWARRR
きゃーっ
EEEEEE
Sensei!
Let's go on that one next!
Another thriller?
How many are you going to ride?
It's been a while since I've been to an amusement park.
オエ
BLEH
Hurry up!
きゃーっ
EEEEEE

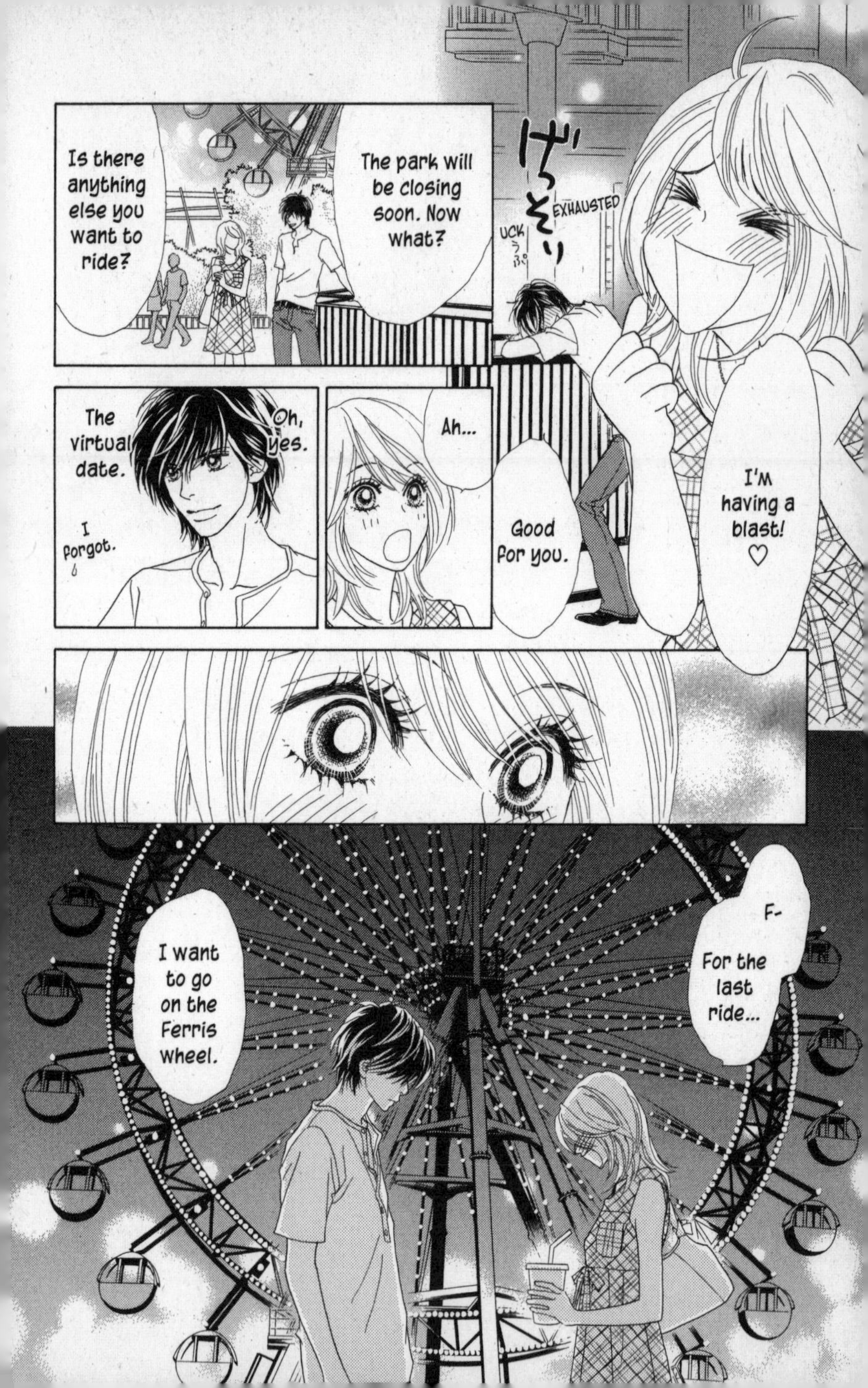
I'M having a blast! ♡
げっそり
EXHAUSTED
うぷ
UCK
Good for you.
The park will be closing soon. Now what?
Is there anything else you want to ride?
Ah...
Oh, yes.
The virtual date.
I forgot.
F-
For the last ride...
I want to go on the Ferris wheel.

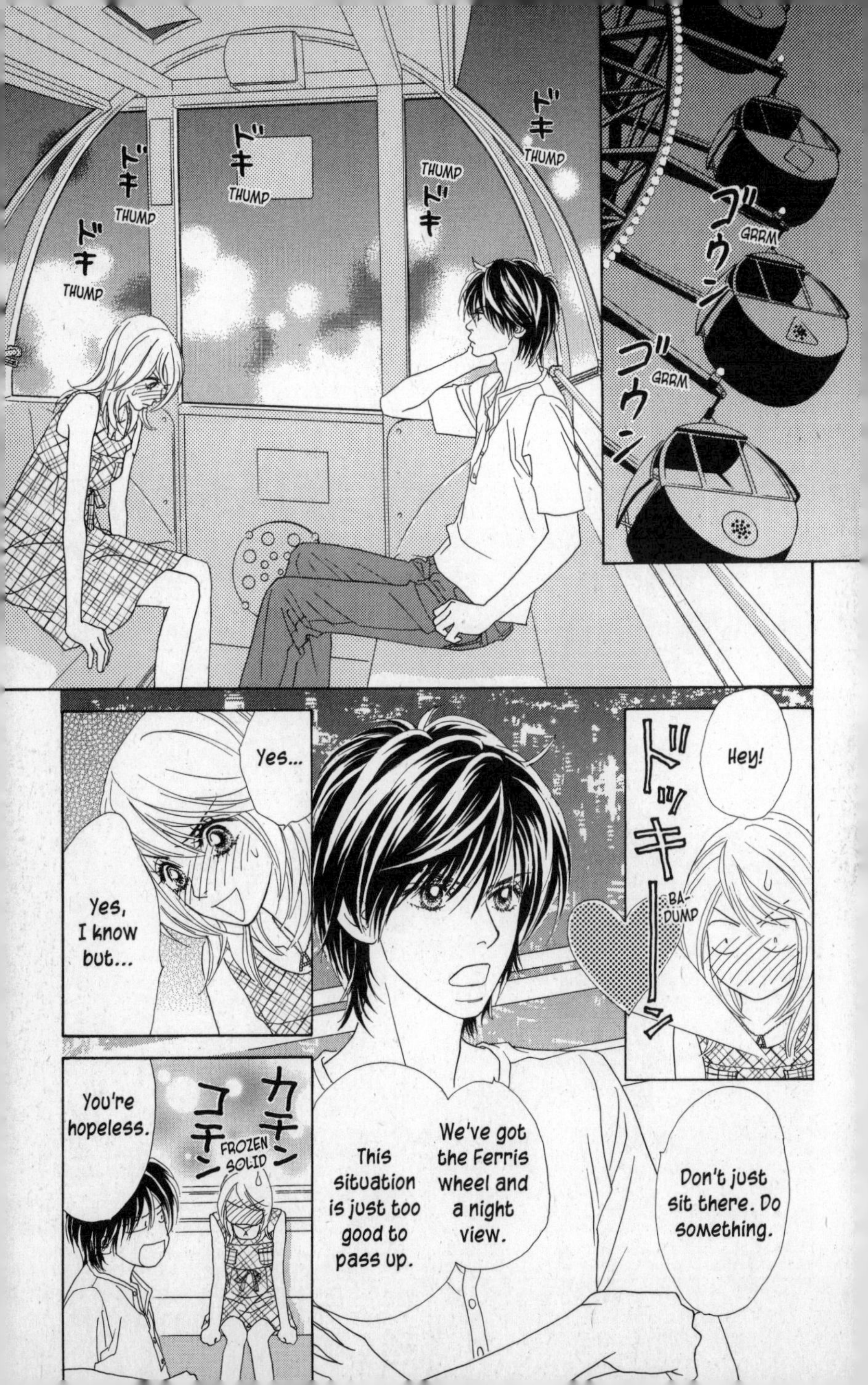

ゴウン
GRRM
ゴウン
GRRM
ドキ
THUMP
THUMP
ドキ
ドキ
THUMP
ドキ
THUMP
ドキ
THUMP
Hey!
ドッキーン
BA-DUMP
Don't just sit there. Do something.
We've got the Ferris wheel and a night view.
This situation is just too good to pass up.
Yes...
Yes, I know but...
You're hopeless.
カチンコチン
FROZEN SOLID

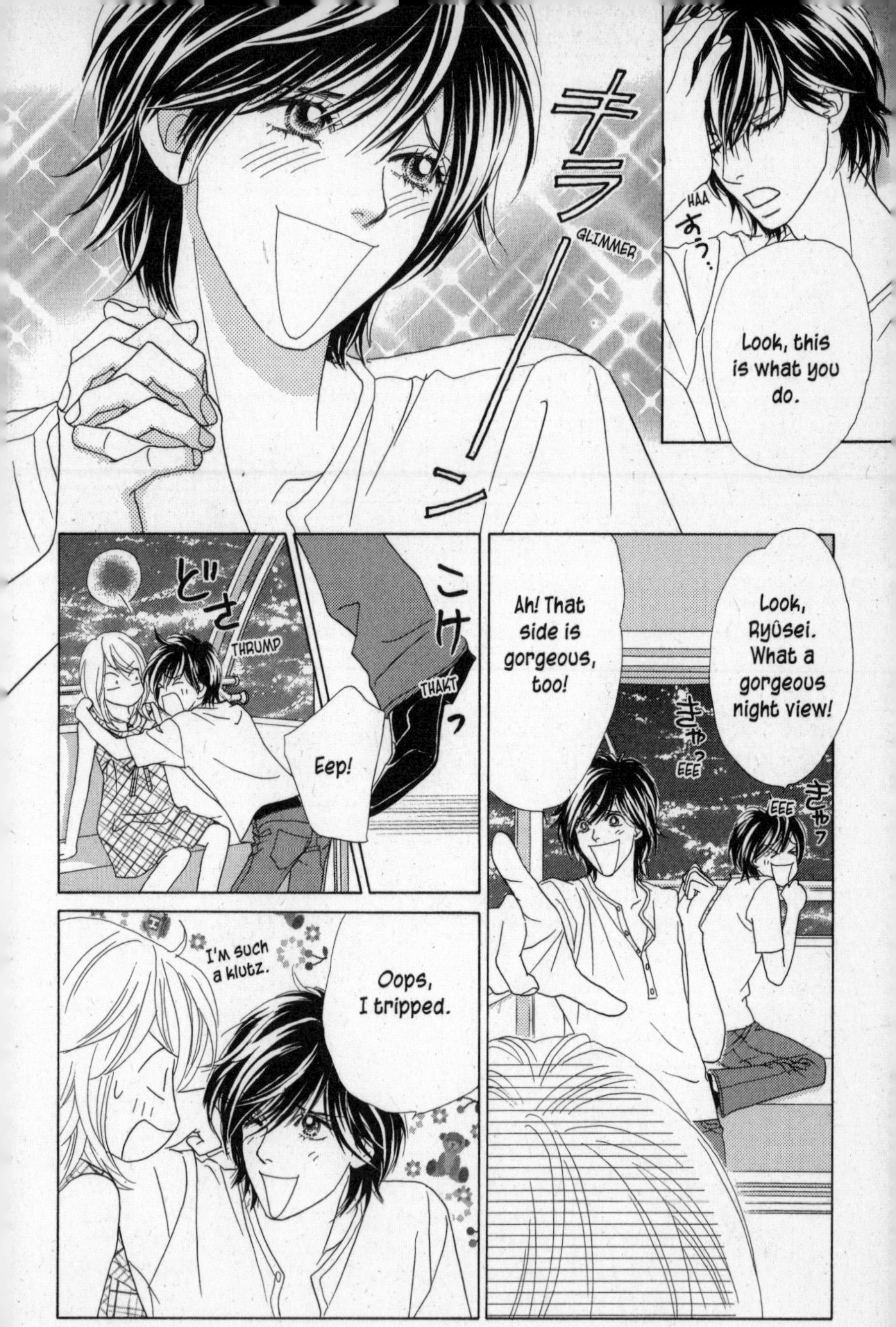
すぅ…
HAA
Look, this is what you do.
キラーン
GLIMMER
Look, Ryûsei. What a gorgeous night view!
きゃっ
EEE
Ah! That side is gorgeous, too!
きゃっ
EEE
こけっ
THAKT
Eep!
どさ
THRUMP
Oops, I tripped.
I'm such a klutz.

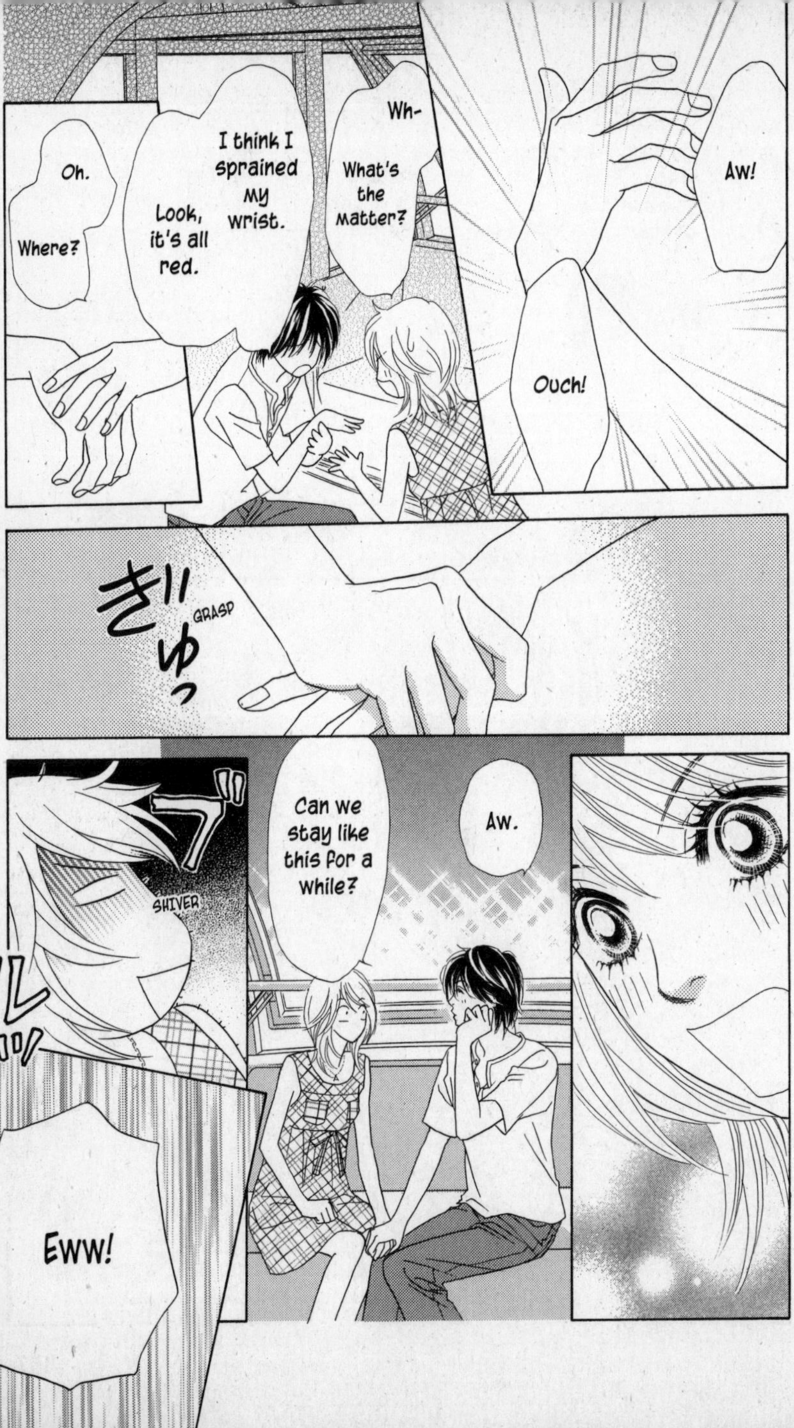
Aw!
Ouch!
Wh-
What's the matter?
I think I sprained my wrist.
Look, it's all red.
Oh.
Where?
ぎゅっ
GRASP
Aw.
Can we stay like this for a while?
ブルッ
SHIVER
Eww!

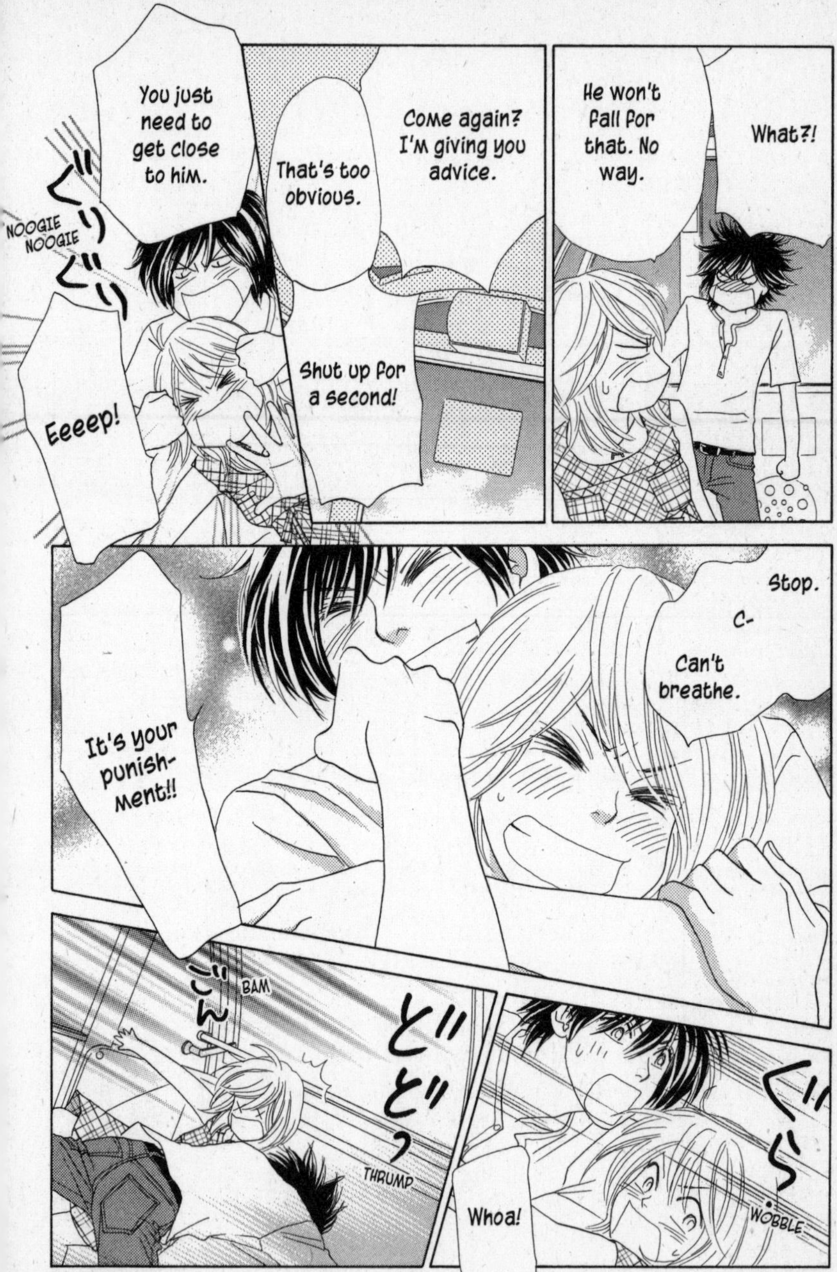
What?!
He won't fall for that. No way.
Come again? I'm giving you advice.
That's too obvious.
Shut up for a second!
You just need to get close to him.
ぐりぐり
NOOGIE NOOGIE
Eeeep!
Stop.
C-
Can't breathe.
It's your punishment!!
ぐら
WOBBLE
Whoa!
どどっ
THRUMP
ごん
BAM

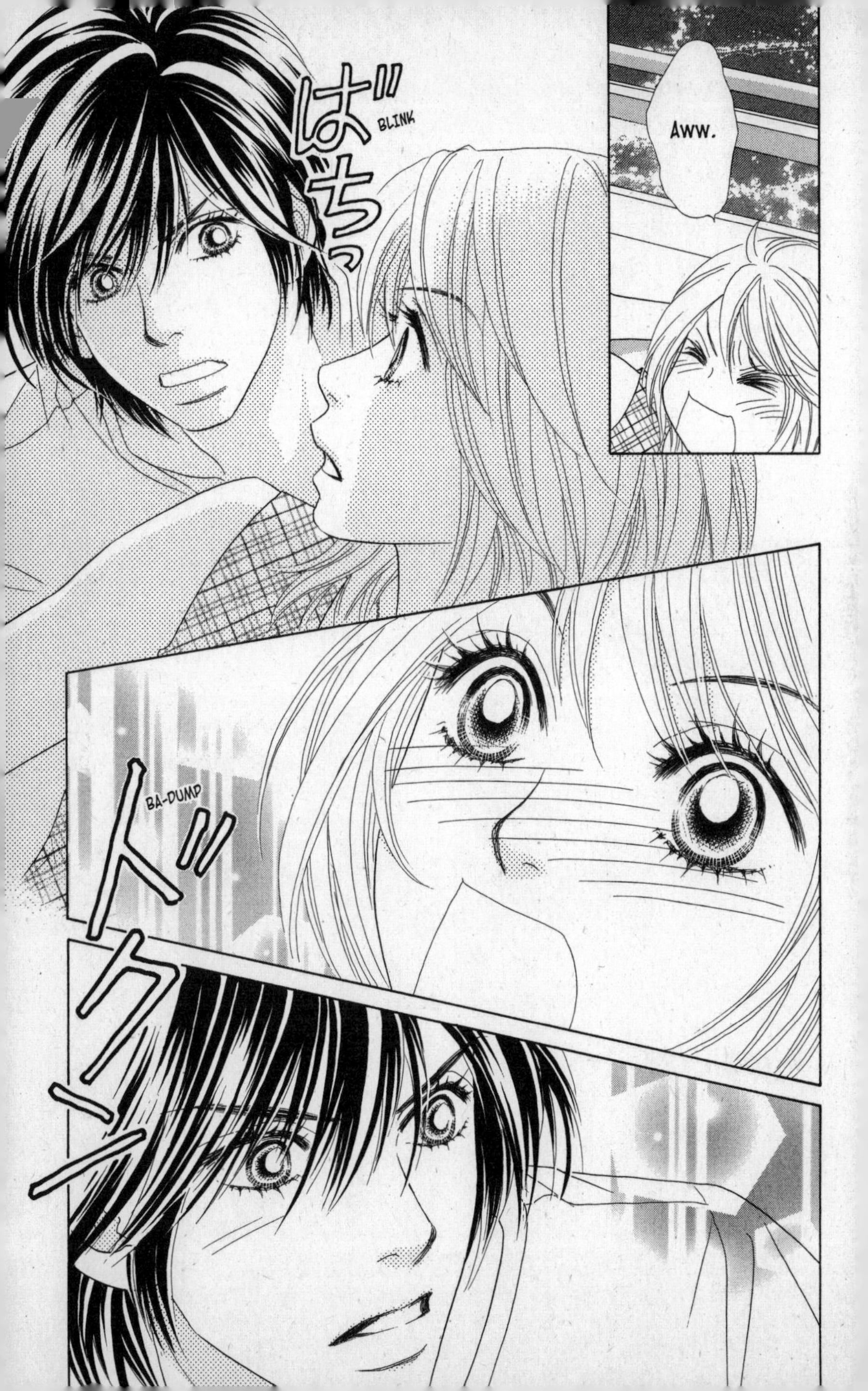
Aww.
ばちっ
BLINK
ドクン
BA-DUMP

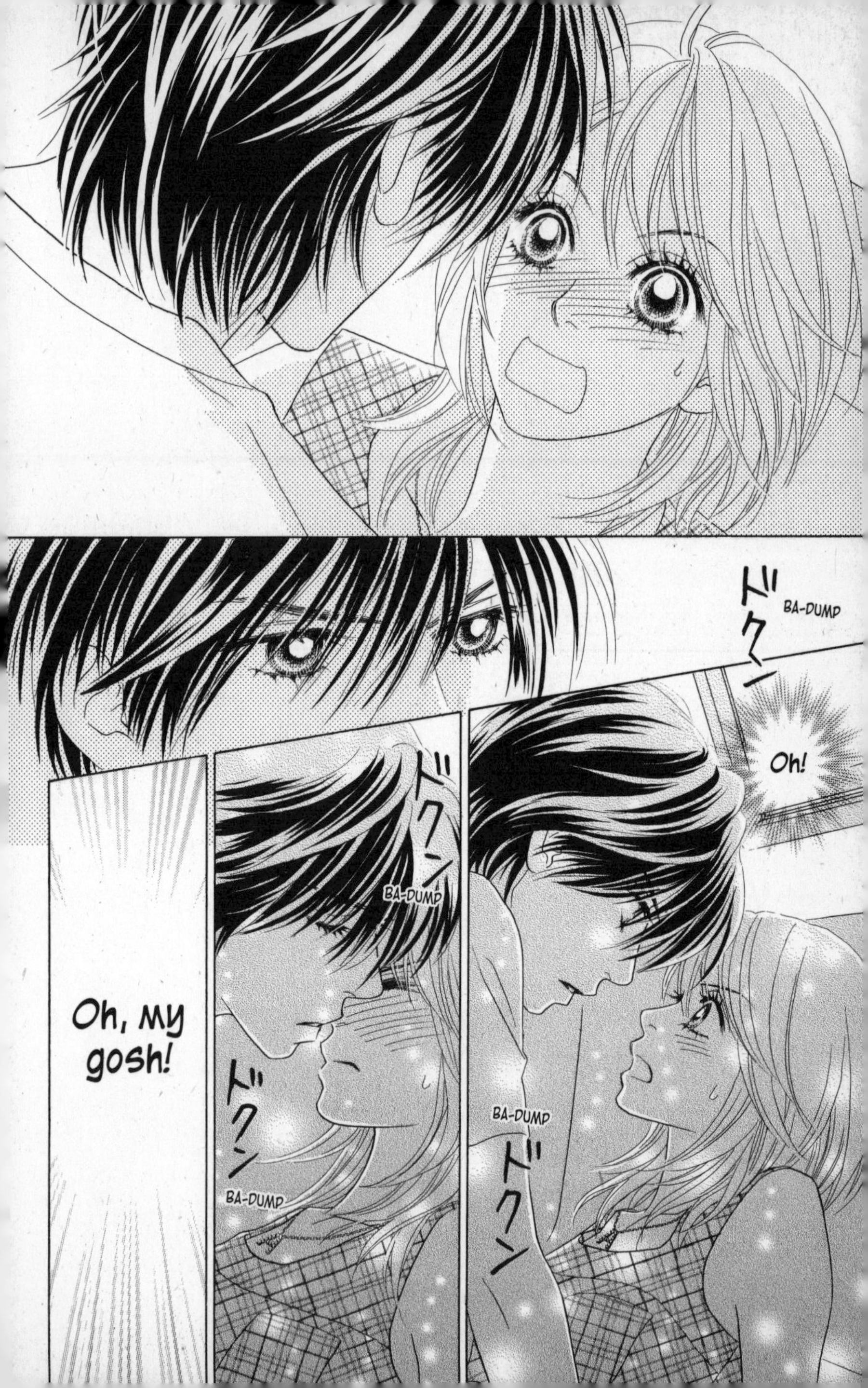
ドクン
BA-DUMP
Oh!
BA-DUMP
ドクン
ドクン
BA-DUMP
ドクン
BA-DUMP
Oh, my gosh!

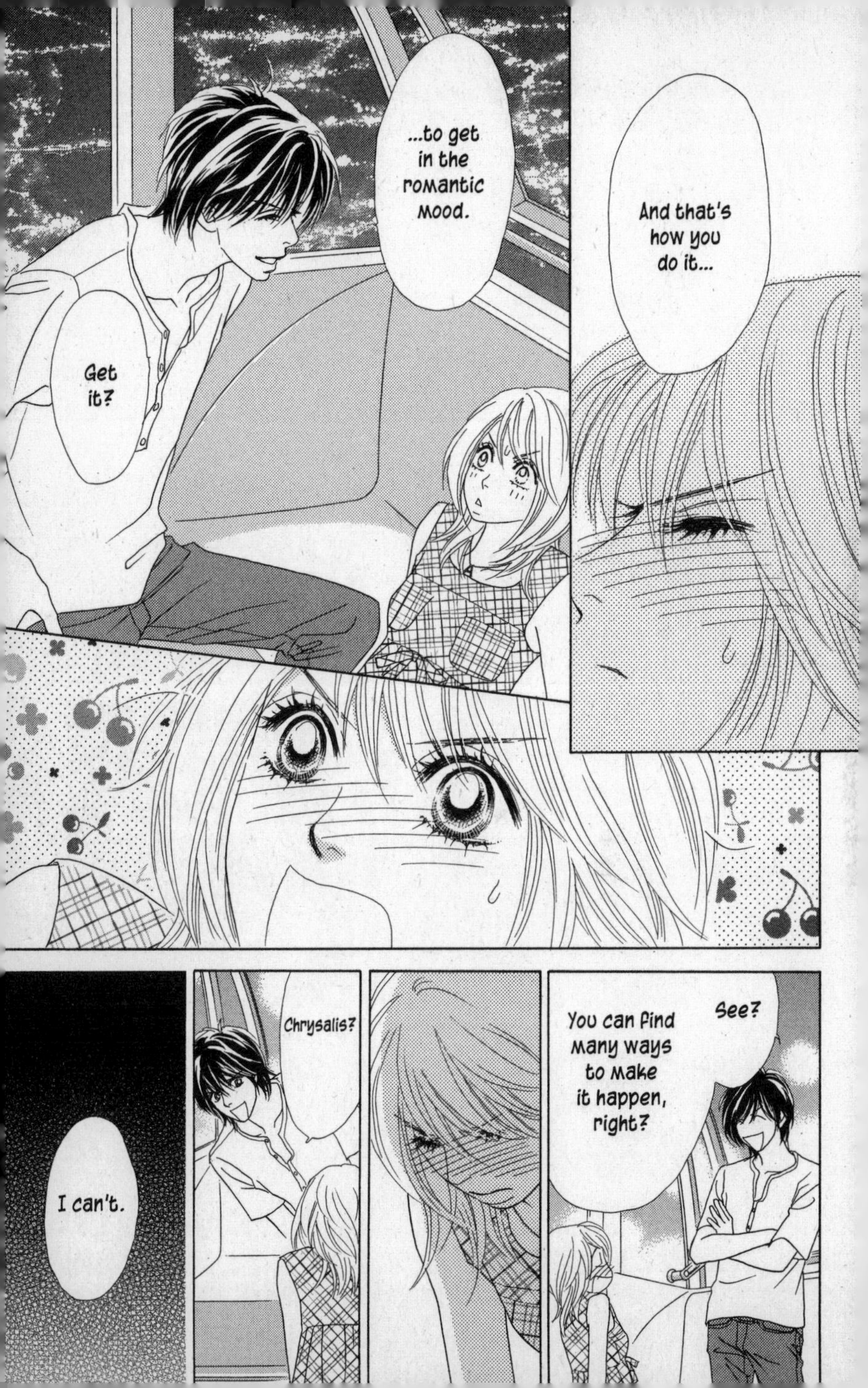
And that's how you do it...
...to get in the romantic mood.
Get it?
See?
You can find many ways to make it happen, right?
Chrysalis?
I can't.

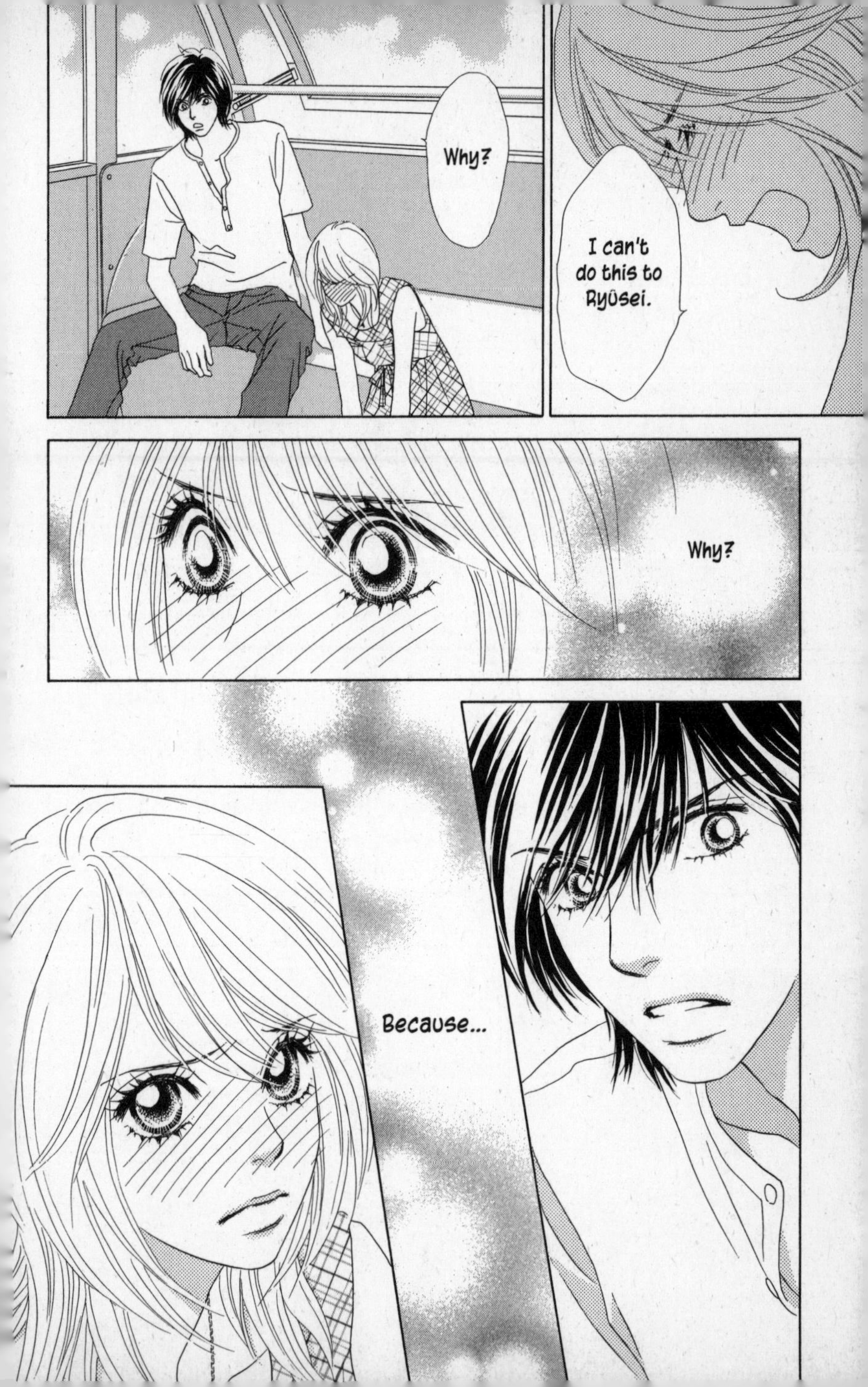
I can't do this to Ryûsei.
Why?
Why?
Because...

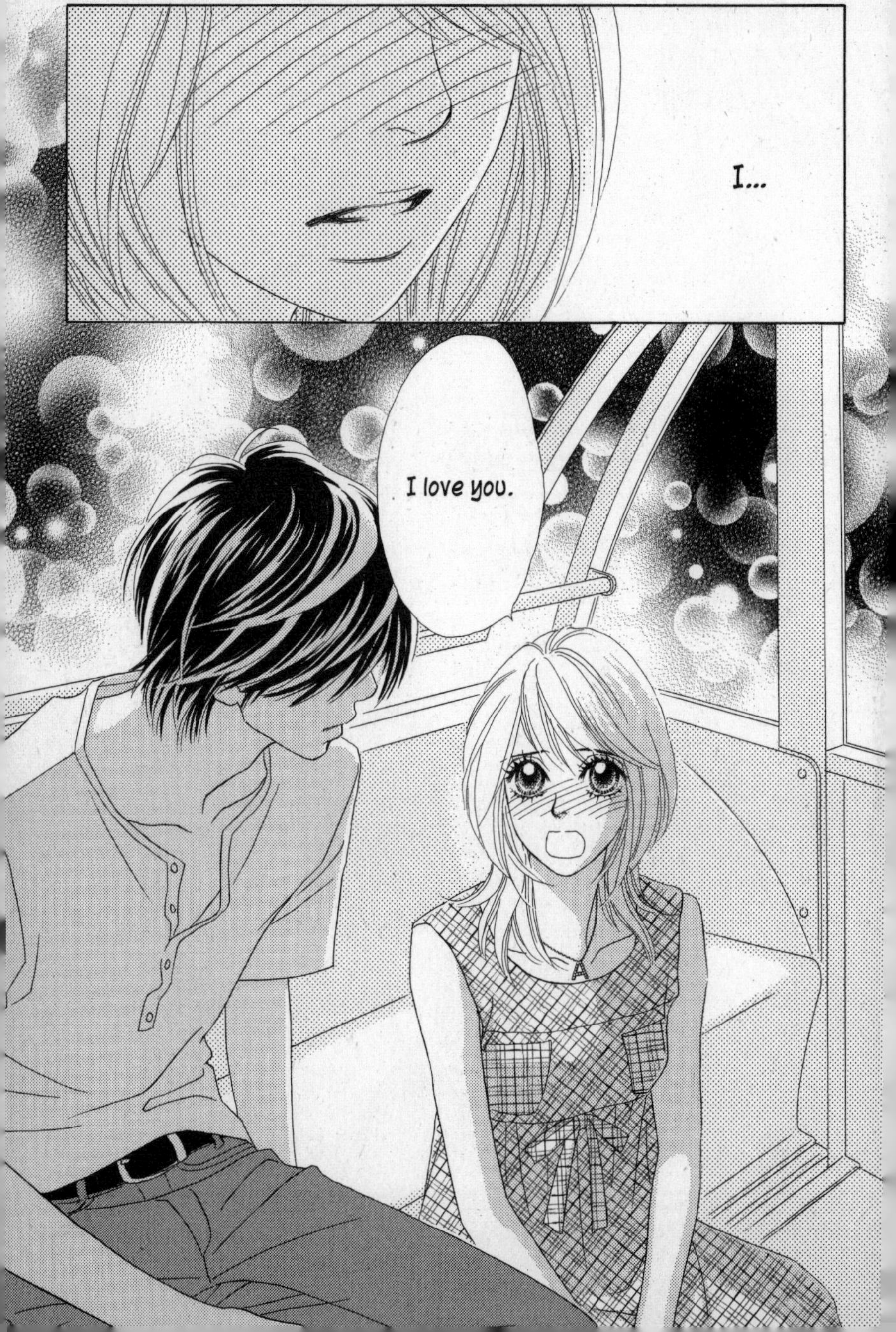
I...
I love you.

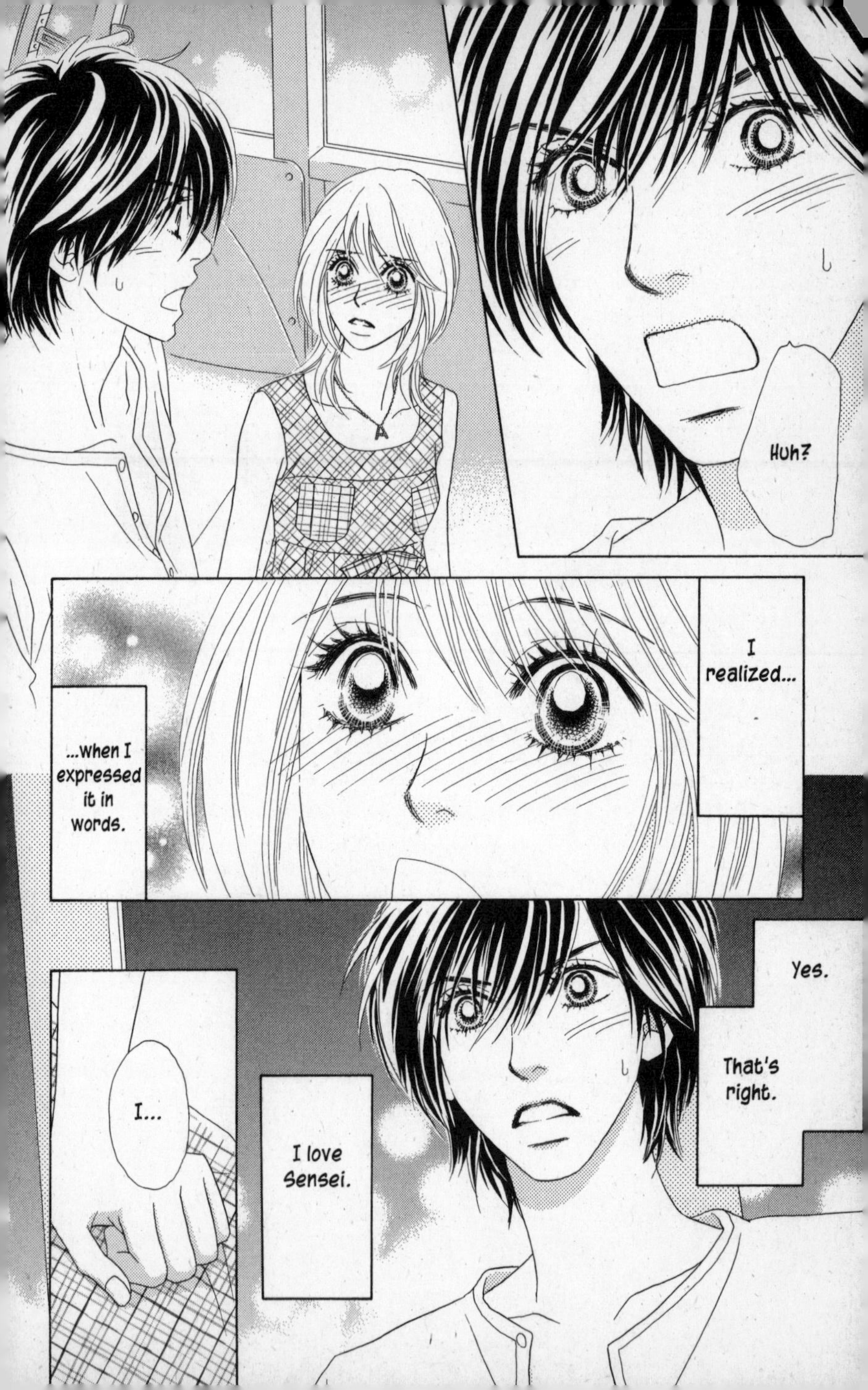
Huh?
I realized...
...when I expressed it in words.
Yes.
That's right.
I love Sensei.
I...

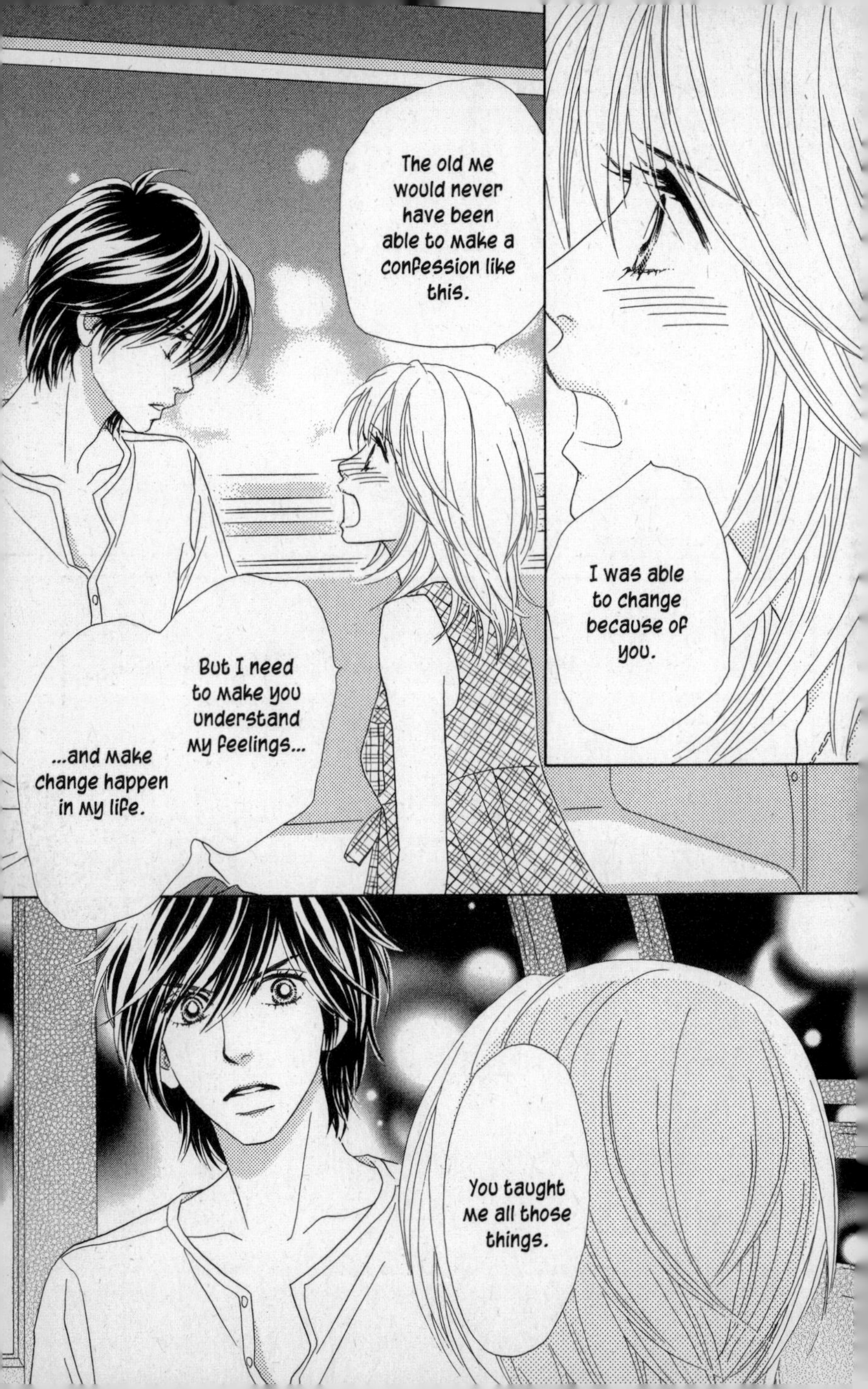
I was able to change because of you.
The old me would never have been able to make a confession like this.
But I need to make you understand my feelings...
...and make change happen in my life.
You taught me all those things.

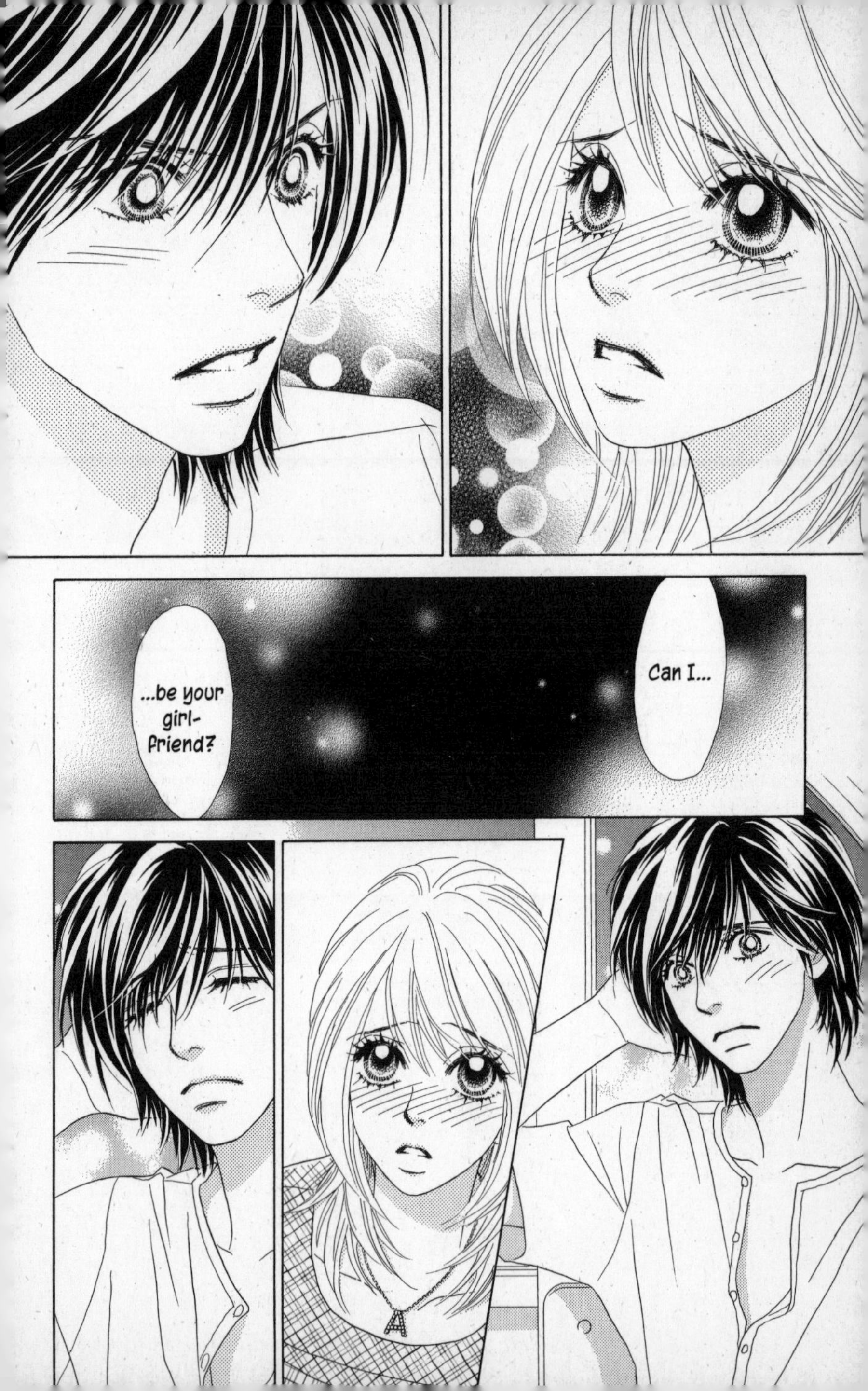
Can I...
...be your girl-friend?

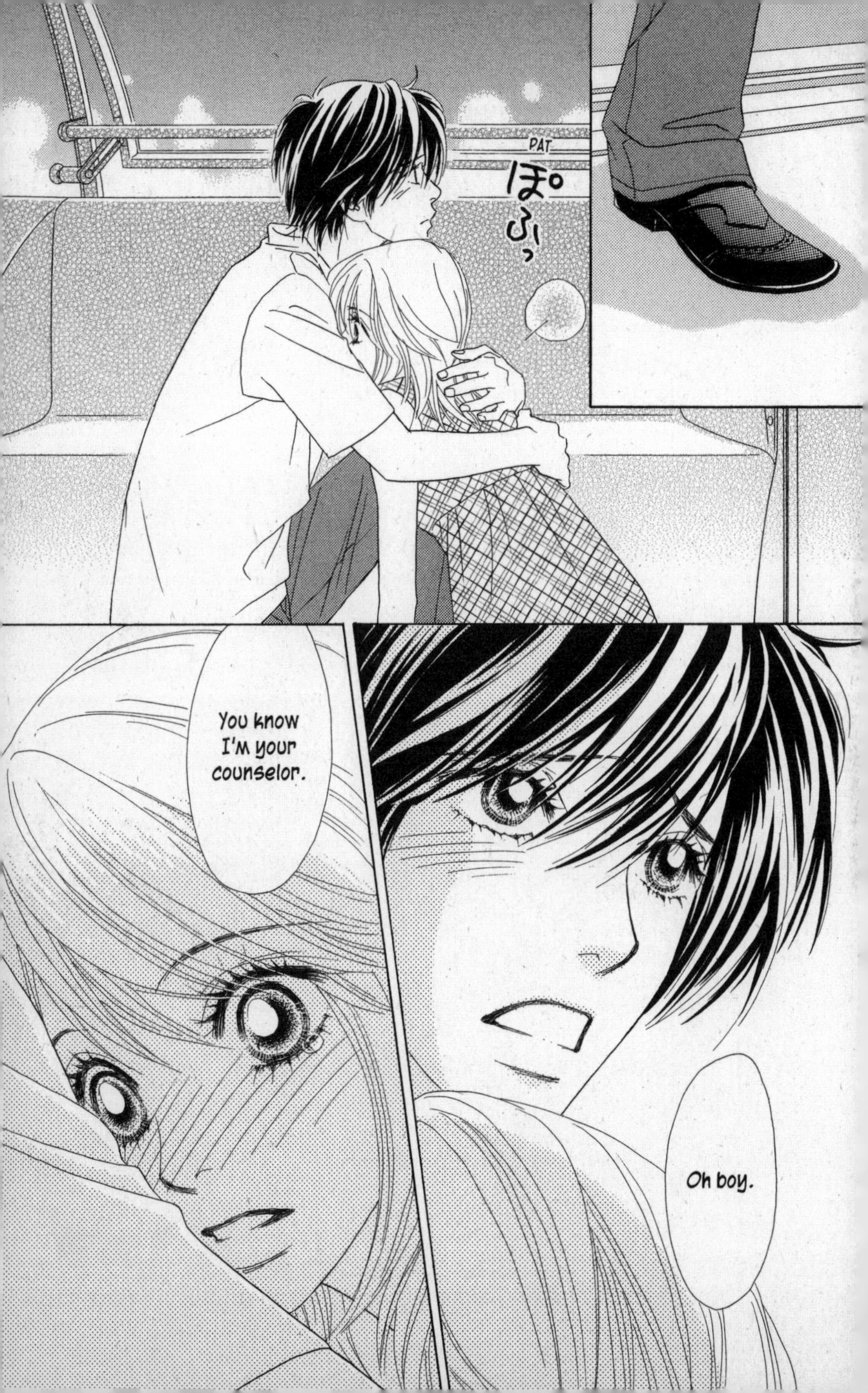
PAT
ぽふっ
Oh boy.
You know I'm your counselor.

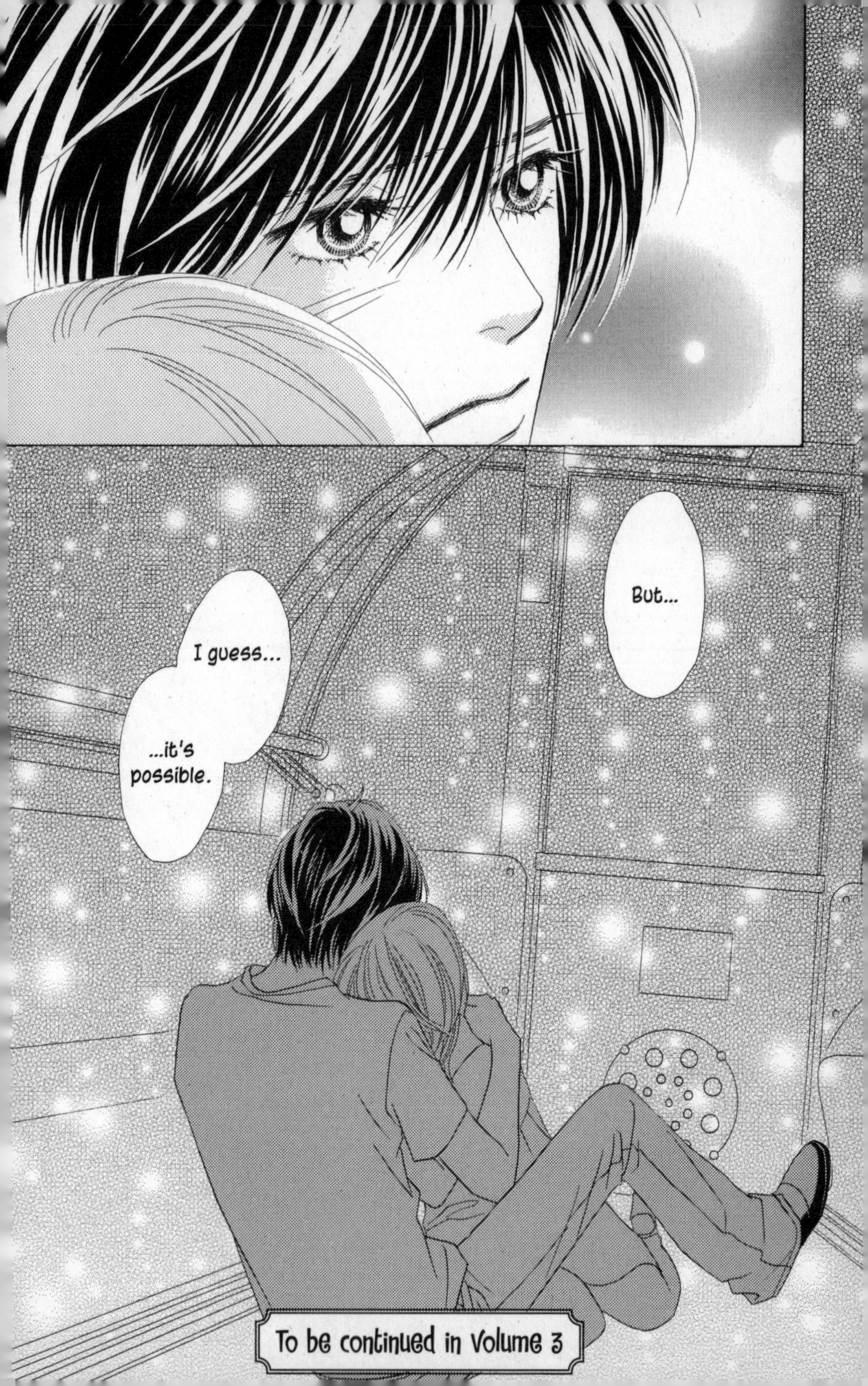
But...
I guess...
...it's possible.
To be continued in Volume 3

Staff

A i k o   A m e m o r i
T o m o m i   K a s u e
S a t s u k i   F u r u k a w a
A k i k o   K a w a s h i m a
A y u m i   Y o s h i d a

Editor
T o s h i y u k i   T a n a k a

May 9, 2007

M i w a   U e d a

Bonus Page

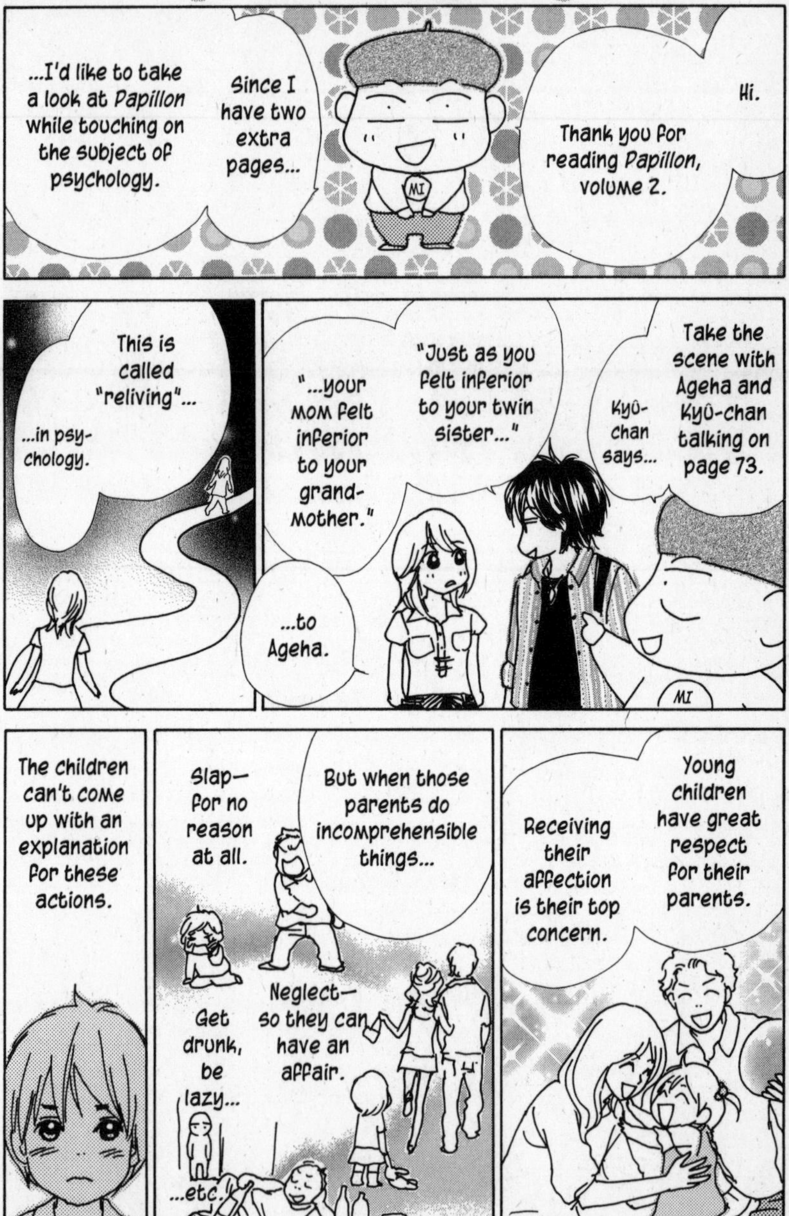
Hi.
Thank you for reading Papillon, volume 2.
Since I have two extra pages...
...I'd like to take a look at Papillon while touching on the subject of psychology.
MI
Take the scene with Ageha and Kyô-chan talking on page 73.
Kyô-chan says...
"Just as you felt inferior to your twin sister..."
"...your MOM felt inferior to your grand-mother."
...to Ageha.
MI
This is called "reliving"...
...in psy-chology.
Young children have great respect for their parents.
Receiving their affection is their top concern.
But when those parents do incomprehensible things...
Slap—for no reason at all.
Neglect—so they can have an affair.
Get drunk, be lazy...
...etc.
The children can't come up with an explanation for these actions.

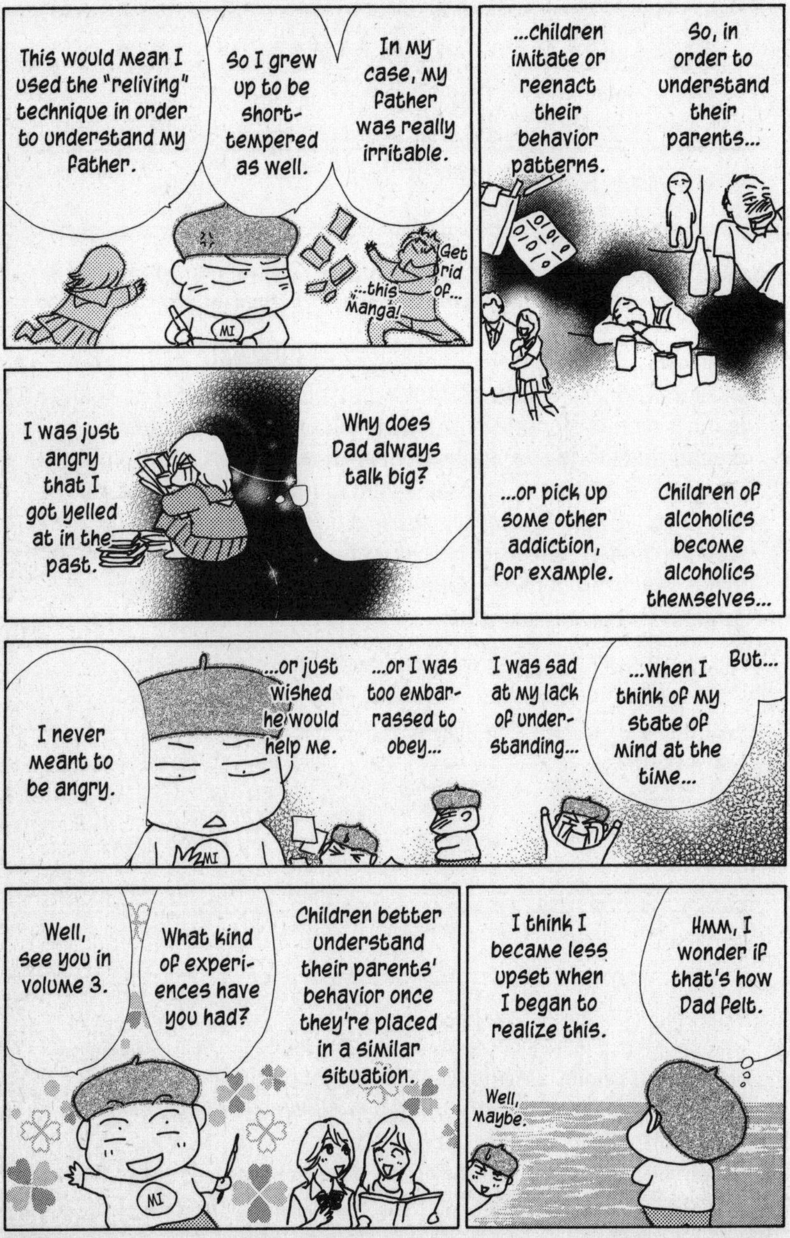
So, in order to understand their parents...
...children imitate or reenact their behavior patterns.
Children of alcoholics become alcoholics themselves...
...or pick up some other addiction, for example.
In my case, my father was really irritable.
So I grew up to be short-tempered as well.
This would mean I used the "reliving" technique in order to understand my father.
Get rid of...
...this manga!
Why does Dad always talk big?
I was just angry that I got yelled at in the past.
But...
...when I think of my state of mind at the time...
I was sad at my lack of understanding...
...or I was too embarrassed to obey...
...or just wished he would help me.
I never meant to be angry.
HMM, I wonder if that's how Dad felt.
I think I became less upset when I began to realize this.
Well, maybe.
Children better understand their parents' behavior once they're placed in a similar situation.
What kind of experiences have you had?
Well, see you in volume 3.

SPECIAL THANKS

I would like to take this opportunity to thank some people for their help.

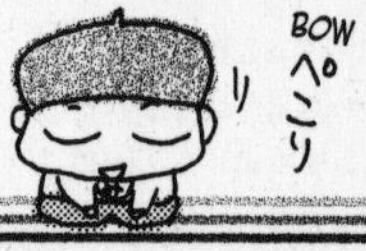
BOW
ぺこり

Yasuyoshi Kitabata-san

- Psychological Counselor, Seminar Trainer, and Industrial Counselor
- Member of the Japan Industrial Counselors Association

Yasuyoshi-san has done psychoanalysis of my manga characters on several occasions for me. This time, I asked for his advice on Ageha and her mother's approach to reconciliation. Calling her "mom" several times in the hospital was to open up Ageha's heart, since the word "mom" has a nice soft sound to it that can bring out our emotions. He says he uses this method on people who show no reaction to their parents in his counseling. Repeatedly saying "mom" to your mother will fill you with heartrending tearful emotion. I'm grateful for that discussion.

Yasuyoshi-san's Web magazine and books are very helpful in learning to understand relationships, and I recommend them.

Yasuyoshi-san's website:	http://www.counselingstyle.com/
Web magazine:	*Koi no Gift wo Tsukamu Hito, Koi no Wana ni Ochiru Hito*
Publication List:	*"Kandô" to "Shiawase" no Hôsoku*
	Koi wo Tsukamu Onna, Koi wo Otosu Onna
	Ienakatta "Suki" Korenara Ieru

Sat-chan

Thank you for gathering information and materials when I had trouble coming up with Kyû-chan's background. ♡ While your story as a college student was helpful, a counselor like Kyû-chan seemed unrealistic. Since he is a fictional character, I'm going to loosely draw him without focusing on reality.

I hope you can give me some advice if I have any questions again. Thank you so much.

Martin-sensei

Martin-sensei has continued to help me since volume 1. I thank him for mentioning *Papillon* on his blog and bringing up *Peach Girl* in his Web magazine. He used a scene in *Peach Girl* to explain a secret of relationships. His psychoanalysis of my manga was surprising and has offered new discoveries that I have found very interesting. If anyone is interested, check out Martin-san's Web magazine.

The back issue with the article on *Peach Girl*:
• *Renai Kyôshitsu PREMIUM No.255, Kimochi wo Tsutaeru, Sono Saki ni*

By the way, Kyû-chan was set up to be a cross between several counselors I know, but Martin-san claims he closely resembles him (laughs). I guess that means anyone interested in Kyû-chan's advice should go to Martin-san. In addition to his forum, Martin-san offers counseling over email, by telephone, and in person. If you're seeking advice, please check out his website.

Furthermore, Martin-san will have a new book out:
• *Ai sare Aura "Himitsu no Hôsoku: Aitai toki ni Aeru Kiseki no Renaijutsu*

I can feel Martin-san's enthusiasm through the long subtitle (laughs). The book was due out in late June 2007. Please look for it at a bookstore.

Haracchi and his wife, Akko-chan

Haracchi has told me of his past experience as a school guidance counselor. Since he had free time with very few students seeking help, he organized a health newsletter for his school. I wonder why people find it embarrassing to seek counseling.

Since Haracchi has been too busy to meet me, I have to thank Akko-chan for playing messenger for me. I really appreciate them.

I also want to thank everyone from my heart for their advice and support.

About the Creator

MIWA UEDA was born on September 29, in Hyogo, Japan.
Her original series, *Peach Girl*, won the Kodansha Shojo Manga
of the Year Award in 1999. *Papillon* is her latest creation.

Translation Notes

Japanese is a tricky language for most Westerners, and translation is often more art than science. For your edification and reading pleasure, here are notes on some of the places where we could have gone in a different direction with our translation of the work, or where a Japanese cultural reference is used.

Butterfly and Flower

The full Japanese title of this series is *Papillon: Chô to Hana*. Ageha and Hana's names contain the Japanese characters *chô* and *hana*, which mean "butterfly" and "flower" respectively. The title, *Papillon*, is French for "butterfly"—a good title for a story about a girl undergoing an amazing transformation, like a caterpillar becoming a butterfly.

Kyû-chan

Ichijiku's nickname comes from a Japanese character in his last name, which can also be read as *kyû*.

Love Hotel, page 30

A "love hotel" is a special type of short-stay hotel—rates are often offered by the hour—intended for couples looking for sexual intimacy.

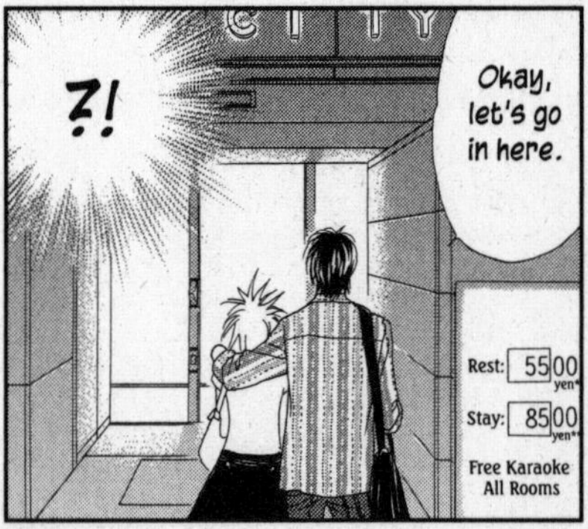
Okay, let's go in here.
?!
Rest: 5500 yen
Stay: 8500 yen
Free Karaoke All Rooms

Postpartum Depression, page 61

Postpartum depression is caused by the stresses and hormonal changes that follow childbirth. It can appear during the first year after childbirth and continue thereafter for a long time. Common symptoms are mood swings, feelings of worthlessness and rejection, and sleep disturbances.

Preview of *Papillon*, Volume 3

We're pleased to present you a preview from volume 3. Please check our website (www.delreymanga.com) to see when this volume will be available in English. For now you'll have to make do with Japanese!

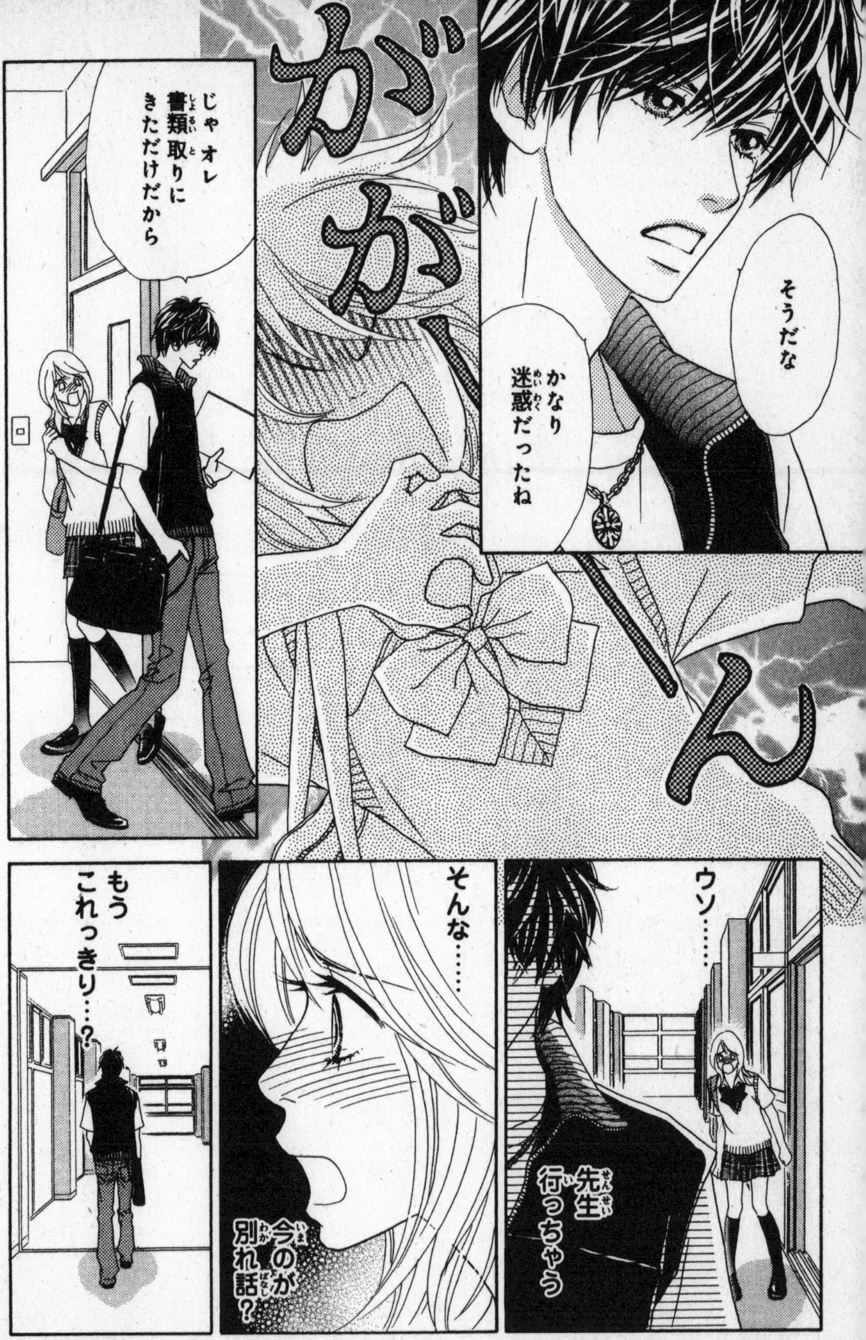
そうだな
かなり迷惑だったね
ががーん
じゃ オレ 書類取りにきただけだから
ウソ……
先生行っちゃう
そんな……
今のが別れ話？
もう これっきり…？

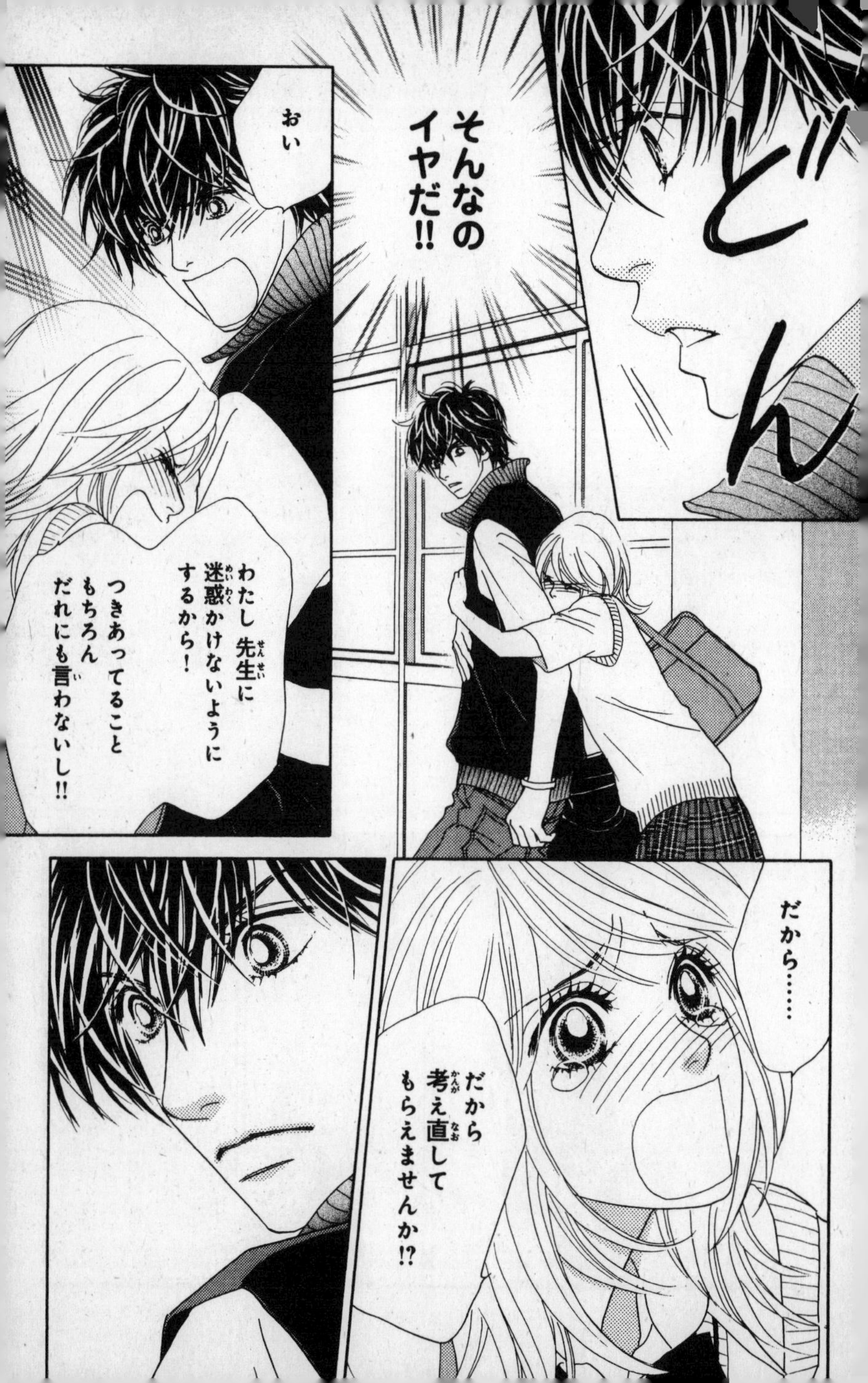
どん
そんなのイヤだ!!
おい
わたし 先生に迷惑かけないようにするから!
つきあってることもちろんだれにも言わないし!!
だから……
だから考え直してもらえませんか!?

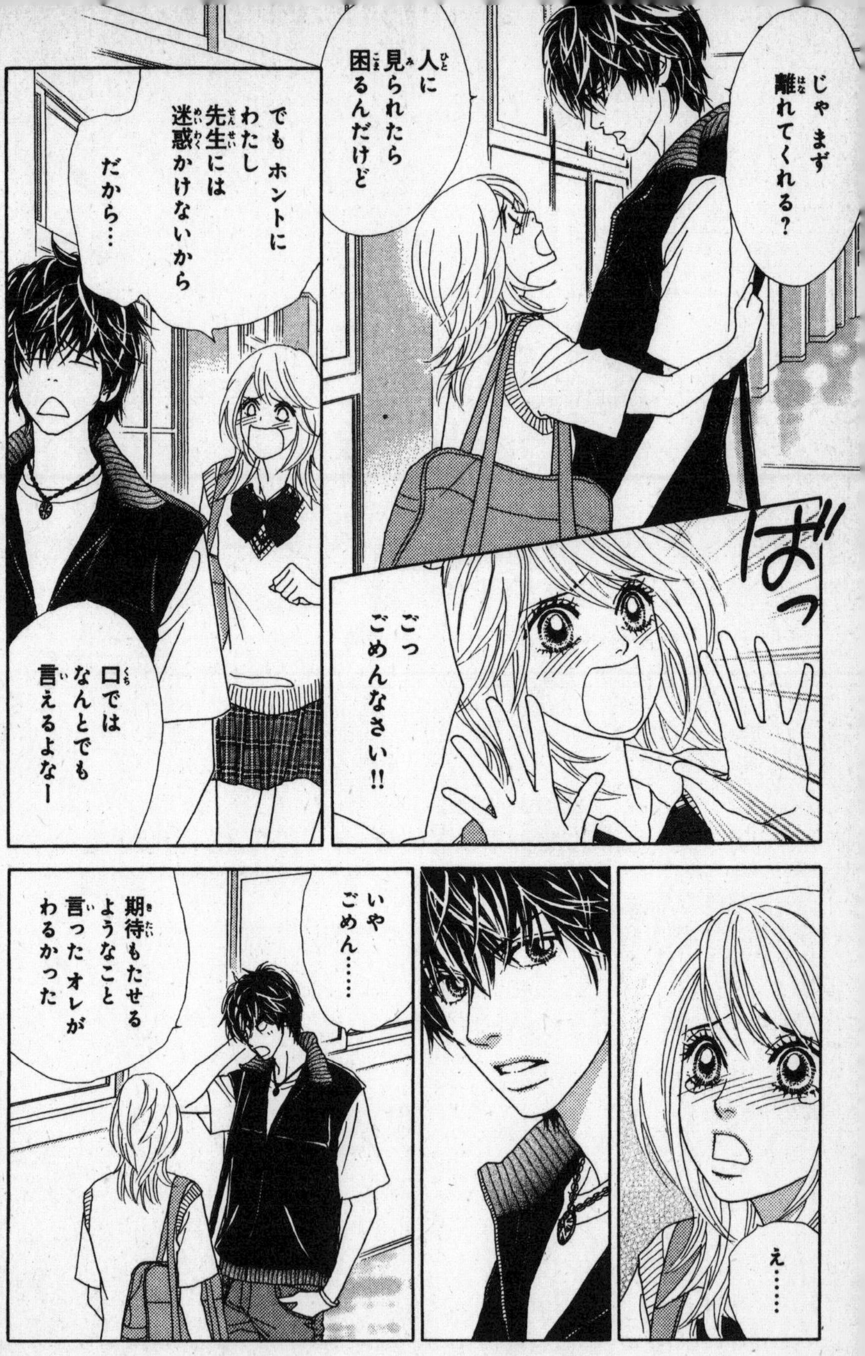
じゃ まず離れてくれる?
人に見られたら困るんだけど
ばっ
ごっ ごめんなさい!!
でも ホントに わたし 先生には 迷惑かけないから
だから…
口では なんとでも 言えるよなー
え……
いや ごめん……
期待もたせる ようなこと 言った オレが わるかった

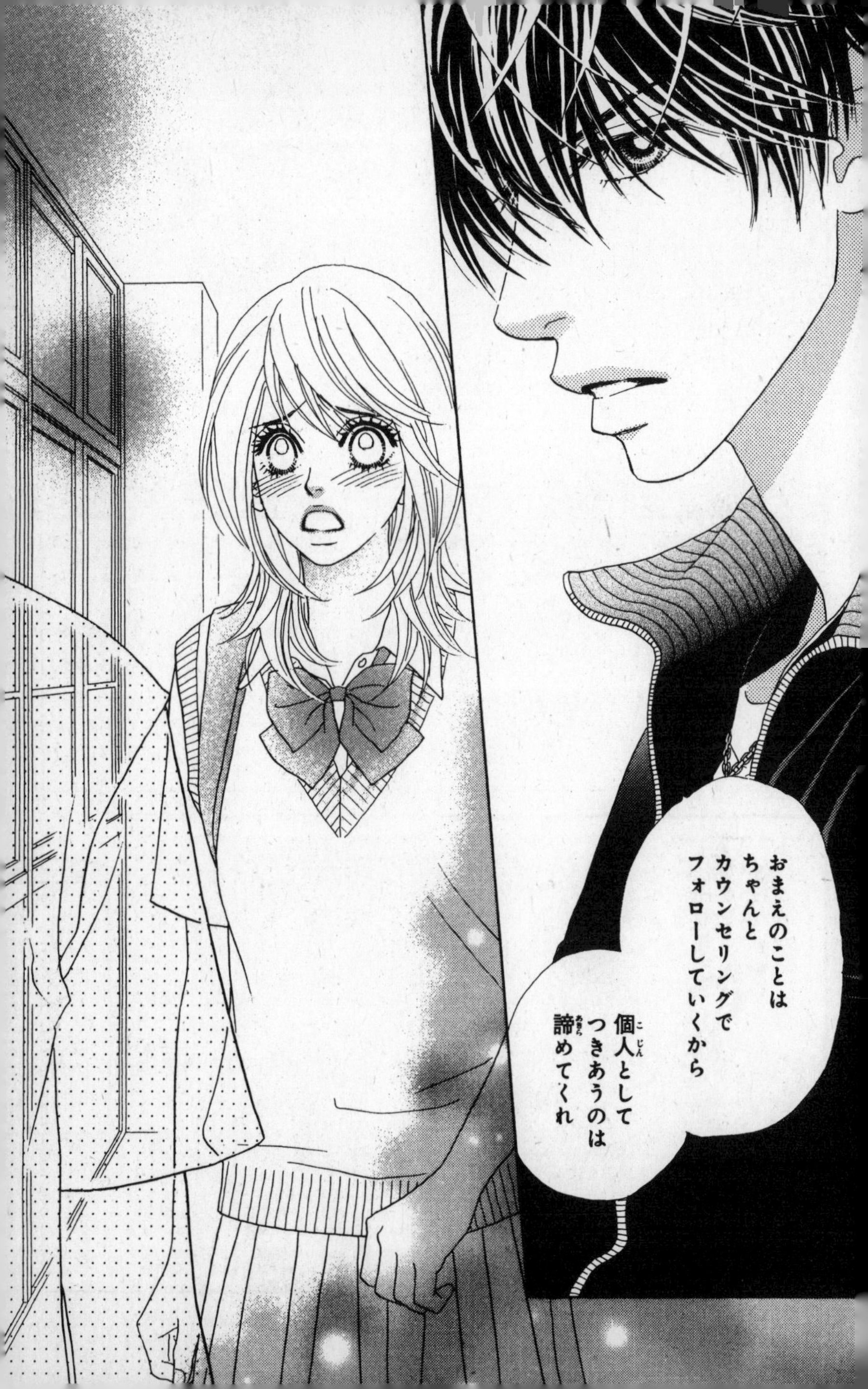
おまえのことはちゃんとカウンセリングでフォローしていくから
個人とマつきあうのは諦めてくれ

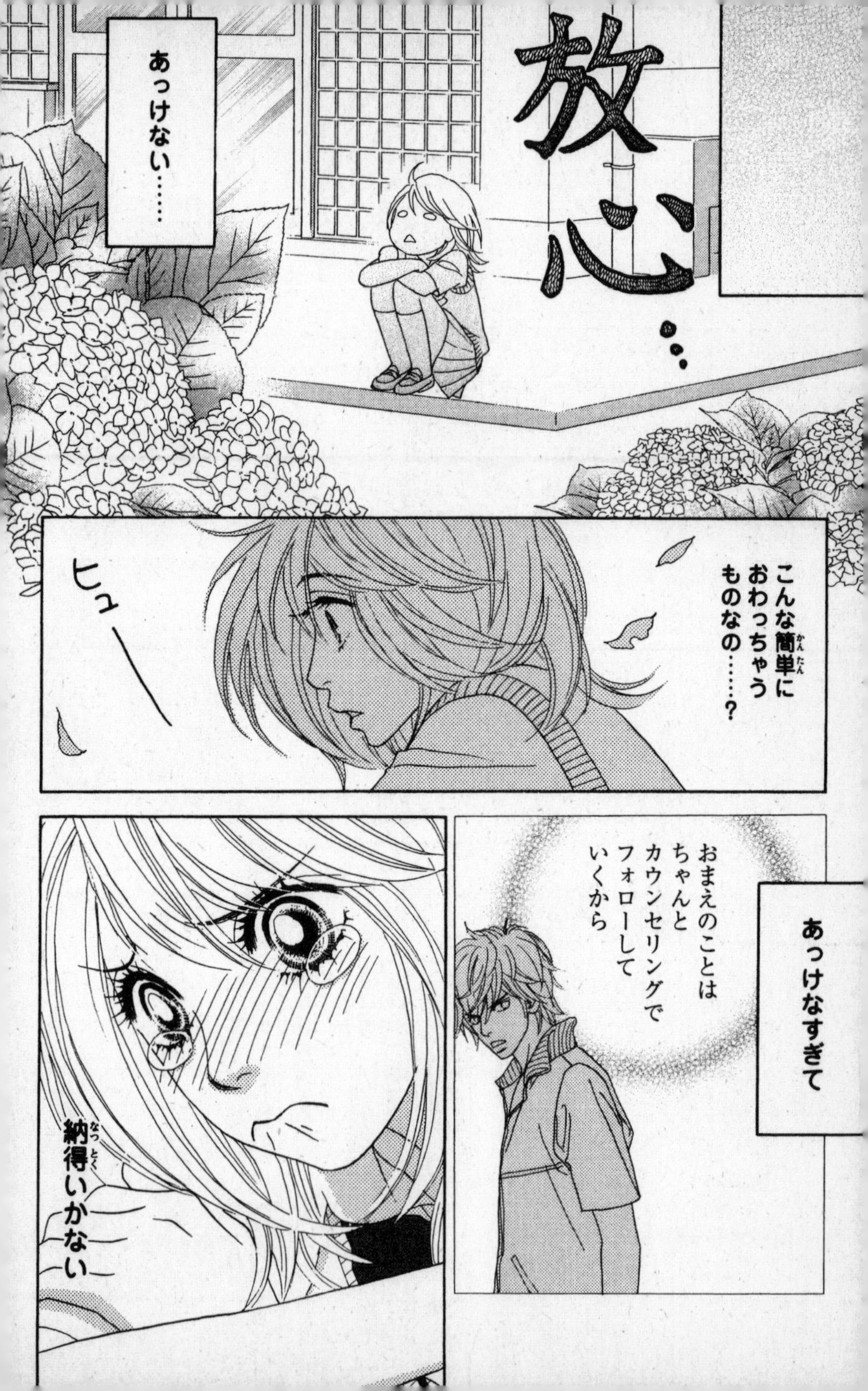
放心…
あっけない……
こんな簡単におわっちゃうものなの……?
ヒュー
あっけなすぎて
おまえのことはちゃんとカウンセリングでフォローしていくから
納得いかない

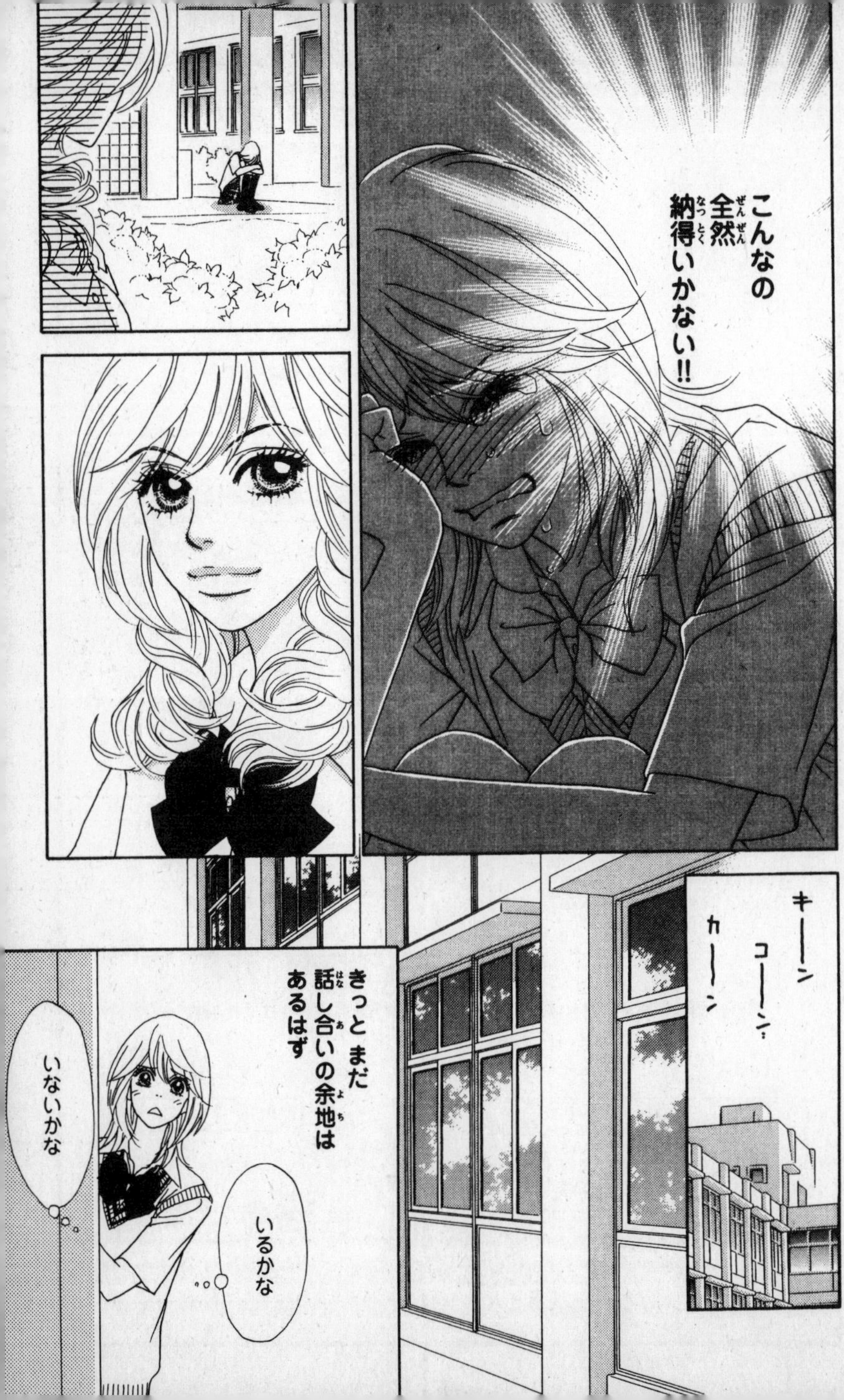
こんなの全然納得いかない!!
キーン
コーン
カーン
きっとまだ話し合いの余地はあるはず
いるかな
いないかな

STORY BY SURT LIM
ART BY HIROFUMI SUGIMOTO

A DEL REY MANGA ORIGINAL

Exploring the woods, young Kasumi encounters an ancient tree god, who bestows upon her the power of invisibility. Together with classmates who have had similar experiences, Kasumi forms the Magic Play Club, dedicated to using their powers for good while avoiding sinister forces that would exploit them.

Special extras in each volume! Read them all!

KITCHEN PRINCESS

STORY BY MIYUKI KOBAYASHI
MANGA BY NATSUMI ANDO
CREATOR OF ZODIAC P.I.

HUNGRY HEART

Najika is a great cook and likes to make meals for the people she loves. But something is missing from her life. When she was a child, she met a boy who touched her heart— and now Najika is determined to find him. The only clue she has is a silver spoon that leads her to the prestigious Seika Academy.

Attending Seika will be a challenge. Every kid at the school has a special talent, and the girls in Najika's class think she doesn't deserve to be there. But Sora and Daichi, two popular brothers who barely speak to each other, recognize Najika's cooking for what it is—magical. Could one of the boys be Najika's mysterious prince?

Special extras in each volume! Read them all!

Kamichama Karin Chu

BY KOGE-DONBO

A GODDESS IN LOVE!

Karin is your lovable girl next door—if the girl next door also happens to be a goddess! Karin has a magic ring that gives her the power to do anything she'd like. Though what she'd like most is to live happily ever after with Kazune, the boy of her dreams. Magic brought Kazune to her, but it also has a way of complicating things. It's not easy to be a goddess and a girl in love!

• Sequel series to the fan-favorite *Kamichama Karin*

Special extras in each volume! Read them all!

VISIT WWW.DELREYMANGA.COM TO:
• Read sample pages
• View release date calendars for upcoming volumes
• Sign up for Del Rey's free manga e-newsletter
• Find out the latest about new Del Rey Manga series

RATING T AGES 13+

DEL REY MANGA

The Otaku's Choice™

Yozakura Quartet

BY SUZUHITO YASUDA

A DIFFERENT SET OF SUPERTEENS!

Hime is a superheroine. Ao can read minds. Kotoha can conjure up anything with the right word. And Akina . . . well, he's just a regular guy, surrounded by three girls with superpowers! Together, they are the Hizumi Everyday Life Consultation Office, dedicated to protect the town of Sakurashin. And with demon dogs and supernatural threats around every corner, there's plenty to keep them busy!

Special extras in each volume! Read them all!

VISIT WWW.DELREYMANGA.COM TO:
- Read sample pages
- View release date calendars for upcoming volumes
- Sign up for Del Rey's free manga e-newsletter
- Find out the latest about new Del Rey Manga series

minima!

BY MACHIKO SAKURAI

A LITTLE LIVING DOLL!

What would you do if your favorite toy came to life and became your best friend? Well, that's just what happens to Ame Oikawa, a shy schoolgirl. Nicori is a super-cute doll with a mind of its own—and a plan to make Ame's dreams come true!

Special extras in each volume! Read them all!